The Republic Besieged
Civil War in Spain 1936-1939

The Republic Besieged
Civil War in Spain 1936-1939

Edited by

PAUL PRESTON AND ANN L. MACKENZIE

EDINBURGH UNIVERSITY PRESS

DP269
.R4
1996X

First published 1996 by
Edinburgh University Press
Edinburgh, EH8 9LF

British Library Cataloguing-in-Publication Data
A British Library CIP Record is available

ISBN   07486 0868 0   Cased
        07486 0861 3   Paper

The Editors are profoundly indebted to the Cañada Blanch Foundation and to the University of Glasgow for subventions which have generously enabled publication of *The Republic Besieged: Civil War in Spain 1936-1939*.

Printed and bound in the European Community
by J W Arrowsmith Ltd, Bristol.

In Memory of

E. Allison Peers

UNIVERSITY
of
GLASGOW

CONTENTS

Preface ANN L. MACKENZIE i

Introduction PAUL PRESTON v

PART I
International Hostility to the Second Republic

The Gentle General: The Official British Perception of General
Franco during the Spanish Civil War
ENRIQUE MORADIELLOS 1

Mussolini's Spanish Adventure: From Limited Risk to War
PAUL PRESTON 21

Nazi Germany's Intervention in the Spanish Civil War and the
Foundation of HISMA/ROWAK
CHRISTIAN LEITZ 53

'We Are with You': Solidarity and Self-interest in Soviet Policy
towards Republican Spain, 1936-1939
DENIS SMYTH 87

Battleground of Reputations: Ireland and the Spanish Civil War
R. A. STRADLING 107

PART II
The Forging of a War Effort

'From the Summit to the Abyss': The Contradictions of
Individualism and Collectivism in Spanish Anarchism
CHRIS EALHAM 135

War, Modernity and Reform: The Premiership of Juan Negrín,
1937-1939
HELEN GRAHAM 163

Civil War, Violence and the Construction of Francoism
MICHAEL RICHARDS 197

'Obligación de opinar': The Limits of Pluralism in Manuel
Azaña's *La velada en Benicarló* 241
JAMES WHISTON ... ...

'The Grand Camouflage': Julián Gorkin, Burnett Bolloten and
the Spanish Civil War
HERBERT RUTLEDGE SOUTHWORTH 261

Index 313

Notes on Contributors

PAUL PRESTON is the Príncipe de Asturias Professor of Contemporary Spanish History and Director of the Vicente Cañada Blanch Centre for Contemporary Spanish Studies at the London School of Economics and Political Science. His books include *The Coming of the Spanish Civil War: Reform, Reaction and Revolution in the Second Spanish Republic 1931-1936* (London: Routledge [2nd ed.], 1994); *The Triumph of Democracy in Spain* (London/New York: Methuen, 1986); *The Spanish Civil War 1936-1939* (London: Weidenfeld & Nicolson, 1986) and *Franco: A Biography* (London: Harper-Collins, 1993).

ANN L. MACKENZIE is Ivy McClelland Research Professor of Spanish at the University of Glasgow. She is author of, among other works, *La escuela de Calderón: estudio e investigación* (Liverpool: Liverpool U. P., 1993); and *Francisco de Rojas Zorrilla y Agustín Moreto: análisis* (Liverpool: Liverpool U. P., 1994); editor and, with Kenneth Muir, translator of Pedro Calderón, *Schism in England (La cisma de Inglaterra)* (Warminster: Aris & Phillips, 1990); and author, with Adrian Allan, of an edition and study of E. Allison Peers, *Redbrick University Revisited: The Autobiography of 'Bruce Truscot'* (forthcoming 1996). She is General Editor of the *Bulletin of Hispanic Studies*.

ENRIQUE MORADIELLOS is Lecturer in History at the Universidad de Extremadura at Cáceres. He is the author of several books including *Neutralidad benévola: el Gobierno británico y la insurrección militar española de 1936* (Oviedo: Pentalfa, 1990) and *La perfidia de Albión: el Gobierno británico y la guerra de España* (Madrid: Siglo XXI, 1996).

CHRISTIAN LEITZ is Lecturer in History at the University of the West of England, Bristol. He wrote a doctoral thesis at St Antony's College, Oxford, on the economic relations between Nazi Germany and Franco Spain, 1936-1945.

DENIS SMYTH is Professor of European History at the University of Toronto. He is author of *Diplomacy and Strategy of Survival: British Policy and Franco's Spain, 1940-41* (Cambridge: Cambridge U. P., 1986) and, with Paul Preston, of *Spain, the EEC and NATO* (London: Royal Institute of International Affairs/Routledge and Kegan Paul, 1984).

R. A. STRADLING is Reader in History at University of Wales, Cardiff. He is the author of several books on early modern Spain including *Philip IV and the Government of Spain* (Cambridge: Cambridge U. P., 1988) and *The Armada of Flanders* (Cambridge: Cambridge U. P., 1992) as well as, with Meirion Hughes, *The English Musical Renaissance 1860-1940: Construction and Deconstruction* (London: Routledge, 1993).

CHRIS EALHAM is Lecturer in European Studies at University of Wales, College of Cardiff. He wrote his London University doctoral thesis on 'Policing the Recession: Law and Order in Republican Barcelona, 1930-1936'.

HELEN GRAHAM is Lecturer in History at Royal Holloway and Bedford New College in the University of London. She is the author of *Socialism and War: The Spanish Socialist Party in Power and Crisis, 1936-1939* (Cambridge: Cambridge U. P., 1991); editor, with Paul Preston, of *The Popular Front in Europe* (London: Macmillan, 1987); editor, with Martin Alexander, of *The French and Spanish Popular Fronts: Comparative Perspectives* (Cambridge: Cambridge U. P., 1989); editor, with Jo Labanyi, of *Spanish Cultural Studies, An Introduction: The Struggle for Modernity* (Oxford: Oxford U. P., 1995).

MICHAEL RICHARDS is a British Academy Post-Doctoral Fellow at the University of Sheffield and author of a University of London doctoral thesis on economic autarchy and political and social repression during and after the Civil War in Spain.

JAMES WHISTON is a Fellow and Senior Lecturer in the Department of Spanish and Portuguese at Trinity College, Dublin. He is the author of a Critical Guide, *Juan Valera, Pepita Jiménez* (London: Grant & Cutler, 1977); *The Early Stages of Galdós's 'Lo prohibido'* (London: Tamesis Books, 1983); and, most recently, *Antonio Machado's Writings and the Spanish Civil War* (Liverpool: Liverpool U. P., 1996).

HERBERT RUTLEDGE SOUTHWORTH, now retired, has been a journalist, broadcaster and historian. He wrote his first article on the Spanish Civil War in 1936 in *The Washington Post*. Subsequently, he worked in New York as deputy editor of *News of Spain* for the Spanish Republican Government. He served with the U.S. Office of War Information in North Africa during the Second World War. In 1946, he founded Radio Tangier which he managed until 1960. He wrote his doctorate at the Sorbonne under the supervision of Pierre Vilar. He has taught at the University of Vincennes (Paris) and has been Regents Professor at the University of California, San Diego. He is author of *El mito de la cruzada de Franco* (Paris: Ruedo Ibérico, 1963); *Antifalange* (Paris: Ruedo Ibérico, 1967) and *Guernica! Guernica!: A Study of Journalism, Propaganda and History* (Berkeley: Univ. of California, 1977).

Preface

This book is the first volume in a projected series of major works of research into Spanish history, culture and society, to be published under the auspices of the Department of Hispanic Studies, University of Glasgow and the Vicente Cañada Blanch Centre for Contemporary Spanish Studies at the London School of Economics and Political Science. The series, which will be jointly edited and directed by Ann Mackenzie and Paul Preston, is part of a proposed larger enterprise of collaboration involving scholars in Britain, Spain and throughout the world. This series of Research Studies on Spain is designed to stimulate and publish research into the history of Spanish civilization in all its aspects — political, social, religious, literary, artistic, international — from the Golden Age through to the twentieth century.

This first volume of the series has its origins in an idea conceived by Paul Preston several years ago. In 1984, in order to make available to a wide readership key aspects of research being undertaken on Spain during the 1930s, he had edited and published a collection of studies dealing with *Revolution and War in Spain 1931-1939*.[1] In the decade that followed major researches continued to be carried out in this field, and he formed the opinion that a second volume of collected studies — as successor to *Revolution and War in Spain* — should be published. Numerous other commitments, however, not least his monumental biography of *Franco*, prevented him from realizing his intention. Then, in 1994, there came a suggestion from Ann Mackenzie: would he edit, with her, a collection of essays to commemorate, in 1996, the sixtieth anniversary of the Spanish Civil War? An application made to the Cañada Blanch Foundation for a grant to publish the book proved successful. The University of Glasgow, following Ann Mackenzie's

---

1   (London: Methuen 1984).

appointment in 1995 to a Chair at that institution, also agreed
to assist the costs of publication. Thanks to these subventions,
the Editors were able to realize the original project and publish
a coherent collection of studies representative of current
researches into the history and politics, the character and
predicament, of the Spanish Republic Besieged 1936-1939.

* * * * *

A significant number of publications and other academic
happenings, of which this book is one, have followed the
centenary, in 1991, of the birth of E. Allison Peers. These
diverse studies and events have been designed to honour his
prodigious contributions, as scholar and university teacher, to
the advancement of learning and development of Hispanic
Studies in Britain and throughout the world. In 1994 Geoffrey
Ribbans delivered the Fifth E. Allison Peers Lecture at the
University of Liverpool, offering an objective interpretation of
the life and work of 'E. Allison Peers: A Centenary Reappraisal'.
An exhibition entitled *Redbrick Revisited: The University of
Liverpool 1920-1952*, held at Liverpool University in that same
year, celebrated the career of Allison Peers as Gilmour
Professor of Spanish and recorded his considerable influence
upon changes in British universities during the critical period
of post-war reconstruction — achieved most notably through
the books which he wrote pseudonymously about 'Redbrick'
Universities. In 1995 Peers' previously unpublished Memoirs,
together with a Critical Introduction and Notes elucidating
their significance, entitled *Redbrick University Revisited: The
Autobiography of 'Bruce Truscot'*, were sent to press and will
shortly be published.[2] A recently issued Special Number of the
Bulletin of Hispanic Studies, financed by the Gulbenkian
Foundation, commemorated Peers' foundation of the journal
more than seventy years ago, and also recognized Peers'
pioneering work to develop in Britain the study of *Portugal: Its
Culture, Influence and Civilization*. Soon forthcoming is a

---

2   Edited by Ann L. Mackenzie and Adrian R. Allan (forthcoming, 1996).

Homage Volume of *Essays in Memory of E. Allison Peers*, jointly published by the Modern Humanities Research Association and Liverpool University Press, which acknowledges the enduring importance of Peers' researches into Spanish literature and culture, observed most notably in his surveys and analyses of the Romantic Movement in Spain and his *Studies of the Spanish Mystics*.

The present book differs from other studies already dedicated to Allison Peers in that it celebrates, rather than his achievements as a literary critic, journal-editor and educationist, his work as a historian. In a series of influential books written in the late 1930s and early 1940s, Peers documented and illuminated contemporary conflicts, issues and preoccupations affecting and transforming the State, Church and Society in Spain. These books, during the decades when they were published, established Peers as the most trusted commentator on the Spanish Civil War — as,

> on this so controversial topic, the one dispassionate, reliable guide and mentor of the English-speaking world amidst a welter of confusing emotionalisms.[3]

Even nowadays, between fifty and sixty years after they were written, *The Spanish Tragedy 1930-1936: Dictatorship, Republic, Chaos* (1936); *Catalonia Infelix* (1937); *The Spanish Dilemma* (1940); and *Spain in Eclipse* (1943), revealing Peers' extraordinary knowledge of Contemporary Spain, are, as Geoffrey Ribbans has commented,

> a valuable source of purely political history, of great documentary, and at times eye-witness, value.[4]

Among more than fifty books which Peers completed in 'an incredible rhythm of production', these histories of 'The Spanish Tragedy' represent some of the most enduring results of his researches. For these works Allison Peers deserves to be

---

3   See William C. Atkinson, 'In Memoriam', *Memorial Number, Bulletin of Hispanic Studies*, XXX (1953), No. 117, 1-5, at p. 4.

4   I borrow this quotation, with the one immediately following, from Geoffrey Ribbans, 'E. Allison Peers: A Centenary Reappraisal', published in *Essays in Memory of E. Allison Peers*, ed. Ann L. Mackenzie (Liverpool: Liverpool U. P./London: Modern Humanities Research Association, 1996).

remembered with esteem and gratitude by all scholars concerned to deepen our historical understanding of Spain before, during and after the Civil War.

* * * * *

The Editors place on record their profound indebtedness to the University of Glasgow and the Vicente Cañada Blanch Foundation for generous subventions, without which joint assistance this project could not have been realized. They are particularly grateful to Professor Sir Graeme Davies, Principal of the University of Glasgow, for his decisive encouragement at a critical stage in the book's preparation. Equally they are indebted to the Cañada Blanch Foundation for support that has been moral as well as financial — support which, remarkably, did not waver when the concise book of studies originally proposed, which had been expected to fill only one hundred and twenty pages, more than doubled its length to become a History of *The Republic Besieged: Civil War in Spain 1936-1939*.

Ann L. Mackenzie

January 1996.

Introduction[1]

PAUL PRESTON

In 1996, there will be commemorations of the sixtieth anniversary of the outbreak of the Spanish Civil War. It is likely to be the last such substantial commemoration which will enjoy the participation of surviving protagonists of the war most of whom are now in their eighth decade. There can be little doubting the significance of the Spanish Civil War, both as 'the last great cause' and as a defining moment on the road to the Second World War. In Spain, Mussolini and Hitler drew together in the Rome-Berlin Axis as they witnessed the pusillanimity of the democratic powers.[2] Scholarly research and anniversaries, however, are not usually comfortable bedfellows. It is in the nature of research that it rarely comes to fruition in time to be published on an appropriate anniversary. The previous major commemoration of the Spanish Civil War in 1986 stimulated a great surge of publishing activity in Great Britain, which included reprints of major works by Raymond Carr and Hugh Thomas, a work of synthesis, graphic collections and valuable memoirs and other material concerning the International Brigades, but little in the way of major new advances in research.[3] In the United States,

---

1   I would like to thank the Vicente Cañada Blanch Foundation for its generous support for this volume and also of the individual research of several of the contributors.

2   See Paul Preston, *The Spanish Civil War 1936-1939* (London: Weidenfeld & Nicolson, 1986), 1-7.

3   Among the books published in 1986 were *Images of the Spanish Civil War*, with an introduction by Raymond Carr (London: George Allen & Unwin); *No Pasarán: Photographs and Posters of the Spanish Civil War*, ed. Frances Morris (Bristol: Arnolfini); *Cockburn in Spain: Despatches from the Spanish*

the anniversary was marked only by the publication of books about the Abraham Lincoln Brigade.[4]

In Spain itself, there was less made of the fiftieth anniversary than might have been expected. That was a consequence of the so-called 'pacto del olvido' (the pact of forgetfulness). As part of the general desire of the great majority of the Spanish people to ensure a bloodless transition to democracy, there was a tacit, collective agreement that there would be no settling of accounts after the death of Franco. A determination to prevent a repetition of Civil-War violence eventually overcame any longing for revenge. This collective determination to contribute by whatever means to the re-establishment of democracy had its advocates within the historical profession. The consequence was a reticence in universities about teaching the history of the period of the war and its aftermath and, in research, a marked reluctance to publish work which might in some way reopen old wounds. This was reflected in a refusal by the Socialist Government to sanction any official commemoration of the fiftieth anniversary of the Civil War in 1986.[5] Despite its crucial value in political

---

Civil War, edited by James Pettifer (London: Lawrence & Wishart); *Voices from the Spanish Civil War: Personal Recollections of Scottish Volunteers in Republican Spain 1936-39*, ed. Ian MacDougall (Edinburgh: Polygon Press); Walter Gregory, *The Shallow Grave: A Memoir of the Spanish Civil War* (London: Victor Gollancz); and *International Brigade Memorial Archive: Catalogue 1986* (London: Marx Memorial Library). There were reprints of Raymond Carr, *The Civil War in Spain* (London: Weidenfeld & Nicolson, first published 19??) and Hugh Thomas, *The Spanish Civil War* (London: Hamish Hamilton, first published 19??). The work of synthesis was my own book on the war (see above, note 2).

4   See Carl Geiser, *Prisoners of the Good Fight: The Spanish Civil War 1936-1939* (Westport, Connecticut: Lawrence Hill & Co.) and Marion Merriman and Warren Lerude, *American Commander in Spain: Robert Hale Merriman and the Abraham Lincoln Brigade* (Reno: Univ. of Nevada Press).

5   The trend towards a 'value-free' history of the Civil War during the first decade of the transition period was made explicit in Juan Luis Cebrián, 'Para una nueva cultura política', his introduction to the fiftieth-anniversary collection of articles published in the newspaper of which he was then editor, *El País*, *La guerra de España 1936-1939* (Madrid: *El País*, 1986). The impossibility of forgetting the past was clear in both the fiftieth-anniversary history produced by *Historia 16*, *La guerra civil*, ed. Julio Aróstegui *et al.*, 24 vols (Madrid: Información y Revistas, 1986-88) and in the proceedings of a major conference held in Salamanca in September 1986 (Julio Aróstegui,

terms and its importance as a measure of the great political maturity of a Spanish populace traumatized by both the Civil War and the experience of the Franco dictatorship, the 'pacto del olvido' was always going to be difficult for the historians.[6] In fact, in Catalonia, major research on disagreeable aspects of the Spanish Civil War had proceeded despite the 'pact'.[7] Elsewhere, the uneasy truce with the past was broken within five years as a stream of important works began to appear about the repression in the Nationalist zone during the war and in Franco's Spain thereafter.[8]

In the ten years since the last flurry of non-specialist interest in the Spanish Civil War, research has also moved on substantially in Britain.   Inevitably, logistical considerations mean that the kind of detailed local research now being undertaken in Spain can rarely be matched by foreign scholars — although chapters 6 and 8 of the present volume show that it can be done. In consequence, much of the recent research being

---

Historia y memoria de la guerra civil, 3 vols [Valladolid: Junta de Castilla y León, 1988]).

6   See, for example, Francisco Moreno Gómez, *La guerra civil en Córdoba (1936-1939)* (Madrid: Editorial Alpuerto, 1985).

7   See Joan Villarroya i Font, *Els bombardeigs de Barcelona durant la guerra civil (1936-1939)* (Barcelona: Abadia de Montserrat, 1981); Hilari Raguer, *Divendres de passió: vida i mort de Manuel Carrasco i Formiguera* (Barcelona: Abadia de Montserrat, 1984); Josep M. Solé i Sabaté, *La repressió franquista a Catalunya 1938-1953* (Barcelona: Edicions 62, 1985); Josep Massot i Muntaner, *Vida i miracles del 'Conde Rossi': Mallorca, agost-desembre 1936, Málaga, gener-febrer 1937* (Barcelona: Abadia de Montserrat, 1988) and *Georges Bernanos i la guerra civil* (Barcelona: Abadia de Montserrat, 1989); Josep M. Solé i Sabaté and Joan Villarroya i Font, *La repressió a la reraguarda de Catalunya (1936-1939)*, 2 vols (Barcelona: Abadia de Montserrat, 1989-90).

8   Julián Casanova, Ángela Cenarro, Julita Cifuentes, María Pilar Maluenda and María Pilar Salomón, *El pasado oculto: fascismo y violencia en Aragón (1936-1939)* (Madrid: Siglo XXI, 1992); María Cristina Rivero Noval, *La ruptura de la paz civil: represión en la Rioja (1936-1939)* (Logroño: Instituto de Estudios Riojanos, 1992); Julia Cifuentes Chueca and Pilar Maluenda Pons, *El asalto a la República: los orígenes del franquismo en Zaragoza (1936-1939)* (Zaragoza: Institución Fernando el Católico, 1995); Vicent Gabarda, *Els afusellaments al País Valencià (1938-1956)* (Valencia: Edicions Alfons el Magnànim, 1993); Francisco Cobo Romero, *La guerra civil y la represión franquista en la provincia de Jaén 1936-1950* (Jaén: Diputación Provincial, 1993); Encarnación Barranquero Texeira, *Málaga entre la guerra y la posguerra: el franquismo* (Málaga: Editorial Arguval, 1994).

conducted outside Spain has been concerned with broader considerations of the politics of both zones and the international dimensions of the war. The purpose of this volume is to make available to a wider audience the results of the research in progress of some of the growing number of scholars working on these aspects of the Spanish Civil War.

Local research in Spain and elsewhere has enriched our view of the crisis of the 1930s and it has also reinforced one of the two central facts about the Spanish Civil War: in its origins, it was a series of *Spanish* social wars and many of the difficulties faced within the Republican zone derived from the incomplete resolution of some of those conflicts. Foreign, as well as Spanish scholars,[9] have contributed to confirming the other central truth about the war: in its course and outcome, it was an episode in a greater European Civil War that ended in 1945.[10] The ultimate defeat of the Spanish Republic came after a three-year siege in which it was besieged from without and from within; from outside, by the forces of international Fascism and their unwitting accomplices among the democratic states and, from inside, by the forces of the extreme left who put their own revolutionary ambitions before the effort to build a centralized war effort.

The rising took place on the evening of 17 July in Spain's Moroccan colony and in the Peninsula itself on the morning of 18 July. The plotters were confident that it would all be over in a few days. Had they just had the Republican government to contend with, their predictions might have come true. In fact, Spain was soon divided along the lines of the electoral geography of February 1936 — the coup was successful in the

---

9   The pioneer in this regard was Ángel Viñas; see his *La Alemania nazi y el 18 de julio* (Madrid: Alianza Editorial, 1974) and *El oro de Moscú: alfa y omega de un mito franquista* (Barcelona: Grijalbo, 1979). More recently, important works include Ismael Saz Campos, *Mussolini contra la II República: hostilidad, conspiraciones, intervención (1931-1936)* (Valencia: Edicions Alfons el Magnànim, 1986); Enrique Moradiellos, *Neutralidad benévola: el gobierno británico y la insurrección militar española de 1936* (Oviedo: Pentalfa, 1990); and Juan Avilés Farré, *Pasión y farsa: franceses y británicos ante la guerra civil española* (Madrid: Eudema, 1994).

10   Paul Preston, 'The Great Civil War: European Politics, 1914-1945', in *The Oxford History of Contemporary Europe*, ed. Tim Blanning (Oxford: Oxford U. P., 1995), 148-81.

Catholic small-holding areas which voted for the CEDA. However, in the left-wing strongholds of industrial Spain and the great estates of the deep south, the uprising was defeated by the spontaneous action of the working-class organizations. Within a matter of days, the country was split into two war zones and there was every reason to suppose that the Republic would be able to crush the rising. While power in the streets lay with the workers and the militia organizations, there was still a bourgeois Republican government which had legitimacy in the international arena, control of the nation's gold and currency reserves and virtually all of Spain's industrial capacity. There was not that much to choose between the armed forces of both sides. What the working-class militias lacked in training they made up in an enthusiasm that could not be matched by the conscripts of the rebel army. That situation was exemplified in the navy where left-wing sailors had mutinied against their right-wing officers.

There would, however, be two factors which would soon make all the difference between the two sides — the ferocious African Army and the help of the Fascist Powers. At first, the colonial army under Franco, was blockaded in Morocco by the fleet. However, while the Republican Government in Madrid met only hesitance from its sister Popular Front government in Paris and covert hostility from London, Franco was quickly able to persuade the local representatives of Nazi Germany and Fascist Italy that he was the man to back. As Enrique Moradiellos shows in chapter 1, Franco also managed to persuade the local British authorities in North Africa that he was fighting a 'frankly Communist' enemy and that they should close the facilities of the ports of Tangier and Gibraltar to the Republican forces. Altogether more decisive was his success with the Italians and Germans. Again, as is demonstrated in chapters 2 and 3, his 'blind faith' in his own success and his powers of persuasion were crucial. Both the Italian authorities in Tangier and local representatives of the Nazi Party were sufficiently convinced by him that they put his case to Mussolini and Hitler respectively. Their decision-making processes were, of course, then conditioned by their own calculations of the opportunities offered by the Spanish crisis to alter the European balance of power to the detriment of Britain and France. Nevertheless, it is significant that, in London, the insurgents were soon known as 'General Franco's forces' and, in Rome, as 'i franchisti' — and this two months before Franco was elected as single commander of the rebel forces. As Dr Moradiellos demonstrates, the confident prophecy of important figures in Whitehall that Franco would see the benefits to Spain of friendship with Britain was not fulfilled.[11]

By the end of July, Junkers 52 and Savoia-Marchetti transport aircraft were arriving to permit the airlift of the bloodthirsty Foreign Legion across the Straits of Gibraltar. That crucial early aid was soon followed by a regular stream of high technology assistance. In contrast to the state-of-the-art equipment arriving from Germany and Italy, complete with technicians, spare parts and the correct workshop manuals, the Republic, shunned by the democracies, had to send its ill-equipped and bookish emissaries to operate in the open arms market and, in consequence, make do with over-priced and obsolete equipment from private arms dealers. However, whereas unstinted Italian aid would severely damage Italian military effectiveness, the Germans, as Christian Leitz demonstrates in chapter 3, were ruthless in ensuring a return on their investment in terms of strategic raw materials and growing penetration of the Spanish mining industry.

Western European diplomats stationed in Moscow had reported to their governments that the initial reaction of the Soviet Union was one of deep embarrassment about the events in Spain. The Kremlin did not want the rising and the revolution which it provoked to undermine its delicately laid plans for an alliance with France. However, by mid-August, as Denis Smyth shows in chapter 4, it was apparent to the Soviet hierarchy that an even greater disaster would befall those plans if the Spanish Republic fell. That would severely alter the European balance of power, leaving France with three Fascist states on her borders. Eventually, it was reluctantly decided to send help. The tanks and planes which arrived in the autumn were, together with the arrival of the International Brigades, to

---

11 On Franco's pro-Axis sentiments after the Spanish Civil War, see Denis Smyth, *Diplomacy and Strategy of Survival: British Policy and Franco's Spain, 1940-41* (Cambridge: Cambridge U. P., 1986), *passim* and Paul Preston, *Franco: A Biography* (London: Harper-Collins, 1993), 323-531.

save Madrid in November 1936. However, they were also to be used to justify the intervention of Hitler and Mussolini. The motivation of both was principally to undermine the Anglo-French hegemony of international relations but they were sure of a sympathetic ear in London when they claimed to be fighting Bolshevism.

The volunteers who fought to save Madrid were described by German and Italian diplomats to their receptive British and French colleagues as agents of Moscow sent to Spain to establish a Communist outpost in Western Europe. In fact, their reasons for going had nothing to do with any such schemes. They were among the first in Europe to take up arms against the Fascist menace. Italian, German and Austrian refugees saw the Spanish Civil War as their first chance to fight back against Fascism. French (the most numerous contingent), British and North-American volunteers went to Spain out of concern about what defeat for the Republic might mean both in international terms and also in their own countries as a boost for the extreme right. In that sense, they were fighting national as well as international conflicts on Spanish soil. An extreme example of this is provided by the Irish who, as Robert Stradling shows in chapter 5, were to be found on both sides, fighting in Spain essentially Irish battles. The pro-Republican volunteers from all over Europe and the Americas were the first in the field in a war which would not end until 1945. These 'premature antifascists' were reviled on their return home to Britain, treated as the 'scum of the earth' in French internment camps or regarded as dangerous and un-American in the United States. Despite this, the surviving volunteers fought in the Second World War — after all, the anti-Fascist war was their war.

The Spanish Republic was fighting not only Franco and his armies but also, to an ever greater degree, the military and economic might of Mussolini and Hitler. Besieged from outside, the Republic also had massive internal problems unknown in Franco's brutally militarized zone. The crumpling of the bourgeois state in the first days of the war saw the rapid emergence of revolutionary organs of parallel power. A massive popular collectivization of agriculture and industry took place. Exhilarating to participants and observers like George Orwell and Franz Borkenau, the great collectivist experiments of the autumn of 1936 did little to create a war machine. That task, as is demonstrated by Helen Graham in chapter 7, would lie at the heart of the undeclared civil war which would rage within the Republican zone until mid-1937. Socialist leaders like Prieto and Juan Negrín were convinced that a conventional state, with central control of the economy and the institutional instruments of mass mobilization, was essential if there was to be an efficacious war effort.

Even the marginalized President of the Republic, Manuel Azaña, shared this goal. However, as James Whiston shows in chapter 9, it is a measure of his abdication from the struggle that his views were expressed in oblique form in his novel-cum-dialogue, *La velada en Benicarló*. The Communists and the Soviet advisers agreed — not only was this common sense but the playing down of the revolutionary activities of Trotskyists and anarchists was necessary to reassure the bourgeois democracies with which the Soviet Union sought understanding. In chapter 6, Chris Ealham explains why the traditional theory and practice of Spanish anarchism was inimical to the aims of Negrín and his Soviet advisers. The anti-statist thinking of the libertarian movement, the Confederación Nacional del Trabajo, the Federación Anarquista Ibérica and the Federación Ibérica de Juventudes Libertarias, led them to pose their revolutionary goals in opposition to the Republican state. Deeply damaging to the central economic coordination of the war effort, this also led to crippling internecine hostilities within the Republican zone. The activities of 'uncontrollables' who engaged in robbery and violence for their own ends undermined the efforts of successive Republican governments to project an image of bourgeois normality. This in turn permitted the coalition of Republicans, moderate Socialists and Communists to justify the crushing of a revolution which could be portrayed as objectively playing into the hands of Fascism.

It was in large part against the indisciplined individualism of the anarchists that, henceforth, there would be a struggle to establish a Popular Front government which fulfilled the expectations of the architects of the Popular Front electoral coalition of February 1936. That was eventually established under the premiership of Negrín from May 1937. Despite having crushed the revolution, incorporated the working-class militias into the regular forces and dismantled the collectives, it still did not achieve victory — not because the policies were wrong but because of the strength of the international forces arrayed against the Republic.

With the Spanish Republic abandoned by the Western Powers and opposed by Franco, Hitler and Mussolini, only the Soviet Union came to its aid. Of course, Stalin did not do so out of any idealism or sentiment. Rather the case was that, threatened by expansionist Germany, he was hoping like his Czarist predecessors to limit the threat by seeking an encircling alliance with France. He feared rightly that, if Franco won the war with the help of Hitler, France would crumble. Accordingly, he set out to give sufficient aid to the Republic to keep it alive while ensuring that the revolutionary elements on the left were prevented from provoking the conservative decision-makers in London from supporting the Axis in an anti-Bolshevik crusade. It is appalling that the revolutionary *élan* of the Spanish people, the Republic's greatest asset, should have been squandered or that the sincere revolutionaries of the POUM should have been smeared as Nazi agents and bloodily suppressed by the agents of the NKVD. It is certainly true, as Denis Smyth argues, that Stalin's rational quest for respectability did nothing to alter the contempt felt in Whitehall for the Spanish Republic.

However, as Herbert Southworth demonstrates in chapter 10, one of the consequences of the Cold War was the successful dissemination of the idea that it was the Stalinist repression which led to Franco's victory. In the historiography of the Spanish Civil War sponsored by the CIA-funded Congress for Cultural Freedom, minor episodes of the internecine struggles within the Republican zone are allowed to dwarf the wider issues of the war. The success of that historiography has obscured the fact that Hitler, Mussolini, Franco and Chamberlain were responsible for that victory, not Stalin. It is difficult to imagine how a revolutionary Spain could have succeeded without the support of Russian arms. Indeed, without Russian arms and the International Brigades, Madrid would probably have fallen in November 1936 and Franco been victorious long before the anarchists and Trotskyists of Barcelona became an issue.

The consequences of his victory are examined in chapter 8 by Michael Richards. Franco was determined to win the war slowly and thoroughly. His ambition was not a swift and stylish victory but a thorough-going demolition of everything related to the Republic as the first step towards the permanence of his own regime. If he did not aspire to a thousand-year Reich, he made it clear in many speeches that he intended to eradicate socialism, communism, anarchism, liberal democracy and freemasonry from Spain for centuries to come. Part of that project was accomplished by a slow war of attrition in which many Republicans were killed and many communities annihilated. Systematic and deliberate massacres such as those at Badajoz, Malaga and Guernica had an immediate objective within the war but also a longer-term aim of demoralizing the Republican population.[12] To put it crudely, Franco intended that those Republicans who were not killed in the war or forced into exile would be left too traumatized ever to oppose his regime. Michael Richards explains what that really meant in terms of losses of ideals, of hope, of identity, of dignity, of material comfort, of personal security. He shows how, by the deliberate and systematic use of terror, the conditions were created in which the struggle for mere survival erased any possibility of political opposition. Franco's regime would be the institutionalization of his victory in the Spanish Civil War. The Great Powers would acquiesce in its survival just as they had acquiesced in its creation.

---

12 See Paul Preston, 'General Franco as Military Leader', *Transactions of The Royal Historical Society*, 6th Series, IV (1994), 21-41.

PART I

INTERNATIONAL HOSTILITY TO THE SECOND REPUBLIC

1

The Gentle General:
The Official British Perception of General Franco during the Spanish Civil War

ENRIQUE MORADIELLOS

Just before the outbreak of the Spanish Civil War, information on Francisco Franco in official circles was decidedly scanty, despite the fact that the future Caudillo had been a guest of the British Government in January 1935, as the Spanish representative at the funeral of George V. It was far less detailed than that available on his famous aviator brother and significantly more sparse than information on Generals Sanjurjo, Berenguer and Goded, whose political activity had in recent years been intense. It was limited to a biographical note in the routine report which the British Embassy in Madrid had to compile on 'leading personalities' for use by the Foreign Office and the government. Nevertheless, the note written in January 1936 by the Ambassador, Sir Henry Chilton, already emphasized the professional merits, political possibilism and anti-revolutionary zeal of the ascendent general. It read as follows:

> Franco, Major General Francisco. Born at Ferrol on the 14th December 1892. An infantry officer who served with great distinction in Morocco, where he commanded the Foreign Legion from 1923 to 1926. He played a conspicuous part in the occupation of the Ajdir sector, for which he was promoted to Brigadier-General. On creating the General Military Academy at Saragossa in 1928, General Primo de Rivera appointed him its first Commandant. When this academy was closed under the first Republican Government, General Franco was appointed to the 15th Infantry Brigade. In 1933 he became Military Commander of

the Balearic Islands.   In February 1935 he was appointed Commander-in-chief, Morocco, but was called home in May, after Sr. Gil Robles had become War Minister, to be chief of the Central General Staff.   He was promoted to his present rank in March 1934.   A fearless officer, clever tactician, popular commander, General Franco is one of the most prominent officers in the Spanish Army, and has now the almost unique record among senior officers of being as much appreciated by Republican War Ministers as he was formerly by Ministers under the Monarchy. He is regarded as a 'national power'.   He acted as principal adviser to the War Minister in many aspects of the military campaign in October 1934 in Asturias.   General Franco belongs to a family of distinguished soldiers.   His brother, Don Ramón, is the well-known airman.[1]

During the critical semester between the Popular Front victory in February 1936 and the military insurrection in July information on Franco received in London remained exiguous. This is surprising because, given Britain's important economic and strategic interests in Spain, analysts in the Embassy and in the Western (Europe) Department in the Foreign Office had closely followed the tense socio-political situation during the Second Republic.[2]   In fact, during this latter period in Conservative governmental circles an interpretation of the Spanish crisis had been developed.   It stressed that Spain was undergoing a pre-revolutionary crisis analogous to that in Russia before the Bolshevik Revolution of October 1917, with an impotent 'Kerenski' Cabinet which was being overwhelmed by the mobilization of the peasants and workers who had brought it to power.   By July these sources almost totally ruled out the possibility of a constitutional resolution of the crisis and expected either an intervention of the army to reimpose order as in 1923 or a civil war which would bring in its train a

---

1   *Records of Leading Personalities in Spain,* 7 January 1936 (Foreign Office Records, Confidential Prints [FO 425], file 413, document W245 [thereafter, FO 425/413 W245]). All British archives referred to are in the Public Record Office (Kew, Surrey). The best and most detailed biography of Franco is Paul Preston, *Franco* (London: Harper-Collins, 1993).

2   *Cf.* Douglas Little, *Malevolent Neutrality. The United States, Great Britain and the Origins of the Spanish Civil War* (Ithaca: Cornell U. P., 1985). Also Enrique Moradiellos, 'The Origins of British Non-Intervention in the Spanish Civil War: Anglo-Spanish Relations in Early 1936', *European History Quarterly,* XXI (1991), No. 3, 339-64.

repetition of the revolutionary events in Russia.

It was in this context that the name of Franco appeared in reports relaying rumours of a military coup picked up by the Madrid Embassy in the spring of 1936. Yet the figure of Franco was only tentatively mentioned, and always appeared after those of the impulsive Goded and the exiled Sanjurjo. It was Goded who, acting as 'Head of the Spanish Army', was responsible for a secret mission to London at the end of May in which the British authorities were warned that a military coup d'état 'designed solely to restore order' was imminent, that it had no Fascist objectives and that it had no connection with Italy.[3]   However, from 18 July, after the outbreak of the military insurrection, the figure of General Franco rapidly acquired importance on the international political stage and he soon shook off his relative anonymity amongst the British governing class.

It was the Ambassador Chilton who, on urgently telegraphing the Foreign Office on 19 July to inform it that 'Senor Gil Robles and General Franco had come out openly against the Government', first emphasized his stature over and above the other generals. Simultaneously, Franco's standing was reinforced by the reports from the British consul in Tetuán (capital of Spanish Morocco), which described him as the 'head of the Army of Africa', precisely the part of the Spanish army with most combat experience, operational capability and prestige abroad.[4]   Indeed, the failure of Generals Goded and Fanjul in Barcelona and Madrid respectively and their immediate detention (prior to their execution within a matter of weeks), along with the accidental death of Sanjurjo in Lisbon, pushed Franco to a position of pre-eminence in a matter of hours.   Furthermore, these unforeseen set-backs eliminated competitors and converted the Moroccan troops into the key

---

3   Note by Mr Shuckburgh, 30 May 1936 (Foreign Office Records, General Correspondence, FO 371/20522 W4919). In a previous despatch by Chilton to the Foreign Office (22 April) he mentioned the rumour that after the military coup 'either General Franco or General Goded' would be 'the dictator' (FO 371/20521 W3720).

4   Despatch from Mr Monck-Mason (British consul at Tetuán) and telegram from Chilton, 18 and 19 July 1936 (FO 371/10523 W6702 and W6626).

force that could break the initial equilibrium in Spain between the military insurgents on the one hand and the worker and pro-government militias, on the other.

Franco himself built his reputation by very successfully undertaking wide-ranging international negotiations aimed at securing vital foreign support. At the same time as he contacted local representatives of the Fascist governments of Rome and Berlin to obtain aircraft to transport his troops to Seville, the General held a series of meetings with the British consul in Tetuán, Mr Monck-Mason, to ask the British Government to close the ports of Gibraltar and Tangier to the Republican navy, which was blockading the Straits.

At his first meeting with the British consul on 20 July, Franco maintained that he was fighting against a 'frankly Communist' enemy, and stated that for this reason the United Kingdom should close its port facilities. The British Government, after receiving this request along with a contrary one from the Republican authorities, on 22 July decided *de facto* to accept Franco's demand and neutralized the ports of Gibraltar and Tangier for the duration of the War. To a large extent, this reaction reflected the British authorities' fears about the presence in Gibraltar of a fleet 'commanded and manned by Communists' (according to the Governor of Gibraltar). More importantly, it followed on from their conclusion that in Spain 'military forces' were combating 'a virtual Soviet' under the umbrella of a lifeless, phantasmagoric government, which was, as a result, unworthy of either indirect or direct support. Such a government, as a mask for Bolshevik expansionism, deserved, in the eyes of London, no more than the arms embargo which would soon be imposed with the signing of the Non-Intervention Pact by all the European Powers.[5]

---

[5]   Dispatch from Mr Monck-Mason, 21 July 1936; telegram from the Gibraltar Governor, 22 July 1936; telegram from the Embassy secretary, 21 July 1936 (FO 371/20523 W6758, W6747 and W6575); Cabinet Minutes and Conclusions, 22 July 1936; Cabinet Office Records, Cabinet Minutes (CAB 23), file 85 (thereafter, CAB 23/85). For an overview of British policy during the war see Jill Edwards, *The British Government and the Spanish Civil War* (London: Macmillan, 1979). Also, Enrique Moradiellos, 'Appeasement and Non-Intervention: British Policy during the Spanish Civil War', in *Britain and*

In these initial (daily) meetings with the British consul in Tetuán, Franco transmitted the image of a prudent and sincere leader who accepted the difficulties he faced and who had to look for aircraft and other help from abroad. On 29 July, after the arrival of the first planes sent secretly by Hitler and Mussolini, Franco 'very optimistically' informed the consul that '[he] had now a larger number of aeroplanes than the Government forces', and that he would use them to transport his troops over to the mainland and initiate the march on Madrid. He also affirmed that, 'he did not attempt to conceal the fact that the reduction of Madrid would take some time to effect'. Such a show of prudence and sincerity led the consul to conclude that: 'There can be no doubt that General Franco is extremely anxious to do nothing that might entail complications with Great Britain'.[6] In this way, together with his success in obtaining Italian-German aid, by the end of July Franco had attained a pre-eminent position amongst the insurgents in the European chancilleries and mass media, far above the other generals and the anonymous National Defence Junta officially established in Burgos.

This could be seen in the first debate on the Spanish conflict in the British House of Commons. On 31 July, a leading figure in the Labour Party, Philip Noel-Baker, maintained that the Republican Government still retained the right to buy British arms in order to defend itself and bitterly denounced the attempted coup by 'General Franco and his fellow-conspirators'. Even the anodyne minutes of British Cabinet meetings reflect a significant change of emphasis. Hence, while in the meeting of the Cabinet Committee on Foreign Policy on 27 July the rebels were referred to simply as the 'Spanish Insurgents', when it met again on 25 August the phrase 'General Franco's forces' predominated. By this time, in the British right-wing and Catholic press, Franco had been elevated to the position of head of an anti-Communist crusade. Thus, on 20 July, the London daily, *The Morning Post*, stated that 'General Franco is the strong man of the movement'. Seven days later the *The Daily*

---

the Threat to Stability in Europe, 1918-1945, ed. P. Caterrall and J. C. Morris (London: Leicester U. P., 1993), 94-104.
6   Despatches from Mr Monck-Mason, 24 and 30 July 1936 (FO 371/20524 and 20525, W6989 and W7492).

Mail published the first interview Franco had given to a foreign newspaper under the headline, 'GENERAL FRANCO TALKS', in which he was presented as the 'commander-in-chief of the southern anti-red Army'. The general's message could not have been more direct and straight-forward:

> Communism triumphant spells the destruction of Western Civilization and religion. We appeal to the great nations for sympathy in our struggle against destructive Bolshevism.[7]

With respect to official British Conservative circles, although never admitted in public, the promotion of Franco into the representative of the insurgent forces had very positive, even though hidden, effects. Given Franco's record and his cautious personality, the British authorities were convinced that they were faced with a nationalist and counter-revolutionary military movement, which had no aggressive fascistic ambitions to revise the international *status quo*, as was the case with Italy and Germany. Franco's insurrection was therefore perceived as posing no threat to the country's strategic position (the security of the British naval base in Gibraltar) or to its economic interests (the continuation of substantial British investments and the dominance of U.K. companies over Spanish commerce).

In brief, Franco did not appear to be either a dangerous doctrinaire politician (like Adolf Hitler) or an unpredictable Fascist demagogue (like Benito Mussolini). Rather he was viewed as a good Spanish military man, who was prudent, conservative and nationalist, and who had risen up only to combat chaos and the spectre of social revolution which had now raised its head in the Republican rearguard. Moreover, as Britain's old and faithful Portuguese allies never tired of repeating, Franco intended 'the establishment of a regime resembling the Portuguese rather than a Fascist State'.

---

7   *Parliamentary Debates. House of Commons*, 31 July 1936, column 1891. Minutes of the Committee on Foreign Policy (limited to the most important ministers and charged with evaluating the diplomatic strategy of the country). Cabinet Office Records, Committee on Foreign Policy (CAB 27), file 622 (thereafter, CAB 27/622). On the impact of the war on British public opinion see the classic study by Kenneth W. Watkins, *Britain Divided. The Effects of the Spanish Civil War on British Political Opinion* (London: Thomas Nelson, 1963).

Whichever side won the war, Britain could count on two decisive elements to guarantee her position in Spain: in the first place British financial and economic strength, which was of crucial importance for the Spanish economy, and, secondly, the military supremacy of the Royal Navy in the area. Nevertheless, Franco's victory in the Civil War was viewed as a 'splendid' prospect because, in the revealing words of a senior official within the Foreign Office, 'the alternative to Franco is Communism tempered by anarchy'.[8]

It was because of this reasoned political confidence in Franco, and in the nature of the insurrection he headed, that the British authorities contemplated his quest for Italo-German aid and its deliverance without excessive concern. Moreover, Franco was quick to send a telegram to London on 8 August giving a formal guarantee that there would be no territorial agreements with Rome or Berlin in recompense:

> Sent via Lisbon Stop Categorically deny the story spread in that country about supposed promise of bases in Morocco to any Power Stop Spanish National Movement will respect treaties in vigour with all loyalty Stop General Franco.[9]

As the reactions in the Foreign Office indicate, this denial was accepted as sincere and truthful. Sir George Mounsey, Assistant Under-Secretary in charge of Western Europe, noted laconically that: 'It is not a Spanish characteristic to bargain away his property'. Mr Shuckburgh, clerk officer responsible for Spanish affairs in the Western Department, added afterwards, 'we can probably rely on the General's nationalistic feeling to prevent anything of that sort'. Nevertheless, in order to prevent any misunderstandings Anthony Eden, Secretary of the Foreign Office, asked for and obtained approval from the Cabinet to transmit a warning, *suaviter in modo*, to the unpredictable Mussolini laying out the tolerable limits for Great Britain of his support for Franco. These were respect for the

---

8   Minute by Gladwyn Jebb, 25 November 1936 (FO 371/20570 W15915). The above adjective is taken from a private letter (1 August 1936) by David Margesson, Conservative Chief Whip, to his friend Neville Chamberlain, then Chancellor of the Exchequer and Prime Minister *in pectore* (in J. Edwards, *op. cit.*, 99). The Portuguese guarantee is taken from a despatch from the Chargé d'Affaires in Lisbon, 16 August 1936 (FO 371/20531 W8783).

9   Telegram and minutes, 11 August 1936 (FO 371/20528 W8158).

territorial integrity of Spain and the *status quo* in the Western Mediterranean.[10]

The evolution of the political situation in the insurgent camp accentuated British confidence in General Franco. Given the great expansion of the Fascist Falange Española on the back of the wartime social mobilization, his maintenance of tight military control over the anti-Republican coalition was much appreciated in London. On 25 September Mr Oswald Scott, First Secretary of the Embassy (evacuated to Hendaye near the Franco-Spanish border), sent a dense report to London which was to be of key importance in the definitive crystallization of the official British position. In it he argued that a victory for the Republic would result in an inexorable Balkanization of Spain combined with total Soviet dominance. In addition, a note enclosed by the Commercial Secretary added that: 'This will be the end of our financial stake in Spain and the ruin of our commerce for years'. In contrast, the expected victory of the insurgents would bring a badly needed stability to the country on the basis of rule by General Franco with the support of the social-Catholic masses, who would act as a bulwark against Falange extremism:

> General Franco has a wider vision and contemplates probably a liberal military dictatorship, with the Roman Catholic Church re-established but kept aloof from politics, and measures of social, industrial and agrarian reform designed to preclude a recurrence of the conditions which in recent years made unrest inevitable among the working and peasant classes. If Sr. Gil Robles were to be able to reassume control of Acción Popular and the CEDA he might quite well be found co-operating with General Franco but his absence from Spain in the early days of the revolt has for the time being destroyed his prestige and popularity and opened the road for the extreme elements of Falange Española. [...] This [collaboration between Franco and Gil Robles] should afford a combination with sufficient vision, discipline and administrative ability to produce a government capable of giving the country what it has looked for in vain for years: firm leadership, progressive ideals, education (not on purely clerical lines), and perhaps even equal justice.

---

10   Telegram and minute, 13 and 21 August 1936 (FO 371/20532 W8997); Cabinet Minutes, 2 September 1936 (CAB 23/85).

The Commercial Secretary added, in his accompanying note, that he saw as achievable the British hope that it would be possible to intensify future relations with the new Spanish regime through the old, well established, recourse to the diplomacy of pound sterling:

> I do not think that Germany and Italy will be able to exert a special influence on Spanish Commercial policy. As long as the United Kingdom remains a large market for Spanish exports, we shall have adequate means of protecting ourselves. Commerce usually depends upon self-interests, and gratitude rarely plays an important part.

Both reports were subject to a close examination by high-ranking civil servants in the Foreign Office, and they were sent to other ministries (War, Admiralty, Air, Board of Trade and the Treasury) for their information. On the basis of these reports, the desk officer in charge of Spanish affairs in the Foreign Office elaborated a crucial minute which took up the generalized identification of Franco as 'the protagonist of a liberal dictatorship', whose establishment would be favourable for the interests of the United Kingdom. Given its sincerity it is worth quoting at length:

> I suggest that our chances of regaining our influence in Spain during this period [the postwar] are considerable, owing to the fact that the Spanish revolution, unlike the Fascist and Nazi revolutions, will have been won primarily by the military, who traditionally look to the United Kingdom and France rather than to Germany and Italy. [...] It is therefore a British interest that a liberal military rather than a Fascist dictatorship should emerge (1) in order to counteract Italian and German influence, (2) in order to stabilise the internal situation.[11]

---

11 Minute by Mr Montagu-Pollock in response to the reports by Mr Scott and Mr Pack cited, 9 October 1936 (FO 371/20540 W12454). Mr Pack reaffirmed his opinion in an extensive report (30 October 1936) in which he pointed out that 'when the war is over Spain will be in need of imports considerably above her normal requirement [...], will be short of foreign exchange and there will be a grave need for extensive foreign credits [...]. In any case the obvious country in which to obtain such foreign credits will be Great Britain. The inference is that we shall, in the future, be in a very strong position for negotiating any commercial agreement with the new Spanish Government, even though we may have offended them in the course of the

These arguments and the expectation of a rapid end to the war guided the conduct of the British authorities during the whole of the first semester of the Civil War. They were behind the official policy of collective Non-Intervention, whose real aims were less impartial than they were declared to be. These were, in reality, to confine the war to Spain and at the same time to block the support of Britain's French ally to the Republic, prevent an Anglo-French alliance with the Soviet Union on the Spanish problem, and side-step any conflict with Germany and Italy as a result of their aid to Franco. Winston Churchill had defined these aims succintly in a private letter to Eden on 7 August:

> It seems to me most important to make Blum [French Socialist Premier] stay with us strictly neutral, even if Germany and Italy continue to back the rebels and Russia sends money to the Government.[12]

However, the unexpected Republican resistance in Madrid at the end of 1936, thanks to Soviet military aid, destroyed the expectation of a short military conflict. At the same time, the sudden intensification of Italo-German military and diplomatic support undermined the credibility of the European system of collective Non-Intervention. In these circumstances the unanimity of the British leadership regarding the policies followed began to break down. The growing Italo-German intervention and collaboration, along with the signs of Fascist growth in the Francoist zone, led Anthony Eden and his collaborators in the Foreign Office to consider necessary a re-evaluation of the potential danger for British interests and a redesign of the country's policies with respect to what was now perceived as likely to be a long war.

On the last day of December 1936, Sir Robert Vansittart, Permanent Under-Secretary at the Foreign Office, presented to the Cabinet a dense secret report on *The World Situation and British Rearmament*. According to this document, the principal threat to the far-flung and weakened British Empire was to be

---

war' (FO 371/20519 W14919).

12 Foreign Office Records, Eden Papers (FO 954), file 27. *Cf.* E. Moradiellos, 'British Political Strategy in the Face of the Military Rising of 1936 in Spain', *Contemporary European History*, I (1992), No. 2, 123-37.

found in German revisionism and its attempt to create a front with Italy (and Japan) which was nominally anti-Communist, but which could be turned against the United Kingdom. Faced with this danger, the British response should be to maintain the present policy of appeasement, negotiation and limited rearmament, while exploring the possibilities of separating Italy from Germany and avoiding the nightmare of an exhausting conflict on three separate fronts. In this respect, the report called attention to the potential risks which the present policy of tacit tolerance towards the Nazi-Fascist activities in Spain could have:

> The two dictator States are creating a third; and, by recognising General Franco's government before he is sure of winning, they have committed themselves irretrievably to making a success of his venture, thus limiting niceties as to means. This may well bring the dictators still closer together, anyhow for a while, though here again there are already signs that Italy is disquieted by the thoroughness of the German effort, and might conceivably be prised loose. It is true that the Soviet government, which seems lately bereft of statesmanship or even card-sense, is largely responsible for making Spain the scene and cause of the bloodiest form of that very ideological struggle that we are seeking to prevent. The fact remains that the new totalitarian partners, who have been keeping their domains on a positive war-footing for the past few years, have cheerfully accepted the opportunity, and with their great quantities of surplus war material have turned ideological cannibalism into something even more concretely inimical to our interests. It is ironically true that, the crisis once precipitated, the victory of the Right would be no worse for us than the victory of the Left — a very extreme Left — which would spread a dividing and disintegrating contagion into France and from France into ourselves, and would so alter the European kaleidoscope as to present Germany with hegemony ready made. On the other hand, if Franco wins, the now combined weight of the two larger autocrats — unless natural causes and our own skill diminish their unity — will be too great for him, and he will be pulled more completely into their camp than his past proclivities and present interests render natural. We shall then be faced by at least a temporarily working combination of dictators, major, minor and minimus.[13]

---

[13] Reproduced in *Documents on British Foreign Policy, 1918-1945,*

These same doubts were expressed concurrently by Anthony Eden in Cabinet in order to force a firmer Non-Intervention policy whose objective would be to favour a mediated settlement which would prevent the establishment of a Spanish regime closely associated with the German-Italian Axis. However, these worries were not shared by the other members of the British Government nor by high-ranking policy makers and military strategists. In the words of the influential Sir Maurice Hankey, Secretary to the Cabinet and of the Committee on Imperial Defence:

> I take a less serious view than he of the German and Italian adventures in Spain. General Franco is still a long way off victory, even if he captures Madrid, and, even if he wins, he may easily quarrel with his erstwhile supporters. Gratitude is not a strong tie in Politics.[14]

Hence, after the transformation of the conflict into a long war at the end of 1936, the British leaders decided to maintain their Non-Intervention policy, and their tacit acceptance of an Italo-German aid which, at the end of the day, served to counter Soviet support for the Republic. The fact was that it seemed clear that this Nazi-Fascist help was in no way modifying the nature of the insurgent camp. Sir George Mounsey recalled in this regard: 'We have all along being inclined to discount the permanence of any German or Italian influence in Spain. Franco has had to lean on those two Powers because no help was forthcoming from any other quarter'. In any case, the marginal 'Spanish affair' could not be allowed to undermine the key policy of European appeasement and the possibility of separating Italy from Germany, especially because the resort to the 'diplomacy of pound sterling' would always be available in Spain. In March 1937, Neville Chamberlain, then Chancellor of the Exchequer and two months later to be Prime Minister, headed the opposition to the policy of firmness favoured by Eden with this key argument:

Series 2, vol. XVII (London: H.M.S.O., 1979), appendix II, 779-80.

14 'Some Remarks on Sir Robert Vansittart's Memorandum', January 1937 (Cabinet Office Records, series 63 [Hankey Papers], file 51: CAB 63/51). On the efforts made by Eden see the minutes of the meeting of the Cabinet Committee on Foreign Policy, 8 January 1937 (CAB 27/628).

It had to be remembered that we were dealing not only with the Spanish insurgents, but, behind them, with the Germans and Italians. General Franco was not a free agent. No doubt he hoped to win, but hardly without assistance from the Germans and Italians. Consequently he was unlikely to agree to any undertaking which was unacceptable to the Germans and Italians unless we were able to do something disagreeable to him in return. The Germans and Italians would not allow him to do so. To insist up to the point proposed in the Secretary of State's Memorandum therefore, was not only useless but must lead to a very serious situation with Germany and Italy. If and when General Franco had won the Civil War, however, the situation would be very different, and no doubt he would be looking round for help from other countries besides Germany and Italy. That would be the moment at which to put strong pressure upon him. [...] that would be the time for action.[15]

The decision of the British Government to maintain unaltered its policy of unconditional Non-Intervention — in practice so favourable to the insurgents — was accompanied by a confirmation of its secret confidence in General Franco. This reaffirmation was not unrelated to the measures taken by the General and his victories on the battlefield, and was not even undermined by the crisis provoked by the naval blockade of Bilbao in April 1937. After the key conquest of the city, and of its industrial hinterland two months later, Franco renewed his pledge to respect British interests in Spain both through his unofficial representative in London, the Duke of Alba, and through the Portuguese Government. At the same time, the General communicated his acceptance of the British presence in Gibraltar and 'his desire that the nations of the Iberian Peninsula should work together within the orbit of British foreign policy'.[16]

Moreover, the recent changes in the structure of the regime and, above all, the forced unification of all the right wing political parties in April seemed to confirm the military's predominance over the extremist elements within the

---

15 Cabinet Minutes and Conclusions, 3 March 1937 (CAB 23/87). The previous quotation in a minute, 3 April 1937 (FO 371/21288 W6244).

16 Minute by Lord Cranborne, 28 June 1936 (FO 800/296 [Foreign Office Records, series 800, 'Private Collections', file 296, 'Cranborne Papers']); despatch from Eden to the Ambassador in Lisbon, 28 June 1936 (FO 425/414).

Nationalist coalition, and the increasingly unassailable position of Franco at its head. Both these phenomena were seen as reassuring in official British circles, which continued to maintain a mythical vision of Franco as an affable and 'liberal' general, who was the most effective antidote to Falangist extremism and the best solution to the Spanish tragedy. Thus, on 13 July 1937 a minute by Mr Walter Roberts, Head of the Western (Europe) Department at the Foreign Office, insisted that General Franco was 'a man of liberal ideas surrounded by reactionaries' and that his triumph and the consolidation of authoritarian rule under his person was in the British interest:

> I have always thought that in the event of a Nationalist victory General Franco, if he were to survive as a political leader, would have to maintain for a time a regime which did not include concessions to former enemies, and that it would only be *after* his position was fully established that he could afford to make a beginning with his liberal programme. If I am right, it would probably be in the interests of future peace in Spain that this position should be accepted by foreign governments, and in particular by His Majesty's Government, and that we should resist the clamour for the immediate restoration of a parliamentary regime, which would almost inevitably lead to General Franco being overthrown by his extremist supporters and to a further period of civil war.[17]

Mr Roberts' reasoning was backed up with more firmly grounded arguments by Lord Cranborne, Parliamentary Under-Secretary of State at the Foreign Office, in an extensive report dated 21 July. Cranborne argued that fears expressed by some official analysts, along with leaders of the Labour Party and some Conservatives, regarding the security of Gibraltar and British naval hegemony in the Mediterranean in the event of a Francoist victory with Italo-German help were unfounded. His confidence was based on the persuasive power of the pound sterling and the dissuasive capability of the Royal Navy:

> I suggest that we are far too apt to assume that General Franco must be regarded as an inevitable danger to us. If he is for the moment hostile, it is largely the result of the present conjunction of circumstances. [...] But there are other and far more enduring

---

17   Minute, 13 July 1937 (FO 371/21295 W12237).

considerations which must incline him, in the long run, towards friendship with England. There is the fact that we want nothing from him, that we do not intend to sue his extremity to extract from him embarrassing concessions. There is the fact that we are the richest country in Europe, and have indeed in the past played far the greatest part in financing the development of Spain. There is the fact that we have the greatest fleet in the world, well placed alternatively to blockade or assist in the protection of his coasts. There is the fact of our long friendship with Portugal. All these are considerations that must be constantly in his mind. [...] A Franco Spain is not necessarily a weakness to the British Empire — it might easily be a strength. But it rests with us to take the first step, if the foundations of future friendship are to be well and truly laid.[18]

During the second half of 1937, in accordance with these ideas, British policy was frankly favourable to the Franco regime on a series of bilateral and diplomatic fronts. In particular, in November 1937, the British Cabinet recognized the Francoist administration as *de facto* Government in Spain and there then followed an exchange of diplomatic agents between London and Burgos. The new British agent, Sir Robert Hodgson, held his first meeting with General Franco on 31 January 1938, and his impressions served to validate the General and the majority view already held within the Foreign Office:

He has a very attractive personality. He is small of stature, probably no more than 5 feet and 6 inches, stockily built, and, I understand, 46 years of age. His hair, which was originally black, is now turning a steel grey and curls over his temples. He has a soft voice and speaks gently and rapidly. His charm lies in his eyes, which are of a yellow brown, intelligent, vivacious, and have a marked kindliness of expression. [...] General Franco told me that at the time when the 'movement' broke out he was busy studying English. His lessons had been brusquely interrupted. He then asserted his friendly feelings towards England, mentioning the good feeling which had united the two countries in the past and referring briefly to old history and the Duke of Wellington's campaign. He spoke, too, of the cultural ties which united so many Spanish families with England and of the favourable dispositions which the simple folk in this country entertained towards things

---

18 FO 371/21298 W14857.

English.   Both countries had a maritime tradition and their position on the map was a tie between them. [...] He also ... spoke of Anglo-Spanish relations in a manner which justifies the belief that the cordial tone he used to me was a true index of his sentiments.[19]

After the resignation of Anthony Eden as Secretary of the Foreign Office in February 1938 because of disagreements over the tolerance of Italian intervention, the pro-Francoist proclivities of Neville Chamberlain's Cabinet were further accentuated.   The British leadership was not prepared to allow the Spanish affair to get in the way of the improvement of Anglo-Italian relations, and saw the victory of Franco as a necessary contribution to this aim.   As the private secretary of Lord Halifax, the new Foreign Secretary, stated in his diary on 5 June: 'In Spain the Government are praying for Franco's victory'.   A clear example of this was the pressure put on the French Government in June 1938 definitively to close the southern border with Republican Spain to the supply of Soviet arms.   The success of this policy signified the blockage of the last open route for the importation of arms and munitions to the Republican army.   Franco confidentially expressed his gratitude to Chamberlain for this and other measures in a personal message transmitted by Lord Phillimore on 3 July:

> His Excellency wished me to greet Mr Chamberlain in his name and to thank him heartily for the friendship which he has shown towards Spain and to remind him that by his policy he is defending the same ideals and principles as we are and working in the interests of world peace and civilization.[20]

The offer of neutrality made by Franco in September 1938, during the diplomatic crisis which concluded with the Munich Pact and the partition of Czechoslovakia, temporarily calmed any British anxieties regarding Francoist foreign policy. However, the subsequent deterioration of the situation in Europe and the clear symptoms of growing Fascist influence within the Franco regime rekindled fears within some sectors of

---

19   Despatch, 1 February 1938 (FO 425/415).

20   Message from General Franco, 3 July 1938 (FO 800/323 ['Halifax Papers']).   The previous quotation is in *The Diplomatic Diaries of Oliver Harvey, 1937-1940* (London: Collins, 1970), 148.

the Foreign Office.

In November 1938, various reports sent from Spain contradicted the image harboured by the British of the Spanish Caudillo. Some dispatches stated that Franco 'is now very much under the influence of the Falangists', and especially that his brother-in-law and Minister of the Interior, Ramón Serrano Suñer, was 'very pro-German'. Field-Marshal Sir Philip Chetwode, president of the International Commission for the Exchange of Prisoners, confessed in a private letter to Lord Halifax, that with regard to clemency and humanity Franco 'is worse than the Reds'. Meanwhile, reports from British military attachés on both sides of the conflict stressed that Franco was a mediocre strategist and that his conduct of the war left much to be desired.[21]

With the definitive Nationalist victory in March 1939, Franco's limitations became clear, as did his determination to retain his post without taking any steps towards a Monarchist restoration. The new British Ambassador, Sir Maurice Peterson, who met Franco on 11 April, found him 'a friendly and sincere, although simple-minded, man', whose only 'genuine' obsession was Communism. According to Peterson, Franco shared 'the obstinacy, as well as the chivalry, with which the Spanish tradition credits the Galician' and 'goes on beating the anti-Communist drum because he does not know what other note to sound'.[22]

By this time, the British authorities had reached the conclusion that 'Franco is going to be a big noise for a considerable time to come — a second Primo de Rivera', and that this situation 'would probably suit us best'. Reports insisted that Franco 'enjoys his position', was delighted with the shows of support he had received, and 'is taking root in his capacity as Head of State'. Consequently, 'he is unlikely to step down in favour of anyone else for some considerable time to

---

21 Despatch from the British Ambassador in Paris, 9 November 1938 (FO 371/22631 W14907); private letter from Chetwode to Halifax, 14 November 1938 (FO 800/323); reports from Major Mahony and Major Richards, 7 November and 9 October 1938 (FO 425/415).

22 Despatches by Peterson, 12 April, 9 June 1939 (FO 425/416 and FO 371/24130 W9645).

come'.[23] This, it was felt, could be a guarantee of neutrality in the case of war with Germany because, in the words of a confidential report prepared in July 1939 by the War Office (Directorate of Military Operations and Intelligence), Franco, like the rest of the Spanish generals, 'is fully alive to the dangers which might threaten Spanish Morocco, the Balearics, the Canaries, etc., should Spain excite the hostility of the Democracies'. The same report went on to repeat the favourable impression of Franco which had been predominant in official circles during the Civil War:

> General Franco is a well know Spanish type: Dignified, austere, simple, a devout Catholic, a bland even-tempered, non 'intellectual', Middle Class personality. A good general with a reputation for calmness and cautiousness, but no Napoleon or Frederick The Great. Everything about him is the antithesis of the tub thumping fire-breathing Nazi or Fascist. He gives the impression of being a gentle and humane personality upon whom greatness has been thrust unasked for. He commands complete loyalty from the Generals and therefore from the Army; for the present his position as Head of the State is unchallenged.[24]

Unfortunately for Britain, with the onset of the Second World War, the Foreign Office would soon discover the other side of the gentle general, despite the fact that he was quick to declare Spain's neutrality. At the end of September 1939 Franco received a visit from the Conservative MP, Lord Lloyd, who found him 'quite friendly', but also stated that he was 'full of German propaganda with no real knowledge of what is going on in the world'. Furthermore, according to Lord Lloyd, 'he fully believed the German stories about our naval reverses, and thought that the French would run out of the war'.[25] Meanwhile, within Spain a whole system of secret aid for the German war effort was being put into operation: the official press showed its preference for a German victory without any reservations; Spanish ports were made available as secret bases for the supply of Nazi submarines; and the Spanish military and police authorities gave logistic aid to the German secret

23 Despatch and telegram by Peterson, 3 May, 13 July 1939 (FO 371/24129 and 24131, W7368 and W10625).

24   Report by Major Mahony, 26 July 1939 (FO 371/24131 W11396).

25   Minute, 1 November 1939 (FO 371/23170 C17246).

services.[26] On 9 October 1939 Ambassador Peterson summed up with the following words the significance of these facts: 'the *tempo* of the German drive in Spain has accelerated'.[27]

In conclusion, the gentle general began to show another side of his personality, that of a *dictator minimus*, annoying, irritating and expectant. And once he was launched on his game of war and bluff, for the British the worst was yet to come.

---

26 Minute on Spanish Press and Neutrality, 11 September 1939; note from the Naval Staff, Admiralty, 3 October 1939 (FO 371/23170 C13685 and C17705). *Cf.* Charles B. Burdick, 'Moro: The Resupply of German Submarines in Spain, 1939-1942', *Central European History*, III (1970), No. 3, 256-84.

27 Despatch, 9 October 1939 (FO 371/23168 C16669).

2

Mussolini's Spanish Adventure: From Limited Risk to War[1]

PAUL PRESTON

The Spanish officers who rose in rebellion on 17-18 July 1936 dramatically miscalculated the scale of the task facing them. They had anticipated a classic *pronunciamiento* and assumed that, within a matter of days or at most a couple of weeks, they would control Spain. In general, they had not expected the scale of working-class resistance on the Spanish mainland. More particularly, given that the naval officer corps was solidly anti-Republican, they did not foresee the mutiny which placed the fleet in Government hands and permitted the blockade in Morocco of the most powerful rebel forces, the professional Army of Africa, commanded by General Franco. Accordingly, in the days immediately following the uprising, both Franco and General Emilio Mola, the leader of the military rebels on the Spanish mainland, sent requests for help to Fascist Italy and Nazi Germany. The earliest formal requests from both to reach the German Foreign Office were dismissed out of hand and it was only when emissaries from Franco with Nazi Party connections reached Hitler on the evening of 25 July that a decision was taken to help the Spaniards.[2] Messengers reached Rome as early as 21 July but another four days were to pass before Mussolini began to incline towards taking a hand and a

---

1   This paper has benefited enormously from the help in terms of advice and materials so kindly given me by Lucio Ceva, MacGregor Knox, Ismael Saz and Brian R. Sullivan.

2   Ángel Viñas, *La Alemania nazi y el 18 de julio* (Madrid: Alianza, [2ª ed.] 1977), 308-52; Paul Preston, *Franco: A Biography* (London: Harper Collins, 1993), 154-60.

further two or possibly three before he decided irrevocably to grant the Spanish requests. Despite his lengthy hesitation, the Duce's decision was taken in ignorance of that of Hitler albeit at about the same time or shortly thereafter.[3]

The initial resolutions of both dictators were remarkably similar. They were to send the aircraft and other materials necessary to assist General Franco to transport his forces from Spanish Morocco to the mainland. Over the next weeks and months their commitment to Franco's cause would increase considerably. None the less, Hitler was to remain relatively circumspect, sending important equipment and the crack, technologically advanced, but small, Condor Legion. In contrast, Mussolini's involvement increased to the point at which Italy was, in everything but name, at war with the Spanish Republic. In consequence, his contribution to Franco's victory was decisive. In the process, Mussolini willingly moved into the orbit of the Third Reich and he permitted financial and physical resources to be deployed on a scale which severely diminished Italian military effectiveness in the Second World War.

Given the sheer scale of Mussolini's involvement in Spain, fighting a full-scale external war, it is remarkable how relatively cursory is its treatment at the hands of historians.[4] It is perhaps understandable that there has been little evaluation of the Italian contribution to Franco's victory since it did not suit Francoist historians to seek explanations for the Caudillo's success other than his own genius and, since 1945, Italian historians have not been inclined to dwell on Mussolini's few triumphs in terms of military aggression. The precise calculation of the financial and military costs to Italy of the Duce's Spanish entanglement is a difficult subject which has

3   There is no basis for the assertion of Denis Mack Smith, *Mussolini's Roman Empire* (London: Longman, 1976), 99, that Mussolini made his decision 'Only when he heard that the Germans had agreed to assist'.

4   Maxwell H. H. Macartney and Paul Cremona, *Italy's Foreign and Colonial Policy 1914-1937* (London: Oxford U. P., 1938) and C. J. Lowe and F. Marzari, *Italian Foreign Policy 1870-1940* (London: Routledge & Kegan Paul, 1975) each have only four passing references to the Spanish Civil War. R. J. B. Bosworth, *Italy and the Wider World 1860-1960* (London: Routledge, 1996) has two.

recently begun to receive the treatment which it demands.[5] However, it remains curious that, with the notable exception of the work of the Spanish historian Ismael Saz, two crucial and interrelated questions have not been fully explored.[6] The first is how and why was the initial decision taken in favour of agreeing to the requests of the Spanish rebels. The second concerns the reasons, including Spanish and German pressures, for the escalation of Italian commitment.

The assumptions made by the bulk of the extant historiography are that the initial Italian commitment to Spain was partly a response to reports that French aircraft and munitions were being sent to the Spanish Republic and partly an ideological anti-Communist commitment to preventing the Soviet Union gaining a foothold in the Mediterranean. It is further accepted that the decision was delayed only until the arrival of an emissary, the Spanish Monarchist Antonio Goicoechea, who could confirm the links beween the 1936 uprising and an earlier agreement made by Mussolini in 1934 to assist the Spanish Right to overthrow the Second Republic.

---

5   Generale Mario Montanari, 'L'impegno italiano nella guerra di Spagna', in *Memorie Storiche Militari 1980* (Rome: Ufficio Storico dello Stato Maggiore dell'Esercito, 1981), 121-52; Lucio Ceva, 'Influence de la guerre d'Espagne sur l'armement et les conceptions d'emploi de l'aviation de l'Italie Fasciste', in Fondation pour les Études de Défence Nationale, *Adaptation de l'arme aérienne aux conflits contemporains et processus d'indépendance des armées de l'Air des origines à la fin de la Seconde Guerre mondiale* (Paris: Service Historique de l'Armée de l'Air, 1985), 191-99; Lucio Ceva, 'L'evoluzione dei materiali bellici in Italia', in *L'Italia e la politica di potenza in Europa (1938-40)*, ed. Ennio di Nolfo, Romain H. Rainero and Brunello Vigezzi (Milan: Marzorati Editore, 1981), especially pp. 359-80; Lucio Ceva, 'L'ultima vittoria del fascismo Spagna 1938-1939', *Italia Contemporanea*, (settembre 1994), No. 196, 519-35; Lucio Ceva, 'Conseguenze politico-militari dell'intervento italo-fascista nella guerra civile spagnola', in *La guerra civile spagnola tra politica e letteratura*, eds. G. S. Sacerdotti, A. Colombo and A. Pasinato (Florence: Shakespeare & Co., 1995), 215-29; Angelo Emiliani, 'Costi e conseguenze dell'intervento italiano nella guerra di Spagna' (unpublished paper); Brian R. Sullivan, 'Fascist Italy's Military Involvement in the Spanish Civil War', *The Journal of Military History*, LIX (October 1995), No. 4, 697-727.

6   The author's debts to the exemplary study by Ismael Saz Campos, *Mussolini contra la II República: hostilidad, conspiraciones, intervención (1931-1936)* (Valencia: Edicions Alfons el Magnànim, 1986) will be apparent in subsequent footnotes.

This is essentially the standard view, to be found in the writings of the official Francoist historian of the war,[7] of the principal biographer of Mussolini,[8] of the biographer of the Italian Foreign Minister, Galeazzo Ciano,[9] of the author of the most thorough study of Italian intervention in Spain,[10] and of a large proportion of the voluminous bibliography on the Spanish Civil War. The widespread currency of this version owes much to the existence of a convenient and colourful document containing Goicoechea's own fanciful account of how, on 25 July 1936, he persuaded Ciano to release the Italian assistance which he had negotiated in March 1934.[11]

In fact, Goicoechea had little to do with the Duce's intervention in Spain. Nor was that initiative the fruit of a rash determination to take on both France and Russia in the Mediterranean. Rather it came as the culmination of a complex and anything but spontaneous decision-making process. Ultimately, the long-term commitment would become as personal and capricious as other initiatives by Mussolini, but the original decision was influenced by evaluation of information and pressures from various sources. The input to be considered consisted of the requests and accompanying claims of several Spanish emissaries, of reports from Italian representatives in Spain and Spanish Morocco regarding the likely outcome of the conflict, of information from Italian Embassies in London, Paris and Moscow — but not Berlin —[12] about the likely reaction to the Spanish conflict of Britain,

---

7   Joaquín Arrarás, *Historia de la Cruzada española*, 8 vols, 36 tomos, (Madrid: Ediciones Españolas, 1939-43), III, 126.

8   Renzo de Felice, *Mussolini il duce: lo stato totalitario 1936-1940* (Turin: Einaudi, 1981), 365.

9   Giordano Bruno Guerri, *Galeazzo Ciano: una vita 1903-1944* (Milan: Bompiani, 1979), 227-29.

10   John F. Coverdale, *Italian Intervention in the Spanish Civil War* (Princeton NJ: Princeton U. P., 1975), 72-74.

11   Goicoechea's version appears in José Gutiérrez Ravé, *Antonio Goicoechea* (Madrid: Celebridades, 1965), 34-36.

12   Italo-German conversations held in Rome and Berlin about the Spanish Civil War during the first two weeks of the conflict between deal in generalities about evacuating respective nationals and the dangers of French and Russian involvement. Not until 4 August was there any interchange of information about intervention.

France and Russia, and, to a much lesser extent, of the views of important elements of the Italian establishment, the hierarchy of the Fascist Party, the Church and the Armed Forces.

In the first couple of days, there was little hard information reaching Rome about the situation in Spain. Along with most of the diplomatic corps, the Italian Ambassador, Orazio Pedrazzi, had already taken up residence in his summer quarters in the elegant Basque resort of San Sebastian. In the wake of news that the uprising in Madrid had been defeated and the most effective rebel troops isolated in Morocco, Pedrazzi was deeply pessimistic. He departed rapidly to an hotel in St Jean de Luz on the other side of the frontier. The first gloomy reports that he managed to get through to Rome did nothing to incline Mussolini to intervene.[13]   Pedrazzi's predecessor, Raffaele Guariglia, also went to St Jean de Luz in order to get his Spanish fiancée out of San Sebastian and was so negatively impressed by the uphill task facing the military rebels that he sent a pessimistic report to Rome along with an hysterical claim that the Republic was receiving massive assistance from France.[14]

The first request for Italian help for the Spanish military rebels was carried to Rome by Luis Bolín, the correspondent in England of the Monarchist newspaper *ABC*. Bolín had chartered, and flown as far as Casablanca in, the De Havilland Dragon Rapide which was to go on to the Canary Islands to take Franco to Morocco. When the aircraft stopped at Casablanca on the return, Bolín joined Franco on the last stage of his journey to Tetuán in Spanish Morocco. On arrival, it was made clear that the ferocious Army of Africa, with its 47,000 well-armed and well-trained men, was effectively blockaded in Africa by the Spanish fleet now in the hands of its loyal Republican crews. Franco swiftly instructed Bolín to go to Rome to seek help. He gave him a sheet of paper containing the cryptic message 'I

---

13 Pedrazzi to MAE, 18 July 1936, Archivio Storico del Ministero degli Affari Esteri (ASMAE), Politica, Spagna, busta 11, telegrama 173; 20 July 1936, ASMAE, Spagna Fondo di Guerra (SFG), b.1; José Ignacio Escobar, *Así empezó* (Madrid: G. del Toro, 1974), 65-66; Coverdale, *Italian Intervention*, 68-69.

14 Raffaele Guariglia, *Ricordi 1922-1946* (Naples: Edizioni Scientifiche Italiane, 1949), 325. His first wife had died, see p. 210.

authorize Don Luis Antonio Bolín to negotiate urgently in England, Germany or Italy the purchase of aircraft and supplies for the Spanish non-Marxist Army'. When Bolín asked what kind of aircraft and supplies, Franco added a scribbled footnote in pencil '12 bombers, 3 fighters with bombs (and bombing equipment) of from 50 to 100 kilos. One thousand 50-kilo bombs and 100 more weighing about 500 kilos'. Bolín was to get further authorization for his mission from General José Sanjurjo Sacanell, the nominal head of the military uprising, who was in Lisbon. On 20 July, armed with another signature, Bolín flew in the Dragon Rapide from Lisbon to Biarritz, where he spent the evening in the company of the Conde de los Andes (Francisco Moreno y Zulueta) and the Marqués de Luca de Tena, the owner of *ABC*. Andes telephoned the exiled Spanish King Alfonso XIII who was on holiday in Czechoslovakia. He agreed to help in persuading the Fascist authorities to grant the necessary military assistance. The Dragon Rapide took Bolín to Marseilles on the morning of 21 July whence he continued his journey by commercial aircraft. He arrived in a hot and muggy Rome later the same afternoon only to find his first efforts to gain entrance to the Palazzo Venezia rebuffed by a good-natured guard.[15] That evening, Bolín received a telephone call from Alfonso XIII announcing that his equerry, the Marqués de Viana, was leaving for Rome with a letter of introduction. On the following day, 22 July, accompanied by Viana and armed with the letter from the King, Bolín secured a meeting with the Spanish-speaking Ministro degli Affari Esteri, Galeazzo Ciano.[16]

It was the Spaniards' good fortune that Mussolini had himself relinquished the post of Ministro degli Affari Esteri barely six weeks earlier on 9 June and appointed his son-in-law. The dismissal of his Under-Secretary at the Ministero degli Affari Esteri, the cautious anti-German (and therefore) pro-Austrian Fulvio Suvich, represented an abandonment of his

15 *Daily Express*, 26 June 1938; Luis Bolín, *Spain: The Vital Years* (Philadelphia: J. B. Lippincott, 1967), pp. 52-54, 159-67; Antonio González Betes, *Franco y el Dragón Rapide* (Madrid: Ediciones Rialp, 1987), 186-89.

16 Alfonso XIII to Mussolini, 20 July 1936, *I Documenti Diplomatici Italiani*, 8ª serie, vol. IV (Rome: Istituto Poligrafico e Zecca dello Stato, 1993), 648-49; Bolín, *Spain*, 167-68; Saz, *Mussolini contra la II República*, 243.

role of guarantor of Austrian independence and a move towards closer relations with Hitler. The thirty-four year-old Ciano was something of a lightweight — handsome and quick-witted but more given to the social pleasures of the 'notte romana' than to long hours with diplomatic papers. He came to the post after being Minister of Press and Propaganda and a spell in Ethiopia at the head of the *Squadriglia La Disperata*. It was assumed that he owed his preferment to the fact that he was the son of the influential Fascist Party hierarch, Admiral Costanzo Ciano, and, more importantly, to his marriage in 1930 to Mussolini's daughter, Edda. Mussolini's own sons, Bruno and Vittorio, had shown little political talent and the Duce was mistrustful of the more intelligent members of the Fascist hierarchy. Accordingly, his benevolence towards Ciano made it perhaps inevitable that his son-in-law should harbour ambitions of one day succeeding the Duce. Certainly, familiarity with his father-in-law had intensified his tendency to arrogance and to precipitate decision-making.[17]

Ciano had helped popularize the idea that the Abyssinian war had made Italy again a great power. His promotion was seen in the diplomatic corps as representing a fascistization of the Palazzo Chigi. He believed that his mission was to make Italian foreign policy fully Fascist. He was determined not to fall into the sin perceived as having been committed by Dino Grandi, Undersecretary from May 1925 to September 1929 and then Minister until July 1932, of letting the traditional career diplomats blunt his Fascist thrust. In fact, if Grandi had a Fascist thrust, it had been blunted more by the realities of the Great Power relationships within which he had to function. Henceforth, ambassadors and other diplomats would not be permitted to speak directly with the Duce. The British Ambassador, Sir Eric Drummond, commented 'In future, heads of missions will have to approach Signor Mussolini through the

---

17 Yvon de Begnac, *Palazzo Venezia: storia di un regime* (Rome: Editrice La Rocca, 1950), 571-84; Guerri, *Ciano*, 159-85; Mario Donosti, *Mussolini e l'Europa: la politica estera fascista* (Rome: Edizioni Leonardo, 1945), 43-44; Giorgio Pini and Duilio Susmel, *Mussolini: l'uomo e l'opera*, 4 vols (Firenze: La Fenice, 1953-55), III, 357. For an incident which showed the sexual decadence of Ciano, see José Antonio Girón de Velasco, *Si la memoria no me falla* (Barcelona: Editorial Planeta, 1994), 46.

channel of a young and inexperienced man'. Drummond also quoted an Italian observer as perceiving Ciano as 'another diaphragm between Mussolini and the world'.[18] Within a year of taking up the post, the Count would boast to Rudolf Hess that 'in Italy, the most Fascist-minded Ministry is the Foreign Ministry'. In private, he would lament the time it took 'to conquer the Palazzo Chigi' saying 'only I know what a struggle I have to make these goats keep step to the Fascist march'.[19] He was exaggerating for the benefit of Hess — the career diplomats had often not been able to restrain Mussolini before 1936 and the Ministry itself was not entirely opposed to the Duce's expansionism.

Nevertheless, a process of greater fascistization would be carried out by means of the *Gabinetto*, an inner cabinet staffed by like-minded young Fascists and headed by the one-time head of propaganda services, Ottavio De Peppo. The head of his personal secretariat ('capo della segreteria particolare del ministro'), and deputy to De Peppo, was his close friend, Filippo Anfuso. Mussolini's first Ambassador to Franco, Roberto Cantalupo, later bitterly described the *Gabinetto* as 'a court of young gentlemen with too many expectations, sick with snobbery, ambitious, very cultured but untrained'. Experienced functionaries were by-passed and humiliated. Previously, Mussolini's tendency to ill-considered daring was slightly inhibited by the weight of diplomatic input that he encountered in the Ministry. Henceforth, there would be a tendency for foreign policy to be concocted out of his whims and the encouragement of the easily enthused Ciano.[20]

---

18 Drummond to Eden, 12 June 1936, R3491/241/22, in *British Documents on Foreign Affairs* Part II, Series F, vol. 12 (Washington: University Publications of America, 1992), 60-62. On Grandi, see Felix Gilbert, 'Ciano and his Ambassadors', in *The Diplomats 1919-1939*, ed. Gordon A. Craig and Felix Gilbert (Princeton: Princeton U. P., 1953), 513; MacGregor Knox, 'I testi "aggiustati" dei discorsi segreti di Grandi' and Paolo Nello, 'A proposito dei discorsi segreti di Dino Grandi', *Passato e Presente: Rivista di Storia Contemporanea*, (1987), No. 13; Paolo Nello, *Un fedele disubbidiente: Dino Grandi da Palazzo Chigi al 25 Luglio* (Bologna: Il Mulino, 1993).

19 [Galeazzo Ciano], diary entries for 27 October and 20 November 1937 (*Ciano's Diary 1937-1938* [London: Methuen, 1952], pp. 25, 35).

20 'una corte di giovanottini di troppe speranze, malati di snobismo e ambiziosi, molto colti ma inesperti' (Roberto Cantalupo, *Fu la Spagna.*

In any case, a combination of the success in Abyssinia and national resentment at League of Nations sanctions meant that the Duce was at the height of his popularity, bursting with self-confidence and not inclined to listen to reasoned criticism. Ciano and Mussolini would interact in such a way as to move towards the view that war between Fascism and the democracies was inevitable. Ciano took over at a time when the big question for Italy was the future of her relations with Great Britain.[21] The outbreak of the Spanish Civil War six weeks later coincided with efforts by the Western Powers to put an end to the legacy of bitterness over sanctions and re-establish normal relations with Rome. On 22 July, apparently unconcerned that he might in any way undermine this development, Ciano reacted with enthusiasm to his Spanish visitors, spontaneously declaring 'We must put an end to the Communist threat in the Mediterranean' although adding cautiously 'You realize, of course, that I must speak to a certain person before giving you a definite assurance. Why not see me tomorrow?'[22] However, when the enthusiastic Ciano saw the marginally more cautious Mussolini, the Duce had already received *and* rejected a request from Franco.

As soon as the first news of the uprising had arrived, the Italian Minister Plenipotentiary in Tangier, Pier Filippo de Rossi del Lion Nero, had sent his military attaché, Major Giuseppe Luccardi, to Tetuán to report on the situation. In Tetuán on 20 July, Franco saw Luccardi twice and had duplicated the request already sent via Bolín, asking him if the Italian Government would supply transport aircraft. He also requested the opening of a clandestine radio link with Luccardi.[23] Luccardi's telegram communicating these requests to Italian Military Intelligence (SIM) arrived on the morning of 21 July. Given the implications of such requests, the head of the SIM, General Mario Roatta, passed copies to Mussolini. He also discussed the telegram with his assistant Colonel Emilio

---

Ambasciata presso Franco. Febbraio-Aprile 1937 [Milano: Mondadori, 1948], pp. .50-52, 67-68); De Felice, *Mussolini il duce: lo stato totalitario*, 340; Gilbert, 'Ciano and his Ambassadors', 517-18.

21 Gilbert, 'Ciano and his Ambassadors', 524-26.

22 Bolín, *Spain*, 168.

23 Luccardi to Ministero della Guerra, 20 July 1936, *DDI*, 8ª, IV, 640-41.

Faldella, who claimed in 1972 with the full benefit of hindsight, that he said prophetically 'Spain is like quicksand ('come una sabbia mobile'). You put your hand in and your whole body disappears. If things go badly, we'll get the blame; if they go well, we'll be forgotten. But we must do something without being openly committed'.[24]

Meanwhile, on the same day, 21 July, Franco saw Luccardi again and, manifesting real anxiety, made a more reasoned request for eight transport aircraft which he desperately needed for an airlift of his troops across the Straits. His case was a skilfully aimed appeal to Mussolini, offering flattery, certain success, future subservience and a bargain price. Franco declared that his objective was to establish 'a Republican government in the Fascist style adapted for the Spanish people'. He implied that he was sole leader of the military uprising, saying that he had four armies at his command, in Andalusia, Burgos, Valladolid and Zaragoza. He stated that the struggle was unavoidable to prevent the establishment of a Soviet state in Spain. He claimed success would be assured if the limited request for eight Italian transport aircraft was granted. Finally, he promised that if Italy smiled on his cause, 'future relations will be more than friendly' ('più che amichevoli').[25] The request opened up the tempting prospect of a client state to the West and on France's southern borders. However, the situation was far too confused to tempt the Duce into a precipitate response. On Mussolini's direct orders, Roatta instructed Luccardi to tell Franco that no such aircraft were available and refused the request for regular radio contact lest it be discovered and perceived as official Italian collusion with Franco.[26]

Accordingly, Luccardi told Franco that the air transport demands occasioned by the rainy season in Ethiopia severely limited the availability of aircraft. Franco continued to insist, saying 'such a service secretly provided by Italy would never be

24 De Felice, *Mussolini il duce: lo stato totalitario*, 364-65.

25 Luccardi to Ministero della Guerra, 21 July 1936, *DDI*, 8ª, IV, 652.

26 Roatta to Luccardi, 21 July 1936, *DDI*, 8ª, IV, 651; Alberto Rovighi and Filippo Stefani, *La partecipazione italiana alla guerra civile Spagnola*, 2 vols, each in two parts *Testi* and *Allegati* (Rome: Ufficio Storico dello Stato Maggiore dell'Esercito, 1992-93), I, *Testo*, 76-77.

forgotten'. Luccardi also reported that Franco had been heard describing the failure to send aircraft as 'miopia política' and that Italian help 'would have permitted the influence of Rome to prevail over that of Berlin in the future politics of Spain'.[27] De Rossi's sympathy for Franco had already been made clear. He had abused his position as Chairman of the Control Committee which administered Tangiers to prevent the refuelling of the Spanish Republican warships that were blockading the rebels. Now, on 23 July, he also made Franco's case to the Ministero degli Affari Esteri.[28] The arguments that Franco intended to establish a Fascist state in Spain and combat Bolshevism in the Mediterranean were received with sympathy by Ciano. However, when Mussolini saw De Rossi's telegram later in the day, he is alleged by Ciano to have written 'NO' in blue pencil at the bottom of the telegram and, on another, the Duce wrote 'Atti' (short for 'agli atti' = shelve or file).[29] This suggested that the Duce was being altogether more sensible than his son-in-law. His caution derived from the fact that reports were coming in that the French Prime Minister, Léon Blum, and his Minister of Aviation, Pierre Cot, had decided to respond favourably to requests from the Spanish Government for military aid. For the Duce to help Franco at this stage would thus be to risk a confrontation with France. Apart from the wild allegations from Guariglia about French arms deliveries, the Italian Ambassador in Paris, Vittorio Cerruti, had reported on 22 July that the Spanish Government had requested military equipment from France and, on 23 July, that 20,000 10 kilo bombs had been sent to Marseilles for onward delivery to Spain, that twenty-five Potez bombers were about to fly to Madrid and that their crews would stay on to train Spanish airmen.[30]

Thus, when the expectant Bolín and Viana returned to the Ministry on 23 July, they were met by an embarrassed Filippo

---

27 Luccardi to Ministero della Guerra, 22 and 23 July 1936, *DDI*, 8ª, IV, pp. 659-60, 663.

28 De Rossi to Ciano, 23 July 1936, *DDI*, 8ª, IV, 664-65.

29 The story about Mussolini's annotations on the telegrams was told by Ciano to Cantalupo just before the latter departed for Spain as Ambassador to Franco (Cantalupo, *Fu la Spagna*, 63).

30 Cerruti to Ciano, 22 July, ASMAE, Spagna Fondo di Guerra (SFG), b.12, tel.7131; 23 July 1936, *DDI*, 8ª, IV, 669-70.

Anfuso, who told them regretfully that their requests could not be met.[31] They insisted on seeing Ciano again and managed to do so two days later. At that point, he revealed quite truthfully that he and the Duce were inhibited by concern for the international repercussions of open Italian intervention in the Spanish Civil War. Bolín insisted that the battle against Communism already involved Italy. What Ciano did not tell them was that he was actively engaged, through his correspondence with Tangier, in evaluating the seriousness of General Franco's rebellion in the hope of overcoming Mussolini's initial scepticism.

By 24 July, the situation in Rome was changing in Franco's favour in part because of his success in bringing Luccardi over to his cause. He saw the military attaché yet again and regaled him with horror stories of the rampages of 'Marxists' in southern Spain and allegations that the French were sending aircraft to Barcelona. Luccardi was moved to send another telegram to Rome reiterating the request made by 'questa bella e generosa figura di soldato'.[32] In immediate reply to Luccardi's telegram, Ciano — acting, it would appear, on his own initiative — sent three telegrams in quick succession to De Rossi asking for his assessment of Franco's possibilities of success and for confirmation that the aerodrome at Melilla was under Franco's control, and instructing him to suggest that he set up a Spanish government in Morocco as a legal cloak for possible Italian assistance.[33] What was now interesting Rome above all was Franco's chances of success.

In the meanwhile, on 25 July, Ciano received another Spanish delegation headed by Antonio Goicoechea, the leader of the Monarchist Party, Renovación Española. Goicoechea's version of events is as follows. Three days earlier, General Mola had summoned Goicoechea to his headquarters in Burgos to discuss methods of securing international assistance and commissioned him to go to Rome.[34] Mola hoped that, since

---

31 Bolín, *Spain*, 168-69; Saz, *Mussolini*, 180-82.

32 Luccardi to Ministero della Guerra, Ciano to De Rossi, 24 July 1936, *DDI*, 8ª, IV, 686-87.

33 Ciano to De Rossi, 24 July 1936, *DDI*, 8ª, IV, 687.

34 Gutiérrez Ravé, *Antonio Goicoechea*, 34-36. See also Arrarás, *Cruzada*, III, 126.

Goicoechea had negotiated a pact with Mussolini in March 1931, he would be well received in Rome. He drove to Biarritz and then flew onto Rome, accompanied by the Monarchist intellectual, Pedro Sainz Rodríguez, and the Carlist, Luis María Zunzunegui. They arrived in Rome on the evening of 24 July but had to wait until the following morning to be received by Ciano. At that point, Ciano told Goicoechea that Italy had held off sending aid only until someone arrived to confirm the links between the present military uprising and the arrangements made in 1934. Totally satisfied that Goicoechea was the appropriate authority, Ciano then said that the twelve aircraft which had merely been awaiting this confirmation would soon be at Franco's disposal. There remained only the question of payment. The price was one million pounds sterling and Goicoechea swiftly arranged, against his own signature, that the funds be advanced by the millionaire businessman Juan March.[35]

Goicoechea's account has had an extraordinary effect on subsequent historiography. Mussolini's biographer, Renzo De Felice, has described his mission as 'il passo decisivo'. In this, he is following the American historian of Italian intervention, John F. Coverdale, who refers to it as 'the request for aid that finally provoked Italy's intervention in the Civil War'.[36] There is no record of the visit in Ciano's surviving papers although, since the Ministero degli Affari Esteri papers are not complete,

---

35 Goicoechea's version appears in Gutiérrez Ravé, *Antonio Goicoechea*, 34-36. Goicoechea's authorship of the document has been questioned by Ángel Viñas, *La Alemania nazi y el 18 de julio*, 308-10. However, when interviewed by the author in Madrid in March 1970, Gutiérrez Ravé insisted that Goicoechea wrote it. On the 1934 pact see *How Mussolini Provoked the Spanish Civil War: Documentary Evidence* (London: United Editorial, 1938), *passim*.

36 De Felice, *Mussolini*, 365; Coverdale, *Italian Intervention*, 72-74. Coverdale accepts the Goicoechea document at its face value. For a critique of both, see Ismael Saz, 'La historiografía italiana y la guerra civil española', in *Historia y memoria de la guerra civil*, ed. Julio Aróstegui, 3 vols (Valladolid: Junta de Castilla y León, 1988), I, 85-106. The idea that the Spaniards paid for the aircraft persists in Rovighi and Stefani, *La partecipazione italiana*, I, *Testo*, 77; Ferdinando Pedriali, *Guerra di Spagna e Aviazione Italiana* (Rome: Ufficio Storico dell'Aeronautica Militare Italiana, 1992), 33, and José Luis de Mesa, *El regreso de las legiones (la ayuda militar italiana e la España Nacional 1936-1939)* (Granada: García Hispan Editor, 1994), 16.

that certainly does not mean that it did not take place. There is no record of Bolín's visit either although, in that case, there does exist some corroborating evidence. None the less, even accepting that Goicoechea did indeed visit Ciano, his account of his mission is so riddled with errors and inconsistencies of detail as to cast serious doubt on his veracity. He claims that his mission had come about because of the failure of previous missions to Rome by the Marqués de Luca de Tena and by Luis Bolín. This is absurd on both counts. Luca de Tena did not go to Rome until 5 August.[37] Bolín's mission had still not failed since, on 22 July when Mola apparently told Goicoechea that it had, he was only making his first visit to Ciano. In any case, Mola had no way of knowing about Bolín's progress.[38]

Goicoechea presents his meeting with Mola as having taken place à deux. He fails to mention that it came about at a meeting called by Mola with those senior Monarchist figures who had found their way to Burgos. The other Monarchists present at the meeting with Mola included José Ignacio Escobar, the owner of the ultra-rightist Monarchist newspaper La Época, as well as Sainz Rodríguez and Zunzunegui. According to Sainz Rodríguez, he and Zunzunegui accompanied Goicoechea throughout the journey and not just from Biarritz. Goicoechea failed to mention that Escobar was given a parallel mission to Berlin. Goicoechea claimed to have flown from Biarritz to Rome in the Dragon Rapide which had brought Franco from the Canary Islands to Morocco, but Escobar, who described in convincing detail their brief sojourn in Biarritz, claimed that they continued their journey in a private plane belonging to Juan March as far as Marseilles where they transferred to a commercial aircraft. Even stranger is that Goicoechea should claim to have talked to Ciano about aircraft for Franco since his mission was to get ten million rifle cartridges for Mola — a narrow request which helped convince the Italians that Mola was altogether less serious than

37   Juan Ignacio Luca de Tena, Mis amigos muertos (Barcelona: Editorial Planeta, 1971), 25-27; Saz, Mussolini contra la segunda República, 188, n.121.

38   The exiguous communications between Franco and Mola made no mention of Bolín, see José Manuel Martínez Bande, 'Del alzamiento a la guerra civil verano de 1936: correspondencia Franco/Mola', Historia y Vida, (1975), No. 93.

Franco.[39] Even if aircraft had been part of Goicoechea's agenda, it is difficult to believe that Ciano, for whom 'la bella figura' was so important and who was so clearly enjoying the role of patronizing the Spanish emissaries, should have been so clumsy as to mention money. In fact, Ciano did not raise the question of payment until very much later.[40] The only money which changed hands at a relatively early stage of the Spanish Civil War was in connection with three Savoia-Marchetti S.55X flying boats purchased with funds from Juan March for service as bombers in the Balearic Islands. The money for those aircraft was attributed by the Monarchists only later to the twelve aircraft sent from Sardinia in order to inflate their role in securing Mussolini's crucial assistance for Franco.[41]

Goicoechea was not the only senior Monarchist to claim credit for Italian intervention. That was a reflection of the fact that, with the Falange and the Army dominant in the Francoist zone, the Monarchists wanted to stake a claim to a crucial role in the Caudillo's success. The owner of the Monarchist newspaper, *ABC*, the Marqués de Luca de Tena, recounted his own negotiations with Ciano although he mistakenly dates the crucial decision to 'the early days of August'.[42] Sainz Rodríguez, in his own memoirs, forgetting all about Goicoechea, presents himself as the person responsible for persuading Ciano to intervene in Spain. In fact, his task had been to negotiate the purchase of the three seaplanes. He also claims to have persuaded Luca de Tena not to visit Ciano at all.[43] The imprecision of the Monarchists' memoirs suggests that none of them was involved in anything more than inconsequential conversations with Ciano who, after the key decisions had been made, was happy to give them good news which each attributed

---

39 Escobar, *Así empezó*, 55-69; Pedro Sainz Rodríguez, *Testimonio y recuerdos* (Barcelona: Editorial Planeta, 1978), 233.

40 Colloquio Ciano-Canaris, 28 August 1936, *DDI*, 8ª, IV, 896. See also Ramón Serrano Suñer, *Entre Hendaya y Gibraltar* (Madrid: Ediciones Españolas, 1947), 46-47.

41 Saz, *Mussolini contra la II República*, 189-90; Gerald Howson, *Aircraft of the Spanish Civil War 1936-1939* (London: Putnam, 1990), 267-68; Ramón Garriga, *Juan March y su tiempo* (Barcelona: Editorial Planeta, 1976), 380.

42 Juan Ignacio Luca de Tena, *Mis amigos muertos*, 25-27.

43 Sainz Rodríguez, *Testimonio y recuerdos*, 233-37.

to his own diplomacy. Altogether more important was the local relationship between Luccardi and De Rossi and Franco not least because it ensured that Rome saw Franco as the principal rebel leader. In consequence, assistance would be directed at him and not towards Mola.

It goes without saying that the requests from the Spanish rebels and the evaluations of Luccardi and De Rossi had to be considered in a broader decision-making context. One of Mussolini's principal concerns was the position of France and the possibility of a close relationship developing between the two Popular Front Governments of Paris and Madrid. However, this is not to say that Mussolini intervened in the Spanish Civil War only defensively because he feared French intervention and regarded it as equivalent to Russian aid.[44] Despite the report from Guariglia, Mussolini knew that the initial French decision to help the Spanish Republic had been abandoned largely as a reaction to the massive right-wing press campaign mounted after leaks from the military attaché at the Spanish Republican Embassy in Paris, Major Antonio Barroso. Ironically, the French *volte-face* had also been made partly as a consequence of rumours and press speculation in Paris about possible German and Italian intervention.[45] These events were followed closely in Rome through detailed reports from the Italian Embassy which was liberally supplied with information from rebel sympathizers within the Spanish Embassy. Cerruti had reported on 22 and 23 July not only on Spanish Republican

---

44 Emilio Faldella, *Venti mesi di guerra in Spagna* (Florence: Le Monnier, 1939), 67; Jesús Salas Larrázabal, *Intervención extranjera en la guerra de España* (Madrid: Editora Nacional, 1974), 31; Coverdale, *Italian Intervention*, 75-76; Mesa, *El regreso*, 16. In this regard, the semi-official Italian Fascist history by General Biondi Morra is revealing. While maintaining the fiction of Italian neutrality, he presents France and Russia virtually as belligerents on behalf of Franco. Accordingly, the Italian people, not the Government, spontaneously volunteered to go and fight. See Francesco Belforte, (pseudonym of Generale Francesco Biondi Morra), *La guerra civile in Spagna,* 4 vols (Milano: ISPI, 1938-39), II, pp. 46-66, 179-85. He also asserts that 'French aid was merely a further manifestation of Russian intervention' (57).

45 David Wingeate Pike, *Les français et la guerre d'Espagne 1936-1939* (Paris: Presses Universitaires de France, 1975), 79-93; Clerk to F.O., 24 July 1936, FO371/20523, W6881/62/41, 25 July 1936, FO371/20524, W6960/62/41.

requests for French aid, but also on the French reaction. He was also able to provide accurate information on the efforts of rebel sympathizers within the Spanish Embassy to sabotage Hispano-French relations and on the sympathy for the Spanish rebels within French military circles. By 25 July, Cerruti was reporting on the success of the rightist press offensive and of how pressure from London was paralysing the Blum Cabinet and making it think again about help for Spain. All of these despatches were seen and signed by Mussolini. Despite a hysterical telegram from Pedrazzi about French aid to 'the Spanish Bolsheviks', there is no doubt that the Duce and Ciano knew for certain by 25 July that the French had decided definitively not to help the Spanish Republic.[46]

The likely attitude of Britain was also of some concern to Mussolini. Accordingly, he was significantly impressed by small gestures of British hostility towards the Madrid Government and by the belief that London had put pressure on Blum not to help the Spanish Republic. Mussolini was convinced that a victory for the Spanish Republic would open the doors to Communism in Spain. It was an explicit assumption of Italian policy that the British would not only not object to an effort to stop this happening but would also see things in the same terms. The Duce assumed that he would ultimately face a life-or-death confrontation with Britain, but for the moment he was biding his time, seeking a temporary *rapprochement*. Given that Britain could not sustain a war on three fronts against Germany Japan and Italy, there was a propensity in London towards some kind of agreement with Mussolini. However, in view of the enormous importance of the Mediterranean to imperial defence, there was little that Britain could offer Italy. Nevertheless, hints of a growing cordiality could be seen in the lifting on 15 July of sanctions in force against Italy since November 1935, the withdrawal of additional naval forces posted to the Mediterranean during the Abyssinian crisis and the decision on 27 July to abandon 'assurances' of support in the Eastern Mediterranean for Greece, Yugoslavia and Turkey. The bases for agreement were

46 Cerruti to Ciano, 22 July 1936, Pedrazzi to Ciano, 26 July, *DDI*, 8ª, IV, pp. 656-57, 704; Saz, *Mussolini*, pp. 198-201, 210.

sufficiently fragile to make Rome aware that precipitate action with regard to the Spanish Civil War might easily have soured Anglo-Italian relations.[47]

This, together with fear of outright confrontation with the French whom he assumed to be about to aid the Spanish Republic, account for why Mussolini, prior to 25 July, rebuffed the first requests from the Spanish military rebels. His concern had to be balanced against the attractive possibility of preventing an alliance of the French and Spanish Popular Fronts in the Western Mediterranean. Moreover, he had good reason to feel that the Spanish rebels were not without support within the British establishment. Not least, Sir Samuel Hoare, as First Lord of the Admiralty, and Admiral Sir A. Ernle Chatfield, the First Sea Lord and Chief of the Naval Staff, were enthusiasts for the Nationalist cause.[48] Information reaching Rome as Mussolini and Ciano considered granting Franco's insistent requests strongly confirmed their suspicions that their action would enjoy the covert approval of Britain. On 27 June, Luccardi informed Rome that the British naval authorities in Gibraltar had invited Franco to send a Spanish general to make an official request that Republican vessels be neither refuelled nor permitted to use Gibraltarian territorial waters. In contrast, a Republican general in mufti ('in borghese'), wishing to talk to the British authorities, had been refused entry to the Rock.[49] On 28 July, the Count made it clear to Edward Ingram, the British Chargé d'Affaires in Rome, that he believed that Portuguese support for the Spanish military rebels would not be possible without British encouragement.[50] That this was a reasonable supposition was revealed when Franco himself, in an interview with the Toulouse daily *La Dépêche*, declared 'The

47 Dino Grandi, *Il mio paese: Ricordi autobiografici* (Bologna: Il Mulino, 1985), 415-16.

48 Ismael Saz, 'El fracaso del éxito: Italia en la guerra de España', in *Espacio, Tiempo y Forma: Revista de la Facultad de Geografía e Historia de la Universidad Nacional de Educación a Distancia*, Serie V, Historia Contemporánea, tomo V (Madrid: UNED, 1992), 105-11; Jill Edwards, *The British Government and the Spanish Civil War, 1936-1939* (London: Macmillan, 1979), pp. 16-20, 101-05.

49 Luccardi to Ministero della Guerra, 27 July 1936, *DDI*, 8ª, IV, 706-07.

50 Ingram to Eden, 28 July 1936, *Documents on British Foreign Affairs 1919-1939*, Second Series, vol. XVII, 31-32.

question is not just a national but an international one. Certainly, Great Britain, Germany and Italy should view our plans with sympathy'.[51]

A further significant consideration in Mussolini's decision to intervene in Spain was the likely role of the Soviet Union. According to his later rhetoric, Mussolini participated in the Civil War because he wanted to fight Communism.[52] On 25 July, Ciano received the German Ambassador in Rome, Ulrich von Hassell, and told him with empty bravado that 'we share with the Reich government the anxiety about seeing the Soviets establishing themselves at the gates of the Mediterranean'. On 6 August 1936, Ciano spoke on the telephone to von Hassell, and claimed mendaciously that the Soviets and the French were 'unreservedly supporting the Spanish Government, which in reality hardly existed any longer but was entirely in the hands of Communists'.[53] In fact, Mussolini was well aware that the French had drawn back from supporting the Republic and that the USSR was deeply embarrassed by the situation in Spain. Given that, for all his sincere anti-Communism, the Duce could not contemplate a military conflict with the Soviet Union, his decision to intervene in Spain was influenced by knowledge that originally the Kremlin did not intend to do anything that might bring about a Republican victory.

The USSR was extremely slow to come to the aid of the Spanish Republic and, once it did, the guiding principle behind its policy could hardly have been further removed from the goal of spreading revolution. Although diplomatic relations with Spain had been established on 27-28 July 1933, Moscow did not even name a diplomatic representative until 29 August 1936, over six weeks after the military uprising. If anything, Moscow's concern was the fact that the Germans and Italians were using the threat of Soviet intervention as a justification for

---

51 Published on 30 July but given on 28 July (Pike, *Les français*, 92).

52 He told his wife that 'Bolshevism in Spain means Bolshevism in France, which means Bolshevism next door and in fact a serious threat to bolshevise Europe' (Raquele Mussolini, *My Life with Mussolini* [London: Robert Hale, 1959], 91). See also Belforte, *La guerra civile*, II, 303-07.

53 Colloquio di Ciano con von Hassell, 25 July 1936, *DDI*, 8ª, IV, 696-97; Hassell to Wilhelmstrasse, 6 August 1936, *Documents on German Foreign Policy* Series D, vol. III (London: H.M.S.O., 1951), 30-31.

their own involvement in Spain. On 27 July, Mussolini had received a detailed report sent four days earlier by Vicenzo Berardis, Chargé d'Affaires at the Italian Embassy in Moscow, about the Kremlin's 'great embarrassment' regarding the Spanish Civil War. A rebel victory would seriously undermine Franco-Soviet collaboration and a left-wing victory by 'armed workers' would inspire a wave of international anti-Communism which would counteract efforts made to 'normalize' Soviet diplomacy in the context of the policy of collective security. According to Berardis, the Soviet intention was to endeavour to maintain a position of 'prudent neutrality'. A highly placed Soviet source had told him that 'in the Kremlin, they were extremely annoyed and perplexed by the events in Spain and that in no circumstances would the Soviet Government let itself get involved in the internal events of the Peninsula where there was nothing to gain and everything to lose'. It was Soviet policy to maintain neutrality with regard to Spain and do no more than make platonic declarations of sympathy for the Spanish Republic.[54] Along with indications of French weakness, reports on Russian embarrassment convinced Mussolini and Ciano that any Italian aid to Franco would be all the more decisive. Eventually, Moscow would intervene, but the decision to do so came about well after Mussolini had committed himself to meeting Franco's first pleas for help.

It will be recalled that, while awaiting the Duce's decision, Ciano had sent three telegrams to De Rossi seeking more information about Franco's prospects of success. De Rossi had sent Luccardi to see Franco on 25 July. The rebel general had told him that five of Spain's eight military regions, the Balearic Islands, the Canary Islands and all of Spanish Morocco were 'in his possession' ('in suo possesso'). Sensing that Ciano at least was increasingly inclined to help him, Franco had inflated his request to twelve transport aircraft, twelve reconnaissance aircraft and ten fighters as well as transport ships, anti-aircraft guns and munitions. He also reiterated the point that the sooner the assistance arrived the more certain his success

---

54 Berardis to Ciano, 23 July 1936, ASMAE, Spagna Fondo di Guerra (SFG), b.12, tel.2295/906, reprinted *DDI*, 8ª, IV, 675-77; Saz, *Mussolini*, 206-07.

would be.[55]

At some point on 25 or 26 July, Mussolini had inclined to the possibility of aid for Franco and ordered his three military Ministries to prepare, on a contingency basis, possible shipments and for aircraft to be seconded from their squadrons.[56] On 27 July, Ciano informed De Rossi that aircraft were gathering in Sardinia and would be able to reach Melilla in five hours and that a cargo ship was being loaded with munitions and aviation fuel ready to sail. This was a reference to the cargo ship *Emilio Morandi* which was in fact secretly loaded in La Spezia during the night of 27-28 July.[57] At the point at which Ciano's telegram was sent to De Rossi, no irrevocable decision had yet been taken. Ciano asked De Rossi to get a report on the situation from Franco 'without undertaking obligations or making promises of any kind'. Within one hour, De Rossi replied that Franco had total faith in his victory although he was anxious to 'reinforce his attack troops in mainland Spain'. Reinforcing the notion that Franco was sole leader of the uprising, De Rossi himself referred to 'the Franco movement'.[58]

Mussolini was inclined by 25 July to help Franco as a result of the telegrams from Luccardi and De Rossi, reports of French paralysis and hints of British acquiescence. He seems definitively to have made his own mind up about helping Franco only after the receipt on 27 July both of Berardis' report on the Kremlin's attitude to the Spanish crisis and of another important telegram. On that day, Italian military intelligence, SIM, informed the Ministero degli Esteri that Yvon Delbos had instructed all French diplomatic missions that France was maintaining a policy of non-intervention with regard to Spain and that all deliveries of material to Spain, whether from the

---

55   De Rossi to Ciano, 25, *DDI*, 8ª, IV, 690-91.

56   Pedriali, *Guerra di Spagna*, 33.

57   Ferdinando Bargoni, *L'impegno navale italiano durante la guerra civile spagnola (1936-1939)* (Roma: Ufficio Storico della Marina Militare-USM, 1992), 67.

58   Ciano to De Rossi, De Rossi to Ciano 27 July 1936, *DDI*, 8ª, IV, 705-06.

State or from private industry, were prohibited.[59] Together with the certainty that neither the French nor the Russians had any intention of intervening, De Rossi's latest reply was sufficient to galvanize Mussolini into action. Keen as he was on a march to the ocean in order to break with the 'servitù del Canale di Suez', the Duce now felt that Franco was a safe enough bet to justify the risk. The prize was a satellite Spain and thus access to the Atlantic.[60] Ciano received Bolín and Viana again and told them 'Everything is settled. My Consul in Tangier has seen General Franco. We are sending you bombers and fighters, in due course we may send more'. On 28 July, Ciano telegrammed De Rossi to say that the aircraft could be in Melilla within six hours of receiving word from Franco about arrangements for landing.[61]

In fact, it was not until Tuesday 28 July that Lieutenant Colonel Ruggero Bonomi, Commander of the School of Aerial Navigation at Orbetello, was summoned to the Ministry of Aviation, where he was received by General Giuseppe Valle, the Chief of Staff of the Regia Aeronautica and Under-Secretary of the Ministry of Aviation. General Valle gave him the job of leading a squadron of twelve bombers from Sardinia to Morocco. Shortly after Bonomi arrived with his staff at Elmas aerodrome near Cagliari, on the morning of 29 July, twelve Savoia-Marchetti S.81 Pipistrello bombers, drawn from the 55ª, 57ª and 58ª *squadriglie* of the *Regia Aeronautica* flew in. Their Italian airforce markings were crudely painted over in grey. At seven o'clock in the evening, General Valle himself arrived to brief the crews. He was accompanied by Bolín and a Consul in the Fascist Milizia, Ettore Muti, a fanatical adventurer who had served in Ciano's squadron in Ethiopia. Valle instructed the crews that, on arrival in Morocco, they should join the Spanish Foreign Legion as a cover. At dawn on 30 July, they took off to

---

59 Servizio Informazioni Militari al Ministero degli Esteri, 27 July 1936, *DDI*, 8ª, IV, 707.

60 MacGregor Knox, 'Il fascismo e la politica estera italiana', in *La politica estera italiana (1860-1985)*, a cura di Richard J. B. Bosworth e Sergio Romano (Bologna: Il Mulino, 1991), 326.

61 Bolín, *Spain*, 169-71; Ciano to De Rossi, 28 July 1936, *DDI*, 8ª, IV, 710; Saz, *Mussolini*, 181-91; Roberto Cantalupo, *Fu la Spagna*, 63.

fly to Nador in Spanish Morocco.[62]   They were followed by twelve sea-borne Fiat C.R.32 fighters.[63]

From the Spanish side, the decisive contact had not been Bolín, Viana or Goicoechea but Franco who, in persuading Luccardi and De Rossi that he was in charge of the rising and that he was going to win, secured Mussolini's early support for himself.   Of equal importance for the Duce were the reports from his diplomats.   After the point of no return, all of the feedback from London reinforced the assumption that the British would do nothing to impede Italian help for Franco. Even as the first Italian aircraft were on their way to Morocco, the Italian Chargé in London, Leonardo Vitetti, reported on the widespread sympathy to be found within the highest reaches of the Conservative Party for the Spanish rebels and for Italian Fascism.   Vitetti's conclusions derived from conversations with Conservative M.P.s, Captain David Margesson, the Conservative leader of the House, with senior Tories at the Carlton Club and with representatives of the Rothemere press.   Tory Members of Parliament told him of their conviction that the events in Spain were the direct consequence of 'subversive Soviet propaganda' and of their anxiety to see the Spanish Left crushed.   The right-wing Leo Amery, who had been First Lord of the Admiralty in the early 1920s, had told him that the Spanish War raised 'the problem of the defence of Europe against the threat of Bolshevism'.   Ciano was delighted and encouraged further contacts.[64]   Vitetti reported that British support for French proposals for non-intervention was based entirely on the belief that it was a useful device for preventing French help to the Spanish Republic.[65]   Within months,

---

62   Valle flew with them on the first part of their journey according to Rovighi and Stefani, *La partecipazione italiana*, I, *Testo*, 78. However, this is not mentioned either by the official Italian Airforce historian of the Spanish Civil War nor by Bolín in his memoirs.   See Pedriali, *Guerra di Spagna e Aviazione Italiana*, 34-35; Bolín, *Spain*, 170-71; Howson, *Aircraft of the Spanish Civil War*, 273-75.

63   Pedriali, *Guerra di Spagna*, 34-35; Rovighi and Stefani, *La partecipazione italiana*, I, *Testo*, 78; Bolín, *Spain*, 170-71; Howson, *Aircraft of the Spanish Civil War*, 273-75.

64   Vitetti to Ciano, 29 July, 3 August, Ciano to Vitetti, 30 July 1936, *DDI*, 8ª, IV, pp. 711-13, 719-20, 736-7; Saz, *Mussolini*, 204-05.

65   Vitetti to Ciano, 3 August 1936, *DDI*, 8ª, IV, 739.

Mussolini would tell Göring in the Palazzo Venezia that 'The English Conservatives have a great fear of Bolshevism, and this fear could very well be exploited politically'.[66] In early August, Vitetti reported that he had been told by the Spanish inventor of the autogyro, Juan de la Cierva, that he had bought all the aircraft available on the free market in Britain and was about to send them to Mola. He said that 'the British authorities had given him every facility even though they knew only too well that the aircraft are destined for the Spanish rebels'.[67]

Ciano and Mussolini were thus convinced that Italian aid to the Spanish rebels would not meet with opposition from London. They were right. Cantalupo commented later on the strangeness of Chamberlain's position — wanting to appear neutral while working for Franco's victory. Ciano informed Cantalupo in December 1936 of his conviction that the Non-Intervention Committee had been invented by the British to facilitate a reconciliation with Italy. In February 1937, he confided in Cantalupo his certainty that the British were delighted to see Italian blood spilt to keep Communism out of Spain.[68] One month later, Ciano told Drummond that he could not believe that Britain could be hostile to Italy because of the help given to Franco.[69] The only significant British concern regarding Italian intervention in Spain was that Italy might have designs on the Balearic Islands. This concern predated the outbreak of the Spanish Civil War and led to regular British efforts to elicit Italian assurances to the contrary.[70]

Neither Mussolini nor Ciano were inhibited in their decision-making by the possible reaction of Britain. The Italian decision to intervene in the Spanish Civil War was taken sometime between 25 and 27 July. It was taken after repeated

---

66 On 23 January 1937, Galeazzo Ciano, *L'Europa verso la catastrofe* (Milan: Mondadori, 1948), 136.
67 Vitetti to Ciano, 6 August 1936, *DDI*, 8ª, IV, 773-74.
68 Cantalupo, *Fu la Spagna*, pp. 61, 63, 75.
69 Drummond to Eden, 31 March 1937, R2340/1/22, *BDFA*, Series F, vol. 13, 21.
70 Shuckburgh to Vansittart, 30 May, FO371/20522, W4919/62/41; Vitetti to Ciano, 8, 9 August, *DDI*, 8ª, IV, pp. 775, 783; Ingram to Eden, 13 August, and minute by Shuckburgh, 21 August 1936, FO371/20532, W8997/62/41. See also Coverdale, *Italian Intervention*, 147-48; Saz, *Mussolini*, 210-11.

requests for reassurance rather than the most careful investigation into Franco's possibilities of ultimate success. The investigation that was carried out consisted largely of Luccardi's transmission (rather than assessment) of (convincing) assertions from Franco. After concluding that a small quantity of Italian equipment could be decisive for the military rebellion in Spain and provide massive rewards in terms of extended influence in the Western Mediterranean, and after being provided with overwhelming evidence that its provision was not likely to provoke a dangerous reaction from London, Paris or Moscow, Mussolini decided to help Franco. At this stage, it is important to note that both the Duce and Ciano accepted Franco's claims that a limited — but still substantial — amount of help, the Savoia-Marchetti bombers and the Fiat C.R.32 fighters sent from Sardinia, would rapidly tip the balance in favour of the rebels.[71]

Strong headwinds had reduced the speed of the Savoia-Marchetti S.81s. Only nine of the original twelve arrived. With fuel running low, one came down in the sea, one landed and one crashed in French Morocco.[72] News of their dramatic arrival was telegraphed to Paris where it was then decisive in the French decision to push for non-intervention. The initiative for an agreement emanated from the French.[73] Nevertheless, there can be little doubt of British enthusiasm for the notion. Immediately before the French Cabinet meeting which took the final decision on non-intervention, the British Ambassador in Paris, Sir George Clerk, pressed Delbos to permit no supply of commercial aircraft to Spain.[74]

Grandi's retrospective claim that 'L'adesione del governo italiano al patto di non intervento in Spagna fu da principio sincera' is more laughable even than his bare-faced lies at the

---

71 De Felice, *Mussolini*, 367. However, that is not the same as accepting Grandi's assertion that it was a question of 'aiuti modesti e con una testimonianza di simpatia appena apprezzabile' (Grandi, *Il mio paese*, 418).

72 De Rossi to Ciano, 31 July 1936, *DDI*, 8ᵃ, IV, 728-29; Pedriali, *Guerra di Spagna*, 35-36.

73 Cambon to Eden, 2 August, Eden to Cambon, 3 August, 1936, FO371/20526, W7504/62/41.

74 Clerk to F.O., 7, 8 August 1936, FO371/20528, W7964/62/41; W7981/62/41; Thomas to Cadogan, 11 August 1936, FO371/20531, W8676/62/41.

time.[75] After the crash-landings of three of the original aircraft, the official Italian line was that some kind of private venture was afoot.[76] On 3 August, the French Ambassador in Rome, Charles de Pineton, Comte de Chambrun, spoke to Ciano. He passed on the urgent appeal from Blum for a non-intervention agreement on Spain and also raised the question of the two Savoia-Marchettis which had crashed in French Morocco. Ciano put him off by saying that Mussolini was absent. The Duce was indeed in Riccione whence he sent Ciano notes for a reply to the non-intervention invitation, according to which Italy agreed in principle but required it to be made clear if the agreement were to be extended to the activities of political parties and private citizens and also regarding the proposed methods of control.[77] Two days later, he received Chambrun again. Lying without compunction, Ciano told Chambrun that an inquiry was under way and that he was 'in a position to deny any, even indirect, interference by the Fascist Government'. Two days later, he again told Chambrun that 'although an inquiry was at present in progress, I could state that they were not planes in service with an Italian air force unit, but machines supplied by a private firm to private Spanish citizens and that, finally, the Government had absolutely no knowledge of the affair'. On the next day, 6 August, by which time the heads of Italian and German military intelligence were already liaising on support for Franco, Ciano told Chambrun that Italy accepted the principle of non-intervention. Following the script provided by Mussolini, he expressed flagrantly hypocritical concern that expressions of solidarity with the Spanish Republic within the democracies, in the form of demonstrations, press campaigns, subscriptions of money and the enrolment of volunteers, constituted 'a flagrant and perilous form of intervention' and asked for more details of proposed control methods.[78] On the

---

75 Grandi, *Il mio paese*, 418; conversation Eden and Grandi, 25 November 1936, FO371/20550, W16668/62/41.

76 Ingram to F.O., 1 August 1936, FO371/20526, W7525/62/41.

77 Colloquio di Ciano con Chambrun, 3 August, Mussolini to Ciano, 5 August 1936, *DDI*, 8ª, IV, pp. 738-39, 749-50.

78 Colloquio di Ciano con Chambrun, 5 August 1936, *DDI*, 8ª, IV, 750; Ciano, *L'Europa*, 51-52. *Cf.* Ingram to F.O., 4 and 6 August 1936, FO371/20526, W7698/62/41 and FO371/20527, W7921/62/41.

next day, he received the British Chargé d'Affaires, Edward Ingram, told him of Italy's acceptance of the principle of non-intervention and piously went on to insist that restrictions be extended to cover propaganda and other support for the belligerents.[79]   Ciano also continued to protest indignantly to Chambrun about alleged deliveries of French equipment to the Spanish Republic while demanding that the Italian airmen who had crash-landed in French North Africa be released without trial.[80]

Ciano and Mussolini proceeded in the confidence that Britain approved of what they were up to. It was reported in Rome that when Mussolini had had the British Chargé in Rome, Edward Ingram, informed that he was going to send aircraft to Franco, he had received the reply that 'the Foreign Office had understood the Italian initiative in its precise significance'.[81]   In mid-August, Ciano was still mendaciously fending off British requests for an Italian commitment to non-intervention.[82]   Their conviction that neither France nor Russia was likely to intervene in Spain was stronger than ever. Further despatches from Berardis in Moscow painted a picture of a Kremlin ever more worried by events in Spain and deeply relieved by the apparent international agreement over non-intervention. Soviet aid to Spain seemed likely to go no further than collections among Russian workers and violent attacks on Italy in the press.[83]   Despite the embarrassment of the crash-landing in French North Africa, there had been no negative repercussions to their risk-taking. Not only had they got away with it, but the return on their investment seemed to be rapid and it took the form of an intensification of the relation with Nazi Germany.

The first official communication from Germany that Hitler was committed to helping Franco came at a meeting in Bolzano on 4 August between the German and Italian Intelligence chiefs, Admiral Wilhelm Canaris and Roatta. However, since

79 Colloquio di Ciano con Ingram, 6 August 1936, *DDI*, 8ª, IV, 757-58.

80 Colloquio Ciano/Chambrun, *DDI*, 8ª, IV, 785.

81 Nino D'Aroma, *Vent'anni insieme: Vittorio Emanuele e Mussolini* (Bologna: Editoriale Capelli, 1957), 242.

82 Ingram to Eden, 18 August 1936, FO371/20572, W9621/9549/41.

83 Berardis to Ciano, 6 August 1936, *DDI*, 8ª, IV, 758-62.

pairs of German Junkers Ju 52s had started to fly to Morocco via the Italian mainland and Sardinia on 29 July, it is inconceivable that Italian Military Intelligence was unaware that Hitler was helping Franco. The meeting at Bolzano was held at the request of Canaris who was somewhat economical with the truth. He informed Roatta that the German government, via the Ministry of Aviation and without informing the Foreign Ministry, had sent four Junkers transport planes by air and a shipload of munitions. He did not mention that a further six were flying to Morocco and ten being taken by sea. Canaris requested that Italy supply, at German expense, aviation fuel to the Spanish rebels and also permit German aircraft flying to Spain to refuel in Italy. Roatta and Canaris agreed to set up a daily exchange of telegrams to permit coordination on Spain thereby going a step nearer to the broader Italo-German coordination with regard to Spain sought by Ciano.[84]

The seeds of the later escalation of Italian aid can be seen in a desperate telegram from De Rossi to Ciano of 19 August. Transmitting a request from Franco, he urged that risks be taken on his behalf. He underlined the rebel general's achievements to date and made great play of the legal government's advantages in terms of its 'privileged position in international law', its financial resources and its control of the Mediterranean sea ports. According to De Rossi, the situation was similar to that a month previously except on a much greater scale. 'Speedy Italian commitment to ample assistance then permitted Franco to turn around his difficult predicament and gave him the freedom of movement to become master of Western Spain and occupy the Sierra de Guadarrama before the capital. But, from such positions, solid and important that they are, he can only with difficulty go forward and secure above all possession of the capital if he does not have new resources to make up the deficiencies in his armament and to balance the help constantly sent by the forces of international subversion,

---

84 SIM to MAE, 5 August, *DDI*, 8ª, IV, 751-52. Howson, *Aircraft of the Spanish Civil War*, 207. By 8 August, Luccardi was able to report to Rome that ten Junkers had arrived by air and that the announced ship with the other equipment had reached Cádiz (Luccardi to Ministero della Guerra, 9 August 1936, *DDI*, 8ª, IV, 780).

especially the French Popular Front ...'. The telegram was seen by Mussolini.[85] De Rossi's knowledge of Franco's situation derived from the fact that the rebel general now clearly saw him as an efficacious channel to the Duce. Luccardi flew to Seville on the following day to confer with Franco who made a cunning allegation concerning the recent attempt by the Republic to recapture Mallorca. Fully aware of the Duce's interest in the Balearic Islands, Franco claimed that the presence of numerous French citizens among the invaders signified that the Republic had ceded the Balearic Islands to France in return for aid. De Rossi's telegram recounting this was also seen by Mussolini. Luccardi brought back with him the news that Franco was about to provide a list of all the equipment that he needed 'in order that he can rapidly conclude his offensive against the loyalists and assume full control of the government of Spain'. Complaining that Republican daylight bombing raids were impeding the advance of his columns, Franco's request, forwarded by Luccardi, was for motor torpedo boats (presumably to neutralize the continuing blockade of Morocco), a squadron of light bombers, twenty-four armoured cars, two hundred light machine guns with one million cartridges, twenty thousand gas masks and poison gas bombs.[86]

The request was largely successful. Soon there would be an Italian force in Mallorca. Then, as Franco encountered ever greater difficulties in his march on Madrid, he turned to Italy as a matter of course. And the more that Mussolini said 'yes', the more difficult it became to say 'no' since, for all that the democracies turned a blind eye, the world knew that the cause of Franco was the cause of the Duce. Within a month, he had moved imperceptibly but catastrophically from his initial cautiously reached decision in favour of limited aid towards the open-ended commitment that, within five months, would see Italy effectively at war with the Spanish Republic. That first decision may be assumed to have been taken almost exclusively by Mussolini and Ciano. The subsequent escalation of Italian commitment to the Spanish rebels seems to have taken into

---

85 De Rossi to Ciano, 19 August 1936, *DDI*, 8ª, IV, 823-24.
86 De Rossi to Ciano, 20, 22 August, Luccardi to Ministero della Guerra, 21 August 1936, *DDI*, 8ª, IV, pp. 827, 829, 852-53, 861.

account the likely views of important elements of the Italian establishment only when they were in agreement with the Duce. The ideological fervour manifested by Mussolini and Ciano found an echo among the majority of Catholics who endorsed the Vatican's enthusiastic support for intervention against atheism in Spain.[87] It was also in tune with the wishes of prominent members of the Fascist Party, like Achille Starace and Roberto Farinacci, who were anxious to have their 'Guerra Fascista' and play a part in the creation of the Fascist empire to match the military intervention in Abyssinia. None the less, the ultimate decision was Mussolini's alone. He was, without doubt, influenced by the enthusiasm of Ciano. However, his own inclinations had already been revealed by his declared commitment to a 'svolta totalitaria' (totalitarian turn) of the regime by which he wished to put an end to the bourgeois comfort of Italian daily life and create a warrior culture.[88] In contrast to the Vatican and the Fascist Party, the military establishment, particularly Marshals Balbo and Badoglio, was more cautious. They believed that intervention should be avoided on the grounds that the Armed Forces needed time and resources to reorganize and recuperate from their efforts in Abyssinia. Balbo thought the Duce was crazy. Cantalupo found him glassy-eyed and other-worldly ('lo sguardo alquanto fisso, lento e vitreo, astratto dalle cose e dalle persone che gli erano davanti'). Ciano told Cantalupo 'he has tasted great glory, he looks down on us from on high and we seem tiny. He lives in a world apart. Perhaps it is better like that. If we leave him on Olympus he can undertake great tasks. As far as we are concerned, let us respect the concentration of his spirit and think about the affairs of this world'. In fact, Ciano was using his position to push Mussolini towards deeper commitment in Spain. Certainly, the Duce was increasingly isolated, in touch with the world only through the filter of sycophants, irritable, deaf to any criticism, tending to talk in private with deliberate

---

87 Aldo Albónico, 'Accenti critici di parte fascista e cattolica alla "Cruzada" ', in *Italia y la guerra civil española* (Madrid: Consejo Superior de Investigaciones Científicas, 1986), 1-9. *Cf.* Giordano Bruno Guerri, *Fascisti: Gli italiani di Mussolini; il regime degli italiani* (Milan: Mondadori, 1995), 216.

88 De Felice, *Mussolini*, 375-81; Saz, 'El fracaso del éxito', 114.

pronunciation as if addressing a mass rally (Cantalupo: 'le sue parole scandite come se ci fosse stato un gran pubblico a raccoglierle'). Several leading Fascists were worried that, since the Abyssinian War, Mussolini had changed.[89] It is hardly surprising that he was susceptible to requests from Franco linked to insinuations of future subservience.

---

89 Cantalupo, *Fu la Spagna*, pp. 50, 55-56; Mack Smith, *Mussolini's Roman Empire*, 99; Claudio G. Segrè, *Italo Balbo: A Fascist Life* (Berkeley/Los Angeles: Univ. of California, 1987), 342-43; De Felice, *Mussolini il duce: lo stato totalitario*, 254-84.

3

Nazi Germany's Intervention in the Spanish Civil War and the Foundation of HISMA/ROWAK

CHRISTIAN LEITZ

On 21 July 1936, Johannes E. F. Bernhardt, a German citizen resident in Tetuán, the capital of Spanish Morocco, offered his assistance to General Francisco Franco, one of the leaders of the Spanish rebellion of 17 July against the Spanish Republican Government in Madrid.[1] Though Bernhardt's decision seemed almost insolent considering the nonentity he was, it became the initial step towards Germany's intervention in the Spanish Civil War. Tetuán turned out to be Bernhardt's spring-board for becoming one of the most influential Germans in Franco Spain during the Civil War and the Second World War.

As sales director he had contributed significantly to the expansion of the company H. & O. Wilmer, Sucesores de H. Tönnies which acted as a trade representative in Spanish Morocco of several German companies. Alongside promoting and selling German products such as cables, freezers, kitchen equipment, and electrical and optical goods, Bernhardt also became involved in the local production of practice targets for the Spanish artillery. He had therefore plenty of opportunities to become acquainted with Spanish army officers. Significantly, among these were many officers who were to play important roles in the rebellion and subsequent Civil War

---

1   German Federal Archive Koblenz (BA) R121/842, unsigned, undated report *Entwicklung vom Juli 1936 bis Dezember 1937*; A. Viñas, *La Alemania nazi y el 18 de julio, antecedentes de la intervención alemana en la guerra civil española* (Madrid: Alianza, 1974 [1st edn.]; 1976 [2nd ed.]), 279.

against the Spanish Government, most notably General Emilio Mola, Lieutenant-Colonel Juan Yagüe Blanco, Lieutenant-Colonel Juan Beigbeder y Atienza, and Lieutenant-Colonel Carlos Asensio Cabanillas.[2]

It is therefore likely that Bernhardt's decision to approach Franco had more to do with his business contacts than with his position within the small Nazi Party organization in Spanish Morocco.[3] In fact, only when he had already offered his services to Franco, did he contact the local Nazi leader, Adolf Langenheim. By then Franco had already responded positively to Bernhardt's offer.[4] Despite the superior position of Langenheim — according to the British Consul-General in Tetuán 'virtually the German Consul' in Spanish Morocco — it was Bernhardt who took the initiative.[5] He used the ensuing developments to emerge out of the obscurity of his work in Spanish Morocco, while Langenheim ceased to be of any importance despite his presence at one of the most decisive moments in the development of the relationship between Nazi Germany and — what was to become — Franco Spain.[6]

Franco and his fellow insurgents had clearly not expected that what was to be a swift rebellion would ultimately turn into a full-scale Civil War. However, the obvious slow progress of the rebels on the mainland made it ever more crucial for Franco's troops in Spanish Morocco to be rapidly available. Franco was in charge of about 5,000 soldiers of the Spanish Foreign Legion, 17,000 Moorish *Regulares*, and 17,000 Spanish conscripts, undoubtedly the best troops in the Spanish army at the time.[7]

---

2   Viñas, *La Alemania nazi* (2nd ed.), 292 f.

3   On Bernhardt's role in the local Nazi group, see *ibid.*, 281, 283, 290f. and BA R7/738, unsigned memorandum *Entstehung, Entwicklung und gegenwärtiger Stand des ROWAK/SOFINDUS — Konzerns*, 15/3/1940; see also H.-H. Abendroth, *Mittelsmann zwischen Franco und Hitler: Johannes Bernhardt erinnert 1936* (Marktheidenfeld: W. Schleunung,1978), 10.

4   BA R121/842, unsigned, undated report *Entwicklung*.

5   Public Record Office London (PRO) FO371/20525/7487, Letter, E. Gye to FO, 31/7/1936.

6   See below.

7   M. de Madariaga, 'The Intervention of Moroccan Troops in the Spanish Civil War', *European History Quarterly*, XXII (1992), 77.

The initial plan had been to ferry these troops across the Straits of Gibraltar on board ships of the Spanish navy. However, the rebels had not expected that most of the Spanish seamen would refuse orders to take over their ships. After the transport of only several hundred Moroccan troops across, the sea route was blocked by ships loyal to the Republic.[8]   In addition, air transport was severely restricted by the lack of adequate planes available to the insurgents.[9]

It was at this critical point that Bernhardt approached Franco, and the general reacted immediately. He decided that Bernhardt, and Langenheim as the highest Nazi dignitary in Spanish Morocco, should deliver a message to the Nazi leadership in Germany. In his short letter to the German Führer, Adolf Hitler, Franco asked for ten transport planes, anti-aircraft machine guns, five fighter planes and some other equipment.[10]   A telegram was also sent to General Erich Kühlental, German military attaché in Paris. This message, in which Franco asked for ten planes 'for the transport of troops',[11] was communicated to the German Foreign Ministry on 23 July. The Ministry immediately decided against the request and made it clear that it had no intention of involving Germany in the unfolding struggle in Spain.[12]

On 25 July, Hans Heinrich Dieckhoff, director of the political section of the Foreign Ministry and a future Ambassador to Franco Spain, set out some of the reasons for the negative response to Franco's request. According to his memorandum, which was written in reaction to the arrival of

---

8   M. Tuñón de Lara et al., La guerra civil española 50 años después (Madrid: Labor, 1985), 202. By 21 July two cruisers, two destroyers, three gunboats and seven submarines were blockading the coast of Spanish Morocco (H. Thomas, The Spanish Civil War [London: Penguin, 1988], 231; S. Payne, Politics and the Military in Modern Spain [Stanford: Stanford U. P., 1967], 353).

9   Figures vary between 40 and 100 planes. See J. Coverdale, Italian Intervention in the Spanish Civil War (Princeton: Princeton U. P., 1975), 68; Tuñón de Lara, op. cit., 205; J. Salas Larrazabal, Intervención extranjera en la guerra de España (Madrid: Editora Nacional, 1974), 63.

10   Viñas, La Alemania nazi (2nd ed.), 339.

11   Akten zur deutschen Auswärtigen Politik (ADAP), D, III, doc.2, 5, Telegram, Wegener (Tangier) to German Foreign Ministry, 22/7/1936.

12   Viñas, La Alemania nazi (2nd ed.), 323.

Bernhardt and Langenheim in Germany, the German colony in Spain and German merchantmen and warships in Spanish waters would be under threat should it become known that Germany was supplying the rebels with weapons. In addition, international complications might arise if Germany interfered in a country with friendly links to France and Britain.[13]

However, events were already unfolding which would lead to the eventual intervention of Germany in the Civil War. On 23 July Franco's mission, consisting of Bernhardt, Langenheim and a Spanish representative, Captain Francisco Arranz Monasterio, had departed for Berlin where they arrived on 25 July. The two German envoys immediately met the head of the Nazi Auslandsorganisation (AO), Ernst Bohle, who reacted with great interest to their message. Bohle was extremely keen to promote the position of the AO in the external affairs of the Reich.[14] If Franco's request was granted with the help of the AO, the organization would have achieved a triumph over its official rival, the Foreign Ministry. The latter, after all, had clearly rejected the idea of supporting the rebels. However, Bohle concluded that he could not personally take a decision on such an important matter. He therefore arranged for a meeting with the Deputy Führer, Rudolf Hess.

After listening to Bernhardt and Langenheim, Hess, in turn, also concluded that such a weighty matter could only be decided by Hitler himself. Consequently, he rang up Hitler, who agreed to see both envoys at Bayreuth where he was attending the Wagner Festival. According to Bernhardt, on the evening of 25 July, Hitler received Franco's two German envoys in the presence of only one other person, Dr Wolfgang Kraneck, head of the AO Legal Office.[15] However, the latter was apparently completely ignored by Hitler. After he had listened to Bernhardt and asked him several questions, Hitler eventually decided in favour of Franco's request. Evidently, the Führer's crucial decision was already taken when he invited Hermann Göring, General Werner von Blomberg, the War Minister, and

---

13 ADAP, D, III, doc.10, 11f., Memorandum by Dieckhoff, 25/7/1936; Viñas, *La Alemania nazi* (2nd ed.), 333.

14 On Bohle see D. M. McKale, *The Swastika outside Germany* (Kent, Ohio: Kent State Univ., 1977), *passim*.

15 On Kraneck see *ibid.*, 51.

Captain Coupette, commander of the Naval Shipping Administration Section of the High Command of the Navy (OKM), to join him and his guests.[16] Initially, both Göring and von Blomberg appeared reluctant to support Franco's request.[17] When Hitler then emphasized his decision, both duly changed their minds.

Under the code name *Unternehmen Feuerzauber* (Operation Magic Fire) the organization of a support operation was immediately set into motion. Admiral Lindau and General Erhard Milch arrived in Bayreuth on the morning of 26 July, and the former was put in charge of the preparations for the transport operation. Back at the Reich Air Ministry (RLM), on Göring's orders, Milch instructed General Helmuth Wilberg to set up *Sonderstab W* (Special Staff W) which was to control the organization of the whole supply operation.[18] The German intervention in Spain had commenced.

Two questions have occupied historians of the Spanish Civil War ever since Hitler agreed to intervene in Spain. Firstly, whether the Nazi regime had any knowledge of the preparations for the military rebellion, or, more importantly, whether it played an active role in the preparations? And secondly, what was the motivation behind Hitler's decision to intervene?

In his pioneering study *La Alemania nazi y el 18 de julio* Ángel Viñas has demonstrated in detail that Hitler's decision at Bayreuth was taken quickly and spontaneously and that contacts between German officials and the leaders of the rebellion-to-come were negligible in the years immediately before 1936. Though Hitler had admired Primo de Rivera's

---

16 Abendroth, 'Die deutsche Intervention im spanischen Bürgerkrieg. Ein Diskussionsbeitrag', in *Vierteljahreshefte für Zeitgeschichte*, I (1982), 120.

17 Viñas, 'El Tercer Reich y el estallido de la guerra civil', in *Historia 16*, VIII (no date), 52; Abendroth, 'Die deutsche Intervention', 121 and 126; R. Proctor, *Hitler's Luftwaffe in the Spanish Civil War* (Westport: Greenwood Press, 1983), 18.

18 Viñas, 'El Tercer Reich', 54. For a detailed description of the developments in Germany directly after the meeting at Bayreuth see the epilogue to Viñas, *La Alemania nazi* (2nd ed.).

coup in 1923, he appeared to have had no interest in Spain.[19] Viñas' conclusion is confirmed by Wolfgang Schieder who emphasizes the very minor role Spain played in Hitler's long-term planning right up to the military coup.[20] Yet, attempts have been made to prove that some of the Spanish rebels not only had contacts with individual German officials before the coup, but that the German Government was aware of the plans for a rebellion, indeed, that it was involved in the preparations for it. Marxist historians, most notably Marion Einhorn, agree that German diplomats and the Nazi leadership had worked towards the rebellion for years and that Hitler's decision to intervene was not spontaneous but planned.[21]

Other historians have also subscribed to this view. Dante Puzzo insists that on his visit to Germany in early 1936 General José Sanjurjo, the designated leader of the coup, gained the promise of German support for the planned military insurrection against the Spanish Republic. Puzzo's theory, however, does not hold water, particularly as he insists that Sanjurjo ensured the use of German aircraft for the transport of troops from Morocco to Spain if the Spanish navy remained loyal to the Republic.[22] In fact, the future rebels anticipated the availability of the Spanish navy which meant that there was no need to arrange for German aircraft.

Johannes Bernhardt's activities before the insurrection are of particular interest to Stanley Payne. Although Payne does not maintain that German officials were instrumental in the preparations for the rebellion, he has tried to demonstrate that Bernhardt was already involved in the activities of anti-Republican plotters before the coup. Payne argues that Bernhardt visited Berlin in June 1936 'to convince Nazi officials

---

19 Viñas, *La Alemania nazi, passim*.

20 W. Schieder, *Spanischer Bürgerkrieg und Vierjahresplan* (Darmstadt: Wissenschaftliche Buchgesellschaft, 1978), 330.

21 See M. Einhorn, *Die ökonomischen Hintergründe der faschistischen deutschen Intervention in Spanien, 1936-1939* (Berlin: Akademie-Verlag, 1962), pp. 87 and 89.

22 D. Puzzo, *Spain and the Great Powers 1936-1941* (New York/ London: Columbia U. P., 1962), 47.

that Germany should support the projected rebellion'.[23] However, despite their extensive examination of Bernhardt's life and career, neither Viñas nor Hans-Henning Abendroth have detected any information about such an involvement. The author of this essay has also failed to find any evidence to corroborate Payne's claim.

Viñas does not deny that contacts between individual Germans and future leaders, participants or just sympathizers of the insurrection had occurred after Hitler's *Machtergreifung*. The most intriguing example is the case of Josef Veltjens, a World War I flying ace, and employee of a company with a major interest in arms sales since the late 1920s.[24] Despite the lack of conclusive evidence, it appears that Veltjens had some contact with General Mola's ring of conspirators about the sale of German arms to the conspirators. The main piece of evidence indicating such contacts is contained in a German Foreign Ministry document of 6 July 1936. It reveals that Spanish Fascists had negotiated with 'Herr Feltjen' [*sic!*] about the secret smuggling of weapons from Germany. The Ministry, however, had 'not the slightest interest in it'.[25]   Although Veltjens did eventually become involved in Germany's intervention in the Spanish Civil War,[26] there is no evidence to suggest that Hitler's decision to support Franco was related to past contacts between Germans, official and private, and Spanish conspirators.[27] Unless such evidence emerges, it has to be concluded that Germany's direct involvement with the

---

23 Payne, *Politics and the Military*, 355 f. (based on C Foltz Jr, *The Masquerade in Spain* [Boston: Houghton Mifflin Co., 1948], 46 f.).

24 Viñas, *La Alemania nazi* (2nd ed.), 139 f.

25 *Documents on German Foreign Policy* (DGFP), D, III, 1, von Bülow to Voelckers, 6 July 1936. For information on Veltjens' pre-Civil War career see Viñas, *La Alemania nazi* (2nd ed.), 138 ff. and 274 f.; R. Whealey, *Hitler and Spain: The Nazi Role in the Spanish Civil War* (Lexington: Univ. Press of Kentucky, 1989), 81; H.-H. Abendroth, *Hitler in der spanischen Arena: Die deutsch-spanischen Beziehungen im Spannungsfeld der europäischen Interessenpolitik vom Ausbruch des Bürgerkrieges bis zum Ausbruch des Weltkrieges 1936-1939* (Paderborn: Schöningh, 1973), 19f.

26 See below.

27 See also W. L. Bernecker, 'Alemania y la guerra civil española', in *España y Alemania en la edad contemporánea*, ed. W. L. Bernecker (Frankfurt am Main: Vervuert, 1992), 138 f.

rebellion in Spain started with Hitler's decision on 25 July 1936.

In fact, the only available evidence of German Government contacts with Spanish military personnel during the first half of 1936 undermines somewhat the theory that the Nazi regime supported the conspiracy.   In late April 1936 the German Government showed no reluctance in allowing the Friedrich Krupp A.G. to conclude two armaments deals with the War Ministry of the Spanish Popular Front Government.[28] It seems fairly unlikely that such permits would have been issued in a matter of days if the Nazi regime had already been in league with the conspirators.

As far as the second question is concerned, there can be no doubt[29] that Hitler's foremost motive for Germany's intervention was ideological.   From the information he had gathered, particularly from Bernhardt and Langenheim, Hitler clearly concluded that he had to help the rebels to rescue Spain from Communism.[30]   Explaining his decision to an initially reluctant Joachim von Ribbentrop, Hitler emphasized 'that Germany could not accept a Communist Spain under any circumstances'.[31] Ernst von Weizsäcker of the German Foreign Ministry underlined the anti-Communist factor when he concluded that 'a red neighbour to France would, *realpolitisch*, constitute a negative factor for Germany's policies'.[32] Viewed in

---

28   Imperial War Museum, Krupp Files (IWM Krupp), File 15a, AGK to Krupp, 24/4/1936; Krupp to AGK, 28/4/1936; von Bülow to Krupp, 30/4/1936.

29   See Bernhardt's own statement to Abendroth, in Abendroth, *Mittelsmann*, 32 f., and 'Deutschlands Rolle', 481; Viñas, *La Alemania nazi* (1st ed.), 233 f.

30   Abendroth, *Mittelsmann*, 32; Viñas, *La Alemania nazi* (1st ed.), 62; G. Stone, 'The European Great Powers and the Spanish Civil War, 1936-1939', in *Paths to War: New Essays on the Origins of the Second World War*, ed. E. Robertson and R. Boyce (London/Basingstoke: Macmillan, 1989), 200 f.; A. Adamthwaite, *The Making of the Second World War* (London: Allen & Unwin, 1979), 55.   For a detailed discussion of the 'anti-Communist motive' see Bernecker, 'Alemania y la guerra civil española', in *España y Alemania*, ed. W. L. Bernecker, 139-46.

31   Hitler to Ribbentrop, 26/7/1936, in J. v. Ribbentrop, *Zwischen London und Moskau: Erinnerungen und letzte Aufzeichnungen* (Leoni-am-Starnberger See: Druffel Verlag, 1953), 88.

32   L. Hill, *Die Weizsäcker-Papiere, 1933-1950* (Frankfurt/Main: Propyläen, 1974), 104.

reverse, the Nazi regime probably concluded that the elimination of the Popular Front Government in Spain might have a negative effect on the recently elected French Popular Front.[33]

Moreover, the ideological argument for intervention in Spain was closely related to strategic considerations. Victory for the francophile Popular Front in Spain would be of strategic advantage to France, particularly in view of Spain's usefulness as a land-bridge to the French colonies, and troops in North Africa. It might even provide the Soviet Union with a further ally to complement the Franco-Soviet pact. Victory for the insurrection, however, might see the French Republic surrounded by potentially hostile Fascist or semi-Fascist states.[34] Moreover, Hitler apparently argued in December 1936 'that Spain was a convenient sideshow which absorbed the energies of the other Great Powers, thus leaving Germany a freer hand to pursue its ambitions in the East'.[35] A combination of mainly ideological as well as strategic considerations thus led Hitler to initiate Germany's intervention in favour of Franco. Despite the insistence of some historians that economic considerations contributed to Hitler's initial decision,[36] they became significant only after the meeting at Bayreuth.

It has been pointed out that the first organizational step of Germany's intervention was the foundation of *Sonderstab W* under General Wilberg. On Wilberg's orders a freight

---

33 Whealey, 'Foreign Intervention in the Spanish Civil War', in *The Republic and the Civil War in Spain*, ed. R. Carr (London/Basingstoke: Macmillan, 1971), 215.

34 Immediately after the outbreak of the Civil War, the French Government was already anxious about such possible negative repercussions for France, should the rebels succeed in Spain (Abendroth, 'Deutschland, Frankreich und der Spanische Bürgerkrieg 1936-1939', in *Deutschland und Frankreich 1936-1939*, ed. K. Hildebrand and K. F. Werner [Munich: Artemis Verlag, 1981], 453 f.).

35 Whealey, 'Foreign Intervention', 219.

36 See, for example, G. T. Harper, *German Economic Policy in Spain during the Spanish Civil War, 1936-1939* (The Hague/Paris: Mouton, 1967), 16 f.; Puzzo, *Spain and the Great Powers*, 43 f.; G. Weinberg, *The Foreign Policy of Hitler's Germany I* (Chicago: Univ. of Chicago Press, 1970), 289; H. Dahms, *La guerra española de 1936* (Madrid: Rialp, 1966), 169.

contracting company in Hamburg, Mathias Rohde & Jörgens Co., was employed to provide ships for the clandestine transport of supplies to Spain. In the meantime, Bernhardt and his fellow envoys arrived back in Tetuán on 28 July on board a German plane flown by Alfred Henke.[37] After removing the symbols of nationality from his plane, Henke immediately undertook the first German transport of rebel troops across the Straits to Seville.[38] Not surprisingly, one of Berlin's main concerns was the camouflaging of the German supply and transport operations. As it was not sufficient simply to remove German symbols, a more organized system was introduced. In the event, a private company was created which, being officially Spanish, would handle all the operational details.

Registered in Tetuán on 31 July 1936 under the name of Carranza & Bernhardt, Transportes en General, with Fernando de Carranza y Fernández-Reguera, a retired navy captain and friend of Franco, and Bernhardt as joint owners, it became better known under the name of HISMA, an abbreviation of its commercial name Hispano-Marroquí de Transportes, Sociedad Limitada.[39] As its first main task HISMA was simply to act as an 'administrative organization and payments office for German help given to the Nationalist movement of Spain'. In practice, this translated into organizing the transportation of Franco's troops and their equipment to the mainland, camouflaging these transports, and arranging the acquisition of additional war *matériel* from private companies. Yet, HISMA's role did not remain restricted to the administration of the initial small amount of German aid. Parallel to the growth of the scale of German intervention, HISMA's size and influence was to increase over the course of the following year. As HISMA's sole managing director with full administrative

---

37 Viñas, *La Alemania nazi* (2nd ed.), 385 and 392; Whealey, *Hitler and Spain*, 7.

38 Abendroth, *Hitler in der spanischen Arena*, 41.

39 BA R7/738, unsigned memorandum *Entstehung*, 15/3/1940; BA R121/842, unsigned, undated report *Entwicklung*; Viñas, *La Alemania nazi* (2nd ed.), 385 ff. The name HISMA can apparently be put down to a suggestion made by Franco (see Abendroth, *Mittelsmann*, 41).

authority, Bernhardt became the main individual beneficiary of its expansion.[40]

HISMA's foundation on 31 July coincided with the departure of the first German ship, the *Usaramo*, with material destined for Franco.   It left Hamburg with eighty-five passengers[41] and seven hundred and seventy-three items of cargo.[42] These items included ten Junkers-52, six Heinkel-51, anti-aircraft guns, bombs, ammunition, and various other pieces of equipment for the crews of the aircraft which were to transport Franco's troops across the Straits.[43]   At the same time, a further ten Junkers-52 were already on their way to Nationalist Spain. At the beginning of August they landed in Tetuán and immediately commenced the transport of Franco's troops to Jerez de la Frontera and Seville.[44]   By the second week of October German planes had transported thirteen thousand, five hundred and twenty-three Moroccan troops and over two hundred and seventy metric tons of arms across the Straits.[45] The impact of this first major air-lift in history was enhanced by the Italian help for Franco which commenced on 29 July with the departure of the first supply ship from Italy.[46]

Owing to the arrival of Franco's troops in the south west of Spain in August, the military situation of the Republic deteriorated steadily.   The capture of Badajoz on 14 August provided the Nationalists with unrestricted access to Portugal which proved to be an extremely helpful ally of the Nationalists, albeit under the cover of formal neutrality.   In early August 1936, Franco's brother, Nicolás Franco, established himself as

---

40 BA R7/738, unsigned memorandum *Entstehung*, 15/3/1940; BA R121/842, unsigned, undated report *Entwicklung*.

41 Abendroth, *Hitler in der spanischen Arena*, 41; Whealey, *Hitler and Spain*, 74.

42 Federal Archive Freiburg (BA/MA) RM20/1222, First entry in list *Sonderdampfer nach Spanien bis einschliesslich 5.1.1937*.

43 BA/MA RL2 IV/1 D1, Report about Unternehmen Feuerzauber, by General Schweickhard, 8/3/1940; BA/MA RM20/1222; Viñas, *La Alemania nazi* (2nd ed.), 392.

44 BA R121/842, unsigned, undated report *Entwicklung*.

45 Whealey, 'Foreign Intervention', 217.

46 For the events surrounding Italy's intervention in the Spanish Civil War see the article by Paul Preston in this volume and Coverdale, *Italian Intervention, passim*.

Franco's procurement officer in Lisbon under the cover name of Aurelio Fernando Aguilar.[47] He became a significant link to Germany, which started to transport material via Lisbon to Nationalist Spain in August 1936.[48] HISMA actively sought contact with the Salazar government to arrange for such operations. On 13 August, the *Kamerun* left Hamburg, followed by the *Wigbert* on the following day. Both ships eventually unloaded their cargoes — mainly aviation gasoline, bombs, ammunition and two Junkers-52 — in Lisbon.[49] Despite British pressure on the Portuguese Government to keep out of the conflict,[50] Portugal continued to be a conduit for goods destined for the Nationalists. According to British Intelligence approximately 320,000 rifles and 555,000 revolvers were dispatched from Germany via Portugal to the Nationalist forces between January 1937 and August 1938.[51]

It thus becomes clear that Franco continued to receive German supplies after the initial contingent and even though the expected rapid Nationalist victory had not come about. Hitler had committed himself to continue supplies until the air-lift was completed. However, the Nazi regime had to ask itself whether it should prolong its intervention beyond the completion of the air-lift. In the event, the decision was in Franco's favour when, on 24 August, Hitler came to the conclusion that 'General Franco should be supported with supplies and militarily as much as possible. Any active German participation in the fighting, however, should not take place for the time being'.[52] A possible future military involvement by German troops was therefore not ruled out.

---

47 ADAP, D, III, doc.26, 24, Letter, Du Moulin to German Foreign Ministry, 3/8/1936.

48 In April 1938 Nicolás Franco was officially appointed as Franco Spain's Ambassador at Lisbon (G. Stone, *The Oldest Ally: Britain and the Portuguese Connection, 1936-1941* [Woodbridge: Boydell & Brewer, 1994], 14).

49 ADAP, D, III, doc.52, 47, Letter, Du Moulin to German Foreign Ministry, 22/8/1936; BA/MA RM20/1222, *Sonderdampfer nach Spanien bis einschließlich 5.1.1937*; Viñas, *Guerra, dinero, dictadura: ayuda fascista y autarquía en la España de Franco* (Barcelona: Editorial Crítica, 1984), 56 f.

50 ADAP, D, III, doc.77, 67; see also Stone, *The Oldest Ally*, 10.

51 Stone, *The Oldest Ally*, 10.

52 Abendroth, *Hitler in der spanischen Arena*, 53.

By the beginning of August, Franco had moved his headquarters to Seville, where most of his Moroccan troops were being landed. When, on 7 August, HISMA duly established its second branch there, it laid the groundwork for a pattern for the entire Civil War, namely to create HISMA branches close to Franco's respective headquarters.[53] Once Franco had been embraced as Head of State and Generalissimo by the Nationalist *Junta de Defensa Nacional* on 29 September 1936, HISMA's close proximity to the newly established leader of the Nationalist troops and territory augured well for a more effective relationship. Certainly, it was in Franco's interest to be able to communicate his supply requirements to the relevant German authority as quickly as possible.

Increasingly, other factors came to have an impact on the relationship between HISMA and Franco. With the rebels in need of Germany's support for a far longer period than anticipated, more detailed attention was paid to the problem of Franco's mounting debts and the possible economic benefits which might arise. On 30 July Göring, whom Hitler had put in charge of the Spanish operation, was already pondering the payment of German deliveries of war *matériel* with iron ore.[54] It is easy to see why Göring would have considered such a form of payment. While the Republic relied on the gold reserves of the Bank of Spain to finance most of its war effort, the Nationalists had to find other ways to pay for their supplies.[55] As Robert Whealey has pointed out, the Nationalists 'had the backing of millionaires', such as Juan March Ordinas, and, in general, they found it easier to obtain credit from international financial circles than the Republican Government.[56] Apart

---

53 BA R121/842, unsigned, undated report *Entwicklung*.

54 Viñas, *La Alemania nazi* (1st ed.), 434; Abendroth, 'Deutschlands Rolle', 481.

55 For the financing of the Civil War see Viñas, *Guerra, dinero, dictadura; política comercial exterior de España I*, 'Gold, the Soviet Union, and the Spanish Civil War', *European Studies Review*, IX (1979), 105-28 and 'The Financing of the Spanish Civil War', in *Revolution and War in Spain 1931-1939*, ed. Paul Preston (London: Methuen, 1984). See also Whealey, *Hitler and Spain*, and 'How Franco Financed his War — Reconsidered', in M. Blinkhorn, *Spain in Conflict 1931-1939* (London: Sage, 1986).

56 See Viñas, *Política comercial exterior*, 289 for detailed accounts of individual loans granted to Franco during the Civil War.

from compelling private persons to hand over all their foreign currency holdings and valuables,[57] both sides continued with the export of as many international trade commodities as possible. As a whole, eleven per cent of the Nationalist Civil War budget was made up of foreign exchange from current exports, profits and dividends on foreign investments owned by wealthy Nationalist partisans, seized precious metals and repatriated earnings of Spaniards working overseas.[58]

Yet, this leaves a substantial share of the Nationalist budget unaccounted for. Ultimately, Franco was forced to request increasing amounts of German and Italian war *matériel* on a credit basis. In the case of Germany demands for repayment increasingly took on the form of demands for Spanish raw materials, though requests for payment in foreign currency were also frequently expressed.[59] In view of Göring's responsibilities within the German government, it seems unsurprising that he happened to be the first Nazi leader to express interest in Spanish raw materials. Three months before the outbreak of the conflict Hitler had ordered Göring to investigate all necessary measures for an improvement of the raw material and foreign currency situation.[60] As Spain produced certain vital raw materials, Göring concluded that payment in such materials could only be beneficial to Germany's economy.

Spain produced substantial amounts of pyrites which constitute an important source of sulphur, as well as iron, copper, lead and zinc.[61] In 1935, pyrite production in Spain amounted to 2.5 million long tons (lts.), roughly twenty per cent

---

57 Viñas, 'The Financing of the Spanish Civil War', 279; Viñas, 'Gold', 120. The value of jewels and coins seized by the Nationalists plus donations of stocks and bonds amounted to Pts 410 million (Whealey, 'How Franco Financed his War — Reconsidered', 257, n. 3).

58 Whealey, 'How Franco Financed his War — Reconsidered', 244; J. Edwards, *The British Government and the Spanish Civil War* (London/ Basingstoke: Macmillan, 1979), 68.

59 See, for example, Archivo Histórico Nacional Madrid (AHN) PG/DGA192, Letter, HISMA to N. Franco, 23/4/1937.

60 G. Thomas, *Geschichte der deutschen Wehr- und Rüstungswirtschaft* (Boppard: Harald Boldt Verlag, 1966), 111 f..

61 C. Harvey, 'Politics and Pyrites during the Spanish Civil War', *Economic History Review*, XXXI (1992), 92.

of world pyrites production. One of Spain's biggest assets was its mercury mining operation at Almadén which supplied about eighty per cent of the world's mercury.[62] In addition, Spain also contributed an important share to European iron ore production. Spain was not only attractive because of her existing raw material production, but also because she possessed huge reserves of a large variety of raw materials, many of which had scarcely been tapped. In 1939, IG Farben reported on Spain's important lead and zinc production and on the potential for expansion of her tin, wolfram (tungsten),[63] gold, bismuth, antimon and sulphur mining.[64]

As a consequence of the growing interest in Spanish raw materials, Göring soon ordered an extension to HISMA's original purpose. Economic factors came to have an impact on the opening of new HISMA branches. An outstanding example for this deployment tactic was the case of Bilbao, the centre of Spain's iron ore mining region. A new HISMA branch was established there in August 1937, immediately after the conquest of the Basque city.[65] HISMA not only constantly extended its geographical sphere of influence, it also enhanced its influence by establishing links with those individuals and organizations involved in Germany's intervention in Spain.

During the course of August 1936 the organizational network behind Germany's intervention in Spain increasingly took shape. On 25 August von Blomberg ordered Lieutenant-Colonel Walter Warlimont to proceed immediately to Spain where he was to act as the representative of Germany's armed forces at Franco's headquarters. Warlimont would be in charge of Germany's forces in Spain and he was supposed to advise Franco on further German supplies of war *matériel*.[66] His

---

62 Edwards, *The British Government*, pp. 82, 92 and 97.

63 On Wolfram see C. Leitz, 'Nazi Germany's Struggle for Spanish Wolfram during the Second World War', *European History Quarterly*, XXV (1995), No. 1, 73-94.

64 NA II, T83, Roll 229, Folder 894, IG Farben report *Spaniens Wirtschaftskräfte*, end of 1939.

65 BA R121/842, unsigned, undated report *Entwicklung*.

66 Viñas, *Guerra, dinero, dictadura*, 59 (based on an unpublished document by W. Warlimont, *Die deutsche Beteiligung am spanischen Bürgerkrieg und einige spätere Folgerungen*).

position at the time, as Head of the Economic Department of the *Heereswaffenamt*, was probably influential in his new appointment in that one of the tasks mentioned in von Blomberg's orders concerned the 'safeguarding of German interests in the ... economic sphere'.[67] Interviewed by Viñas nearly three decades after the Second World War, Warlimont revealed that he was told that the aforementioned economic task included the repayment of German supplies of war *matériel* with supplies of Spanish raw materials.[68]

After his arrival in Spain on 5 September 1936, Warlimont rapidly realized that the growing magnitude of the economic aspect of his mission demanded its separation from his political and military tasks. By now, the question of Spanish payment for German supplies had become the question of the whole economic relationship between the territory controlled by the Nationalists and Germany. Thus, only two weeks after his arrival Warlimont decided to hand over all economic matters to HISMA.[69] After consulting General Wilberg about this matter, he informed Göring about his conclusion.[70] This led to a meeting between Göring, Warlimont, Bernhardt and the head of the *Wehrwirtschaftsstab*, General Georg Thomas, at the end of the month.

In addition to his earlier unspecified demands, Göring had already made it known in early September that he expected some raw materials in return for the Luftwaffe supplies valued at RM 15 million, received by Franco before late August. His list of demands included copper, zinc, tin, iron ores and nickel, with a particular emphasis on cement copper and pyrites.[71] At the meeting, Göring therefore decided to strengthen the position of HISMA *vis-à-vis* the Nationalist administration and elevated it to the official position of 'representative of

---

67 Abendroth, *Hitler in der spanischen Arena*, 124 (based on navy doc. PG 33308 in BA/MA).

68 Viñas, *Guerra, dinero, dictadura*, 59.

69 Abendroth, *Hitler in der spanischen Arena*, 124.

70 BA/MA RL2 IV/I D1, Report about Unternehmen Feuerzauber, by General Schweickhard, 8/3/1940.

71 BA/MA RL2 IV/1 D1, Report about Unternehmen Feuerzauber, by General Schweickhard, 8/3/1940.

Germany's economic interests in Nationalist Spain'.[72] It was determined that HISMA would continue to act as a payment office for the German forces in Spain, but that it would otherwise be independent from the German military command there.[73] Göring's decision was a reflection of the level of his control over Germany's interventionist operations in Spain.[74] Moreover, it was also proof for the further increase of his authority within the Germany economy. By the time of the meeting Hitler had already announced a 'new Four-Year-Programme' for the economy, the control of which Göring immediately usurped. By the time the programme became formalized by an organizational and administrative decree (on 18 October), Göring had already appointed several *Sonderbeauftragte* for various sections of the raw material and foreign currency sectors.[75]

HISMA's economic activities in Nationalist Spain became an additional facet of Göring's control over economic planning in Germany. In the case of HISMA he received assistance from Hess who ordered members of the AO to help with the expansion of the organization. Hess also convinced Göring to appoint AO *Gauamtsleiter* and joint head of the AO's Foreign Trade Office Eberhard von Jagwitz[76] as his authorized representative for economic matters concerning Spain.[77] Thus, Göring had the necessary personnel (members of the AO) and the organizational structure (HISMA) at his disposal to deal with economic matters in Nationalist Spain. Moreover, the

---

72 BA R121/005300, Short undated report about organizational structure of HISMA/ROWAK; Abendroth, *Hitler in der spanischen Arena*, 124.

73 At the beginning of September HISMA had also taken over the financing of the German news service in Nationalist Spain (BA R121/842, unsigned, undated report *Entwicklung*).

74 See Schieder, *Spanischer Bürgerkrieg*, 336.

75 A. Kube, *Pour le Merité und Hakenkreuz: Hermann Göring im Dritten Reich* (Munich: Oldenbourg, 1987), 157 ff. Göring's title 'Plenipotentiary for the Four-Year-Plan' gradually caught on at the end of 1936/beginning of 1937.

76 McKale, *Swastika*, 51. Von Jagwitz ran the Foreign Trade Office in conjunction with Alfred Hess, Rudolf Hess's brother.

77 BA R7/738, unsigned memorandum, *Entstehung*, 15/3/1940; ADAP, D, III, doc.99, 94, Note by Karl Ritter (AA), 15/10/1936; BA/Pots 25.01/7082, Copy of memorandum on a meeting on Spain, 20/11/1936; FCO AA3176, 682859 f., Memorandum on appointment of von Jagwitz, 15/10/1936.

arrival of von Jagwitz heralded the foundation of Rohstoff-Waren-Kompensation Handelsgesellschaft AG (ROWAK) which would be in charge of the German end of the economic relationship. Again, Göring had demonstrated his influence over Germany's economic relations with Nationalist Spain. In fact, on 9 October 1936, Göring's controlling position was emphasized by General Thomas in a meeting between three officials of the Reich Finance Ministry (Assistant Secretaries Meyer and Nasse and Dr Viets), Friedrich Bethke, freshly appointed managing director of ROWAK, and Eberhard von Jagwitz. Thomas made it clear that 'the Spanish issue was not the responsibility of the Wehrmacht any more, but that it had been taken over by General Göring and his staff. It is now to be treated as an economic matter of the Reich over which, on the basis of his orders, General Göring alone has the right to decide'.[78]

In the context of the meeting Thomas alluded to the central role of HISMA and ROWAK which had been founded on Göring's orders on 2 October 1936.[79]   With the help of HISMA/ROWAK, the Nazi state asserted its control over the economic relationship with Nationalist Spain.   By granting ROWAK power of attorney to HISMA on 29 October 1936, the German Government demonstrated that, though officially registered as a Spanish company, HISMA was entirely at the service of the Nazi regime.   Contemporary official and semi-official accounts provide several reasons to explain why a counterpart organization to HISMA had to be created in Germany.   For one, in September HISMA was becoming too zealous in its attempt to export Spanish raw materials to Germany.   Although this could be regarded as a success for the organization, it created problems in Germany as nobody was instructed to distribute such raw materials to individual companies.[80]   In the words of an insider to the organization: 'In the meantime, the ships which HISMA had loaded with raw

---

78   BA/MA RW19/991, Memorandum by Thomas, 9/10/1936.

79   See BA/MA RL2 IV/1 D1, the main military account of Germany's intervention; BA R121/842 and BA R7/738, HISMA/ROWAK's own accounts of their history up to 1940.

80   BA R121/842, unsigned, undated report *Entwicklung*; *ibid.*, Power of attorney, 29/10/1936.

materials and sent on their way to Germany, had arrived there. Yet, no organization existed which was responsible for the running, utilization and accounting for of the raw materials trade'.[81]

In addition, the creation of a central, state-controlled organization could assist the Nazi regime in drawing financial benefits from the import of Spanish raw materials, something which was certainly in their interest in view of the mounting cost of their support for Franco. A clearly defined and structured economic framework became necessary to ensure future economic benefits.[82]

Political motives also contributed to the new arrangement. Private industrial interests and conflicting concerns of other government ministries were usually ignored or even suppressed in favour of the desired HISMA/ROWAK monopoly. A conflict between Göring and these other interested parties ensued until summer 1937, and with Hitler's approval, Göring emerged victorious. HISMA/ROWAK's position remained untouched until the end of the Civil War.

When ROWAK was founded in October 1936, two managing directors, Friedrich Bethke and Anton Wahle, were listed in the official register.[83] In 1938 Bethke followed von Jagwitz into Department V of the Reich Economics Ministry (RWM) where the latter had just been made a special ministerial director for foreign trade.[84] Yet, as managing director of ROWAK, Bethke continued to supervise the day-to-day running of ROWAK, while von Jagwitz remained chairman of ROWAK's advisory committee.[85] In fact, Bethke became one of the most influential

81 BA R7/738, unsigned memorandum *Entstehung*,15/3/1940.

82 BA/MA RL2 IV/1 D1, Report about *Unternehmen Feuerzauber*, by General Schweickhard, 8/3/1940.

83 ROWAK was entered into the Berlin register of companies on 14 October after its partnership agreement had been concluded on the tenth (BA R121/837, Record in the Berlin county court register, 14/10/1936).

84 Whealey, *Hitler and Spain*, 80.

85 BA R2/22, Memorandum by Berger (RFM), 8/10/1938; BA R2/23, Letter, von Jagwitz to Dr Müller (RFM), 22/12/1938; BA R2/27, Audit of ROWAK by Deutsche Revisions- und Treuhand AG, 31/12/1937; BA R7/738, Unsigned memorandum *Entstehung*, 15/3/1940; BA R121/819, Docs. on the 6th meeting of ROWAK's advisory committee, October 1940 (?); BA R121/832, Meeting of ROWAK's advisory committee, 4/11/1943.

figures within ROWAK — if not the most important one — and would remain so until the end of World War II.

Back in the autumn of 1936 Bethke and von Jagwitz were still concerned with building up ROWAK. Immediately after its foundation, the new organization was already confronted with a growing number of responsibilities. As one of its first tasks ROWAK became involved in supplying the Nationalist economy with urgently needed goods, such as coal. Such supply operations, together with the organization and distribution of incoming Spanish raw materials, came to constitute important aspects of ROWAK's much wider area of responsibility.

Since Nationalist Spain was not officially recognized by Germany (at the time of the foundation of ROWAK), it was impossible to establish a regular clearing agreement, and impossible to set an official fixed exchange rate. ROWAK was therefore founded to arrange for financing of trade with Nationalist Spain and to assume exchange fluctuation and credit risks for German producers of goods to be exported to that country, in short, to accomplish unofficially what could not be done officially.[86]

Göring put HISMA/ROWAK in charge of the organization of the entire trading relationship, including the organization of a special clearing system, between Germany and the Nationalist territory. This major task included the procuring of maximum amounts of Spanish raw materials and eventually, from spring 1937 onwards, the purchase of mining rights in Spain. With the help of HISMA/ROWAK the Nazi regime clearly aimed for a massive exploitation of Franco's dependence on German military and economic aid.

ROWAK's foundation and Göring's instructions on HISMA/ROWAK's role threw up some important questions. How would ROWAK fit into the whole organizational network which was already dealing with the intervention in Spain? Moreover, where, within the German state, would the organization be placed? Legally, ROWAK was subordinated to Special Section South of Export Department V of the RWM.[87] Yet, before Hjalmar Schacht's resignation as Economics Minister in

---

86 BA R121/1237, Statement by Bethke to the Allies, 18/8/1945.
87 Whealey, *Hitler and Spain*, 78.

November 1937 and the subsequent complete nazification of the Ministry, the RWM had only limited influence in the affairs of ROWAK. Initially, RWM officials — wrongly — assumed that HISMA/ROWAK would only deal with the trade in raw materials and that the HISMA/ROWAK system would merely be a temporary arrangement.[88]   In fact, the RWM had to content itself with being a purely administrative umbrella for ROWAK's activities.   Under Göring's powerful protection, ROWAK was permitted to act independently.   Finally, on 9 November 1936 the RWM itself enforced ROWAK's near-monopolistic position by publishing an administrative order which prohibited private sales or purchases in any part of Spain by any other organization.[89]   In addition, in late 1936 Göring also apparently determined that the War and Foreign Ministries would 'avoid further involvement in the Spanish project'.[90]   The Reich Finance Ministry (RFM), on the other hand, was ordered to supply the necessary funds for the foundation of ROWAK by granting a starting and bridging loan of RM 4 million.[91]

Initially, therefore, ROWAK was officially incorporated into the RWM.   However, only after Schacht's resignation did Göring finally permit the RWM to take proper control of ROWAK.   In fact, Göring's two major confidantes in ROWAK, von Jagwitz and Bethke, were promoted into the RWM in 1938[92] to ensure a continuation of the way ROWAK had been run since its foundation.   None the less, the composition of ROWAK's advisory committee in June 1940 demonstrates that different ministries and organizations continued to be officially involved with ROWAK. Alongside the RWM, the Reich Finance Ministry, the AO, the Reichswerke Hermann Göring and the Deutsche Revisions- und Treuhand-AG were all represented on the committee.[93]   Indeed, HISMA/ROWAK's pivotal role in the

---

88 ADAP, D, III, doc.101, 96 f., Memorandum by Sabath, 16/10/1936.
89 Whealey, *Hitler and Spain*, 79.
90 *Ibid.*, 77.
91 BA R121/1237, Memorandum by Bethke, 8/2/1937.
92 See above.
93 BA R121/819, Docs. on the 6th meeting of ROWAK's advisory committee, Oct. 1940 (?).

economic relationship with Franco Spain was reflected by the involvement of these ministries and organizations.

By late 1936, nearly all exports from Germany to Spain, and vice-versa, had to pass through 'the HISMA/ROWAK system'. Spanish importers of German goods were permitted to negotiate directly with each other. The conclusion of any business deal, however, had to go via HISMA/ROWAK which would generally charge the German exporter a commission. Commission rates depended on the type of export and could change 'according to the kind and extent of the order'. As far as Spanish exports to Germany were concerned, a more limited amount of goods were permitted for import. If a German company wanted to import from Spain, it had to approach ROWAK to ascertain whether the requested goods were allowed for clearing through the account of HISMA/ROWAK. The organization would then supervise the subsequent business deal and again charge a commission for its services.

Thus, trade contacts between German and Spanish companies were fitted into a strict organizational network. In the matter of German war *matériel* deliveries to Spain a slightly different system applied. Contacts between the High Command of the Army (OKW) and ROWAK were run via General Wilberg's *Sonderstab W*.[94] Nationalist orders of war *matériel* would have to be sent from *Sonderstab W* — or if they had been received by HISMA, from there — to ROWAK. Generally, ROWAK then proceeded in one of two ways. It either passed the order on to the Export Association for War Matériel (AGK), the latter being responsible for allocating the order to the relevant arms producers, or it arranged for deliveries from Wehrmacht stocks via *Sonderstab W*.[95]

In any case of transaction, HISMA/ROWAK was certain to receive a handsome financial reward for its involvement. Small wonder, therefore, that the organization was keen to defend its near-monopolistic position. Near-monopolistic because HISMA/ROWAK permitted a limited amount of transactions without

---

94 BA R121/1237, Unsigned report (probably by von Jagwitz), 26/11/1936.

95 BA/MA RM20/1483, OKM Allg. 'Otto' 4/10/1937 — 21/8/1939; BA R121/860, Letter, Bethke to Bernhardt, 23/7/1937.

their direct involvement, in some cases apparently for a hefty commission payment. In one case Rheinmetall paid HISMA a commission of seven and a half per cent as a reward for 'keeping itself out of a business deal'.[96] Near-monopolistic also because, curiously enough, it allowed one private entrepreneur, the aforementioned Josef Veltjens, to enjoy his own small share of the trade between Germany and Nationalist Spain.

Veltjens was given permission to sell war *matériel* directly to the rebels though his activities often intertwined with those of HISMA/ROWAK. Although, after February 1937, he was officially only permitted to supply war *matériel* of non-German origin, Veltjens continued to supply Nationalist Spain with German arms, mainly rifles and ammunition. These arms supplies he usually purchased from ROWAK though he was allowed to sell them to the Nationalists at his own prices.[97] None the less, he remained a relatively small cog in the whole aid machinery. By 30 September 1937 he had purchased RM 7.72 million of war *matériel* from ROWAK while the total expenditure on Germany's intervention amounted to RM 246.92 million for the period 1 August 1936 to 30 September 1937. Although ROWAK received no commission on its deals with Veltjens, it was still a worthwhile operation as Veltjens had to pay for everything he ordered in foreign currency.[98] This, and the fact that his company was regularly employed by ROWAK as a transport organization, specializing in the transportation of explosives,[99] might explain why Veltjens' activities were

---

96 IWM Krupp, File 15a, Memorandum by Vaillant (Krupp), 19/11/1937.

97 BA R121/1237, Three letters, ROWAK to Veltjens, 28/4 and 31/5/1937, 10/3/1939; BA R2/19, Letter, ROWAK to *Sonderstab W*, 22/4/1937, bill No. 16, 22/3/1937; BA R2/20, *Sonderstab W* bills Nos 1 and 2, 9/8 and 24/8/1937. Augusto Miranda, one of Franco's arms buyers in London, reported to Canaris that, several times, he had purchased arms from 'the well-known German arms dealer Veltgens' [*sic!*] (ADAP, D, III, doc.213, 198, Memorandum by von Dörnberg, 26/1/1937).

98 BA R2/20, Report *Aufwendungen für Spanien* by *Sonderstab W*, 6/10/1937; BA R2/27, Report by Deutsche Revisions- und Treuhand AG on an interim audit of ROWAK, May to September 1937.

99 BA R2/27, Payment demands by Veltjens for deliveries undertaken for ROWAK, 25/11/1937; BA R121/1237, Several freight bills issued by Veltjens, 1937; AHN PG/DGA1/925, Bill, HISMA to *Dirección General de Adquisiciones*, 9/10/1937; AHN PG/DGA2/1001, Bill, Hansegesellschaft

tolerated once he had commenced his supply operations. Owing to its official role as the sole 'clearing house' in the trading of goods between Nazi Germany and Nationalist Spain, HISMA/ROWAK ultimately retained control over all transactions, even those conducted by Veltjens.[100]

While HISMA/ROWAK condoned Veltjens' movements, the organization itself ran into serious opposition from some members of the German government. When, in November 1936, the Foreign Ministry furnished the first official German representative to the Franco regime, General Wilhelm Faupel, with the necessary information about the economic relationship between the two states, senior officials in the Ministry clearly showed their hostility to the existing arrangement and reiterated their belief that it would only be used for a transitional period.[101] HISMA/ROWAK, its supporters in the AO, and particularly Göring, did not fail to notice how uncomfortable some senior government officials felt about the influential role of the organization. Yet, they were clearly not prepared to accept such opposition. A controversy was bound to develop, in the first instance particularly over the future of the German-Spanish trade agreement. The agreement had come into force on 9 March 1936 and was to run out on 31 December 1936.[102] The problem arose because the trade agreement had automatically been transferred to the economic relationship with Nationalist Spain after Germany had recognized the Franco regime as the legitimate Government of Spain on 18 November.[103]

After the recognition, official steps towards a new trade agreement could be initiated by both sides. In late 1936, such negotiations posed some danger to the position of HISMA/ROWAK. At least, this change was hoped for by opponents of

---

Aschpurvis & Veltjens to ROWAK, 3/12/1937; see also Whealey, *Hitler and Spain*, 82.

100 IWM Krupp File 15a, Report on a meeting between company officials of Carlos Hinderer & Cia and Krupp, 15/10/1937.

101 ADAP, D, III, doc.132, 123, Memorandum by Sabath, 27/11/1936.

102 ADAP, D, III, doc.163, 153, Telegram, Karl Ritter (AA) to Faupel, Salamanca, 23/12/1936.

103 ADAP, D, III, doc.123, 113f., Telegram, Hans Dieckhoff to all German diplomatic missions, 17/11/1936.

HISMA/ROWAK in Germany and Nationalist Spain. At first, the problem was shelved for a short period as the agreement was extended for three months to give both sides an opportunity to plan and then open negotiations.[104] However, the wrangle behind the scenes continued unabated. In early January 1937, a Foreign Ministry memorandum emphasized that HISMA/ROWAK's seemingly monopolistic position should be drastically curtailed, and that normal clearing institutions should be introduced.[105]

This growing conflict of interests in Germany was fuelled by the desire of the Franco administration to conclude 'an intergovernmental clearing and commodity agreement that would regularize trade'. Influential members of the regime, including Nicolás Franco, argued that the financial situation of the Nationalists would benefit more if Spanish raw materials could be sold for foreign currency, and not to pay off debts to Germany.[106] After all, it was argued, debts could be settled after the war. On 20 February 1937, General Francisco Gómez, Conde de Jordana y Souza reiterated to the German Embassy his Government's desire for a normalization of commercial relations with Germany, at least as far as the payment modus was concerned. Franco's Foreign Minister complained about commissions charged for business transactions and about the use of 'intermediaries', though he did not mention HISMA/ROWAK by name. At the same time, Jordana suggested a transitional commercial system on the basis of an *Aski*-account in which Spanish exporters could pay in the sums received for their exports and use the same funds for the payment of imports.[107]

The German Government reacted by arranging a ministerial meeting for 26 February. As part of the preparations for this

104 ADAP, D, III, doc.180, 170, Telegram, German Embassy, Salamanca, to German Foreign Ministry, 1/1/1937.

105 FCO AA3176/D682900 f., Undated, unsigned memorandum, probably January 1937.

106 Abendroth, *Hitler in der spanischen Arena*, 126.

107 MAE R1040/14, Letter, *Comisión de Hacienda* to Nationalist Foreign Ministry, 19/2/1937, and verbal note, Jordana to German Embassy, 20/2/1937; Viñas *et al.*, *Política comercial exterior en España, 1931-1975* (Madrid: Banco Exterior de España, 1979), 166.

meeting, Felix Benzler of the Commercial Section of the Foreign Ministry compiled a very revealing memorandum.   Not surprisingly, the main bone of contention was the conclusion of a new clearing agreement which would endanger the 'present monopolistic position of Rowak/Hisma'.   At the moment, Benzler pointed out, HISMA/ROWAK enjoyed Göring's total support.   In fact, the organization also received some tentative backing from the Foreign Ministry, though with the reservation that any support would only last for the duration of the conflict in Spain.   Schacht was unreservedly in favour of a new clearing agreement and, ergo, against the organization.   According to Benzler, he was still supported by the Reich Finance Ministry and the Food Ministry, though the latter seemed to be about to adopt the position of the Foreign Ministry.   Benzler concluded that the meeting was clearly intended to decide on this important matter and to resolve some of the aforementioned disagreements.   No disagreement, however, existed about the need to convince Franco to agree to a new trade agreement which would give Germany better trading conditions.[108]   This desired new trade agreement was supposed to strengthen Germany's position in view of the fact that, after a successful conclusion of the Civil War, the Nazis would no longer be able to rely on Franco's dependence on Germany.   Attempts by Italy and Britain to conclude trading agreements with the Franco administration in late 1936 had only underlined this fear.[109]

At the actual ministerial meeting Schacht surprisingly agreed not to press for a new trade and clearing agreement with Franco Spain.[110]   There is no definite evidence to account for Schacht's decision.   It can only be assumed that, in the face of growing support for Göring's position amongst other ministers,

---

108 ADAP, D, III, doc.223, 207 ff., Memorandum by Felix Benzler (AA), 23/2/1937.

109 Franco signed a treaty with Italy on 28 November 1936 part of which covered general economic matters.   Both states accorded to each other preferred nation treatment. The German Government feared that this would make Franco dependent on Italy, and would weaken Germany's position (ADAP, D, III, doc.142, 132, Telegram, von Neurath to German Embassy in Rome, 5/12/1936).

110 ADAP, D, III, doc.231, 214, Memorandum by Karl Ritter, 17/3/1937; FCO AA 2946H/D576095-100, Memorandum by von Jagwitz, 1/12/1937.

Schacht acquiesced to buy time. In the end, the outcome of the meeting left HISMA/ROWAK in a consolidated position, yet conflict between supporters and opponents of HISMA/ROWAK persisted. In a conversation with Karl Ritter in March 1937, von Jagwitz attacked Wilhelm Ullmann of the Deutsche Überseeische Bank (Banco Alemán Transatlántico). Ullmann had apparently approached the Franco Government about the need to normalize trade relations with Germany. Von Jagwitz was convinced that it was this 'unauthorized initiative' which, in February, had led to Jordana's request for the conclusion of a new trade and clearing agreement.[111] Although it seems highly unlikely that an individual German businessman could influence the Franco Government on such an important matter, the issue serves to re-emphasize the mutual mistrust between supporters and opponents of HISMA/ROWAK. Clearly, many German businessmen were concerned about the increasing intervention of new organizations, such as HISMA/ROWAK, and National Socialist officials in the running and direction of Germany's trade. The case of Germany's economic relations with Franco Spain proved to be a significant example for this development.

Complaints about such special organizations and arrangements[112] eventually led von Jagwitz to compile a comprehensive defence of HISMA/ROWAK in his memorandum *Durchsetzung nationalsozialistischer Grundsätze in der Wirtschaft*. He emphasized that Spain provided an excellent example that it was possible to direct Germany's foreign trade according to National Socialist principles. German industry had been 'helpless' in the face of the abnormal circumstances created by the Spanish Civil War. As it had clearly failed and as this failure would have created enormous damage to the German economy, it had been absolutely essential to create an organization which was able to react positively to new circumstances. At the same time, this new organization would be able to extract unforeseen amounts of important raw

---

111 ADAP, D, III, doc.231, 213 f., Memorandum by Ritter about a conversation with von Jagwitz, 17/3/1937.

112 See particularly BA R7/3411, Memorandum by Dr Max Ilgner, 6/4/1937.

materials from Spain. Von Jagwitz declared that German industry had reacted irresponsibly to the situation by sending representatives to Nationalist Spain who were to compete for the purchase of Spanish goods as well as the sale of their own goods. No thought had been given to the problems this would cause. Von Jagwitz's main argument against this kind of attitude was that unrestrained competition could only push up the prices of Spanish goods. Fortunately, however, HISMA/ ROWAK managed to succeed over the 'egoism of the free economy'. Von Jagwitz concluded that German companies had by now recognized the need to subordinate themselves to the new trading system and he underlined his belief in HISMA/ ROWAK by referring to the economic and financial success of the organization.[113]

Von Jagwitz's memorandum of August 1937 turned into a written confirmation of the triumph of his organization against its opponents.[114] In May, Franco had finally dropped his demand for a clearing agreement. He thereby virtually accepted the existing HISMA/ROWAK system. German pressure on Franco had succeeded.[115] During negotiations in Burgos in April[116] the German delegation had argued against the opening of direct trade links between individual companies. Indeed, Franco was implicitly warned that to reject the existing clearing system would have serious implications for the financing of German war *matériel* deliveries to Spain.[117] General Franco's decision to abandon his demand for a clearing agreement can be interpreted as a direct reaction to this threat. The discussions over a new trade agreement found their conclusion in July when several important protocols were signed. In the first protocol, signed on 12 July, both sides

---

113 See FCO/AA 3176/D682984-87, Report by ROWAK on its first 6.5 months, 4/5/1937 on the economic performance of HISMA/ROWAK.

114 BA R121/860, Memorandum *Durchsetzung nationalsozialistischer Grundsätze in der Wirtschaft* by von Jagwitz, 26/8/1937; FCO AA2946H/D576095-100, Memorandum by von Jagwitz, 13/12/1937. See also Abendroth, *Hitler in der spanischen Arena*, 129.

115 ADAP, D, III, doc.263, 248 f., Telegram, Faupel to German Foreign Ministry, 21/5/1937.

116 Abendroth, *Hitler in der spanischen Arena*, 130.

117 ADAP, D, III, doc.256, 244 f., Telegram, Ritter to German Embassy in Salamanca, 13/5/1937.

agreed to postpone a comprehensive economic agreement as long as the present conditions of war prevailed.[118]

Whereas the first protocol catered for the future, the second, signed three days later, was concerned with present economic matters. Both sides promised, if possible, to supply each other with raw materials, food and manufactured products. The protocol was kept very general, and did not go into specific arrangements for trade.[119] The last protocol was mainly concerned with the debt question. It was decided to postpone a decision on repayment. Crucially, the Franco Government agreed to supply Germany with raw materials as security and part payment on the debt. Furthermore, the Spaniards conceded to Germany the right to invest in economic interests in the Nationalist territory. Indeed, the regime would accept the formation of Spanish companies with German specialists and German capital to find and mine raw materials as long as these companies complied with Nationalist jurisdiction. Additionally, Germany promised to help Franco Spain in the reconstruction of the country and the stimulation of Spanish production.[120] All three protocols appeared to underline the strong position of the German Government. Economically, Franco Spain appeared to be bound to Germany very closely. For the time being, Franco had to accept Germany's economic expansion in Spain. On the other hand, many parts of the protocols were kept sufficiently vague to give Franco some leeway. Firstly, the debt question was to be settled in later negotiations. Secondly, the supply of raw materials was left to Franco's discretion, though he certainly remained pressed to fulfil German requests. Thirdly, Germany's desire to build up a mining empire had to be in accordance with Nationalist law. As it turned out, laws could be altered to limit Germany's economic expansion. Finally, Franco could hope that a victorious conclusion of the Civil War and thus an end to his military dependence on Germany, would allow him to reduce Germany's influence in Spain.

---

118 ADAP, D, III, doc.392, 347 f., Protocol signed by Faupel, Wucher, Jordana, Bau, 12/7/1937.

119 ADAP, D, III, doc.394, 350 f., Protocol, 15/7/1937.

120 ADAP, D, III, doc.397, 354 f., Protocol, 16/7/1937.

Though certainly a very crucial issue, the conflict about its existence and the extent of its influence over the economic relationship between Germany and Franco Spain did not constitute the only matter HISMA/ROWAK had to deal with after the foundation of ROWAK. Other political and military developments had an impact on the organization. One such development was Hitler's decision in late 1936 to increase Germany's military presence in Spain by sending a substantial military force, the Condor Legion. Hitler had been extremely disappointed about the slow progress of the Nationalist troops, particularly in their attempt to capture Madrid. However, the Führer was even more annoyed about what he regarded as Franco's mistaken strategy.[121] In the end, Franco had to accept the establishment of the Legion in order to receive more German aid.[122]

The first transport of troops left Stettin on 7 November. By 18 November, 92 planes and more than 3,800 troops as well as tanks, anti-aircraft guns and signal equipment had already been transported to Spain.[123] While General Hugo Sperrle was appointed first commander of the legion, Warlimont was called back to Germany.[124] German troops already in Spain were integrated into the Condor Legion. Although the Legion was led by a German commander, it was subordinated to Franco's military command.[125] Its maximum strength at any one time during the Civil War never exceeded more than around 5,600 men.[126]

With regard to HISMA's relationship to the Legion, it is essential to emphasize the role of Wilhelm Faupel. On the day of Germany's official recognition of the Franco Government,[127]

---

121 ADAP, D, III, doc.113, 106 ff., Order of the German War Minister, 30/10/1936.

122 Whealey, *Hitler and Spain*, 49.

123 Whealey, *Hitler and Spain*, 50; Whealey, 'Foreign Intervention', 218.

124 Abendroth, *Hitler in der spanischen Arena*, 63.

125 ADAP, D, III, doc. 113, 106 f., Order of the German War Minister, 30/10/1936.

126 Whealey, *Hitler and Spain*, 101 f.

127 Hitler and Mussolini recognized Franco's Government on 18 November 1936 inspite of the fact that Franco had not yet captured Madrid, an initial pre-condition for the recognition (ADAP, D, III, 99 f., Note of the publishers referring to 87-99 of Ciano's papers *L'Europa verso la catastrofe*.

Hitler appointed Faupel German Chargé d'Affaires in Franco Spain,[128] despite the insistence of the Foreign Ministry on sending one of its diplomats, Eberhard von Stohrer, to Nationalist Spain. However, the AO had convinced Hitler about Faupel, and 'AO-Ambassador' Faupel left Germany as her first official representative to the Franco Government.[129] According to Abendroth the AO had clearly come to regard Spain as its domain. After all, AO members Bernhardt and Langenheim had been instrumental in Hitler's decision to intervene in Spain, and Bernhardt had become an important figure as director of HISMA. Moreover, ROWAK was largely led and staffed by members of the AO. Having established a firm role in the economic relationship between the two states, the AO was very keen to extend this influence to the diplomatic field. Although Faupel was not a member of the AO, his beliefs and his experience in Latin America were sufficient to convince the organization of his usefulness.[130]   Faupel arrived in Salamanca   on 28 November 1936 to take over Germany's diplomatic representation in Franco Spain.   The Foreign Ministry had to content itself with appointing two of their men, Schwendemann and Enge, as Faupel's diplomatic and economic advisers. A further important advisory role was taken up by Warlimont who returned to Spain as Faupel's military adviser.[131]

It is evident that the German Foreign Ministry played a more marginal role in Germany's intervention in Spain. Clearly, the Nazi Party and one of its organizations, the AO, were in the driving seat. Although German embassy officials in Nationalist Spain were involved in the day-to-day running of Germany's relationship with Nationalist Spain, the major decisions were usually taken by NSDAP officials, most notably

---

See also ADAP, D, III, docs.109 and 110, 103 f.; ADAP, D, III, doc.122, 113, Telegram, von Neurath to German Embassy in Portugal, 17/11/1936).

128 ADAP, D, III, doc. 125, 117, Memorandum by von Neurath, 18/11/1936.

129 Faupel arrived as German Chargé d'Affaires. He became Ambassador on 11 February 1937, ADAP, D, III, 206, n.2.

130 For more information on Faupel, see Abendroth, *Hitler in der spanischen Arena*, 104.

131 Proctor, *Hitler's Luftwaffe*, 72.

by Hermann Göring. While Göring had not contributed to the initial decision to intervene in Spain — a decision evidently taken by Hitler alone — he managed to acquire a dominant role thereafter. This is particularly true of the economic aspect of Germany's intervention and the development of an economic relationship with Nationalist Spain.[132]   There is no evidence that Hitler was consulted when Göring elevated HISMA to a central role in the economic relationship between the Nationalist territory and Germany in the autumn of 1936. As part of this expansion Göring arranged for the transfer of AO members to HISMA, and soon after that to ROWAK, which owed its existence solely to Göring's orders.

After the initial arrangements Göring continued to remain closely involved in the future development of HISMA/ROWAK. Not only did he give the organization control of the entire economic relationship and clearing system between Nazi Germany and Nationalist Spain, he also intervened against the attempted interference of German officials opposed to the new system.   Although the RWM was nominally in charge of HISMA/ROWAK, ultimate authority rested with Göring. In the crucial ministerial meeting in early 1937, Göring prevented any alteration to the HISMA/ROWAK system by its opponents. Göring's defence of the system even warded off Nationalist Spanish demands for a normalization of the trading relationship. He had become convinced of HISMA/ROWAK's usefulness to Germany's needs, but likewise also to his own quest for more power. No evidence could be found that Hitler, at any point, showed his disapproval of Göring's decisions, or intervened actively in favour of opponents of the HISMA/ ROWAK system.   After Hitler's initial decision to support Franco, he only intervened again on two further occasions in 1936, first, when he decided to continue and expand Germany's intervention in August, and second, when he ordered the creation and dispatch of the Condor Legion in October. By the end of 1936, however, and for the remainder of the Civil War, Göring was firmly in charge of Germany's intervention in

---

132 See C. Leitz, 'Hermann Göring and Nazi Germany's Economic Exploitation of Nationalist Spain, 1936-1939', *German History*, XIV (1996), No. 1.

Spain, not least in the economic field via HISMA/ROWAK. In fact, Göring came to rely on HISMA/ROWAK to draw the maximum economic benefit from Germany's intervention in Spain. Although his attempt to turn Spain into an economic dependent of Nazi Germany failed, and HISMA was deprived of its influential role during the course of 1939, ROWAK continued to play a central role in the economic relationship between Nazi Germany and Franco Spain until the end of the Second World War.

4

'We Are with You': Solidarity and Self-interest in Soviet Policy towards Republican Spain, 1936-1939[1]

DENIS SMYTH

On 3 August 1936, a crowd of around 150,000 people thronged Moscow's Red Square. It was a female worker from the 'Red Dawn' factory, E. Bystrova, who expressed the purpose of this gathering most eloquently:

> Our hearts are with those who at this moment are giving up their lives in the mountains and streets of Spain, defending the liberty of their people. We send our greeting of fraternal solidarity, our proletarian greeting to the Spanish men and women workers, to the Spanish wives and mothers, to all the Spanish people. We say to you: remember that you are not alone, that we are with you.[2]

Although the *Pravda* journalist Mijail 'Koltsov', maintained that the Muscovite manifestation had not been pre-planned, and had been organized at the shortest notice, foreign diplomatic observers did not doubt that it represented the official Soviet attitude, on that date, towards the recent military uprising against the Spanish Republic.[3] Indeed, Republican

---

1 This essay is a revised and expanded version of a paper read before the Irish Conference of Historians held at Maynooth from 16-19 June 1983 (*Historical Studies XV* [Belfast: Appletree Press, 1985], 223-37).

2 Mijail Koltsov, *Diario de la guerra española* (Madrid: Akal, 1978), 7-8; International Editorial Board, *International Solidarity with the Spanish Republic* (Moscow: Progress Publishers, 1975), 300.

3 Koltsov, *Diario* 7; *Documents on British Foreign Policy, 1919-1939*, ed. W. N. Medlicott and Douglas, Series 2 (hereafter cited as *DBFP*), XVII, *Western Pact Negotiations: Outbreak of the Spanish Civil War, June 23, 1936-January 2, 1937* (London: HMSO, 1979), 83.

Spain's Ambassador to the USSR, Dr Marcelino Pascua, reminded his government, on several occasions, during his accreditation to Moscow from October onwards, that Soviet 'public opinion' was so 'absolutely directed and controlled' that it could be viewed as a reliable guide to the Soviet regime's inclinations and intentions, at any given moment.[4] Moreover, there was no denying the official Soviet Communist inspiration behind the first practical expression of the allegedly spontaneous upwelling of Russian proletarian solidarity with the embattled Spanish Republic. Collections in aid of the 'Spanish fighters for the Republic' were organized in all Soviet factories by the All-Union Central Council of Trade Unions. It was reported that so enthusiastic was the response of Soviet workers to this appeal for support for democracy in Spain that they voted unanimously, in every instance, a 'voluntary' contribution of an identical share of their wages, 0.5 per cent deductible at source. The levy yielded 12,145,000 roubles (c.£500,000 sterling) by 6 August, and amounted to 47,595,000 roubles by the end of October.[5] This financial resource was rapidly translated into humanitarian assistance to Spain: on 18 September, the first Soviet ship to sail for Republican Spain, the *Neva*, departed with a cargo of foodstuffs. Other Soviet ships followed in a sustained effort to deliver alimentary aid to the populous Republican zone of Central and Eastern Spain, an area deprived of its agrarian hinterland in the south and north of the country by the rapid advance of the military rebels on Madrid.[6]

However, Republican Spain needed more than the mere means to keep body and soul together in order to survive, as Franco's Army of Africa advanced on the capital city in the autumn of 1936. Madrid was indeed, as Auden put it, 'the heart', but to keep beating it had to exercise the sinews of modern warfare.[7] Once again, the Soviet Union revealed itself

---

4   Ángel Viñas, *El oro de Moscú: alfa y omega de un mito franquista* (Barcelona: Grijalbo, 1979), 320.

5   *DBFP*, XVII, 83-84; *International Solidarity*, 301-02; Koltsov, *Diario*, 8.

6   *International Solidarity*, 302.

7   W. H. Auden, 'Spain', in *The Penguin book of Spanish Civil War Verse*, ed. Valentine Cunningham (Harmondsworth: Penguin, 1980), 99.

to be willing to provide this vital form of help to the Spanish Republican Civil War effort. During the autumn and winter of 1936-37, twenty-three Soviet merchant ships laden with military equipment, arms and ammunition left Black Sea ports for Spain, while other Russian munitions were smuggled over the Pyrenean frontier. Soviet aircraft and tank crews helped the new Republican Popular Army employ this *matériel* to such effect that Madrid was rescued, a defensive victory won at the Jarama in February, and the Italian Corpo Truppe Volontarie routed at Guadalajara in March 1937.[8]   Moreover, the International Brigades recruited and trained at Moscow's behest by the Comintern and its 'front' organizations proved to be more than just proficient 'shock' troops in the battles that saved Madrid. They also seemed to be the very embodiment of the resolve of 'the fatherland of the working class of all countries' (as Stalin described the USSR in January 1934) to honour its obligation to uphold the Spanish Popular Front against domestic reaction and foreign Fascist intervention.[9] Indeed, Joseph Stalin, the general secretary of the Communist Party of the Soviet Union, claimed that it was precisely this international class consciousness which had prompted Russia to support the beleaguered Spanish Republicans. In a telegram addressed to José Díaz, the general secretary of the Partido Comunista de España (PCE), published on 16 October 1936, Stalin made this declaration:

> The working people of the Soviet Union are only doing their duty in rendering what aid they can to the revolutionary masses of Spain. They are fully aware that the liberation of Spain from the yoke of the fascist reactionaries is not a private concern of Spaniards, but the common cause of all forward-looking and progressive humanity.[10]

Nearly forty years later, the then chairperson of the PCE, Dolores Ibárruri, 'La Pasionaria', repeated Stalin's contention that it was a disinterested internationalism that had induced

---

8   *International Solidarity*, 315.

9   Fernando Claudín, *The Communist Movement: From Comintern to Cominform* (Harmondsworth: Penguin, 1975), 176-77.

10 Ivan Maisky, *Spanish Notebooks* (London: Hutchinson, 1966), 48; *International Solidarity*, 303-04.

the USSR to become engaged in the Spanish conflict: 'it declared from the very first hour of the struggle that the cause of the Spanish Republic was that of all progressive and forward-looking mankind'.[11]

Leaving aside, for the moment, La Pasionaria's analysis of the motives behind Soviet intervention in Spain, her memory is faulty on the question of its timing, for as late as 29 July 1936 (the military revolt against the Republic having broken out during the night of 17-18 July), she herself appealed to all countries to save Spanish democracy, by which date neither in word nor deed had the Soviet Government come out in clear support of Republican Spain.[12] Indeed, on the very day of La Pasionaria's urgent plea for international help, the British Ambassador in Moscow, Viscount Chilston, reported that the officially-controlled Soviet press had displayed a 'great' but only a 'non-commital interest' in the Spanish Civil War since its outbreak. He also recorded a specific Soviet press refutation of a Francoist allegation that a Russian oil tanker had supported an attack by a unit of the Republican fleet on the rebel-held Spanish Moroccan coastline:

> Spanish government has never asked Soviet Union for assistance and we are convinced that they will find in their own country sufficient forces to liquidate this mutiny of fascist generals acting on orders from foreign countries.[13]

Moreover, the Italian Chargé d'Affaires in Moscow, Vicenzo Berardis, had registered an even stronger impression, from as early as 23 July, of Soviet wariness in the face of the unsettling news from Spain:

> A spokesman (for the Soviet leaders) has just now confirmed that they are very annoyed and perplexed at the Kremlin by the events in Spain and that in no circumstances would the Soviet government get itself mixed up in the internal events of the Peninsula where it has everything to lose and nothing to gain. He has also confirmed, cynically, that Moscow would go no further

---

11 *International Solidarity*, 7.

12 *Istoriya Vtoroi Mirovoi Voiny, 1939-1945*, (Moscow: Voenizdat, 1974), II, 52. Paolo Spriano also erroneously asserts that 'the USSR decided to take action from the outset [of the Spanish Civil War], in July-August 1936'. See his *Stalin and the European Communists* (London: Verso, 1985), 23.

13 *DBFP*, 2s, XVII, 36.

than the publication of an article or two expressing platonic sympathy and avoiding the adoption of any official position.[14]

The same Italian diplomat reported to Rome on 6 August that 'the Soviet government had exerted itself to become committed as little as possible' in the Spanish affair.[15]

Yet the events that were to produce an eventual *volte face* in Soviet policy towards the Spanish Civil War also began on 29 July 1936. On that day, the first aircraft of a contingent of twenty German Junkers 52s arrived in Spanish Morocco, and set to work at once, transporting Franco's troops over the Strait of Gibraltar which was dominated by the Spanish Republican fleet. On 30 July, three of the twelve Savoia-Marchetti S.81 bombers sent by Mussolini to augment this air ferry crashed *en route*, two of them on to French Moroccan territory.[16] The news of Fascist intervention in the Spanish conflict on the rebel side was out.[17] According to Chilston's dispatch of 10 August 1936 to the Foreign Office, it was 'the growing weight of evidence that the two principal "Fascist" states were actively assisting the insurgents' that caused the Soviet government to abandon the 'correct and neutral' attitude it had maintained towards the Spanish Civil War during the first fifteen days after its outbreak.[18] The Moscow demonstration of 3 August, already mentioned, the similar meetings held across the Soviet Union and the collection of funds for Republican Spain were intended to signal the Communist State's displeasure at the evidence of foreign Fascist interference in the Spanish troubles. Yet the Soviet response was still cautious. For, though there were advocates of immediate, active Soviet and international Communist support for Republican Spain within the Comintern, the French military attaché in Moscow, Lieutenant-Colonel Simon, informed Paris that there was also a 'moderate group', to which Stalin belonged, which wanted to

---

14 Ministero degli Affari Esteri, *I Documenti Diplomatici Italiani* (Rome, Istituto Poligrafico e Zecca dello Stato, 1993) (hereafter cited as *DDI*), 8ª serie, IV, 676.

15 *Ibid.*, 761.

16 John F.Coverdale, *Italian intervention in the Spanish Civil War* (Princeton N.J.: Princeton U. P., 1975), pp. 3-4, 85-86.

17 *Ibid.*, 4; *DBFP*, XVII, 44.

18 *DBFP*, XVII, 83.

avoid any intervention in the Spanish fight, 'so as not to provoke a reaction from Germany and Italy'.[19]   Indeed, the Soviet Government replied to the Anglo-French project for an international non-intervention agreement on Spain with alacrity, readily affirming its willingness to adhere to the principle of non-intervention in the internal affairs of Spain.[20] The Italian Chargé d'Affaires in the USSR, Berardis, got the impression that 'the French initiative for a non-intervention agreement on Spain has thus been received with intense relief', since it absolved Moscow from making the difficult choice between abandoning the Spanish Left or risking precipitation of a European war.[21]

In subscribing, on 23 August 1936, to the international non-intervention agreement on Spain, which prohibited arms supplies to either of the Spanish contestants, the Soviet Union was lending its support to a scheme which denied the Republican Popular Front its right under international law, as the legitimate government of its country, to acquire the means abroad to supress the domestic rebellion against it.[22] Moreover, as the French Chargé d'Affaires, Payart, told the Quai d'Orsay on 3 September 1936, Soviet adherence to the non-intervention scheme was a victory for 'M. Stalin's currently constructive ideas'. Although it had provoked violent opposition at the heart of the Communist Party of the Soviet Union, Stalin's line of participation in the non-intervention agreement had prevailed. Inspired by 'the two principles of European solidarity and the peaceful coexistence of peoples', Stalin's 'positive policy' represented a deliberate dereliction by 'the fatherland of the working class of all countries' of its duty to help its proletarian progeny in time of need.[23]

Nor did the Soviet Union join the non-intervention powers all the better to render effective aid to its comrades in Spain for as long as possible, as did Fascist Italy and Nazi Germany.

---

19 Ministère des Affaires Étrangères, *Documents diplomatiques Français 1932-1939, 2e série* (hereafter cited as *DDF*), vol. III, *19 Juillet-19 Novembre 1936*, (Paris: Imprimerie Nationale, 1966), 208.
20 *Ibid.*, 338.
21 *DDI*, 8ᵃ, IV, 761.
22 *DDF*, III, 271-72.
23 *Ibid.*, 338.

Some Soviet military experts and perhaps some limited amounts of Soviet small arms did find their way to Republican Spain during the days immediately following Soviet subscription to the non-intervention agreement. However, the first large-scale shipment of Soviet military supplies did not reach Spain until 15 October, when the *Komsomol* docked at Cartagena.[24] Moreover, this breach of promise occurred only after the Kremlin had warned the London-based Non-Intervention Committee, on 7 October 1936, that 'if violations of the agreement for Non-Intervention [were] not immediately stopped the Soviet Government [would] consider itself free from the obligations arising out of the agreement'.[25] An *Izvestiya* editorial of 26 August 1936 had explained Soviet participation in the Non-Intervention agreement on the grounds that the latter scheme was 'apparently directed towards the cessation of this [Fascist] aid to the rebels and to the guaranteeing of the actual non-participation of other countries in Spanish affairs'.[26] If the Non-Intervention agreement proved effective the Soviet Union was prepared, seemingly, to uphold it. However, if the agreement failed to cut the Francoists off from their Fascist providers, then Moscow would examine other ways and means of attaining its policy-goal in Spain.

The Italian Chargé in Moscow defined that Soviet aim in these terms on 13 August 1936: 'Soviet leadership circles have ultimately shaped their attitude to the needs of peace, which is their principal goal'.[27] From the time of his arrival in Moscow, on 7 October 1936, the Spanish Republican representative, Pascua (who was afforded a privileged access to the Kremlin granted to no other Western diplomat at this time) was able to accumulate direct evidence which led him to form an identical view of the predominant purpose of Soviet policy. Pascua informed his government in January 1937 that the Soviet leaders realized that they needed 'several years of peace which would permit the USSR to develop its enormous domestic plans

---

24 Viñas, *El Oro de Moscú*, 152; *idem.*, 'Gold, the Soviet Union and the Spanish Civil War', *European Studies Review*, IX (1979), 110-11.
25 *DBFP*, XVII, 367-69.
26 Quoted by David T. Cattell, *Soviet Diplomacy and the Spanish Civil War* (Berkeley/Los Angeles: Univ. of California Press, 1957), 19.
27 *DDI*, 8ª, IV, 800.

[which were] of such great importance for it and the socio-political world and to consolidate and perfect its still immature military power'. Pascua maintained that the Soviet Communists had relegated the fomenting of Marxist revolutions abroad to a subordinate role in their international strategy:

> The present policy of the USSR is dominated by the idea of the socialist construction of this country ... the socialist construction of the USSR absolutely predominates over everything else not only as a current task, but also as decisive for the future of socialism. This is ... the axis of the question as regards the Soviets.[28]

Pascua had perceived the essential nature of Stalinist foreign policy: the building of 'socialism in one country', the Soviet Union was held to be in the overriding interest not only of Russian workers, but of the whole world's proletariat. Thus was the pre-eminence of *raison d'état* in Soviet foreign policy reconciled with revolutionary internationalism. To complete their massive socio-economic transformation of the USSR through the Five-Year Plans, the Soviet Communists needed a quiet international existence, free from external distraction and foreign interruption. Peace and security were their principal international aims. The protection of their gigantic exercise in socio-economic engineering was, Pascua recognized, the factor which conditioned every foreign policy move made by the Soviet Government: 'all the political game is being subordinated to the colossal and essential task of the Soviet leaders'.[29]   It was firmly within this herarchy of policy priorities that the Spanish problem was evaluated by the Soviet Government. Pascua even concluded that the Spanish War was in itself a minor matter in Moscow's international calculations.[30]   The sole criterion of strategic significance apparently applied by the Kremlin in the mid-1930s to international affairs was the possible impact of a foreign development upon the security of the one land where Socialism was under construction. This point was discerned also by Berardis, who advised his Foreign Minister, Galeazzo Ciano, on 20 August 1938, that the reason the USSR so

---

28   Viñas, *El Oro de Moscú*, pp. 320, 323.

29   *Ibid.*, 321.

30   Manuel Azaña, *Obras completas*, 4 vols (Mexico D.F.: Oasis, 1966-68), IV, *Memorias políticas y de guerra*, 734.

earnestly desired the successful conclusion of a non-intervention accord on Spain was its 'fear of international complications'.[31] Such was the grand strategic perspective from which Soviet policy towards the Spanish Civil War was formulated.

The Soviet Ambassador in London, Ivan Maisky, tried to impress this very point upon the British Foreign Secretary, Anthony Eden, on 3 November 1936. In a conversation with Eden, Maisky gave what he himself described as 'an exposition of the motives which had actuated the Soviet government in the Spanish conflict':

> He [Maisky] was emphatic that the Soviet government's admitted sympathy with the government in Spain was not due to their desire to set up a communist regime in that country. I [Eden] remarked that the Ambassador could hardly be surprised if other people thought differently in view of the declared objective of the upholders of communism to make their method of government universal. The Ambassador replied that it was quite true that this was their ultimate objective but it was a very distant one — nobody [in] Russia today thought that could be achieved for instance in our lifetime — and the Soviet government's purpose in attempting to assist the Spanish government was far more immediate than that ... The Soviet government were convinced that if General Franco were to win the encouragement given to Germany and Italy would be such as to bring nearer the day when another active aggression would be committed — this time perhaps in central or eastern Europe. That was a state of affairs that Russia wished at all costs to avoid and that was her main reason for wishing the Spanish government to win in this civil strife.[32]

The Foreign Office's Soviet expert, Laurence Collier, accepted 'Maisky's account of his government's motives' as 'substantially accurate'.[33] Stalin's Spanish policy was an integrated part of Soviet international strategy as a whole. It was the general strategic implications of Fascist intervention in Spain which prompted Soviet concern over that country and their eventual engagement there.[34]

---

31 *DDI*, 8ª, IV, 849.

32 *DBFP*, XVII, 495-96.

33 *Ibid.*, 496.

34 See, e.g., Soviet Ministry of Foreign Affairs, *Dokumenty Vneshnei Politiki SSSR*, (hereafter cited as *D.V.P.SSSR*) XIX (Moscow: Izdatelstvo

The Kremlin had been alarmed for some time at the seemingly endemic antagonism of Nazi Germany towards the Soviet State and, as Maisky had impressed upon Eden, Moscow wanted to thwart any success for Hitler in Spain which might encourage him to undertake military adventures eastwards. The Soviet Union had already moved to counter the potential threat to its security, posed by the developing block of right-wing states formed by Germany, Italy and Japan, by altering its own ideological and diplomatic course during 1934-35. Forsaking political sectarianism and revolutionary isolationism, Stalin had sought anti-Fascist allies among the bourgeois democratic parties and states.[35] The main result of the effort to create a popular front at the international level was the Soviet-French Treaty of Mutual Assistance of 2 May 1935, by which both powers promised 'immediate' joint consultation if either were 'threatened with or in danger of aggression' and also pledged 'reciprocally' to render each other aid and assistance in case of 'an unprovoked aggression on the part of a European state' on either country.[36] Although right-wing reluctance in France to bind their country to Communist Russia delayed the parliamentary ratification of the treaty until March 1936, its confirmation then was followed soon afterwards by the election victory of the French Popular Front coalition under Léon Blum. This happy coincidence appears to have reawakened the Soviet interest in concluding a military convention with France that would develop their diplomatic association into an effective military alliance. The Soviet leadership pursued this project especially actively from the early summer of 1936 until the spring of 1937, the same period during which it had also to form its basic line of foreign policy towards the Spanish Civil War. The hope that France might become Soviet Russia's military partner was the main positive influence (and, of course, it was clearly connected with the

Politicheskoi, 1974), 475.

35 Isaac Deutscher, *Stalin: A Political Biography* (Harmondsworth: Pelican, [revised ed.] 1966), 407-12; Claudín, *Communist Movement*, 174-79; E. H. Carr *The Twilight of Comintern, 1930-1935* (London: Macmillan, 1982), pp. 116-55, 403-27.

36 J. A. S. Grenville, *The Major International Treaties, 1914-1973: A History and Guide with Texts*, (London: Methuen, 1974), 152-53.

major negative influence on Soviet policy at that time, anxiety about Hitler's Germany) affecting Moscow's attitude towards the Spanish Civil War, during the crucial months of late 1936 and early 1937. It was only subsequent to the Soviet elaboration of a stable policy-line on Spain that the Kremlin's hopes for an alliance with France were to be definitively disappointed by opposition from within the French Government and the army's general staff.[37]

It was, then, the Soviet preoccupation with protecting the strategic position of their potential ally, France, that produced the twists and turns in Russian policy towards Spain in the vital early phases of the Civil War there. Thus, according to intelligence supplied by informers to the Parisian Prefecture of Police, on 25 July 1936, Soviet representatives had been warned by their government to beware of any demonstration of sympathy towards Republican Spain which might place France in an awkward position *vis-à-vis* England and thereby imperil Stalin's plans for an anti-Nazi bloc.[38] Equally, Viscount Chilston realized that it was precisely this concern which had induced Moscow to abandon its initially aloof attitude towards the Spanish struggle. On 10 August 1936 the British Ambassador relayed home Karl Radek's refutation, in *Izvestiya* of 4 August, of the Nazi charge that the Spanish War was Moscow's work:

---

37 John E. Dreifort, 'The French Popular Front and the Franco-Soviet Pact, 1936-37: A Dilemma in Foreign Policy', *Journal of Contemporary History*, XI (1976), 217-36; Robert J. Young, *In command of France: French Foreign Policy and Military Planning, 1933-1940* (Cambridge, Mass.: Harvard U. P., 1978), 145-50; Anthony Adamthwaite, *France and the Coming of the Second World War* (London: Cass, 1977), 47-50.

Stalin did also explore the possibility of a *rapprochement* with Nazi Germany in later 1936 to early 1937. However, Hitler was more impressed by the Soviets' strenuous efforts to forge a strategic partnership with Britain and France, than by Moscow's professed willingness to mend Russo-German fences (Jonathan Haslam, *The Soviet Union and the Struggle for Collective Security in Europe 1933-1939* [New York: St Martins Press, 1984], 127-28; see also Jiri Hochman, *The Soviet Union and the Failure of Collective Security, 1934-1938* [Ithaca/London: Cornell U. P., 1984], 111-15).

38 Carlos Serrano, *L'enjeu espagnol: PCF et guerre d'Espagne* (Paris: Messidor-Éditions Sociales, 1987), 51.

The louder the German Fascists shout about Bolshevik or French intervention in Spain, the plainer it becomes that they are preparing for serious action not only against Spain but against France also.

Chilston emphasized the importance of this latter statement by commenting on it thus:

This last sentence reveals of course the kernel of the Soviet government's problem.   Lenin prophesied long ago that Spain would be the first to follow in Russia's footsteps, but Spain and the world revolution can wait; meanwhile any danger to France is a danger to the Soviet Union.[39]

The Soviets were quick to grasp that the Spanish conflict might well result in acute danger for France.   On 14 August 1936 *Pravda* editorialized in this vein:

It is absolutely essential to submit to serious study the possible consequences   of   Spanish   events   for   the   future,   for   the independence and for the security of France.[40]

A Fascist regime in Spain, in alliance with Hitler or Mussolini, or both, could create a military threat along France's previously secure Pyrenean frontier and might even interrupt metropolitan lines of communication with French North Africa, where large-scale forces were stationed in time of European peace. As has been mentioned above, the Soviet Government did sign the international non-intervention agreement on Spain, in late August 1936, in spite of its growing alarm about the possible repercussions of a Fascist victory there.   However, as the People's Commissar for Foreign Affairs, Maxim Litvinov, declared at the League of Nations on 8 September 1936, 'the Soviet government has associated itself with the Declaration on Non-Intervention in Spanish affairs only because a friendly power [i.e. France] feared an international conflict if we did not do so'.[41] Recognizing that Blum's Popular Front Government was too divided on the issue of aid to the Spanish Republic to

---

39   *DBFP*, XVII, 84-85.

40   Cited by Cattell, *Soviet Diplomacy*, 6.   The Soviet party line on the strategic threat France would confront in the event of an insurgent victory in Spain was faithfully echoed by the French Communists (see, for example, Pierre Broué, *Staline et la révolution* [Paris: Fayard, 1993], 74-75).

41   Cattell, *Soviet Diplomacy*, 39.

take practical steps to safeguard French strategic interests in Spain, the Soviets apparently rallied to the non-intervention agreement in the hope that the scheme would succeed in its purpose of localizing the conflict by ending foreign Fascist assistance to Franco. Yet, when continuing Italo-German aid brought the Spanish military rebels to the brink of victory in late September and early October 1936, the Soviet Government resolved to intervene to save Republican Spain because it realized that the French government was too paralysed by internal dissent over Spain to take action to help itself.[42] Stalin was emphatic that this determination to defend France was the sole motive behind his intervention in Spain, when he discussed the matter with Pascua early in 1937:

> Spain, according to them [Soviet leaders] is not suitable for Communism, nor prepared to adopt it and [even] less to have it imposed on her, nor even if she adopted it or they imposed it on her, could it last, surrounded by hostile bourgeois regimes. In opposing the triumph of Italy and Germany, they are trying to prevent any weakening in France's power or military situation.[43]

Moreover, the final influence impelling the USSR to become involved in the Spanish conflict was the awareness that not only would France, the linchpin of the embryonic Soviet defensive network, be defended, but that a collective security system might be extended to embrace other democratic powers, particularly Britain. The defence of Republican Spain against Fascist aggression might provide convenient ground for co-operation between the Soviet Union and the Western democracies, a working partnership that could develop into a fully-fledged military alliance with Britain and France, thereby realising the Kremlin's general design for the protection of Communist Russia against Nazi Germany. Certainly, this was the hope expressed by the Soviet Ambassador to Germany, Yakob Z. Suritz, in a letter he sent to Moscow, on 12 October 1936: 'It is possible that our decisive declaration in the Spanish question might have a healthy influence and lead to the consolidation of the elements opposing Fascism'.[44]

---

42 *DBFP*, XVII, 475-76.
43 Azaña, *Obras completas*, IV, 618.
44 *D.V.P.SSSR*, XIX, 475.

The role of Soviet advisers and Spanish Communists in restraining, reversing and even repressing the revolutionary process inside the Republican zone of Spain seems explained, in part at least, by Stalin's determination that the regime there should present a moderate, bourgeois democratic image to capitalist politicians in Britain and France, who might be persuaded to mount a joint Anglo-French-Soviet rescue operation on its behalf. Stalin counselled Republican Spain's Socialist Premier, Francisco Largo Caballero, on this point in a letter of 21 December 1936:

> The urban petty and middle bourgeoisie must be attracted to the government side ... The leaders of the Republican party should not be repulsed; on the contrary they should be drawn in, brought close to the government, persuaded to get down to the job in harness with the government ... This is necessary in order to prevent the enemies of Spain from presenting it as a Communist Republic, and thus to avert their open intervention, which represents the greatest danger to Republican Spain.[45]

A radical Spanish Republic, moreover, would frighten off conservatives in Britain and France whose co-operation the Soviets sought in joint action over the Civil War, with the immediate aim of saving Republican Spain, but with the more fundamental purpose of obtaining Anglo-French membership of an anti-Nazi block which would guarantee the strategic security of the USSR. Indeed, the new French Ambassador in Moscow, Robert Coulondre, explicitly warned Soviet officials, including Litvinov, on a number of occasions, in late November to early December 1936, that a success for the anarchists and communists in Spain could have adverse effects on Franco-Soviet relations.[46] In fact, acute Spanish Republican observers discerned a clear Soviet unwillingness to help their cause on a scale greater than that which the British and French would complement or tolerate. Thus, the president of the Spanish Republic, Manuel Azaña, was sure, in August 1937, that the Soviet Union would avoid any action in support of Republican Spain that could injure seriously Moscow's relations

---

45 Cited by Claudín, *Communist Movement*, 707.
46 *DDF*, IV, *20 Novembre 1936-19 Février 1937*, (Paris: Imprimerie Nationale, 1967), 248.

with Britain or jeopardize its pursuit of 'Western friendships'.[47] Again, Pascua informed his government in January 1937 that Soviet support for the Spanish Republican cause was 'conditional on a clearer and more effective French attitude, doubtless subordinate to English solidarity'.[48]

It was in order to be able to project a credible image to Paris and London of the Spanish Republic as a moderate bourgeois democracy that the Soviets spearheaded a socio-economic counter-revolution inside Republican Spain.   This process dismantled agrarian collectives, returned collectivized industries to private enterprise, destroyed (with admittedly sectarian ideological zeal) the 'Trotskyist' Partido Obrero de Unificación Marxista and absorbed the socialist and anarcho-syndicalist militia into a new regular formation, the Popular Army of the Republic.[49] The inevitable result of this exercise in repression was the destruction of the popular *élan* of the masses of Republican Spain, whose very talent for spontaneous, direct action had saved the Republic in the first days of the military *pronunciamiento* against it, between 18 and 20 July 1936. The people's energy had to be controlled and the revolutionary process channelled if the Civil War was to be won. However, the brutal Communist suppression of Republican Spain's left-wing socialist and anarcho-syndicalist revolution perhaps deprived the Spanish Republic of some of its domestic power-base.   Only foreign aid, the elusive intervention of Britain and France, could have saved the demoralized and divided Republic. But the Soviet Communist strategy failed to achieve its goal: British indifference and French indecision doomed Republican Spain.

Moscow, however, continued to exercise a moderating influence on political and social developments within Republican Spain for the effective duration of the Spanish Civil War, in the hope of ultimate strategic association with the

---

47 Azaña, *Obras completas*, IV, 734.

48 Viñas, *El Oro de Moscú*, 322.

49 For an extreme version of this view, see Burnett Bolloten, *The Spanish Civil War: Revolution and Counterrevolution* (New York/London: Harvester Press, 1979), 249-531. A more plausible account may be seen in Helen Graham's chapter in this volume, 'War, Modernity and Reform: The Premiership of Juan Negrín 1937-39'.

Western democracies. This courtship of the capitalist powers in the Spanish cockpit was pursued notwithstanding its lack of return and the condemnation it drew down on Spanish Communists from other leftists. Indeed, a significant dissenting voice was raised even within the Spanish Communist Party as the fortunes of Civil War turned against the Republic, with the progress of the Aragonese offensive launched by the Francoist forces with massive amounts of Fascist equipment and German and Italian aircraft on 9 March 1938. As the outgunned Spanish Republicans retreated before this onslaught, the editors of the Communist Party paper, *Mundo Obrero*, who were based in Madrid and thus situated at some remove from direct control by the party leadership, which was located in Barcelona, expressed open opposition to the official party line on the Civil War. *Mundo Obrero*'s issue for 23 March 1938 contained an article rejecting the view that the fate of Republican Spain depended on its so limiting its socio-political revolution as to ensure that its struggle remained one in defence of bourgeois democracy and national independence, war aims that might appeal to foreign democrats. This article dismissed the argument that 'the only solution for our war is for Spain to be neither Fascist nor Communist, because this is what France wants', and also contended that the Civil War would be won by the Spanish people 'despite the opposition of capitalism'.[50] The Communist Party's leadership moved at once to reimpose conformity with the Kremlin's policy towards the Spanish conflict and a letter to the editors of *Mundo Obrero*, signed by José Díaz, was published on 30 March. It confirmed the party line:

> You affirm that 'the Spanish people will win despite the opposition of capitalism' ... but, politically, it corresponds neither to the situation nor to the policy, of our party and the Communist International. In my report to the November Plenum of our Central Committee, we affirmed:
>
>> That there is a terrain on which all democratic States can unite and act together. It is the terrain of defence of their own

---

50 José Díaz, *Tres años de lucha* (Paris: Ediciones Ebro, 1970), 557; Claudín, *Communist Movement*, 234-35.

existence against the common aggressor: Fascism; it is the terrain of defence against the war that threatens us all.

When we spoke here of 'all the democratic states', we were not thinking only of the Soviet Union, where socialist democracy exists, but also of France, England, Czechoslovakia, of the United States, etc., which are democratic, but capitalist, countries. We want these states to aid us; we think that in aiding us they defend their own interest; we strive to make them understand this and ask for their aid.[51]

As Fernando Claudín notes, Díaz's revealing reference to a war 'that threatens us all' indicates that it was the Russian apprehension about a Fascist attack on the USSR, not the actual war against Spanish democracy, which was the principal inspiration behind this reaffirmation of the official Communist line and, indeed, of that Soviet policy itself.[52]

When the secretary general of France's foreign ministry, Alexis Léger, was told in October 1936 of the Soviets' decision to become involved in the Spanish Civil War, the French diplomat was 'somewhat puzzled by the sudden change in Russian policy'. Believing that 'Stalin had no ideals', that he was a 'realist and an opportunist', Léger could only speculate on the reasons for the *volte-face* in Soviet policy towards Spain. He imagined that 'the idealists in Russia, the followers of Lenin and Trotsky and the advocates of world war and revolution' had been able to force their view upon the reluctant Stalin.[53] Léger's opposite number in the British Foreign Office, Sir Robert Vansittart, was equally perplexed by this shift in Soviet policy, as is evident from his comment on receiving report of it:

It is rather a surprising development seeing that the growth of the German danger in Europe had, since 1933, been until this summer steadily tending to cause Russia to make friends so far as possible

51 Díaz, *Tres años*, 559.
52 Claudín, *Communist Movement*, 714, n.60.
53 *DBFP*, XVII, 475-6. The German Ambassador in Moscow, von Schulenburg, also attributed the Soviet decision to become involved in the Spanish War to the growing influence of forces emanating from 'the basically revolutionary orientation of the Soviet Union' (U.S., British, French Board of Editors, *Documents on German Foreign Policy, 1918-1945, Series D [1937-1945], III, Germany and the Spanish Civil War* [London: HMSO, 1951], 108).

with the Western democracies and to go slower on the revolutionary doctrines.[54]

However, as has been explained above, Stalin's intervention in the Spanish Civil War was not due to a resurgence of revolutionary internationalism in Soviet foreign policy. On the contrary, Soviet engagement in Spain's civil conflict was meant to consolidate, and perhaps complete by military alliance, Moscow's *rapprochement* with the Western powers, in the face of the common Nazi danger. Dr Juan Negrín López, Premier of Republican Spain in the later years of the Civil War, understood the rationale of Soviet policy towards his country, as his declaration before the United States Council on Foreign Relations in May 1939 demonstrates:

> Moscow tried to do for France and England what they should have done for themselves. The promise of Soviet aid to the Spanish Republic was that ultimately Paris and London would awake to the risks involved to themselves in an Italo-German victory in Spain and join the USSR in supporting us. Munich, with its unnecessary surrender to the totalitarians, probably crushed this hope beyond repair. Moscow alone could not have saved us ... France and England never acted as their imperial interests dictated.[55]

Indeed, Litvinov had pleaded with Coulondre, in late November 1936, for an Anglo-French reversion to (stereo)type:

> What we need in France, in the interests of good Franco-Soviet relations, is good patriots ... Likewise, what we need in England is imperialists, good British imperialists ...[56]

Stalin's foreign policy failure in Spain appears, therefore, to have stemmed from the 'objective correctness' of his assessment of the international issues at stake in the conflict there. Calculating carefully the common Spanish ground on which the bourgeois democracies could co-operate with the Soviet Union against the menace of Fascism, Stalin underestimated the subjective factors militating against such a development. Ironically, far from the Spanish earth providing the meeting place for an anti-Nazi convergence between East and West,

---

54 *DBFP*, XVII, 476.
55 Cited by Julio Álvarez del Vayo, *Freedom's battle* (London: Heinemann, 1940), 76-77.
56 *DDF*, IV, 82.

Anglo-French statesmen regarded Soviet encroachment there as a cause for strategic apprehension rather than assurance. Thus, the British Foreign Secretary, Anthony Eden, admitted to Negrín in September 1937 that his Prime Minister, Neville Chamberlain, feared that 'Communism would get its clutches into Western Europe' through the Spanish Civil War.[57] Again, the French Foreign Minister, Yvon Delbos, came to suspect in later 1936 that the Soviets might be trying to use the Spanish struggle as a means of impelling France into direct conflict with Germany.[58]   The instinctive anti-Communism of British statesmen and the doctrinaire antipathy of many French policy-makers towards any Soviet connection frustrated Stalin's design for an international alliance of anti-Fascist Powers. This must have seemed a paradoxical state of affairs to a Communist politician like Stalin who was prepared to subordinate ideological imperatives to, or at least reconcile them with, the exigencies of *Realpolitik*.

---

57 Azaña, *Obras completas*, IV, 805.

58 John E. Dreifort, *Yvon Delbos at the Quai d'Orsay* (Lawrence, Manhattan/Wichita, Kansas: Kansas U. P., 1973), 117.

5

Battleground of Reputations:
Ireland and the Spanish Civil War

R. A. STRADLING

I

Representation

In a recent feature-film set in the Spanish War, a young scouser, Dave Carr — a generic working-class hero who embodies the wish-fulfilment of so many leftist writers — arrives at the Aragon front with a batch of new POUM recruits. Moving in single file up a hillside towards their trenches, they disturb a couple taking advantage of the fleeting absence of war in order to make love under a tree. The male section of this partnership turns out to be the leader of Dave's platoon — Pat Coogan, ex-IRA, dedicated enemy of Fascism and British Imperialism, as reckless in the passions of love as in those excited by political commitment and the heat of battle. A few weeks later, he meets his death in an incident full of ironies. During an attack on an enemy-held village, he is shot — not by an enemy soldier, but by the parish priest, treacherously sniping from his church tower. Coogan is laid to rest in the Spanish earth under the Irish tricolour, whilst his comrades intone 'The Internationale', and his girl makes a speech heavily indebted to La Pasionaria.[1]

The red-headed and red-kerchiefed Coogan is a stereotype, an image epitomizing elements commonly attributed to

---

1   The film *Land and Freedom*, directed by Ken Loach, was made in English and Spanish versions and premiered in Madrid in April 1995. Here and elsewhere, it deservedly filled high-street cinemas for much of the summer.

Irishmen. He is a libertarian rebel, violent and tender by turns, the stuff of which physical courage is made, a soldier and martyr for the cause. These are, to most minds, essences of Irishness. Each is a compelling reason why Irishmen went to Spain, and together they seem to provide an incontestable expression of the faith of one hard-achieved Republic in the final triumph of a dear sister over the forces of oppression. But to rehearse this litany *ad infinitum*, memorializing its meaning in hymns and arias such as Christy Moore's well-known ballad 'Vive el Quinte Brigada' — where the names of the glorious dead are solemnly intoned — is part of a conventional piety which elides the contradictory realities of Ireland's response to the Spanish Civil War. As the film *Land and Freedom* itself reveals, the historical issue is tortuous enough even without the special twists imparted by the Irish dimension. For example, if the 'Fascist' priest had not killed Coogan, our hero might well have ended up — as a member of the 'objectively Fascist' POUM — being eliminated by his Stalinist comrades.[2] Yet even more shocking to liberal sensibilities is the fact that by far the greater number of Irishmen who went to Spain in 1936 were not enlisted in the ranks of the Republic at all, but rather in those of their Nationalist enemies.

II

Reputation

'¡No pasarán! The struggle continues!'. As Coogan's girl announces over his Aragonese grave, so Carr's grieving grand-daughter ritually repeats at the Liverpool cemetery sixty years on. The Spanish Civil War has come to encapsulate modern ideals of progress, to represent the most meaningful chapter in the long march of socialist Everyman. For a minority — particularly surviving veterans on the left — it is still a living and (what is different) a vital site of struggle. This is so

---

2   The main purpose of *Land and Freedom* is to realize on the screen, with the cosmetic alterations necessary to communicate with a modern audience, the political message patented by George Orwell in his *Homage to Catalonia*. There are no more than three grammatical errors in the title of Christy Moore's ballad, but they suggest that Spanish is not his strong suit.

because liberty and progress are always and everywhere under attack, and because resources to defend them in the here-and-now can be derived from the unique Spanish experience. For these reasons too, the past is a matter of reputation; reputation comes from commitment, commitment from sacrifice. Thus those who have fought in a war, or have lost friends, husbands, sons, uncles, lovers will not easily settle for less than absolute justification. It is not simply a jealousy of personal worth. The store of honorific memory, the sense of illustrious value, is collective, abstract and metaphysical. It is unaffected equally by the sordid compromises and bloody divisions of the period itself; by the accreting, and thus changing, historical record of the event we call 'The Spanish Civil War'; or by ephemeral alterations in intellectual fashion. It perhaps resembles more the Catholic doctrine of a boundless well of virtue provided by Christ, his saints and martyrs, than the Marxist notion of surplus material value. In the last analysis — like any myth-complex — it concerns power and power-relations. It provides a fighting fund for those dedicated to freedom in the present and the future. The trenches along the Jarama must be manned and supplied: one day Hill 481, overlooking Gandesa on the Ebro battlefront, will at last be taken.

The community of true progressives, however, must be carefully defined. Not all can belong: above all, the sinister heirs of international Fascism, always masters of disguise, must never approach the shrine. Indeed, by definition, such heretics can have no authentic desire for salvation, but only a mission to steal, defile, diminish or subvert the Ark of the Covenant. Paradoxically, although its value for members is infinite, reputation cannot be shared with others. Any other person or body who lays claim to a benificent heritage deriving from the Spanish War, in doing so detracts from the store of reputation. This vigilance has a specially bitter side in Ireland, where such a claim can be plausibly advanced on behalf of those who took up arms against the cause of the Popular Front. In this case, the sanctions outlined above are uniquely strengthened by those of a populist nationalism also rooted in a mythology of self-perception. The very phrase 'an Irish Fascist' seems perversely oxymoronic, a cultural contradiction in terms. In every sense of the phrase, Fascism has no place in Irish history. To suggest otherwise is somehow to cast a slur on the reputation of the Irish Republic itself as a modern, democratic and progressive state.

In modern Ireland, such has been the public anxiety associated with the whole experience of indigenous Fascism that historical study of it has not been encouraged. Whenever the volunteer unit which went to Spain with General Eoin O'Duffy is recalled, the reaction is an embarrassed silence or a quick resort to the deprecating snigger of anecdote. In contrast, no jokes and no embarrassment are in evidence when their opposite numbers are on parade. The men of the so-called 'Connolly Column' are accepted as nothing less than sentinels of civilization. The monument to their dead installed at the approach to Liberty Hall, the Trade Union headquarters in Ireland's capital city, was 'Unveiled by the Lord Mayor ... as part of the Dublin European City of Culture'. In contrast, there is no public memorial in Ireland to those men who fought and died for another, different set of ideals: in general, to preserve the right of religious belief and practice; in particular, to defend their Catholic faith and the lives of men and women in Holy Orders. These principles are no less civilized than any espoused by their opponents, and the willingness to suffer and die for them is no less worthy of recognition.

In the event, the sacrifice demanded of the Irish Internationals was considerably greater than that imposed on most members of the O'Duffy Brigade. As the poet said, 'too long a sacrifice can make a stone of the heart'.[3] Thus it is not easy for survivors to acknowledge any positive qualities among men of their own nation who were members of an army responsible for the deaths of their comrades; and which (what is more) totally defeated the Republican cause. The present essay is the work of one who admires the volunteers of both sides, and regrets that the process of revision will inevitably be regarded by one of them as an attempt to lessen its store of reputation.

---

3   From W. B. Yeats' 'Easter, 1916'.

III

Politics

As the success of the Loach/Allen film inside and outside Spain demonstrates, its subject matter continues to excite widespread popular interest. At a basic contextual level, the fate of 1930s Spain is perceived as part of the history of several dozen other nations in Europe and the wider world.[4] In most cases it is impossible to state that these nations — whether governments or people — supported one side or the other in the conflict. We know, however, that impressive numbers of their citizens went voluntarily to Spain to fight for the Republic; and that in subsequent years, the community of historians and other intellectuals produced by the nations concerned applauded this act and deplored the pathetic neutralism of their governments. But the Irish case is radically different; it transgresses the norm, subverting many of the assumptions which surround the mythology and the historiography of the war in Spain — of which *Land and Freedom* is merely a particularly influential and current vehicle.

The government of the Free State (Saorstát) certainly stayed neutral, but the population at large supported the Nationalist side, in a substantial minority of cases persistently and vociferously. Whereas in Britain, most pressure was brought to bear on Baldwin's and Chamberlain's governments materially to support the *de jure* government of the Republic, in the Saorstát much more significant pressure was placed upon Eamon de Valera and his Cabinet colleagues to recognize Franco's regime. Indeed, a majority of supporters of De Valera's Fianna Fáil government — the more economically-deprived section of the electorate — disapproved of his non-intervention policy.[5]

---

4   Recent treatments of the war's international dimensions are M. Alpert, *A New International History of the Spanish Civil War* (London: Macmillan, 1994) and J Avilés Farré, *Pasión y farsa: franceses y británicos ante la Guerra Civil Española* (Madrid: Eudema, 1994) .

5   For the general background of Irish history in this period, see J. A. Murphy *Ireland in the Twentieth Century* (Dublin: Gill & MacMillan, 1975) — a useful, short introduction; and the more substantial work by D. Keogh, *Twentieth Century Ireland: Nation and State* (Dublin: Gill & Macmillan, 1995).

Allegiance to Roman Catholicism, both professed and practised, was a palpable feature of Irish society in this decade. This allegiance cut sharply across economic and intellectual divisions, something which stood in contradistinction to the situation in the rest of Europe, including, in notable measure, Spain itself. Even in the British context, it has recently been demonstrated that Catholicism was a seriously disruptive factor in the attempts of working-class organizations to present a united front over the Spanish War.[6] With the *Saorstát*, it is not sufficient to state that the clauses of the previous sentence might be exactly reversed. Even the policies of the Irish Trade Union movement and the Labour Party were dominated by strongly anti-Republican emotions. Though it would be an exaggeration to assert that class was not a major factor in Irish politics, the symbiosis of Catholicism and the cause of national independence — a gradual and often painful process — was a culturally-achieved phenomenon by the 1930s. Social class, or at least the educational orientation that went with it, may have predisposed individuals to accept or reject the pronouncements of the clergy on political issues. But the evidence of Irish public opinion suggests that in 1936, only small numbers of urban working-class males, and middle-class intelligentsia of both sexes, remained indifferent — and fewer still hostile — to the cause of the Catholic Church in Spain.[7]

All this is not to suggest that Irish politics and society were free of bitter or profound divisions. For a start, what is glibly referred to above as 'the cause of national independence' was far from meaning the same thing to all citizens of the Free State. As in other countries, those who demanded that the Dublin Government forswear non-intervention and support for the

---

6   See the relevant sections in T. Buchanan, *The British Labour Movement and the Spanish Civil War* (Cambridge: Cambridge U. P., 1992), esp. chapter 5.

7   For existing work on the broad subject-area of the present essay, including cogent treatment of the domestic Irish context, see D. Keogh, *Ireland and Europe, 1919-48* (Dublin: Gill & MacMillan, 1988) especially pp. 65-97, and J. Bowyer Bell, 'Ireland and the Spanish Civil War 1936 to 1939', in *Strong Words Brave Deeds: The Poetry, Life and Times of Thomas O'Brien in the Spanish Civil War*, ed. H. Gustav Klaus (Dublin: O'Brien Press, 1994), 24-26. (The latter is a slightly updated version of a piece first published in 1969.)

'legitimate' Spanish Republic, were part of the broad left of politics. The difference was that the most active element in their composition was not socialist but radically nationalist groups of the IRA — irreconcilables left isolated by De Valera's formation of the new Fianna Fáil party, and his espousal of the constitutional path, in 1927. Such men regarded national independence as humiliatingly incomplete without the integration of the six northern counties, and therefore considered the war against Britain as still on foot. They had followed De Valera into opposition and Civil War in 1922-23, refusing to accept the Treaty, establishing the partition of the island of Ireland, which their Sinn Féin colleagues had negotiated with Lloyd George.[8] For their part, the latter formed a pro-Treaty grouping, with a clear majority in the *Dáil*. Following victory in the Civil War, they became the governing party of the new nation. The war itself, though lasting less than a year, was a ruthless and bloody affair which poisoned the well of Irish politics, and which even today is still capable of arousing bitter feelings.[9]   In its wake, the IRA was banned, whilst most of those known to have supported the 'insurgency' forfeited any right to government employment. The triumphant party (Cumann na nGhaedheal) ruled Ireland, under the leadership of W. T. Cosgrave, until the indecisive general election of 1932. Ousted from power at last by Fianna Fáil the following year, they split up into mutually recriminatory factions. By 1936, however, they had regrouped in the new Fine Gael party, and were able to provide an effective parliamentary opposition. Their support of Franco and the Spanish Nationalists, and the (variously) contrasting attitudes of their erstwhile enemies, seemed to adumbrate a return to the internecine hostilities of 1922.

Thus, following 1933, the wound in Ireland's side gaped wider and bled more profusely than at any time since the shooting had stopped a decade earlier. Legalized by De Valera after his marginal polls victory of 1932, the IRA began a

---

8   See J. Bowyer Bell, *The Secret Army: A History of the IRA, 1916-1970* (London: Anthony Blond, 1970).

9   Still the most thorough treatment is C Younger, *Ireland's Civil War* (London: Collins, 1968 [paperback repr., 1970]).

campaign of sustained physical intimidation of the opposition. In the confusion of a sudden loss of long-accustomed power and place, the ex-Cosgrave men became convinced that the IRA were being used by their opponents to hound them out of public life. Whilst they saw De Valera as a potential dictator, in fact a process of mutual alienation between Fianna Fáil and the IRA had now become definitive.[10]   The year 1933 witnessed the paramilitary moment. De Valera set up the reserve army force (FCA), in effect a uniformed section of his party, but ostensibly intended to draw the young unemployed away from the IRA. He also sacked the Police Commissioner, General Eoin O'Duffy, founder of the unarmed national police (the Garda Siochána) and proceeded to appoint a new head and membership of this force, more amenable to government needs. Within a few weeks, O'Duffy had accepted the leadership of the Army Comrades Association, a body of ex-army men (i.e. Pro-Treaty veterans of 1922-23); within a few months he and a few collaborators had turned it into a semi-uniformed body which paraded at noisy rallies, and did not flinch from violent confrontation with the IRA.

The Blueshirts — as they later called themselves — were a proto-Fascist organization, reaching at their zenith an enormous membership of forty thousand and adopting a programme derived from Catholic (or 'Christian Democratic') social teaching and Italian Fascist (or 'corporatist') economic ideas. Unlike their adversaries, they never actually declared themselves against the established forms of the constitution. Most thinking Blueshirt supporters would have acknowledged a desire to change the nature of democracy in Ireland, but few accepted the appellation 'Fascist' — except occasionally in the heat of heckling debate, when forced to acknowledge Fascism as the extremest and thus most effective form of resistance to atheistic Communism.[11] Not more than a handful ever wanted

---

10 Bowyer Bell, *Secret Army*, 99-127.

11 For a balanced and thorough account, see M. Manning, *The Blueshirts* (Dublin: Gill & MacMillan, 1970). See also, however, the recent work of M. Cronin, 'The Socioeconomic Background of the Blueshirt Movement in Ireland, 1932-5', *Irish Historical Studies*, XIV (November 1994); and 'The Blueshirt Movement: Ireland's Fascists?', *Journal of Contemporary History*, (April 1995), 311-32. The question of whether the Blueshirts were 'Fascist' can never be

General O'Duffy as dictator, any more than their rivals wished a similar role for Eamon de Valera. Yet for over two years (1933-35) democracy in Ireland took a severe battering. With running battles in the streets of Dublin and Cork, and a kind of guerrilla warfare in the countryside, government seemed caught in a crossfire between the IRA-radical Left alliance and the Blueshirts. A semblance of order had not long been restored — mainly due to fractious leadership divisions inside opposition groupings — when the Spanish Civil War broke out in the summer of 1936.

The declaration of the Spanish Second Republic in 1931 had been greeted with approval in most quarters of Irish opinion. A pervading sense of empathy with many of Spain's democratic-reformist aspirations dulled the edge of Irish reaction to the signs of a visceral anticlericalism which the coming of the Republic unleashed. However, as the single-minded determination of the Spanish Republic to confront and destroy the power of the Church became increasingly apparent, and especially when this policy turned (in the estimation of Catholics) to actual persecution, Irish perceptions began to change. Before the summer of 1936, nevertheless, alarm was muted; indeed, the minatory attitude of the Third Reich towards its Catholic citizens evoked greater attention and condemnation in the press. The military rising of July 1936, and the social revolution it precipitated in various parts of Spain, changed this situation overnight. Immediately, accounts of atrocities against Catholics, and especially against clergy, appeared in the newspapers. The summer months were marked by saturation coverage, fuelled by an apparently endless supply of sensational copy relating the murder of priests. This, in turn, stimulated a chorus of indignation, expressed in press and pulpit, as well as public gatherings from

---

resolved, since the historical issue has been overlaid with innumerable layers of insult, accusation and exculpation. I use 'proto-Fascist' since (a) in the context of the 1930s, a group which paraded in uniform, gave straight-arm salutes, adopted violence as a political tactic, and enunciated a domestic policy influenced by Mussolini's party can hardly be regarded as non-Fascist, but (b) I am persuaded that the majority of its adherents believed they were defending democracy, not undermining it, and few of its rank-and-file thought of themselves as Fascist.

bar-room to council chamber.[12]

The mass murder of religous in 'loyalist' Spain is no longer a matter of serious dispute. Although exact figures will never be agreed, it seems certain that something between seven and ten thousand clergy, including hundreds of nuns and over a dozen bishops, met violent deaths in 1936.[13] Many of the atrocity stories circulated by the contemporary media were full of lurid exaggeration. The element of misrepresentation present here was just as politically-motivated and systematic as the murder campaign itself. It was meant to excite universal fear and hatred of Socialist revolution. In the press and cinema newsreels the terror-gangs were invariably referred to as 'reds'. Nowhere was the intended effect of this campaign more thoroughly achieved than in the Free State. The reiterated warnings of the hierarchy that Ireland itself was being infiltrated by agents of Bolshevik revolution, seemed to be justified. This process was portrayed, in exactly the terms which Stalin was anxious to counter, as part of a world-wide conspiracy orchestrated from Moscow. In Ireland, sympathy for Spanish landowners and other plutocrats whose property was being forcibly expropriated by the people was limited — despite the charitable sanctions of Christianity. But when it came to the killing of priests and nuns, the wanton destruction of churches, and the symbolic abuse of familiar objects of common devotion, feelings ran high. A thrill of anti-Communist fervour ran across Ireland, having a specially keen effect in the rural

---

12 Bowyer Bell, 'Ireland and the Spanish Civil War', 242-45; Keogh, *Ireland and Europe*, 66ff.

13 For a measured general assessment of the anticlerical fury see J. M. Sánchez, *The Spanish Civil War as a Religious Tragedy* (Notre Dame, Indiana: Indiana U. P., 1987). For Catalonia, eyewitness testimony is collected in *La persecució religiosa de 1936 a Catalunya: testimoniatges*, ed. J. Massot I Montaner (Barcelona: Publicacions de l'Abadia de Montserrat, 1987); and the basic monograph is J. M. Solé and J. Villaroya i Font, *La repressió a la reraguarda de Catalunya (1936-39)*, 2 vols (Barcelona: Publicacions de l'Abadia de Montserrat, 1989-90). The main study for Spain as a whole, with statistics which have been much disputed, is A. Montero Moreno, *Historia de la persecución religiosa en España, 1936-1939* (Madrid: Biblioteca de Autores Cristianos, 1961).

towns and villages which held two-thirds of the population.[14] But this majority had little awareness of Spain. To bring about a more focused identification with one victimized section of the Spanish people, and against another, comprising criminal assailants controlled by the agents of an alien power and ideology, some catalyst was needed.

IV

History

Ireland's past was pertinaciously plundered for this purpose. In terms of national education — mostly in the hands of Catholic clerics — it was already a deeply mythologized history, with a powerfully Romantic profile, and this gave its connection with Spain a particularly seductive glow.   In pro-Catholic newspapers, from the nationally-circulating *Cork Examiner* to local editions like the *Tuam Herald*, features appeared celebrating the glorious crusading history of Spain, the profound heritage of its religion and art, the visions of its saints and the sufferings of its martyrs. Given that the nation was experiencing one of its periodic resurgences of mariology, the age-old devotion of ordinary Spaniards to the Blessed Virgin was by no means neglected.[15] It might be suspected, moreover, that the very medium which in 1995 stimulated a wave of

---

14 This conclusion is drawn from secondary sources, already cited; and the newspaper press of the Saorstát in 1936-37. The features outlined were a speciality of the *Irish Independent*, the most popular daily, despite its opposition to Fianna Fáil. The issue of 18 August 1936 contained a long account of priest-hunting in Barcelona and elsewhere reported that: (1) Spanish 'reds' were trained in Moscow; (2) 'Chekas modelled after those of Soviet Russia are slaughtering the citizens wholesale'; (3) churches were being turned into 'red' offices named 'Lenin' or 'Dimitroff'; (4) arms were supplied from Russia and eighteen military advisers had arrived in Cadiz; (and perhaps most impressive) (5) advice on revolution-making was being broadcast in Spanish in Soviet Radio. There was no mention of offences against property — though the paper was owned by a Dublin banker.

15 See e.g. 'Old Toledo' and 'The Irish in Spain ... Soldiers and Statesmen in Spanish Service', *Cork Examiner* (Week-end magazine section), 1 and 22 August 1936; 'Ireland and Spain — Old Memories', *Tuam Herald*, 19 September 1936.

posthumous sympathy for the Spanish revolution was involved in the campaign of 1936 to stifle it as soon as possible. Two of the feature films on general release in small-town cinemas in September 1936 were *The Crusades* and *Castles in Spain*.[16] Meanwhile, on 10 August, General O'Duffy wrote to *The Independent*, asking for volunteers to form an Irish Brigade to fight in Spain 'on the side of the Christian forces'.[17]

In subsequent weeks, readers were reminded that Spain had repeatedly stood by Ireland in its centuries of oppression by English Protestantism. Preaching on a 'Day of Reparation for Spain' in St Mel's Cathedral, Longford, Bishop MacNamee finished with a peroration which — despite its bathetic ending — resembled a call to arms.

> Spain has had intimate relations with our own Ireland. She supported us against religious persecution in the days of Elizabeth. She offered a home to our exiled princes. She trained our greatest Catholic Captain, the hero of Benburb [Owen Roe O'Neill]. So let us pray for Spain.[18]

Spanish Armada survivors (it was dubiously alleged) had been taken in and protected by the Catholic gaels. Above all, the names of the leaders of the diaspora which followed the failure of the Spanish-assisted rebellion against Elizabeth I — the O'Donnell Abu, the O'Neill and the O'Sullivan Mór — were often invoked. W. B. Yeats had used this heritage of the earls, and the central national legacy of the exiled swordsmen (the so-called 'Wild Geese') in marching songs he had written for the Blueshirts in 1934.

> Fail, and that history turns into rubbish,
> All that great past to a trouble of fools;
> Those that come after shall mock at O'Donnell
> Mock at the memory of both O'Neills.[19]

---

16 The latter succeeded the former in the Mall Cinema, Tuan, in the third week of September (*Tuam Herald* 13 September 1936).

17 *Irish Independent*, 10 August 1936.

18 *The Universe*, 18 September 1936.

19 From the first of W. B. Yeats' 'Three Marching Songs'. See F Cullingford, *Yeats, Ireland and Fascism* (London: Macmillan, 1981) for the story behing these effusions.

Taking his cue, O'Duffy cited these epic heroes in expounding Ireland's debt to the religious and military patronage of Spain, which was one inspiration for undertaking his crusade. According to O'Duffy's account, General Mola referred independently to this traditional connection between the two nations during their negotiations in Valladolid.[20] Indeed, some of the Spanish grandee descendants of the ancient Irish chieftains were to take an active interest in the Irish Brigade during its sojourn in Spain. It seems unlikely that this exploitation of historical-romantic sentiment was as powerful an inducement to recruits as the religious motivation *per se* — but the two elements dovetailed perfectly for many young Catholic idealists, and perhaps especially for the potential officer corpos who had missed out on the glorious adventures of 1916-21.

In early November 1936, the undergraduates of the Trinity College Historical Society debated the issues of the Spanish War: the Marquis MacSwiney of Mashanaglass, presiding, intervened strongly in favour of O'Duffy's stance:

> It might be asked why Irish people were mixing in another's peoples affairs. But he [the marquis] would point out that Irish Catholics were granted by King Philip V ... all the rights and privileges of Spanish-born subjects. He did not think that the *Cortes* had ever passed a measure revoling that privilege.[21]

This performance, remarkably *ultra vires* as it was coming from the chair, was enough to persuade his audience, Protestant almost to a man, to support the Republican cause by a vote of over two to one. Yet the pro-loyalist side was also keen to claim the sanction of history. In this camp, however, the focus of sentiment was the more recent past and a more secular inspiration — Wolfe Tone and the Jacobin tradition, O'Donovan Rossa and the early Fenians 'who were linked with Marx and Engels through the International Working Men's Association.'[22]

---

20 E. O'Duffy, *Crusade in Spain* (Dublin: Brown & Nolan, 1938) pp. 16, 24.

21 *Irish Press*, 12 November 1936.

22 M. O'Riordan, *Connolly Column* (Dublin: Free Press, 1979), 53-54. In November 1938, the Duchess of Tetuán — an O'Donnell descendant who patronized O'Duffy — visited the latter's sworn enemy, Frank Ryan, at the

Both the IRA Congress and the Irish Communist Party, who collaborated in organizing Ireland's contribution to the International Brigade, saw the figure of James Connolly, the socialist martyr of the Easter 1916 uprising, as central to their efforts. It was Connolly's name which was later used for the title of an allegedly exclusive Irish battalion. The precipitate (perhaps the main) motive for left-wing intervention was linked to this: the need to counter O'Duffy's initiative, and to save the honour of Ireland which he threatened to besmirch.[23] Moreover, some Irish veterans of the International Brigade were in due course to insist that they, and not their rivals, deserved recognition as the modern 'Wild Geese'.[24]

V

Experience

Over a twenty-two month period stretching from September 1936 to July 1938, nearly one thousand Irishmen went to fight in Spain.[25] This was only the outward sign of Ireland's inward

POW camp in Burgos. Her intercession with Franco may have helped to save Ryan's life. The action was in return for a favour which an Irish O'Donnell had done for a Spanish O'Donnell in the early days of the revolution (*ibid.*, 121).

23   Ryan frequently reiterated this point in his correspondence and other writings; see also 'Irish Volunteers in Spain' by 'C.Q.' in the International Brigade magazine *Volunteer for Liberty*, 11 November 1937.

24   E.g. by Paddy O'Daire, one of the most admirable leaders of the British Battalion, in an interview during the RTE documentary *Even the Olives Are Bleeding* made by Cathal O'Shannon in 1975; according to his *compadre*, J. Monks, O'Daire was inclined to argue this point in the trenches (*With the Reds in Andalucia* [London: privately printed, 1985], 11).

25   No complete lists of volunteers seem to have survived on either side. The lists in M. O'Riordan of pro-government volunteers (*Connolly Column*, 164-67) are deficient in every important respect.   To refer only to the quantitive aspect, material in the Spanish archives indicates the total was nearer 200 than the 146 given by O'Riordan. Estimates of the size of the Irish Brigade range from 600 to over 900; *cf.* H. Thomas, *The Spanish Civil War* (Harmondsworth: Penguin, [3rd ed.] 1975), 979-80, with V. Ennis, 'Some "Catholic Moors" ', unpublished typescript, Irish Military Archives, Dublin. (I wish to thank the archivist, Commandant P. Young, for providing me with a photocopy of the latter and permission to cite it.) General O'Duffy was known

agony.   The Irish people as a whole were emotionally and politically involved in the war to a far greater extent than is represented, and to a deeper extent than any other people in the world — with the possible exception of the Portuguese. At first glance, the total number of volunteers may seem unimpressive. In fact, even in terms of bare statistics, it is remarkable when compared to the record of other countries — for example, given relative population figures, it puts the aggregate of less than two thousand from all the remaining regions of the British Isles into perspective. No other nation (it seems) contributed such comparatively substantial numbers of genuine volunteers to both sides.[26]

Less than three weeks after O'Duffy's public appeal, the *Cork Examiner* reported an official claim that the response had exceeded five thousand men.   Though this figure is not corroborated elsewhere, given the numbers involved in the Blueshirts and their successor organizations, it seems otiose to question its accuracy.[27]   Ireland was being mobilized for an anti-Communist crusade, her fervour focused by the crisis in Spain.   Alongside O'Duffy's initiative, another had been launched by a Dublin businessman and T.D., Patrick Belton, founder of a nationwide organization called the Irish Christian Front — Ireland's answer to the Popular Front. Belton insisted

---

to have kept meticulous records in his Blackrock home, but these were lost or destroyed after his death. They included the papers of his National Corporate Party which organized the recruitment of the Brigade. Figures compiled by the present writer currently project a total of not more than 700 members.

26   Various caveats should be registered here. R. Rosenstone refers to the existence of a French volunteer force ('Compagnie Jean d'Arc'), 500 strong which fought at Jarama (*Historical Dictionary of the Spanish Civil War, 1936-39*, ed. J. Cortada [Westport, Conn./London: Greenwood Press, 1982], 476). I have found no other reference to this unit, which seems not to have any relation to the so-called *camelots du roi* — individuals who enlisted (e.g.) with the *requetés* (see Thomas, *Spanish Civil War*, pp. 768, 980.   Pro-Franco German and Italian units in Spain were, of course, regular armed forces provided by the governments concerned. But the Italian title ('Corpo Truppe Volontarie') — often derided — was not wholly without foundation in fact, and the German force contained many who were not specifically obliged to serve in Spain, both professional and conscript.

27   O'Duffy himself claimed only 'over two thousand' in an interview given a few days earlier (*Cork Examiner* 24 and 27 August 1936). The final figure was — he later asserted — over 6,000 (*Crusade in Spain*, 13-14).

that help to the Spanish Nationalists must be non-military, and in this way he was able to obtain the official endorsement of the Catholic hierarchy, who withheld it from O'Duffy. Belton and his ICF enjoyed a purple patch of quasi-fanatical popularity, organising so-called 'monster rallies' in Dublin and other cities.[28]   The later months of 1936 were punctuated by these jamborees.   Thousands marched under the banners of the Legion of Mary or the Union of Catholic Mothers, gathering in open spaces for speeches spiced with dire warnings of Communist conspiracy and praise of Catholic resistance in Spain.   It was announced that collections would be taken outside the churches for medical and other civilian help to 'Catholic Spain'.   The first of these, held on behalf of the hierarchy in October, raised £43,000; another was held later by the ICF and realized £32,000.[29]

These were enormous donations, largely deriving from a poor, in some respects penurious, community.   Meanwhile, Sunday sermons all over the country contained admiring references to General Franco.   With little opposition, and in most cases unanimously, dozens of local town councils voted through resolutions, based on a prototype passed in Clonmel, calling for official recognition of the 'Burgos government'. Similar motions were passed by Trade Union committees, and at other public meetings up and down the country.   The multi-partisan weight of feeling thus demonstrated was turned on the government by Belton and other opposition leaders.   At first, attempts were made to persuade De Valera's government not to adhere to the non-intervention agreements.   Later, when it was realized that this policy did not in practice disadvantage the Nationalists, the objective became less modest — outright recognition of Franco's regime.[30]   In November 1936, one of the main newspapers in the Nationalist zone proclaimed its

---

28   Bowyer Bell, 'Ireland and the Spanish Civil War', 250-51.

29   O'Riordan, *Connolly Column*, 31.   The first collection was made on the day of Christ the King, a feast of central significance for the Carlist *Requetés*, whose volunteer battalions it seemed at this juncture that the Irish Brigade might join (O'Duffy, *Crusade in Spain*, pp. 13, 180-81, and J. del Burgo, *Conspiración y Guerra Civil* [Madrid: Alfaguara, 1970], 249-50.

30   Keogh, *Ireland and Europe*, pp. 67ff., provides more narrative detail about these events.

confidence in two imminent events: the new *Caudillo*'s capture of Madrid, and the Irish Free State's official recognition of his government. In fact Franco had to wait until the end of the war for both these triumphs.[31]

In the midst of the storm, De Valera remained firm, with a superb sense of opportunism when it came to dividing or wrong-footing his rivals. The *Taoiseach* was a devout Catholic. His position was potentially weakened by the fact that he had never fully repaired the breach with the Church caused by his earlier defiance — now regarded as a disadvantage to Fianna Fáil. He felt it politic to allow his newspaper, the *Irish Press* to display a pro-Catholic — though not pro-Francoist — sympathy over Spain. Perhaps his stand against the populist-clerical tide came more from natural obstinacy than visionary statesmanship. In any case, he rode the crisis with an Olympian style which later became famous. Not only did the Government survive motions of censure, and the bitter confrontation of February 18 1937 — when, after one of the most virulent debates in its history, the Dáil passed a non-intervention measure which made it illegal to send reinforcements to O'Duffy in Spain — but also De Valera won a general election later that year, along with a referundum on his new anti-British constitution.[32] By this time, the peak of national obsession had passed. In Spain attacks on priests and churches had almost ceased; survivors among the former were in custody or hiding, and relatively undamaged examples of the

---

31 *El Adelanto de Salamanca*, 28 November 1936. The hypothetical issue of whether the former event should lead to the latter was certainly raised at Cabinet level by the foreign minister, Seán MacEntee; see his memo of 11 November 1936, Irish National Archives (Dublin) Department of Foreign Affairs, File 277/87. The Republican Government had earlier rejected De Valera's offer to mediate between it and the rebels (Foreign Ministry to Dublin Embassy, 23 August 1936, Archivo del Ministerio de Asuntos Exteriores [Madrid] [Sección del] Archivo de Barcelona, Legajo R415 f. 44).

32 Keogh, *Ireland and Europe*, 83-85. In what seems to be an undated draft of his *Dail* speech of 18 February, MacEntee began with the words: 'No matter what side in the present conflict one's sympathies may lie, and there can be no doubt on which side is the sympathy of the vast majority of the people of this country ...'. In the pencilled corrections, 'no' is replaced with 'little' as a qualifer of 'doubt' and 'vast' has been deleted (Irish National Archives, Foreign Affairs, 227/87).

latter had been boarded up. The *Irish Independent* and the Catholic Sunday press constantly returned to the old martyrdom stories, and made the most of any fresh ones, they could never maintain the level of outrage in their readers whipped up during 1936.[33]   Moreover, they obviously failed to influence many of its 'natural' socio-economic constituency against Fianna Fáil.

One important sociological distinction between the two groups which were travelling to Spain to fight on opposite sides, must be registered at this point. The overwhelming bulk of Irish who went to join the Republicans were from the urban working-class slums (Dublin, Derry, Belfast, Cork). In contrast the Catholic Brigade derived its members equally disproportionately, from small towns and rural farming communities. After many difficulties with domestic organization and overseas transport — which O'Duffy overcame with determination and skill — the latter unit assembled in Spain in the last days of 1936. It has a unique status as the only organized and integral volunteer force to join the Francoist rebels.[34]   It would be an exaggeration to state that its membership represented a cross section of Irish opinion. All the same, it included a notable minority who had fought with the IRA in some or all of the campaigns of 1917-23. Other recruits had been active in the ranks of the labour unions, and there was a token handful of Protestants. For them, the need for unity in the Christian Cause, combined with horror at the priest-killings, overcame confessional considerations and even suspended strong contra-indicative emotions deriving from earlier political experience. Equally notable is the fact that

---

33 For as long as the Irish Brigade remained in Spain, the *Irish Independent* helped justify its constant support by topping-up the righteous outrage factor; see, e.g., its editions of 1, 5, and 12 March 1937.

34 A summary account of the recruitment of the Irish Brigade and its transportation to Spain has been given in my 'Franco's Irish Volunteers', *History Today*, (March 1995), 40-47. For what follows on the military and other experiences of volunteers, the fundamental secondary sources are O'Riordan and O'Duffy (*op. cit.*). However, the political bias of these versions makes excessive dependency unwise. I have thus blended information from a spectrum of interest and witness, but detailed references are restricted to material which is new and/or controversial. Full scholarly apparatus and lists of sources will appear in the book I am compiling on this subject.

many of the political radicals who followed Frank Ryan into the ranks of the International Brigades were also — like their leader himself — practising Catholics. For them, the need for unity amongst a working class engaged in a life-or-death fight against Fascism was more urgent than personal religious convictions. However, alongside the majority group of IRA stalwarts in the ranks of the Irish International Brigaders, there were over a dozen Communist Party members. On the issues of Fascism and Imperialism no measurable gulf existed between such men.

The experiences in Spain of Irishmen on both sides have similarities, but also striking differences. Around eighty of the eventual total of two hundred pro-Republican volunteers, went to Spain in Ryan's original party in December 1936. They arrived at the International Brigade HQ at Albacete not long before Christmas 1936, at approximately the same time as their opponents reached the base at Cáceres. A handful of individual Irishmen were already serving in Republican militia units. Still others, over one hundred in total, were to arrive in small groups, by means of the regular Communist-organized 'underground railway', at various stages until the late summer of 1938. There were soon cases of serious friction between Irish and English members of the XV Brigade, especially the English officers with middle-class accents and regular army attitudes. A baroque series of mistakes and misunderstandings led to a crisis within a month of their arrival. In violent and bitter circumstances, the Irish contingent split up, the majority decamping to join the recently-arrived US battalion. No sooner had this happened than the Nationalist offensive began on the Jarama. During the chaotic and critical three weeks that followed, a dozen Irishmen lost their lives in company with proportionate numbers of American and British comrades. Around forty uninjured survivors seem to have been gradually reintegrated into the British (16th, later 57th) Battalion, which later arrivals were also required to join. Mutual resentments continued, however, since they were rooted not only in national resentments, but also in religious problems which divided Irishmen from each other. As we have seen, most Irish brigaders — not least Frank Ryan himself — were sincere Catholics. Some did not welcome the obligatory ideology lessons in the trenches, and were disturbed by the fact that the practice of their religion was not even available to them when on leave behind the lines.[35]

Those who joined the Republican forces saw considerably more military action — often in horrifying circumstances — and endured greater privation than their Nationalist counterparts. This was, in part, a paradoxical result of the fact that the global numbers of foreign volunteers flocking to the Government side were sufficient to permit the International Brigades as a whole to operate as an autonomous unit.[36] At any one time in its twenty-two month existence, it was mustered roughly at (British) regimental strength — that is, fifteen to twenty thousand — though the ranks were increasingly filled out with native Spaniards in the later stages. It comprised 'mixed brigades', each with its own command staff, transport, communications, artillery and medical sections. Thus the International Brigades were capable of fighting major engagements, and indeed played an important part in most of the great battles of the war (Jarama, Brunete, Teruel, the Ebro). Irishmen were killed and wounded fighting bravely in all these sectors and in many less celebrated confrontations. The fact that the Brigades were of tremendous military significance to the Republic is demonstrated by the fact that the British Battalion (16th, later 57th) of the XV Brigade was only

---

35 For religious policy in the loyalist zone, see F. Díaz Plaja, *La vida cotidiana en la España de la guerra civil* (Madrid: Edaf, 1995), 143-61. On Ryan's attitudes, see S. Cronin, *Frank Ryan: The Search for the Republic* (Dublin: Repsol, 1980), especially pp. 79-81. By August 1937, some access to Catholic services was being allowed in Madrid, and in November, Ryan apparently attended Mass there (*ibid.*, 121-22). Another International, Jim Haughey, was recalled by one comrade as of 'naive Catholic faith', who asked 'prior to the Ebro offensive whether or not the International Brigaders might have a priest to minister to them at the front' (E. Downing, cited by Manus O'Riordan in a letter to C Geiser, 7 April 1993, Marx Memorial Library [London], International Brigade Association Archive Box D-3, File G/1).

36 There is no satisfactory general history of the International Brigades. The best (more or less) objective account is A. Castells, *Las Brigadas Internacionales de la Guerra Civil Española* (Barcelona: Ariel, 1974) which has many and vast lacunae. On the British Battalion, see W. Alexander, *Volunteers for Liberty: Spain 1936-39* (London: Lawrence & Wishart, [2nd ed.] 1986) — the official IBA Communist Party account, but useful once due allowance is made.

once absent from the front for a period of more than a few weeks. Not surprisingly, its overall casualty rate was over forty per cent including about twenty-five per cent dead.

On the Nationalist side, in contrast, some seven hundred Irishmen were simply not enough to play an autonomous role, or even to be used effectively. There were no similar foreign volunteer units with whom they could be constructively deployed: the Germans had specialist units of artillery and air force, the Italians operated almost independently. Moreover, the elite Foreign Legion (or *Tercio*) to which they were affiliated did not operate as an integral force, but formed *Banderas* distributed among various army groups, to be used as the need arose. The XV Bandera (Irlandesa) del Tercio was thus an isolated and under-strength infantry battalion dependent on external Spanish units for all support services. During the very days (mid-February 1937) when it was making its way into the arena of fighting in the valley of the Jarama, to the south of Madrid, Franco decided to call off his offensive. In one sense, this was fortunate for the Irish, since it spared them the appalling losses incurred generally during the battle. However, so trigger-happy were the combatants by the second week of this awful struggle that they were mistaken by their own side for an infiltrating party of Internationals. In the pitched battle which followed four of their number were killed — though they inflicted a high casualty rate on the 'enemy'.[37]   In another

---

37   An Irish officer later estimated that 'over forty' of their attackers — a unit from the Canary Islands — were killed (S. O'Cuinneagáin, *The War in Spain* [Enniscorthy: privately printed, n.d. but 1976], 3). O'Duffy claimed that the opposition 'left more than half their number dead on the field'. Fault for the calamity lay on the Spanish side, and this conclusion was reached by the Army Tribunal (O'Duffy, *Crusade in Spain*, 138-40). Although the Tribunal's records are alleged to be extant, a thorough *in situ* search of catalogues for the *Juticia* and other cognate sub-sections of the *Sección Cuartel General del Generalísimo* of the Military Archives in Ávila failed to locate them. For a general description of Jarama, the only battle in which both groups of volunteers were involved, see Thomas, *Spanish Civil War*, 588-95. For greater military detail see R. Colodny, *The Battle for Madrid* (New York: Paine-Whitman, 1958), J. M. Martínez Bande, *La lucha en torno a Madrid* (Madrid: Editorial San Martín, 1968) and S. Montero Barrado, *Paisajes de la guerra: nueve itinerarios por los frentes de Madrid* (Madrid: Comunidad de Madrid, 1987).

sense, and without knowing it, they had already lost the most crucial casualty: their reputation. From then on the Irish were isolated in a 'quiet sector of a quiet front', and only had one more half-chance of glory. Liaison between the Irish field officers and Spanish general staff was poor, whilst that between O'Duffy and his immediate superior in Toledo was non-existent. When at last the Bandera was ordered 'over the top' it was as part of a large-scale diversionary attack intended to help the Italian advance on Guadalajara, far to the north-west. The operation was never intended to 'succeed' in the obvious sense — the gaining of physical objectives stated and observed — that its participants naturally understood.[38] Even O'Duffy, perhaps not through his own fault, seems to have been ignorant of the strategic context or purpose of the action, in which four of his men were killed and several others wounded. Faced with an apparent threat of mutiny from some officers, he refused to obey his orders to renew the attack the next day.[39] Not long afterwards, the Bandera was moved to another section of the Madrid front. O'Duffy had always insisted that his men would not fight in the north against the strongly Catholic Basque Republic; but it was precisely to this zone that the action of the Nationalist war-effort was now switched.

As among the Internationals, so in the O'Duffyite ranks fissures opened up under pressure. Serious problems originated in March, following the attack described above. Officers suspected it had been a mismanaged manoeuvre which led them into a death-trap for no apparent military reason. Little attempt was made on the Spanish side to explain matters. In any case, the rigid protocol of the *Tercio* ('the Bridegrooms of Death' as their motto had it) rejected anything short of blind

---

38 For the hidden political agenda of military decisions made during the Guadalajara battle, see P Preston, *Franco* (London: Harper-Collins, 1993), 229-33. Nationalist attacks took place all along the Jarama front on 12-15 March 1937. Republican army *partes* (daily reports) for these operations celebrate the successful use of artillery, which (other accounts agree) made the Irish advance towards the heights of Titulcia particularly suicidal (*Partes de la Guerra: Tomo II, Ejército de la República*, ed. J. M. Gárate Córdoba [Madrid: Editorial San Martín, 1978], 241).

39 *Cf.* O'Duffy, *Crusade in Spain*, 161-63, with O'Cuinneagáin, *The War in Spain*, 20-21.

obedience as dishonourable.   During the further period of inaction which followed, O'Duffy lost the loyalty of a number of his officers.   The general's excessive drinking did not help matters, nor his long absences from the front, mostly spent with a few privileged aides in a luxury hotel in the Nationalists's military capital, Salamanca.[40] The former tendency naturally percolated downwards and began to affect discipline. However, the latter example was not imitated, and there were very few desertions. On the contrary, new recruits continued to arrive in Cáceres throughout the period of Irish service, despite rigorous enforcement of the non-intervention agreement by Dublin.[41] Nevertheless, morale and respect were slowly eroded. Most of the rank and file still revered O'Duffy, but without his personal exercise of responsibility authority was badly undermined.

At the end of March 1937, the Colonel-in-Chief of the *Tercio*, Juan Yagüe, made a surprise inspection, as a result of critical reports from Spanish liaison officers, and whilst O'Duffy was away on a jaunt in Seville. By this time, too, Franco had become concerned about the sheer cost of the XV *Bandera*, which was receiving little or no support from Irish sources. Since O'Duffy resisted persistent pressure to allow his men to be integrated fully into the Nationalist army — in effect, to subsume them in a viable operational unit under Spanish command — in mid-April, the Generalísimo decided that disbandment was his only option. A few weeks later the *Bandera* was stood down from the line. During the weeks it took to organize their repatriation, the men were prey to

---

40   Reports quickly reached Dublin that O'Duffy spent little or no time with his men (J. P. Walshe to J Kerney [Irish envoy to Spain], 6 March 1937, Irish National Archives, Foreign Affairs, Letter Book 'B'). The main witness to the Salamanca junketings was the Director of the Irish College in the city, Fr Alexander McCabe, whose reminiscences were at times more cynical than merely sceptical (see D. Keogh, 'An Eywitness to History: Fr Alexander McCabe and the Spanish Civil War, 1936-1939', *Breifne: Journal of Breifne Historical Society*, VIII [1995], No. 30, 445-88). His observations are corroborated in P. Kemp, *Mine were of Trouble* (London: Cassell, 1957), 87-88, and F. McCullagh, *In Franco's Spain* (London: Burns & Oates, 1937), pp. 150-51, 245, 263-64.

41   O'Duffy, *Crusade in Spain*, 169, confirmed by note of Yagüe to Franco, 3 April 1937, Archivo General Militar (Ávila) Cuartel General del Generalísimo, Organización legajo 156.

faction, exacerbated by boredom, rumour and disillusionment. At times, the behaviour of an irresponsible minority must have tested the goodwill of their hosts in Cáceres.[42]

The International Brigades fought on for eighteen months after their despised 'Fascist' compatriots had quitted the field. Not until October 1938 were they disbanded and repatriated as a result of an agreement brokered by the Non-Intervention Powers. Even worse hardship was endured by dozens of their comrades who had become prisoners of war, held in dreadful conditions in a medieval monastery crudely converted into a prison outside Burgos. Most were released at the time of Franco's victory in April 1939.

VI

Memory

When the Irish Brigade arrived home (June 1937) they enjoyed an official civic reception in Dublin and were given a warm welcome in most of the members' home towns. By now, however, they were irreconcilably split into factions, and some were not averse to public rehearsal of their differences and complaints of their treatment in Spain.[43] The Irish public came to realise that glorious accounts of the Brigade's exploits which had occasionally appeared in the papers (especially the *Independent*) were somewhat divorced from reality. O'Duffy

---

42   This account of the dissolution of the *Bandera Irlandesa* is based on a series of documents in O'Duffy, *op. cit.* See especially Yagüe's report to Franco (24 March); O'Duffy's defence of the Bandera to Franco (9 April); and the latter's final decision (issued on 13 April). The Irish journalist, McCullagh, who was based in Salamanca for much of this period, alleged that the Brigade had cost the Nationalists the enormous sum of £170,000 (McCullagh, *In Franco's Spain*, 306). The figure seems exaggerated; none the less, there was a serious financial complication from the point of view of Burgos (see also Keogh, 'An Eye Witness', 485-88).

43   O'Riordan, *Connolly Column*, 101. In contrast, O'Duffy's account at no point betrays any indication that even the slightest disagreement disturbed the glowing relationships between himself and any other party to the enterprise, whether Spanish or Irish.

himself sank into terminal illness and political obscurity, though he helped his men whenever he could, and always responded to appeals from those who had fallen on hard times. Attempts were made by various officers to form a veterans' association which might dedicate itself to repairing bridges and limiting further damage, but to no avail.[44] During the hottest years of the Cold War, the Brigaders were due some honour as a vanguard in the fight against the Communist menace, which had now - just as the priests had predicted in the 1930s — spread atheistic tyranny and persecution to many small, helpless Catholic countries.   In the late 1940s, the party to which most veterans retained allegiance — Fine Gael — entered government for the first time. But any hope veterans nurtured for belated justification was rendered void by the growing distaste for the legacy of the Blueshirts. This was linked to a renewed depreciation of the Brigade's military performance. Brendan Behan's devastating quip that they were the only army ever to return from a war in larger numbers than those they left with became familiar to every citizen of the Republic.[45]   As the years passed, their contribution was increasingly regarded as meaningless even by those who had once prayed for the victory of Franco. In fact, the Catholic Church in Ireland, whose loyal servant O'Duffy had been, never accorded the grateful recognition to him or his men which might have been felt appropriate. Though Ireland remained a deeply Catholic country, the majority mores of politics changed. By the 1960s and the era of the trendy left, veterans were not tempted to recall their campaign in public, whilst children and grandchildren were ashamed of any connection with it. After 1939, at least, most kept their counsel, and died without ever speaking of the experience, let alone leaving any record of it. Many joined the British army after 1940; some felt — once more

---

44 An association was established before the Brigade left Cáceres, and 'a council representative of each of the 32 counties was elected' (O'Duffy, *Crusade in Spain*, 240-41). Capts. O'Cuinneagáin and Quinn were moving spirits behind later attempts to preserve links, 'organising under great difficulties of distance and want of knowledge of survivors' (circular [?1947] sent to veteran Leo McCloskey, Private Collection).

45 Behan's jibe appeared in his *Confessions of an Irish Rebel* (London: Hutchinson, 1965). 133.

— that it was the right thing to do; others were simply soldiers, and always soldiers; and doubtless one or two enlisted with the British just to defy De Valera who had again opted for neutrality. Whatever their reasons, the net effect was that some 'Irish Fascists' died fighting in the great war against Fascism.

The surviving Irish International Brigaders received no public acknowledgement on their return home. On the contrary, veterans have testified that a record of fighting with the 'Reds' rendered them unacceptable as far as potential employers were concerned. Some were kept out of jobs for years through the pernicious influence of various clergy.[46] But they were to have the ultimate reward for struggle and sacrifice, for defeat and victimization. 'You are History: you are Legend' were the prophetic words of 'La Pasionaria' (Dolores Ibárruri) at the stand-down parade of the International Brigades in Barcelona in October 1938. These warriors indeed became part of history and legend. Most of the survivors joined the International Brigade Association, set up before the war ended, in which the small and manageable Irish branch was sustained by an appropriately international organization. By the 1960s, they had acquired the status of visionaries who perceived the evils of Nazism and Fascism well before their political leaders, and were prepared to lay down their lives in order to warn the world. In November 1995, the Parliament of democratic Spain voted to offer honorary Spanish nationality to surviving veterans of the International Brigades.[47] These grizzled super-Republicans can now become — if they so desire — subjects of His Majesty King Juan Carlos I. It is a bizarre consummation.

---

46 See, e.g., Manus O'Riordan, *Portrait of an Irish Anti-Fascist: Frank Edwards, 1907-1983: An Appreciation* (Dublin: privately printed, 1984), Marx Memorial Library, International Brigade Archive Box A-12 Ed/1.

47 G. Jackson, 'Un acto de reconocimiento histórico', *El País*, 7 de diciembre de 1995.

PART II

THE FORGING OF A WAR EFFORT

'From the Summit to the Abyss': The Contradictions of Individualism and Collectivism in Spanish Anarchism

CHRIS EALHAM

Introduction

It was a tremendous irony that the failed military coup d'état of July 1936 which precipitated the Spanish Civil War stimulated precisely what it sought to forestall: a profound and far-reaching social revolution. The subsequent collectivizing economic experiments and the armed workers' militias marked the 'heroic years' of the Iberian libertarian movement: the traditional anarchists of the Federación Anarquista Ibérica (FAI) and the Federación Ibérica de Juventudes Libertarias (FIJL) and the trade union oriented anarcho-syndicalists of the Confederación Nacional del Trabajo (CNT).[1] Yet the glory soon gave way to ignominy, as the twin realities of revolution and civil war laid bare the weaknesses of the libertarians and the limitations of Anarchism as a revolutionary ideology. In the view of Jaume Balius, an anarchist who emerged as one of the

---

1 The literature on the revolution is enormous. Among the most notable studies are: Walter Bernecker, *Colectividades y revolución social. El anarquismo en la guerra civil española, 1936-1939* (Barcelona: Crítica, 1982); Albert Pérez Baró, *Trenta meses de col·lectivisme en Catalunya* (l'Esplugues de Llobregat: Ariel, 1974); Gaston Leval, *Espagne Libertaire (1936-1939)* (Paris: Éditions du Cercle, 1971); Burnett Bolloten, *The Spanish Civil War; Revolution and Counterrevolution* (Chapel Hill, North Carolina: Univ. of North Carolina Press, 1991); Frank Mintz, *La autogestión en la España revolucionaria* (Madrid: La Piqueta, 1974).

most vociferous critics of the CNT-FAI-FIJL hierarchy in the 1930s, 'the CNT was utterly devoid of revolutionary theory. We did not possess a concrete programme. We had no idea where we were going'.[2]

This paper will locate the failure of the Spanish Revolution of 1936-1937 in terms of the contradictory development of the theoretical conceptions of the CNT-FAI-FIJL in the decades before the Civil War. Particular attention will be placed on competing individualist and collectivist revolutionary strategies in Barcelona, the *de facto* capital of Iberian Anarchism and the centre of the Spanish Revolution of 1936-37. This will enable us to see how conflicting views of the individual and collective responsibilities of the anarchist militant converged to produce damaging problems of internal control and discipline within the anarchist movement during the years of the Civil War. These problems culminated in the scourge of the so-called 'incontrolats', who, while outside the control of any particular organization, were part of the 'anarchist family' and, therefore, undermined the hegemony of the CNT-FAI-FIJL .

The Genesis of Anarchist Individualism

The philosophical root of Anarchism is comprised of a profound individualism, an unconditional acceptance of the freedom of the individual to act according to their own will or conscience. It was this same principle which determined the *modus operandi* of the *grupo de afinidad*, the basic element of anarchist practice, which allowed total autonomy to individual members, even if they came into conflict with other anarchists or even members of their *grupo*. Towards the end of the nineteenth century, Ricardo Mella, Anselmo Lorenzo and Federico Urales, the doyens of the modern Spanish anarchist movement, disseminated this doctrine of the individual spirit in

---

2   Los Amigos de Durruti, *Hacia la nueva revolución* (Barcelona: n.p., 1937?), 15. With his customary cruel and sardonic humour, Trotsky compared Anarchism to a hole-ridden umbrella: superficially both appeared to be of some value. But put into action both were useless: Trotsky observed that while the first could not transform society, the second failed to halt the rain. For Trotsky's writings on Spain see his *Escritos sobre España* (Paris: Ruedo Ibérico, 1971).

permanent conflict with authority, capitalism and the State.[3] While these early anarchist pioneers succeeded in spreading their message and establishing a movement and a culture that could survive, or at least endure, state repression, Spanish libertarian theory remained weak. In response to the relative poverty of indigenous anarchist theory, Spanish libertarians borrowed heavily from wider European intellectual trends, both from anarchist sources and the radicalized middle class. The eclectic embrace by Spanish anarchist ideologues of non-proletarian theoretical currents is not a complete surprise, for not only is the genesis of Anarchism found in the radical bourgeois liberalism of the eighteenth and nineteenth centuries but, as an ideological and a philosophical trend, libertarianism evolved in a diverse and ill-defined manner. However, in Spain, these radical bourgeois ideologues had a lasting influence on the development of Spanish anarchist thought and they enhanced the existing individualistic tendencies of the libertarian movement.

Among the non-anarchist writers imported into the Iberian Peninsula by the libertarians was the Norwegian dramatist Henrik Ibsen. From the 1890s Ibsen enjoyed great popularity in libertarian circles and his plays were regularly performed to audiences in workers' theatres across Spain. The themes of individual resistance to falsehood and oppression and the pursuit of truth and justice inherent in works like *An Enemy of the People*, *Peer Gynt* and *A Doll's House* were widely taken as confirmation of the key elements of the anarchist message. Indeed, on May Day 1925 the Scandinavian playwright was praised by *La Revista Blanca*, the standard-bearer of Spanish anarchist intellectuals, as 'the first revolutionary'.[4]

Another imported thinker who enhanced the individualistic leanings of the *fin de siècle* anarchist intelligentsia was the German philosopher Friedrich Nietzsche. From 1898 onwards, before even the translation of Nietzsche's major works into Castilian, *La Revista Blanca* introduced his ideas to a Spanish

3   See José Álvarez Junco, *La ideología política del anarquismo español, 1868-1910* (Madrid: Siglo XXI, 1991); Anselmo Lorenzo, *El proletariado militante* (Barcelona: n.p., 1901 and 1923), 2 vols.

4   *La Revista Blanca*, 15 November 1898 and 1 May 1925; 1 and 15 April, 1 and 15 May, 1 June 1928; 22 February 1935.

audience. While the individualistic aesthetics of Nietzsche's writing made him attractive to intellectuals in general, it was his militant rejection of the exclusive nature of bourgeois society, matched with his advocacy of a violent rupture with the strictures of bourgeois ethics and the renovation of morality, that earned him a following in anarchist circles. His individualistic message was even accepted and endorsed by mainstream libertarian figures such as Mella and Urales. Meanwhile, the Nietzschean incarnation of Zarathustra, the solitary figure prepared to make a stand against the intolerance and indifference of bourgeois society, provided a compelling model for the terrorist advocates of the 'propaganda of the deed', the self-styled anarchist avengers of the crimes of bourgeois society.[5]

It was, however, another German philosopher, Max Stirner, who represented the apogee of individualism in anarchist philosophy.[6] Stirner's *oeuvre* entered Spain around the turn of the century via *La Revista Blanca* and in 1902 *El único y su propiedad* was published, the first Spanish translation of *Der Einzige und sein Eigenthum*, Stirner's *magnum opus*. Nietzsche's individualism paved the way for Stirner, a fact that explains the ease with which middle-class intellectuals close to the anarchist movement, such as the Catalan poet Jaume Brossa and the Basque novelist Pío Baroja, embraced Stirner's ultra-individualistic philosophy.[7] While Nietzsche praised the *Übermensch* (*superhombre*) as a perfect example of human life,

---

5   *La Revista Blanca*, 1 June 1900 and 15 November 1901; Paul Ilie, 'Nietzsche in Spain, 1890-1910', *Publications of the Modern Language Association*, LXXIX (1964), 80-96; Gonzalo Sobejano, *Nietzsche en España* (Madrid: Gredos, 1967), *passim*.; Álvarez Junco, *La ideología política*, 139-69; Rafael Núñez Florencio, *El terrorismo anarquista, 1888-1909* (Barcelona: Siglo XXI, 1983), *passim*.

6   Max Stirner, *Der Einzige und sein Eigenthum* (Berlin: Schuster and Loeffler, 1898). For critiques of Stirner's philosophy see John P. Clark, *Max Stirner's Egoism* (London: Freedom, 1976) and Enrico Ferri, *L'antigiuridismo di Max Stirner* (Milan: A. Guiffrè Editore, 1992).

7   *ERA 80, Els Anarquistes educadors del poble: 'La Revista Blanca' (1898-1905)* (Barcelona: Curial, 1977); E. Armand, *El anarquismo individualista. Lo que es, lo que puede y vale* (Barcelona: Germinal, 1916) and *Reflexiones de un anarquista individualista. Realismo e idealismo mezclados* (Paris: Librería Internacional, n.d.).

Stirner acclaimed the *Einzige* (*único*), the individual ego. Equally, Stirner shared Nietzsche's disgust for the mass of humanity, which he portrayed as a passive, anonymous bloc of mediocrities incapable of breaking with bourgeois social conventions.   In reply, both advocated (individual) rebellion against a society which, they opined, impeded the full development of individual desire.   This rebellion contrasted with collectivist doctrines of solidarity that emphasized the oppression and exploitation of social classes by the capitalist economic system.

Unlike the other imported intellectual apostles of individualism discussed so far, Stirner can be located firmly within those strands of the anarchist tradition that had long glorified the robber.   This trend can be traced to Mikhail Bakunin, one of the founding fathers of European Anarchism, who regarded the 'outlaw' as the prime revolutionary material, 'the genuine and sole revolutionary — a revolutionary without fine phrases, without learned rhetoric, irreconcilable, indefatigable and indomitable, a popular and social revolutionary, non-political and independent of any estate'.[8] Stirner believed in the virtue of vice and he lauded crime in the same way that a poet might worship beauty.   This view was premised on the idealistic assumption that the law and the State possessed no punitive power other than that with which the consciousness of the meek endowed them.   In Stirner's terms, therefore, illegality became a liberating journey of self-actualization that presaged the collapse of authority and power. Although he believed in the destruction of the existing order, for Stirner, it was individual (criminal) will, rather than the proletariat, that would be the grave-digger of the State.   Thus, Stirner rejected all collective morality, whether religious or revolutionary, on the grounds that it represented a debilitating gaol for the individual mind and spirit.   Accordingly, Marxism was denounced as a secular revival of the anti-individualistic philosophy of Christianity, albeit substituting 'God' with new objects of worship like the 'proletariat'.   Instead, adapting Nietzsche's famous dictum, Stirner proclaimed 'the People is

---

8   Cited in Eric Hobsbawm, *Bandits* (Harmondsworth: Pelican, 1985), 110.

dead'. The only value that Stirner accepted was an Epicurean struggle for the hedonistic satisfaction of the senses, irrespective of the consequences for other human beings. *Ipso facto*, this heightened Stirner's incorrigible scorn for the masses and for solidarity; he believed in a pseudo-Darwinian quest for survival in which beggars were to starve, while those with a spirit of resistance and a strong ego would be forced to conquer whatever they needed or desired, invoking their sacred right to violence. The definition of Stirnerism advanced by José Álvarez Junco as 'anti-social individualism' is, therefore, highly justified.[9] In fact, the only collective units Stirner regarded as legitimate were 'Unions of Egoists', tiny groups of individualists and 'conscious illegalists' drawn from the 'dispossessed', an amalgam of paupers, villains, criminals and *déclassé* intellectuals, whom he regarded as the harbingers of change.

Throughout Europe Stirner's message fed into existing anarchist sentiments.[10] As one Italian scholar of the anarchist movement observed, 'individualism slept in the ideological unconscious of many anarchists and the "revelation" of Stirner served to arouse it'. This view is endorsed by Rafael Núñez Florencio, who observed that Stirner's philosophy 'was born in the very heart of Anarchism'.[11] It would be wrong, however, to overstate the influence of Stirner on the ideologues of the Spanish anarchist movement and it seems that the interest of mainstream anarchist thinkers like Urales and Mella in the German egoist was ephemeral.[12] Nevertheless, on the practical plane — and Spanish Anarchism was, after all, essentially a doctrine of action — the influence of Stirnerist individualism was most evident. For example, there is enormous similarity

9   Álvarez Junco, *La ideología política*, 146.
10   See Ettore Zoccoli, *L'anarchia. Gli agitatori. Le idee. I fatti* (Torino: Bocca, 1907); Giacomo Mesnil, *Stirner, Nietzsche e l'anarchismo* (Jesi: Il Pensiero, 1909); Richard Parry, *The Bonnot Gang. The Story of the French Illegalists* (London: Rebel Press, 1987); E. Armand, *L'Anarchisme comme vie et activité individuelle* (Romainville: n.p. 1911); Richard D. Sonn, *Anarchism and Cultural Politics in Fin de Siècle France* (Lincoln: Univ. of Nebraska, 1989), 27.
11   Pier Carlo Masini, *Storia degli anarchici italiani nell'epoca degli attentati* (Milano: Rizzoli, 1981), 195; Núñez Florencio, *El terrorismo anarquista*, 108.
12   Álvarez Junco, *La ideología política*, 147.

between the individualism of Stirner's 'Union of Egoists' and the *grupo de afinidad*, the fundamental unit of anarchist *praxis* in Spain, both of which were characterized by the absolute independence of their individual members. Moreover, although they were always a minority among the variegated anarchist fauna, the pronounced individualism of the disciples of Stirner enabled them to create potent legends and exert a disproportionate influence on the development of libertarian practice in Spain.

One such legend was Achille Vittorio Pini, a Milanese individualist-anarchist. Pini advocated the robbery of the bourgeoisie, or what he dubbed 'individual appropriation', on the grounds that the wealth of the bourgeoisie and their private property was robbed from the workers in the first instance. Exiled in Paris for many years due to his acts of 'repossession', Pini also practised his unique blend of political protest and criminal activity in Barcelona in the early 1890s, where he and his comrades published a newspaper, *El Porvenir Anarquista*, in Italian, French and Spanish.[13] While Pini's stay in the Catalan capital has not yet been widely documented, his 'individual gesture' acquired mythical status among many of the local *grupos de afinidad*.[14]

Pini's sojourn in Barcelona coincided with the rupture of the traditional structures of social control in the city following the urban development, economic expansion and mass immigration precipitated by the 1888 Barcelona World Exhibition. The volatile admixture of a port city with a pronounced bohemian ambience, a low wage economy and a largely unskilled working class of recent peasant origin transformed Barcelona into a 'cocktail of violence, combining the explosiveness of Chicago with the rowdiness of Naples'. In the words of one cultural historian, Barcelona 'attracted the most extreme individualist

---

13 Pier Carlo Masini, *Storia degli anarchici italiani. Da Bakunin a Malatesta (1862-1892)* (Milano: Rizzoli, 1972), 234. Curiously, in his otherwise excellent study of Anarchism in Barcelona during the 1880s and 1890s, Núñez Florencio makes no mention of Pini's stay in the city.

14 Álvarez Junco, *La ideología política*, 494.

rhetoric of destruction'.[15] This material context ensured that the illegalist notions inherent in Stirner's philosophy were often adopted spontaneously by the poorest sections of the Barcelona working class, which were inclined towards crime and theft in order to survive, particularly during times of high unemployment.   With social relations resting on what one inhabitant of the city's tough proletarian neighbourhoods described as 'the continual battle for life', a culture of individual criminality developed in the Catalan capital that legitimized the array of illegal activities acclaimed by Stirner.[16]

The Anarcho-Syndicalist Farrago

The impact of Stirner's ultra-individualism on the European libertarian movement was muted by the upsurge in anarcho-syndicalism at the turn of the century.   In Spain, this process culminated in the creation of the CNT in 1910.   Anarcho-syndicalism assumed the fusion of Anarchism with collective trade unionism, a hybrid which, in the words of the French anarcho-syndicalist Pierre Monatte, 'recalled Anarchism to the awareness of its working class origins'.[17]   In tactical terms, anarcho-syndicalism represented a bid to escape the ghetto where the libertarian movement had been led by the individualistic advocates of 'propaganda of the deed'; it reflected a desire to subjugate the will of the individual to the wider objectives of the collectivity.   The *Carte d'Amiens*, the classic statement of anarcho-syndicalist principle, was a tacit acknowledgement of the failure of the anarchist belief in

---

15   Luis Goytisolo, *Antagonia* (Barcelona: Plaza y Janés, 1993), I, 240; Patricia Leighten, *Re-ordering the Universe.   Picasso and Anarchism, 1897-1914* (Princeton: Princeton U. P., 1989), 15.

16   Baltasar Porcel, *La revuelta permanente* (Barcelona: Planeta, 1978), 103; Emili Salut, *Viveres de revolucionaris.   Apunts històrics del Districte Cinquè* (Barcelona: n.p., 1938), pp. 9-11, 52-57, 114, 123-24, 147-48.

17   Masini, *Storia degli anarchici italiani nell'epoca degli attentati*, 204-05; Monatte cited in James Joll, *The Anarchists* (London: Methuen, 1979), 187.   Like their anarchist predecessors, the Iberian anarcho-syndicalists were theoretically weak and until ideologues like Joan Peiró appeared on the scene in the 1920s, the new creed was heavily reliant on French masters like Fernand Pelloutier, Georges Sorel and Pierre Besnard.

individualism and spontaneity.   By contrast, the anarcho-syndicalists insisted on the need for a central directive organ (*sindicato*) which would organize the working class and their collective energies prior to the expropriation of the bourgeoisie through an insurrectionary general strike.[18]

The aggressive, egoistic individualism inherent in Stirner's philosophy fared badly alongside the promise of solidarity inherent to CNT Anarcho-syndicalism and the growing ranks of *cenetistas* quickly outnumbered the isolated groups of anarchist-individualists.   But the tendency of historians to focus on the mass CNT unions to the detriment of the exclusively libertarian *grupos de afinidad* has given the impression that Spanish Anarchism somehow modernized its practices, eschewing small-group or individual violence in favour of conventional, collective trade union activity.[19]   In fact, the old-style anarchists did not renounce their traditional ideological shibboleths to become revolutionary syndicalists, and the thirty years before the Civil War provide numerous examples of anarchist hostility to anarcho-syndicalism.   Many committed anarchists, including Urales, vehemently opposed the formation of the CNT, which they viewed suspiciously as the harbinger of a bureaucracy that would shackle the spontaneous revolutionary instincts of the masses.   On one occasion the inveterate anti-syndicalist individualism of Urales impelled a group of workers to eject him from a union social centre, an indignity that was compounded by an order that banned the anarchist sage from CNT buildings.[20]

---

18 Xavier Paniagua, *La sociedad libertaria.   Agrarismo e industrialización en el anarquismo español, 1930-1939* (Barcelona: Crítica, 1982), 115-264; Antonio Elorza, *La utopía anarquista bajo la segunda república española* (Madrid: Ayuso, 1973), 387-408.   Despite the evident differences between Anarchism and Anarcho-syndicalism, some historians still employ the two terms interchangeably, as if they had the same meaning.   An example of this is Antonio Fontecha Pedraza, 'Anarcosindicalismo y violencia', *Historia Contemporánea*, XI (1994), 153-79.

19 Examples of this trend include Murray Bookchin, *The Spanish Anarchists.   The Heroic Years, 1868-1936* (New York: Free Life, 1977) and the semi-official history of the CNT by José Peirats, *La CNT en la revolución española* (Cali, Columbia: La Cuchilla, 1988).

20 Paniagua, *La sociedad libertaria*, 83-91, 104-10; Isaac Puente, *El comunismo libertario.   Sus posibilidades de realización en España* (Valencia:

The numerical superiority of the anarcho-syndicalists over the anarchists did not extend to the ideological sphere and the advocates of industrial unionism concentrated on establishing a culture of syndical action, rather than formulating a coherent ideological project for social transformation. This allowed the dwindling number of traditional libertarians to influence the CNT, thereby ensuring that the theoretical confusion and the mélange of collectivism and individualism inherent to Anarchism became translated into Spanish Anarcho-syndicalism, producing an ideological farrago within the CNT. The radical individualistic chic of the anarchists was also evident in many CNT leaders. A case in hand was Salvador 'El Noi del Sucre' Seguí, the most popular of all pre-Civil War CNT leaders, who was assassinated by right-wing gunmen in 1923. Normally regarded as a paragon of anarcho-syndicalist virtue, not least because of his many conflicts with the anarchists, Seguí's ideological origins were shaped more by Nietzsche than by the *Carte d'Amiens* and as a youth, Seguí was an avid member of a pseudo-Nietzschean gang known as 'Els Fills de Puta', which toured the toughest bars of downtown Barcelona in search of excitement and violence. Though Seguí later developed more orthodox syndicalist views, according to those around him, he continued to possess what Pere Foix dubbed a 'savage spirit' and his bohemian-individualistic inclinations resonated in both his attire and his personal ethics.[21]

If individualism survived in the heart of the CNT, it veritably prospered among the anarchist groups which existed around its periphery. At the height of the anarcho-syndicalist

---

n.p., n.d.); Federico Urales, *Los municipios libres. Ante las puertas de la anarquía* (Barcelona: *La Revista Blanca*, 1933); Juan García Oliver, *El eco de los pasos* (Barcelona: Ruedo Ibérico, 1978), 215-16; Teresa Abelló and Enric Olivé, 'El conflicto entre la CNT y la Familia Urales en 1928. La lucha por el mantenimiento del anarquismo puro', *Estudios de Historia Social*, (1985), Nos. 32-33, 317-32.

21 Pere Foix, *Apòstols i mercaders. Seixanta anys de lluita social a Catalunya* (Barcelona: Terra Nova, 1976), 55; Baltasar Porcel, *La revuelta permanente*, 54, 106-07; Salut, *Vivers de revolucionaris*, 147-48; Manuel Cruells, *Salvador Seguí, el Noi del Sucre* (l'Esplugues de Llobregat: Ariel, 1974), 55-59; Eulàlia Vega i Massana, 'Salvador Seguí, el "Noi del Sucre" ', in Alejandro Sánchez, *Barcelona, 1888-1929. Modernidad, ambición y conflictos de una ciudad soñada* (Madrid: Alianza, 1994), 108-12.

groundswell during the first decade of the twentieth century, the Stirnerist descendants of Pini published *El Productor Literario*, a Barcelona newspaper that advised its readership that 'To rob and to kill to live is beautiful, as great as life itself!'.[22] Spanish neutrality during World War One gave a new impetus to the individualist-illegalist trend, as Barcelona's libertine ambience attracted anarchist exiles, draft dodgers and misfits from all over Europe. These anarchist émigrés included the Russian individualist Victor Serge, who had recently completed a jail sentence for his involvement with 'The Bonnot Gang', the infamous French anarchist bank robbers. In Barcelona Serge befriended Costa Iscar, a Catalan anarchist-individualist and pickpocket. Years later, after he had crossed the Rubicon that separated Stirnerist individualism from Bolshevism, Serge evoked the libertarian milieu of Barcelona in his semi-autobiographical novel *Le Naissance de Notre Pouvoir*, describing 'the ego-anarchist poison' embodied in the character Lejeune. In typically Stirnerist fashion, Lejeune declared his contempt for those who preached revolution for the sake of humanity, preferring instead to 'hit the banks. My revolution will be over quickly. I don't believe in theirs. Monarchies, republics, unions—I don't give a damn'.[23]

After World War One the fortunes of the Stirnerist illegalists were boosted. This was part of a more general rise in the standing of the anarchist *grupos de afinidad* following the impasse of the Catalan CNT after 1919, when the main employers' associations opted for a confrontational strategy of 'union-busting'. The anarchists perceived the clamp-down on collective syndical freedoms as a vindication of their strategy of small-group violence and the *grupos de afinidad* came to the fore, ensuring that individualism remained a key element in the

---

22 *El Productor Literario*, 24 February 1906, cited in Núñez Florencio, *El terrorismo anarquista*, 219.

23 Francesc Madrid, *Sangre en Atarazanas* (Barcelona: Antoni López, 1926); Porcel, *La revuelta permanente*, 122-26; Victor Serge, *Birth of Our Power* (London: Writers and Readers, 1977), 29-35. A self-styled 'conscious illegalist' and an expropriator *par excellence*, Jules Bonnot was the most famous of the French Stirnerists and the founder of the so-called 'motor bandits' who were credited with the first ever robbery in which a getaway car was used.

culture of *praxis* of the CNT. The most active of the *grupos de afinidad* was 'Los Solidarios', which included Buenaventura Durruti, Francisco Ascaso and Juan García Oliver, the so-called 'Three Musketeers of Spanish Anarchism', who were not strangers to the philosophy of Nietzsche.[24] These *grupistas* lived a life of illegality, relying on their own individual audacity and initiative, emerging from the shadows to expropriate banks for the 'cause' and 'avenging' and 'eliminating' the 'enemies of the proletariat'.[25]

The new prestige enjoyed by the *grupos de afinidad* and their self-perception that they were the interpreters of the soul of the CNT, precipitated a struggle for control of the unions between the anarchists and the anarcho-syndicalists, both of whom wished to impose their own tactics on the Confederation and transform it in their own image. Increasingly, the CNT was an organization at war with itself and enormous energies were wasted on what were largely vacuous internal debates on strategy that did nothing to resolve the historic confusion over the relative merits of individualism and collectivism and the dichotomy between legality and illegality. Consequently, when General Miguel Primo de Rivera launched his *pronunciamiento* in September 1923 and made himself dictator, the CNT was not in a position to respond. While the union press was censored, in keeping with Primo de Rivera's liberal bonhomie, the CNT was initially allowed a limited legal existence. However, any tolerance towards the anarcho-syndicalists disappeared after May 1924, when anarchist *grupistas* assassinated the newly appointed Barcelona court executioner. This action by an

---

24 The son of a prominent Spanish anarcho-syndicalist described 'Los Solidarios' as being 'ready for any sacrifice, rejecting all compromise, they had an unshakable faith in libertarian Communism ... they took delight in reading *The Conquest of Bread* by Kropotkin, they admired the passionate life of Bakunin (whose ideas they knew only poorly), they discussed Nietzsche and, strangely, the pessimist Schopenhauer' (César M. Lorenzo, *Los anarquistas españoles y el poder* [Paris: Ruedo Ibérico, 1972], 39).

25 Albert Pérez Baró, *Els 'Feliços' anys vint. Memòries d'un militant obrer, 1918-1926* (Palma de Mallorca: Edicions Moll, 1974), 87; Ricardo Sanz, *El sindicalismo y la política. Los 'solidarios' y 'nosotros'* (Toulouse: Imprimerie Dulaurier, 1966), 51-77, 95-118; Abel Paz, *Durruti, el proletariado en armas* (Barcelona: Bruguera, 1978), 27-53; Léon-Ignacio, *Los años del pistolerismo* (Barcelona: Plaza y Janés, 1978), *passim*.

anonymous *grupo de afinidad* provided the authorities with a pretext to force the CNT unions underground, where they stayed until 1930. This episode was portentous: it exemplified the contradictions between the individualistic methods of the largely unaccountable anarchist *grupos de afinidad* and the collective, organizational needs of the libertarian movement that would become so apparent during the Civil War. Prophetically, one anarcho-syndicalist speculated that the killing was the work of 'uncontrollable fanatics'.[26]

The Resurgence of Individualism in the 1920s

Though the dictatorship brought an effective halt to the body of the libertarian movement, the brain continued to function. Throughout the 1920s the censor allowed *La Revista Blanca* to appear, presenting anarchist theoreticians with an opportunity to take stock of the struggles of the preceding period. Urales penned a series of articles on 'the individual and the collective ideal' and 'individualism and human solidarity', in an attempt to synthesize the experiences of the previous thirty years and their ramifications for the relationship between syndicalism, individualism and collectivism. Some of the thinkers who had shaped the individualistic development of Iberian Anarchism, such as Nietzsche, who was largely discredited in anarchist circles following the rise of Italian Fascism and the emergence of Mussolini's nationalist version of the *Übermensch* myth, were publicly rejected by Urales. He also undertook a critique of Stirner's philosophy, which he discarded as 'individualism without either moral or social duties'.[27]

However, instead of producing a new theoretical synthesis and a clear statement of the individual responsibilities of the

---

26 Because the dead executioner had not taken the lives of any anarchists, many CNT members refused to consider this assassination as a classic anarchist *ajusticiamiento*, mistaking it instead as a deliberate provocation by the authorities or by *agents provocateurs* (Adolfo Bueso, *Recuerdos de un cenetista* [l'Esplugues de Llobregat: Ariel, 1976], I, 202-03; Ángel María de Lera, *Ángel Pestaña, retrato de un anarquista* [Barcelona: Argos, 1978], 216).

27 *La Revista Blanca*, 15 March, 1, 15 April, 1 June 1925; 15 September 1926; 1 January 1927; 1 September 1930.

anarchist within the collectivity, Urales repeated the errors of the past. Thus, for all the scorn heaped on Nietzsche's 'erroneous road', radical individualistic aesthetics remained entrenched within the anarchist movement. Similarly, while Stirner was apparently out of fashion with libertarian theoreticians, the German prophet of egoism still found an echo in Urales' rejection of 'universal solidarity'. Moreover, Urales continued to emphasize the importance of gestures inspired by 'the rich ideal of individualism', from which 'Anarchism cannot separate itself'. The unerring support of Urales for an absolute individualism clearly limited his attempt to distance himself from Stirner's philosophy.[28] This same radical individualism permeated the thinking of Urales' daughter, Federica Montseny, an important anarchist theoretician and a leading figure in the Civil War CNT-FAI. Concurring with her father that individual action was the most efficacious form of struggle, Montseny maintained that individualism was 'the basis of life and human progress'.[29]

The individualism of the Urales family found a wider forum through *La Novela Ideal*, the collection of proletarian novels published from 1925 right up until the end of the Civil War. *La Novela Ideal* was an astounding success: there were over five hundred novels published in the series and each edition sold between ten and fifty thousand copies. As a *genre* that celebrated the strength of individual resistance and personal valour against the tyrannical forces of State, Capital and Church, the classic themes of *La Novela Ideal* espoused the theme of human liberation which pervaded the early plays of Ibsen. The novels also frequently conveyed Stirnerist themes, as seen by Mauro Bajatierra's *Fuera de la ley* and Elías García's *Johás el errante*, both of which established a cult of violence and

---

28 *La Revista Blanca*, 1 February, 15 March, 1 April 1925. This point is confirmed by a recent study which concluded that 'al concebir Urales una libertad que no cesa jamás (ni aún al empezar la ajena), y un individuo al cual la sociedad no puede aportar nada, se acerca peligrosamente a la teoría de Max Stirner, quien llevará el Individualismo hasta sus últimas consecuencias ...' (Jorge Rodríguez Burrel, 'Federico Urales: filosofía individualista, anarquismo antisociativo', in *Federico Urales. Una cultura de la acracia, Antropos*, LXXVIII [1987], 49).

29 *La Revista Blanca*, 1 July 1923, 15 December 1927, 15 July 1929.

postulated that the revolution was the supreme manifestation of individualism.[30]

The confused relation between individualism and collectivism was given organizational expression in 1927 with the birth of the FAI. In effect little more than a recreation of the classic nineteenth-century Bakuninist secret anarchist society, the FAI made no attempt to develop anarchist doctrine nor even to synthesize the contradictions of the past. Instead, the mission of the FAI was a rearguard action to maintain anarchist purity in the CNT. Consequently, the FAI attracted the *grupos de afinidad* previously dispersed across Iberia, becoming a rallying-point for those libertarians who were discontented with the dilution of the anarchist message since the development of Anarcho-syndicalism in the first quarter of the twentieth century.[31] The 'Los Solidarios' *grupo de afinidad* provided the operational model for *faísmo*, and their spirit of self-sacrifice and abnegation was expected to be emulated by all FAI members. Even though the individualistic, anti-organizational sentiments of Ascaso, Durruti and García Oliver inhibited them from joining the FAI until 1934, the charismatic power of these living libertarian legends meant that their *grupo de afinidad*, re-named 'Nosotros' in 1931, constituted the *de facto* leadership of the organization. Indeed, according to one young *faísta*, 'Nosotros' was a 'super-FAI' or a 'FAI within the FAI'.[32]

The recrudescence of extreme individualism in the Spanish libertarian movement can be appreciated fully by taking a closer look at the Ascaso, Durruti and García Oliver

---

30 Gonzalo Santonja, *La novela revolucionaria de quiosco, 1905-1939* (Madrid: La productora de ediciones, 1993), 69-81; Marisa Siguan Boehmer, *Literatura popular libertaria* (Barcelona: Península, 1981); Mauro Bajatierra, *Fuera de la ley*, La Novela Ideal, 153 (Barcelona: *La Revista Blanca*, 1929); Elías García, *Johás el errante*, La Novela Ideal, 206 (Barcelona: *La Revista Blanca*, n.d.).

31 The main general source on the FAI is the highly uncritical work by Juan Gómez Casas, *Historia de la FAI* (Bilbao: ZYX, 1977). For a critical study of the FAI in its Barcelona stronghold see my 'Anarchism and Illegality in Barcelona, 1930-1937', *Contemporary European History*, IV (1995), No. 2, 133-51.

32 Fidel Miró, *Cataluña, los trabajadores y el problema de las nacionalidades* (Mexico: Editores Mexicanos Unidos, 1967), 66.

triumvirate. While all the 'Three Musketeers' were *cenetistas*, their participation in collective trade union struggles was always secondary to their militancy in the *grupo de afinidad*. Thus, rather than remain in Spain and organize the CNT clandestinely during the Primo de Rivera dictatorship, the 'Three Musketeers', along with many other *grupistas*, opted for exile. Durruti and Ascaso blazed a trail across the South-American sub-continent and Cuba, expropriating banks and assassinating employers *en route*, before briefly coming to a halt with the bulk of the Spanish exiles in Paris.[33] In the French capital Durruti fell heavily under the influence of Sébastian Faure, the guru of individualist Anarchism and a tireless propagandist for the merits of crime. As far as the rest of the uprooted Spanish libertarians were concerned, not only did the experience of Parisian exile enhance their bohemian tendencies but, in the anarchist café society of 1920s Montmartre, where the legend of the anarchist-criminal Bonnot was very much alive, they were exposed to Stirnerist notions of 'individual repossession', a credo that held obvious attractions for the poverty-stricken émigrés. Individualism was also reflected in *Acción*, a sporadic publication produced by exiled Spanish libertarians, which testified to the influence of French anti-collectivist ideologues like Faure and endorsed individualistic methods of struggle.[34]

Following the collapse of the dictatorship in 1930 and the birth of the Second Republic in 1931, the CNT was legalized and the *grupistas* returned from exile. Slowly but inexorably the FAI enhanced its standing inside the CNT, acquiring control of the most important Catalan unions by the end of 1931, before establishing itself as a hegemonic force inside the CNT Comité Nacional in the years immediately before the Civil War. The complex reasons for the rise of the FAI are beyond the scope of this paper. For our purposes, what is most important is the extent to which the ascendancy of the *faístas* gave new currency

33 Paz, *Durruti*, 61-133; Rai Ferrer, *Durruti, 1896-1936* (Barcelona: Planeta, 1985), 59-60; Salvador Cánovas Cervantes, *Durruti y Ascaso: la CNT y la revolución de julio (historia de la revolución española* (Toulouse: CNT, 1945), 10-12.

34 *Acción*, August 1925.

to the traditional *grupo de afinidad* and the tactics of individual action and small group autonomy. While it would be a gross caricature to suggest that the FAI eschewed collective mobilizations — an unlikely scenario given their standing inside the CNT — as I have shown elsewhere, the *faístas* were the architects of an immense outpouring of individualism within the libertarian movement.[35]

The main forum for extreme individualism during the 1930s was *Iniciales*, a monthly journal aimed at 'true individualists, nudists and vegetarians'. Unashamedly Stirnerist in orientation, *Iniciales* applauded the German *philosophe* as 'the killer of lies'.[36] *Iniciales* was highly critical of all organization, from the CNT unions right across to anarchist bodies like the FAI, all of which it regarded as 'dominating and regulatory' units that turned individuals into 'machines'. According to *Iniciales*, only those who freed themselves from the collective discipline of organization could aspire to be 'authentic revolutionaries'. Meanwhile, *Iniciales* drew on the tradition of Bonnot to articulate a comprehensive justification for illegality, advocating violence and robbery by 'the race of the poor' in their 'quest for life' against 'the usurping bandits in power'.[37]

While the doctrinal aversion of the individualists to collective organization meant that they did not express themselves directly through either the CNT or the FAI, a myriad of historical, political and personal ties bound the Stirnerists to the anarchists who constituted the CNT-FAI leadership in the early 1930s. For example, Antonio 'Dionisios' García Birlan, a prominent individualist of the period, was an associate of the Urales clan. Meanwhile, there were numerous comrades of Ascaso, Durruti and García Oliver who championed

35 By early 1932 *faístas* already occupied key positions in the CNT, with Gregorio Jover, Ricardo Sanz and Juan García Oliver on the Comité Nacional, Francisco Ascaso, José Canela, Patricio Navarro and Ramón Porquet on the Catalan Comité Regional and Segundo Martínez as secretary of the Barcelona Federación Local (see chapter 5 of my unpublished doctoral thesis: 'Policing the Recession: Law and Order in Republican Barcelona, 1930-1936', University of London, 1995).

36 For celebrations of Stirner see especially *Iniciales*, August 1929, January-June, December 1935-February 1936.

37 *Iniciales*, August 1929, December 1930, August, December 1931; May 1932; January, April, November 1934; January-May, September 1935.

the individualist-illegalist cause in the 1930s, including Adolfo Ballano, a regular contributor to *Iniciales* and a one-time member of 'Los Solidarios'.[38] These connections ensured that even though the devotees of Stirner represented a minority inside the libertarian movement in the 1930s, almost certainly amounting to no more than two or three hundred activists, they were still in a position to introduce their perspectives on illegality and expropriation into the wider community of *faístas* and, to a lesser, but none the less significant extent, into the ranks of the *cenetistas*. Indeed, the resonance of illegalist-individualistic ideas in the CNT-FAI was disproportionate to the small numbers of Stirnerists. *Tierra y Libertad*, the weekly newspaper of the FAI, keenly embraced the individualist conception of illegality and viewed theft as a subversive act of rebellion, even exhorting crime as a weapon in the class struggle.[39] Meanwhile, when editiorial control of the CNT daily *Solidaridad Obrera* switched to the FAI, the newspaper progressively adopted a quasi-Stirnerist line, validating the individual 'desire' (*querer*) as part of the 'struggle for life', along with 'violent acts of an individual nature' and a wide gamut of illegal activities, including the counterfeiting of money. In a similarly Stirnerist vein, Mariano 'Marianet' Rodríguez Vázquez, a FIJL activist and secretary of the Barcelona CNT Builders' union, declared that armed robbery was both 'anarchist and revolutionary'.[40]

The experience of the 1930s also demonstrated how the individualistic, anti-syndicalist methods adopted by the FAI (and by the FIJL after their creation in 1932) were often the antechamber to an individualism of ends that bore many similarities to Stirner's philosophy of crime and illegality. This

---

38 Ealham, 'Policing the Recession', chapter 6.

39 García Oliver, *El eco de los pasos*, 188; *Tierra y Libertad*, 26 April, 8 May 1931, 9 June, 11 August, 20, 27 October 1933; *FAI*, 8 January 1935.

40 *Solidaridad Obrera*, 22 March, 20 April, 23 June, 10, 26 August, 16, 23 September, 13 October, 9, 23 November, 7 December 1932; 1, 12 January, 11 February, 8, 14, 18, 25 March, 4, 15-16, 18 April, 23 June, 29 July, 14 October 1933; 15, 24, 26 April 1934; 14, 20 February, 1 March, 15 September 1935; *El Luchador*, 7 July 1933. Though, of course, it is difficult to assess the impact of this message on the CNT rank-and-file, it is worth remembering that the membership of the union oscillated between 500,000 and 1,200,000 in the five years before the Civil War.

was borne out by the numerous examples of anarchists who graduated from the *grupos de afinidad* to quasi-Stirnerist positions of extreme individualism. However, these same cases suggest that the correlation between armed illegality and revolutionary activity was not as great as some anarchists actually believed.   One such example was that of Josep Gardenyes, a veteran of the post-World War One *grupos de afinidad*, who in many ways typified the experience of the anarchists of his generation. Having spent much of the 1920s in exile in Argentina, France and Italy, as well as a spell in jail, Gardenyes emerged as a prominent *faísta* in 1931, frequently addressing meetings in Barcelona alongside the 'Three Musketeers' and participating actively in the 'Agrupación Cultural Faros', one of the main anarchist educational groups in the Catalan capital.   Gardenyes also personified the contradictions between individualism and collectivism in the libertarian movement.   In the view of one of his anarchist contemporaries, Gardenyes was representative of 'the extreme bohemia that hung around part of our movement'. Lacking regular employment, Gardenyes became 'unsettled' and 'degenerate', whereafter he was expelled from the 'Agrupación Cultural Faros' as his egoism was judged to be inimical to the wider interests of the movement.   Gardenyes spent the years before the Civil War in jail, after robbing a cyclist of the meagre sum of twenty-five pesetas.[41]

Although the Stirnerist illegalists were often neither *cenetistas* or *faístas*, they were part of what was known as the 'libertarian family' and, as such, they brought growing embarrassment to the CNT-FAI-FIJL leadership. This unease grew following a series of high-profile cases in which workers were killed by individualists.   In 1933 a waiter from the socialist trade union was killed by a 'Union of Egoists' during a robbery at a Barcelona café. Testifying to the bizarre alliances forged by the Stirnerists, the gang included an anarchist printer employed by the Catalan CNT Regional Committee at the

---

41 García Oliver, *El eco de los pasos*, 115-16; Paz, *Durruti*, 67; Léon-Ignacio, *Los años del pistolerismo*, 242, 314; *Tierra y Libertad*, 4 July, 19 September 1931; *La Batalla*, 7 July 1932; Porcel, *La revuelta permanente*, 126-29. By 1930s standards, twenty-five pesetas was approximately equivalent to three days pay for an unskilled building worker.

Solidaridad Obrera printshop and Charles Levesey, an English bourgeois adventurer and the son of a factory owner. The sterility of individualist violence was reaffirmed in December 1934 when Vicente Aranda Sánchez, a twenty-year old anarchist linked to Barcelona's individualist circles, was convicted of the murder of a young shop worker in a badly bungled robbery and executed. That the father of the dead shop worker was a well-known Barcelona anarchist underlined the random nature of individualist violence.[42]

The growing realization that individualistic violence might corrupt militants and compromise the libertarian movement led to a debate inside the CNT-FAI-FIJL on the question of internal discipline and the need to subjugate the individual will to the exigencies of the organization. Sections of the CNT-FAI-FIJL were distraught that the obsession with spontaneous rebellion made some anarchists far too receptive to random violence and acts that were devoid of any constructive revolutionary content. Such concerns merged with anxieties that the relatively unsupervised expansion of the libertarian movement between 1931 and 1934 had allowed 'undesirable elements' and provocateurs to enter the FAI. Other libertarians feared that Stirnerist-criminality could attract recidivists to the CNT-FAI-FIJL who sought to exploit anarchist ideology as a cloak for their traditional lawbreaking.[43]

A consensus emerged within the hierarchy of the CNT-FAI-FIJL that the exponents of 'individual expropriation' were incompatible with the wider struggle for collective revolutionary transformation. Similarly, 'Marianet' condemned both the 'discredit' the Stirnerists brought to the CNT-FAI and their 'individual expropriations', which he denounced as 'nothing more than the transferral of wealth from one set of hands to another, exclusively for personal benefit'. Rather than the

42 Léon-Ignacio, *Los años del pistolerismo*, 314; *La Vanguardia*, 13, 17-18 August 1933; *Las Noticias*, 2 July 1936; Paz, *Durruti*, 67; *La Vanguardia*, 30 June 1934; *Las Noticias*, 2 July 1936; Chris Ealham, 'Crime and Punishment in 1930s Barcelona', *History Today* (October 1993), 31-37; *La Vanguardia, Las Noticias, La Veu de Catalunya*, 18-22 December 1934.

43 José Luis Gutiérrez Molina, *La idea revolucionaria. El anarquismo organizado en Andalucía y Cádiz durante los años treinta* (Madrid: Madre Tierra, 1993), pp. 65, 77; Pérez Baró, *Els 'Feliços' anys vint*, 87.

agents of liberation, 'Marianet' maintained that an 'abyss' separated the individualists from the anarchist goal of 'general, not individual well-being' and 'collective expropriation'. Similarly, Germinal Esgleas, who had himself been very close to some of the Stirnerists, launched a stern attack on the 'mistaken policy' of his former individualist allies, whom he accused of 'confusing rebellion with terrorism'. Reiterating what he saw as true anarchist morality, Esgleas advocated an 'attack' to 'root out' the individualists, because their acts 'have nothing to do with anarchist doctrine', which aspires to 'the highest of human values', not 'professional banditry'. Finally, in the summer of 1935, a debate on the 'crime epidemic' at a clandestine plenum of the Federación Local de Grupos Anarquistas de Barcelona culminated in a resolution to control the behaviour of anarchist militants by prohibiting individualist criminality.[44]

Civil War, Revolution and the 'Uncontrollables'

The outbreak of Civil War the following year dispelled any illusions within the CNT-FAI-FIJL leadership that the problem of internal control was resolved. When the old state collapsed under the impact of the military coup, the power vacuum in the Republican zone was largely filled by the trade unions. Power lay in the streets of Republican Spain. In Catalonia, the CNT-FAI-FIJL was hegemonic and anarchist militants believed their odyssey was over: their revolution had begun.

Yet the limitations of the 1936 revolution quickly became apparent. Inspired by their libertarian, anti-statist doctrine, the CNT-FAI-FIJL believed that revolution and authority were mutually incompatible. On the streets of Barcelona, the old police force was replaced by revolutionary *patrulles de control*, a seven hundred strong force comprised of all pro-Republican forces, half of whom were recruited from the CNT-FAI-FIJL.[45] But there was no truly revolutionary order and the revolution

---

44 *Solidaridad Obrera*, 18 August 1933, 26 April, 14 July 1934; *La Revista Blanca*, 4 January, 10 May 1935; Paz, *Durruti*, 311-14.

45 Josep Maria Huertas Claveria, *Obrers a Catalunya. Manual d'història del moviment obrer (1840-1975)* (Barcelona: L'Avenç, 1994), 288.

was not given political expression. Thus, while many of the factories and fields of Republican Spain were transformed by socializing and collectivizing economic experiments, the absence of new juridico-political institutions meant that the revolution remained inchoate, unstructured and without order. The lack of co-ordination between the various revolutionary forces resulted in a damaging organizational rivalry, a competition described by the anti-Stalinist Communists of the Partido Obrero de Unificación Marxista (POUM) as 'trade union capitalism'. This failure to foster a new state power constituted the Achilles Heel of the revolution in the Republican zone.[46]

Nowhere was this more vividly seen than in the case of the 'incontrolats'. From the beginning of the Civil War there were complaints in many areas in the Republican zone that 'uncontrollable' elements, apparently beyond the control of all political and syndical organizations, were taking advantage of the collapse of authority to embark on a wave of killings and robberies for their own individual benefit. While it is unfair to attribute all the activities of the 'incontrolats' to the anarchists, there was much evidence to connect them to the libertarian movement. In Catalonia 'incontrolats' were inside the *patrulles de control*, which they used as a cover to perpetrate a series of assassinations and robberies. The anarchists also condemned acts of robbery and pillage by 'uncontrollable' groups of 'undesirables' and 'habitual criminals' in the militias at the battle-front.[47]

Increasingly, problems of individual responsibility and internal control came to dominate the perspectives of the CNT-FAI-FIJL leadership. On 24 July, just a week after the beginning of the Civil War, *Solidaridad Obrera* warned against acts of robbery and other 'criminal outrages', claiming that

---

46   *La Batalla*, 6 December 1936; 9, 28 January, 17, 27 February, 18 March 1937.

47   Joan Llarch, *La muerte de Durruti* (Barcelona: Plaza y Janés, 1985), 97-98, 102; Abel Paz, *Crónica de la Columna de Ferro* (Barcelona: Hacer, 1984), *passim*; Josep Maria Solé i Sabaté and Joan Villarroya i Font, *La repressió a la reraguarda de Catalunya, 1936-1939* (Barcelona: Publicacions de l'Abadia de Montserrat, 1989), I, 59-81; *Diari de Barcelona*, 1, 25 and 27 August 1936; *Treball*, 1-2 August 1936; *La Rambla*, 25 August 1936; *La Humanitat*, 26 August 1936.

'individual or group terrorist action leads to the failure of the worker organization which practises it'. The CNT also appealed to 'revolutionary honour' and implored its militants not to succumb to egotistical individual desires 'prejudicial to the interests of the labouring class'. Yet there was no respite in the activities of the 'incontrolats' and the same week the CNT-FAI-FIJL announced on 'Radio Barcelona' that they had formed 'special patrols' to defend 'civic order' and repress those who were 'staining the triumph with pillage'. However, it soon emerged that these same acts of 'pillage' were being perpetrated by members of the CNT-FAI patrols. Finally, aware that the 'monstrous irresponsibility' of 'groups of thoughtless people (*inconscientes*), outside the control of our movement' might 'discredit our organization' and undermine the credibility of the revolution, on 30 July a FAI manifesto gave notice that 'we will shoot any individual' perpetrating 'acts counterposed to the anarchist spirit'.[48]

But there was no single 'anarchist spirit' and Spanish Anarchism was as convoluted as it was kaleidoscopic. For instance, Joan Peiró, a leading anarcho-syndicalist and also a longstanding member of a FAI-affiliated *grupo de afinidad*, rallied tirelessly against the 'incontrolats', whom he regarded as 'the worst enemies of the people and of the revolution'. In a series of newspaper articles on 'revolutionary dignity', Peiró berated 'the materialism of individuals far more immoral than the bourgeoisie and the capitalists', maintaining that 'revolutions are made by the people for the people, not for the enjoyment of specific individuals ... Robbers and thieves have never honoured a revolution. On the contrary, they have always been the dishonour of every revolution'. With the Stirnerists in mind, Peiró observed that 'if revolutions consisted of robbing and killing people, robbers and professional killers would be the greatest revolutionaries'.[49]

What for Peiró was the object of outrage, represented for the Stirnerists the greatest established truth. The traditional receptiveness of recidivists by a section of the 'anarchist family',

---

48 *Solidaridad Obrera*, 24 and 30 July, 1936; Peirats, *La CNT*, I, 173.
49 Joan Peiró, *Perill a la reraguarda* (Mataró: Edicions Llibertat, 1936), pp. xvii, 41, 127-33.

coupled with the excessive faith in individual action which characterized Spanish libertarianism, precluded a cessation of the antics of the 'incontrolats'. Indeed, they responded with a threat to 'eliminate' the 'renegade' Peiró. Increasingly, the rift within the CNT-FAI-FIJL between the proponents of collective struggle and the advocates of ultra-individualism seemed set to spill over into violence and endanger both the revolution and the fight against Franco. Consequently, the CNT-FAI-FIJL hierarchy moved against those it described as the 'partisans of destruction for destruction's sake' and between 1936 and 1937 several Stirnerists, individualist-anarchists and veterans of the libertarian *grupos de afinidad* involved in robbery, murder and extortion were 'cleansed', including a group of 'incontrolats' headed by Gardenyes, the militant whose ultra-individualism led to his expulsion from the CNT in the years preceding the Civil War.[50] However, the fact that many of the 'incontrolats' emanated from the CNT-FAI-FIJL meant that all the while the anarchists enjoyed hegemony over the revolution, the activities of the 'uncontrollables' were unlikely to disappear completely.

The Shadow of the Counter-Revolution

Like the anarchists, the POUM argued that the 'incontrolats' and those who 'acted autonomously for their own interest and profit' were 'the enemies of the revolution', because their 'adventurism' and 'acts of banditry go against the credit of the revolutionary order'. However, in keeping with their revolutionary communist principles, the POUM located the 'incontrolats' in the context of the failure of the anti-statist libertarians to establish a revolutionary order on the ashes of the old state. Moreover, the POUM warned that the existence of the 'incontrolats' provided the enemies of the revolution, both

---

50 Benjamin Martin, *The Agony of Modernization. Labor and Industrialization in Spain* (Ithaca: ILR Press, 1990), 385; Peiró, *Perill*, 20; *La Batalla*, 31 July 1936; *Solidaridad Obrera*, 9, 24 and 30 July 1936; Juan García Oliver, *El eco de los pasos*, 229-31; Llarch, *La muerte de Durruti*, 24; Portel, *La revuelta permanente*, 129-30. Gardenyes and his comrades, who were caught by the FAI stealing jewels from a flat, were described by Peirats as 'de historial y martirio revolucionario, pero que fueron incapaces de superar un momento de confusión y de debilidad' (*La CNT*, I, 175).

in the Republican and in the Francoist zones, with a platform for eroding the social transformation enacted after July 1936. Thus, the POUM reasoned, the term 'uncontrollable' might become a by-word for all 'revolutionaries who resolutely defend their ideas, particularly when they go against the current'.[51]

This, indeed, is what occurred, for alongside the CNT-FAI-FIJL, the POUM represented a minority in the revolutionary camp and their project of a revolutionary state capable of spearheading the constructive task of social transformation, fighting the Civil War and repressing the activities of the 'incontrolats' was doomed to obscurity. Instead, the growing clamour to 'discipline' the 'incontrolats' was exploited by the middle-class Republicans and the official Communists of the Partido Comunista de España (PCE) and the Partit Socialista Unificat de Catalunya (PSUC), all of whom wished to curtail the post-July 1936 revolutionary changes and strengthen the old Republican state. To this end, the 'irresponsible activities' of the 'incontrolats' endowed the enemies of the revolution in the Republican zone with a pretext to erode the enormous prestige of the revolutionary project among large sectors of the Republican camp, restore the old sources of authority and curb the inchoate power of the *patrulles de control* and the workers' militias. This was most clearly seen in the propaganda line developed by the Republicans and official Communists, based on the caricature of the 'incontrolats' as crypto-Fascist 'provocateurs in the pay of Italo-German Fascism', the 'unconscious tools of Fascism' bent on smashing inter-class 'anti-Fascist unity' and the alliance that existed between Republican Spain and Soviet Russia in the war against Franco. It followed, therefore, that all those who refused to endorse the Civil-War strategy advanced by the Republican-Communist bloc came to be viewed as 'tacitly assisting our enemies', 'enemies of the people' and 'scum' which it proved necessary to 'eliminate' in order to guarantee victory against Franco. Increasingly, the concept of the 'incontrolat' became consubstantial with the

---

51 *La Batalla*, 31 December 1936 and 13 March 1937.

stereotypical view of the 'petit-bourgeois anarchist-deviationist' or 'Trotskyist-Fascist wreckers'.[52]

The official Communists publicly justified their assault on the bastions of revolutionary power in terms of the drive against the 'incontrolats'. Ironically, therefore, the drive against the 'uncontrollables' served as a justification for the 'controlled' provocations of the PCE and the PSUC against their left-wing and revolutionary rivals, particularly the anti-Stalinist Communists of the POUM. Yet it is striking that the political expediency of the identification of the 'uncontrollables' with the revolutionary organizations ignored the numerous cases of murder by 'uncontrollables' in the central area of the Republican zone, where the revolution was least developed and where both the anarchists and the POUM had very few followers. Indeed, according to Benjamin Martin, 'anarchists and *cenetistas* have received a disproportionate amount of blame for the "red terror" '. Moreover, while it is indisputable that the pseudo-revolutionary violence of the 'incontrolats' directed at small businessmen and landowners contributed greatly to the alienation of the Republican middle class, the 'incontrolats' were not responsible for the bulk of the discord in the Republican zone. Instead, the focus on anarchist and POUM 'incontrolats' ignores the 'controlled' campaign of provocation of the PCE and the PSUC against the revolutionary organizations, which culminated in the so-called 'civil war within the Civil War' of May 1937, when the anti-Francoist unity of the Republican camp was broken in order to curb the power of the revolutionary forces.[53]

---

52 Manuel Valldeperes, *Els perills de la reraguarda* (Barcelona: Forja, 1937), pp. 7-10, 23, 25-26, 28; *Treball*, 30 September and 20 November 1936; *La Humanitat*, 2 October and 28 November 1936; *Mundo Obrero*, 14 December 1936.

53 Martin, *The Agony of Modernization*, 384; *La Humanitat*, 31 July 1936; *Diari de Barcelona*, 1 August 1936; *Treball*, 15 August and 20 October 1936; Manuel Cruells, *La societat catalana durant la guerra civil. Crònica d'un periodista polític* (Barcelona: Edhasa, 1978), 73-84; Fundación Andreu Nin, *Los sucesos de mayo de 1937. Una revolución en la República* (Barcelona: Libros Pandora, 1988), *passim*; Manuel Cruells, *Els Fets de Maig. Barcelona 1937* (Barcelona: Editorial Joventut, 1970), 19-125.

Conclusion

To conclude, the period of Revolution and Civil War laid bare numerous contradictions within the Spanish anarchist movement, particularly the inability of the movement to develop an adequate strategy of revolutionary change and the fact that the nature of its proposed social transformation was ill-defined. Also contradictory was the relationship between the individual and collective responsibilities of the anarchist militant. These contradictions had largely been ignored by libertarian theoreticians in the preceding thirty years, the net result of which was that Anarchism destroyed more than it built during the Civil War. The 'incontrolats' were the most notorious example of this process of destruction.

If the chaos of Civil War allowed the 'incontrolats' to come to the fore, their origins are inextricably linked to the development of Iberian libertarianism and the unresolved tensions between the philosophical individualism of Anarchism and the practical collectivism of Anarcho-syndicalism, on the one hand, and the dichotomies of illegality and legality, on the other. The libertarians trusted disproportionately in the vitality, passion and initiative of their militants. At times, this lent itself to an extreme hedonism or epicureanism which, in practical terms, made it difficult for militants to subjugate their own personal quest to satisfy their desires and aspirations to the broader requirements of the movement. This excessive individualism of anarchist ideology proved utterly impervious to notions of 'party discipline' and engendered a culture of indiscipline within the libertarian movement which did not exist inside the Communist parties, whether official or dissident.

This same emphasis on individual will also provided a suitable cover for the individuals who made up the 'incontrolats' and exaggerated the transforming powers of illegalism. In a certain sense, as the harbingers of a new socio-juridico-economic order, all revolutionaries are, *ipso facto*, outside the laws of bourgeois society. However, some anarchists took this truism as evidence that all those outside the law were revolutionary or, at least, nascent rebels. This was especially the case with the followers of the individualist-illegalist ideas of Stirner.

Yet while all Spanish anarchist trends had an individualistic conception at their heart, all individualism did not possess an anarchist essence. Indeed, at a certain point, individualism became inconsistent — anathema in the Stirnerist variant — to the formal anarchist goal of equality. The experience of the 1930s and earlier confirmed that the Stirnerists were inadequate revolutionaries. Nevertheless, Stirnerist ethics were also present within the cardinal tenets of Iberian Anarchism and, according to Ángel Pestaña, a prominent Spanish anarcho-syndicalist, the belief that universal human emancipation would arrive through the sacrifice of the lone avenger allowed Stirnerism to draw on old Spanish anarchist traditions of the 'myth of individual terror'.[54] In the Civil War, these traditions were instrumental in the fall of the CNT-FAI-FIJL, described by one militant as the descent 'from the summit into the abyss'.[55]

---

[54] Ángel Pestaña, *Lo que aprendí en la vida* (Bilbao: ZYX, 1973), II, 63-64.

[55] Ramón Liarte, *El camino de la libertad* (Barcelona: Ediciones Picazo, 1983), 239.

7

War, Modernity and Reform: The Premiership of Juan Negrín 1937-1939

HELEN GRAHAM

In his wartime political objectives as in his earlier academic and intellectual ones,[1] Juan Negrín was a liberal reformer in the tradition of the secularist, elitist and modernizing Institución Libre de Enseñanza.[2] He was born the same year as Franco, in

---

1 University educated in Germany, where he also joined the SPD youth movement, Negrín was clearly a man of formidable intellect. At the age of twenty (in 1912) he received his medical doctorate, (to which he then added another in physiology) thereafter continuing research work in Germany for almost five years. Returning to Spain during the First World War, he ran a laboratory in Madrid's prestigious Residencia de Estudiantes — whose intellectual and artistic élite epitomized the liberal values of the Institución Libre de Enseñanza (see note 2). (A co-*Residente* of Negrín's was Marcelino Pascua, also a medical doctor, who would later occupy the Republic's most crucial wartime ambassadorial post in Moscow.) In 1922, at the age of thirty, Negrín was appointed via the competitive examination of *oposiciones* to the Chair of Physiology at Madrid University. Having joined the PSOE in 1929, he was elected in 1931 as parliamentary deputy for Las Palmas. By 1934 his political commitments (largely in technical committee work) meant Negrín had virtually ceased research work and he would soon also request leave of absence (*excedencia*) from his professorship, thus ceasing to teach. He remained, however, a prime mover of the new University City. As secretary of its development committee from 1931, Negrín invested much unpaid time and his considerable organizational and creative skills in this project. The biographical material on Negrín is rather sparse, but see Santiago Álvarez's biography, *Negrín, personalidad histórica*, 2 vols inc. documents (Madrid: Ediciones de la Torre, 1994); M. Ansó, *Yo fui ministro de Negrín* (Barcelona: Planeta, 1976); J. Llarch, *Negrín ¡Resistir es vencer!* (Barcelona: Planeta, 1985); J. Marichal, 'Juan Negrín. El científico como gobernante', in J. Marichal, *El intelectual y la política* (Madrid: C.S.I.C., 1990).

2 The Institución Libre de Enseñanza [Institute of Independent Education] was founded in Madrid in 1876 by liberal educationalists and

1892, to one of the more conservative families of the Canarian bourgeoisie in Las Palmas de Gran Canaria. But Negrín and Franco epitomized diametrically opposed generational responses to the process of socio-political change which crystalized in Spain with the 1898 imperial collapse and accelerated under the impact of the First World War. While most of the collective responses to this flux had in common an understanding of the centrality of a strong state to Spain's future national development, they would produce entirely different conceptions of the national project which would make and sustain it. Negrín was culturally eclectic, secular/rationalist (though not anticlerical — his brother and sister both entered religious orders), educated extensively abroad (he spent more than eight years in Germany) and extremely well read. In terms of both temperament and experience[3] he could not have been further from the cultural milieux which had formed the rebel military leadership and their civilian backers: the closed world of the barracks and the brutal physical binaries of the colonial campaigns in Morocco had forged a brand of warrior nationalism and a myth of imperial rebirth which were then reinforced by the cultural/intellectual manichaeism of the ultra-Nationalist [casticista[4]] right.

Negrín believed in a classically liberal, 'inclusive' view of the nation state, predicated on a crucial widening of educational access to which he was committed as the key to the social,

---

university teachers — most notably Francisco Giner de los Ríos. Its aim was to provide a non-official, secular education — freed of Catholic dogma — which would nurture the élite needed to modernize Spain.

    3   On Negrín's eclecticism, see Asturian Socialist Teodomiro Menéndez's comment in Marichal, 'Juan Negrín', 89 (see also n. 1 above).

    4   *Casticista*: the adjective derives from *casticismo*, an inward-looking and often intolerant brand of cultural nationalism associated with the Castilian tradition. The term became current in the late nineteenth century, popularized by the writers and thinkers of the Generation of 1898. With its strong racial overtones (*casta*), it was assimilated into Francoist ideology to justify Castilian dominance in the state-making process by presenting Castilian traditions as the most 'typically [i.e. purely] Spanish'.

economic, political and cultural modernization of Spain.[5]   By
the 1930s, however, this integral liberal vision was coming
under great stress across Europe as a vast crisis visibly split
the economic interests of capital from the beliefs and value
systems of political/cultural liberalism: economic retrenchment
was scarcely compatible with the sustained funding of social
reform on which integral liberalism was predicated.   The
Republic under Negrín would fight to defend an integral liberal
project.   But the needs of the war effort, especially one
sustained in conditions of such material inferiority, magnified
the contradictions inherent in that liberal vision — between the
need for a strong state and the belief in a democratically co-
opted nation.

As a liberal and *institucionista*, Negrín's vision of a modern
Spain was neither anti-capitalist nor radically egalitarian in the
social or cultural sense.   His entry into the Spanish Socialist
Party (PSOE) — comparatively late, in 1929 when he was thirty
seven — was not because of any affinity with its proclaimed
classist doctrine but because he saw the party (on the evidence
of its organizational potential and a reformist practice
significantly at odds with that doctrine) as the best instrument
for achieving a liberal reform of Spain's society and polity by
opening her up to liberal European currents and ideas.[6]   In
practice, the PSOE was a moderate social democratic party
which sought power by legal means in order to implement a
welfarist agenda of social and economic reform.[7]   In order to
achieve this a thoroughgoing modernization of the state would
be necessary.   This was the goal with which the parliamentary

---

5   Negrín's newspaper article 'La democratización de la Universidad', in
El Socialista, 28 May 1929, cited in J. Marichal, 'Juan Negrín', 88, as his only
non-medical publication in the pre-war period.

6   *Cf.* the philosophy of the Institución Libre and note that Negrín
advised his students, researchers and colleagues to read the works of
European and other foreign scholars and specialists in their own field (S.
Álvarez, *Negrín, personalidad histórica*, I, 25).

7   *Cf.* Luis Araquistain's comment (before his move into the left Socialist
orbit), that the Socialists had given up their ideal socialist city for that of the
Republicans, cited in Enrique Montero, 'Reform Idealized: The Intellectual
and Ideological Origins of the Second Republic', in *Spanish Cultural Studies:
An Introduction.   The Struggle for Modernity*, ed. Helen Graham and Jo
Labanyi (Oxford: Oxford U. P., 1995), 131.

Socialist Party increasingly identified after the Second Republic was established in April 1931. Probably its most resonant public articulation came in 'La conquista interior de España', the speech delivered at Cuenca in May 1936 by Negrín's then close friend and colleague, the Socialist leader, Indalecio Prieto. In it he exhorted progressive Spaniards to return to the long-standing challenge, the 'interior conquest' of their country — in other words, it was time to abandon revolutionary attempts as unviable (the conclusion Prieto drew from the outcome of the Asturian uprising in October 1934) and return to the task of institutional and social reform. The Cuenca speech perfectly expressed Negrín's own outlook and objectives.

However by 1936 the Socialist movement was seriously divided over the issue of PSOE collaboration in government. In the face of the union-led Left's threats to split ranks, the parliamentary party relinquished its opportunity to enter government and bolster the Republican state in its hour of crisis as support for military sedition spread among the junior officer class. The fear — predominantly Prieto's — of formally splitting the Socialist movement paralysed the party at what was a crucial moment in May 1936. Negrín, who then, as later, viewed the PSOE as a political instrument rather than an end or value in itself, argued, probably more passionately than anyone else, that the party Left was ideologically and strategically bankrupt and that Prieto should thus call its bluff.[8] He did not and his failure of political will which kept the PSOE out of power caused irreparable damage to the Republican project. For whatever the obstacles might have been to defusing the military bomb prior to the coup, they were infinitely less than those which stood in the way of a Republican victory once the war was unleashed.[9] This realization would

---

8   Julián Zugazagoitia, *Guerra y vicisitudes de los españoles* (Barcelona: Editorial Crítica [Grijalbo], 1977), 23-24. *Cf.* also M. Pascua, in S. Álvarez, *Negrín. (Documentos)*, 278. In a sense this option was what Negrín was defending at the Ecija meeting (Seville) when he acted as one of Prieto's armed 'minders' against the violent anger of Socialist youth members and other southern federation Socialists who supported the Left.

9   Inevitably these memories, compounded by the pressures of a war effort continuously waged against the odds, would in the end contribute enormously to the growing estrangement of Prieto and Negrín by mid 1938

have a corrosive effect on the PSOE leadership during the war which intensified Negrín's prime ministerial isolation.[10]

The military rising of 17-18 July 1936 released powerful centrifugal forces which dislocated the fragile apparatus of the state.   In the spaces thus opened up, the popular classes' accumulated experience of direct action and a culture from which the *idea* of the state was very often absent generated many local initiatives to reorganize village or neighbourhood environments which for a time implicitly challenged the existing structure of property.

Negrín was a liberal who believed in the consubstantiality of civil and property rights.   Accordingly, he saw the situation which emerged from the July Days not as an embryonic revolutionary-egalitarian order sustained by the constructive power of the people's will and its genius for improvisation, but as a violent and arbitrary deployment of power consequent on the fragmentation of the state and the collapse of constitutional authority.   As he saw it, the party and union committees which had sprung up to deal, sometimes well and sometimes badly, with the immediate needs of Republican defence, were illegitimate precisely because their power was subject to no constitutional control.   The Republic was also losing vital international credibility as policy makers in the democracies fixed, inevitably if somewhat unfairly (since it was the product of a military coup) on this state of affairs .

To Negrín's mind, moreover, a fragmented state would never possess the resources to defeat its opponents — either within the Republican zone (from social constituencies resisting the process of 'nationalization' accelerating since April 1931, or from an ideological 'fifth column') or those across the lines fighting for a different form of national community.   The Republican state had to be forged in order to win the war, while

---

which further undermined the coherence of the Socialist movement.   A fuller analysis will be provided in my forthcoming book on the Spanish Republic at War 1936-39 (Cambridge: Cambridge U. P., 1997).

   10   For Negrín it was like 'communing with the Void', Gabriel Morón's comment, cited in Helen Graham, *Socialism and War. The Spanish Socialist Party in Power and Crisis 1936-1939* (Cambridge: Cambridge U. P., 1991), 107-08 and *cf.* Fernando Vázquez Ocaña, *Pasión y muerte de la segunda República española* (Ed. Norte, n.d., n.p.; preface, Paris, 1940), *passim.*

the war justified the central liberal state's recuperation of political power and material resources annexed by labour unions, proletarian cantonalists and bourgeois regionalists in the wake of the July rising.[11] The liberal constitutional order integral to this centralizing project was a means of legitimizing Republican state authority. The function of the state was to reorder economic and cultural hierarchy in order to facilitate, in the immediate term, the urgent task of mass mobilization (or 'nationalization') for the war effort, while in the medium term allowing the implementation of reforms compatible with capitalist property relations. If Manuel Azaña had once commented that the Republic began and ended with the state, it was equally the case that the 'historic republicans' in Spain remained notoriously and inveterately incapable of turning their goals into realizable policies.[12] Negrín, on the other hand, was the outstanding politician of the Republican era whose endeavours began to turn that abstraction into a material reality.

This state-building goal was evident in Negrín long before his arrival at the premiership in May 1937. Believing as he did in the idea of a 'rational' or 'guardian' state, Negrín had no interest in parliament as oratorical arena which derived from Mediterranean-clientelist practice. From the beginning, when Negrín had first been elected to the Republican Cortes in 1931, he had committed himself to the technical, behind-the-scenes

11   It is difficult to convey the sheer tangibility of the idea of the state in Negrín, see, e.g., instances in F. Vázquez Ocaña, *Pasión y muerte de la segunda República española*, 59, also his article in S. Álvarez, *Negrín (documentos)*, 252-53; Gil Mugarza, *España en llamas 1936* (Barcelona: Acervo, 1968), 537 (also cited in J. M. García Escudero, *Historia política de las dos Españas* [Madrid: Editora Nacional, 1976], 1745); F. Largo Caballero, 'Notas históricas de la guerra en España 1917-1940' (unpublished manuscript, Madrid: Fundación Pablo Iglesias), 986.

12   Discussed in Helen Graham, 'Community, State and Nation in Republican Spain 1931-38', in *Nationalism and National Identity in the Iberian Peninsula*, ed. A. Smith and C. Mar-Molinero (Oxford: Berg, forthcoming 1996); see also J. M. Macarro Vera, 'Social and Economic Policies of the Spanish Left in Theory and Practice', in *The French and Spanish Popular Fronts. Comparative Perspectives*, ed. M. S. Alexander and H. Graham (Cambridge: Cambridge U. P., 1989) and, for the pre-1930s, Pamela Radcliff, *Politics, Culture and Collective Action in a Spanish City: 1900-1937* (Cambridge: Cambridge U. P., forthcoming 1996).

work in parliamentary committee. (He was a member of the treasury budgets committee.)   In terms of both Negrín's personality and political objectives, he was more concerned with renovating, with establishing underlying structures in order to make things work.[13]

Negrín's experience from the very first stages of the war galvanized his understanding of the need for political and military authority to be concentrated.   When not engaged directly, along with his parliamentary Socialist colleagues, in the task of holding the remnants of government fabric together from the presidential office or navy/air ministry in Madrid, Negrín was to be found observing the Republican military defence at first hand on the Guadarrama sierra, often in far from secure conditions.[14]   Then, from 4 September 1936, as a reluctant Treasury Minister in the Cabinets of the veteran Socialist union leader, Francisco Largo Caballero, Negrín's jurisdictional clashes with the union and neighbourhood committees of the capital were constant in matters of resource-control and supply.[15]

Negrín had accepted the treasury post, at Prieto's behest, as part of the PSOE national executive's team in the new cabinet. Like his parliamentary Socialist colleagues, Negrín had a very low opinion both of Largo's leadership capacity and of the general political calibre and organizational abilities of the PSOE Left which backed the veteran union politician.[16]   The Left's role in helping block PSOE access to the Cabinet in May

---

13 Even as wartime premier, Negrín was not very 'visible'. There are very few photographs since he actively discouraged them. Even the grave in which he was buried in November 1956 in Père Lachaise (Paris) bore no name.

14 Mariano Ansó, *Yo fui ministro de Negrín*, 140; also Marcelino Pascua, cited in S. Álvarez, *Negrín, (Documentos)*, 280; J. Zugazagoitia, *Guerra y vicisitudes*, 122-23.

15 F. Vázquez Ocaña, *Pasión y muerte de la segunda República española*, 59. On Negrín's reluctance see J. Zugazagoitia, *Guerra y vicisitudes*, 154-55, confirmed by Negrín in his speech to the Cortes, 30 September 1938 (Valencia: Ediciones Españolas, 1938), 4, and in the *Epistolario Prieto y Negrín. Puntos de vista sobre el desarrollo y consecuencias de la guerra civil española* (Paris: Imprimerie Nouvelle, 1939), 40.

16 The negative attitude was mutual. For Largo's hostility to Negrín, and for Negrín's sense of party discipline ('estoy con mi partido hasta en sus errores'), see H. Graham, *Socialism and War*, 93-94; *Epistolario Prieto y Negrín*, 40-41.

1936 was the issue which had finally broken, *de facto*, the organizational unity of the Socialist movement.[17] But the party view of its 'left' as an ideologically bankrupt if organizationally highly disruptive element had been growing since the failed October 1934 rising.   Then, the Madrid-based Left's self-proclaimed revolutionary will had vanished into air.   Nor, in spite of much radical rhetoric over the next two years, did the Left ever produce a tangible policy line of its own, much less one capable of building the power structures necessary to orchestrate the anti-capitalist revolution whose imminence it proclaimed.   As Negrín, Prieto and their colleagues well understood, it was the radical mood of the proletarian militia (who had faced down the military rebels in July) and *their* perception of what Largo Caballero and the party left stood for (above all no temporizing with the conspirators) which had determined its central position in the September cabinet.[18] Indeed Negrín's remark on hearing that Largo was to form a government — that it was the victory of October 1934 and worse than if the Nationalists had taken Getafe (the military airfield near Madrid) — should be understood more as a criticism of the Left's political mediocrity and strategic bankruptcy than as an expression of trepidation about its radical policy potential.[19]   (Negrín was also very concerned of course about the negative impression the new government line-up would have on Western government/policy-making opinion internationally.)

With the union-identified Socialist Left holding the core of the Cabinet — premiership and defence, interior and foreign

---

17 H. Graham, *Socialism and War*, 34-41 and 'The Eclipse of the Socialist Left 1934-1937', in *Elites and Power in Twentieth-Century Spain*, ed. F. Lannon and P. Preston (Oxford: Clarendon Press, 1990), 134-39.

18 H. Graham, *Socialism and War*, 55-59 (esp. p. 56) and 'Spain 1936. Resistance and Revolution: The Flaws in the Front', in *Community, Authority and Resistance to Fascism in Europe*, ed. Tim Kirk and Tony McElligott (Cambridge: Cambridge U. P., forthcoming 1996).

19 *Cf.* also Pascua's comments in S. Álvarez, *Negrín (Documentos)*, 278, 281; J. Zugazagoitia, *Guerra y vicisitudes*, 154. The Socialist Left's ideological sterility and strategic bankruptcy were nowhere clearer than in the procedural techniques through which they chose to continue waging the civil war inside the Socialist Party while the Republic itself was fighting for its life (H. Graham, *Socialism and War, passim*).

affairs,[20] Negrín saw himself as an embattled outpost of orderly government amid a tide of deadly, if well intentioned, disorganization and inefficiency. He knew he held a portfolio which was absolutely crucial to the survival of a Republic struggling under the crushing weight of the economic embargo maintained by the Western capitalist democracies (an iceberg of which the specific diplomacy of Non-Intervention was only the tip).

In this context, it was clearly imperative that the Republic secure its gold reserves in a place where they could readily be converted to meet war needs.   In the event, fears that Republican financial resources located in the Western capitalist sector would be blocked, plus signs of Soviet preparedness to aid the Republic in order to prevent its immediate military defeat, meant that dispatching the gold reserves to the Soviet Union became the most viable option. The (inevitably secret) decree to mobilize the gold reserves was one of the last made by José Giral's all-republican Cabinet on 30 August 1936 before it gave way to Largo Caballero's — as a consequence of having been eroded both by Republicanism's temporizing with the rebels and by military and public order disasters.[21] What this meant, as Ángel Viñas clarifies in his definitive study of the gold's shipment,[22] is that the Republican authorities — including the administration of the Bank of Spain, for all that the individual loyalty of many of its high-ranking functionaries was ambiguous — had *already* taken on board that the course of the war — with the rebels targeting Madrid — required the rapid mobilization of its major convertible resources in order to ensure the Republic had the means of waging war. With the arrival of Largo's new Cabinet at this moment, it then fell to Juan Negrín, as the new Treasury Minister, formally to oversee the transfer of the gold. His role, then, was as an executor of

---

20 Although there was really no coherence at all at this 'core' (H. Graham, *Socialism and War*, 78-79, 82-83, 167-97).

21 Most notably the massacre in the Cárcel Modelo on 23 August 1936 (J. Zugazagoitia, *Guerra y vicisitudes*, 128-31; Hugh Thomas, *The Spanish Civil War* [Harmondsworth: Pelican, 1977], 404).

22 *El Oro de Moscú. Alfa y omega de un mito franquista* (Barcelona: Grijalbo, 1979).

existing government policy not as its formulator.[23] Moreover, Negrín's punctiliousness in ensuring that each stage of the transfer was carefully documented, stands in contrast to Largo's own irritation at these safeguards, underscoring Negrín's own highly developed sense of the great responsibility incumbent on those serving the state.[24]

From his treasury post, and later from the premiership,[25] Negrín was working for the re-establishment of an orthodox capitalist economic order but, above all, for economic centralization as a crucial plank in consolidating state power.[26] He began by overhauling the structure and technical working of the treasury itself, although there was a continuity of personnel — the ministry staff being chiefly republican technocrats and senior state functionaries.[27] Negrín's reform of the *carabineros* (customs and frontiers police) — by making them directly responsible to himself as minister and then using them to eject party and union control committees from possession of border posts — tightened central control over foreign exchange. This policy was clearly inspired by a political agenda — the consolidation of the bourgeois state — which also explains the

---

23 *Cf.* Ángel Viñas, *El Oro de Moscú*, 51-55; J. S. Vidarte, *Todos fuimos culpables* (Barcelona: Grijalbo, 1977), 536-39. The kind of fantasy of 'Negrín's treason' recounted in books like *Chantaje a un pueblo* (Madrid: Toro, 1974) by veteran Valencia Socialist and Caballero-supporter, Justo Martínez Amutio, (see p. 42) are scarcely worth refuting since the evidence is so clearly against them. But Marcelino Pascua's withering assessment rings true — that it was an empty, scandal-mongering book in which the author attempted to substantiate his claims by the old trick of presenting himself as something he never was — part of the inner circle of Republican policy makers, Pascua to Viñas, 13 February 1977 (point 6), caja 8 (13), Pascua's personal archive (Archivo Histórico Nacional, Madrid).

24 J. Zugazagoitia, *Guerra y vicisitudes*, 301.

25 Although Negrín's close collaborator, the Left Republican Francisco Méndez Aspe, formally took over the treasury portfolio in April 1938 when Negrín acquired the defence ministry in addition to the premiership, in fact Negrín himself continued to be responsible for the Republic's economic policy until the end of the war.

26 Negrín's treasury work represented his larger goal of putting the state 'back on track' in microcosmic form — *cf.* his hatred of the 'arbitrary spirit' of the July days (F. Vázquez Ocaña, *Pasión y muerte de la segunda República española*, 59-60).

27 Names and details in F. Vázquez Ocaña, *Pasión y muerte de la segunda República española*, 61.

concomitant process of gradually imposing state control over socialized industries. But it is also certain that this sort of economic concentration was as crucial as the militarization of the militia in sustaining the kind of long defensive war imposed upon the Republic by Non-Intervention and arms embargo. Militarization was part of the same state-building agenda of course. But it is worth underlining the obvious point: the Republic had no option but to fight on the Nationalists' terms which meant confronting the most sophisticated military-industrial complex of the day — the Nazi state gearing itself up for war.[28]   In such a battle, foreign exchange was lifeblood. Negrín's comment that 'the war ends for the Republic the day the last gold peseta does' was a shrewd assessment of its perpetual international isolation.[29]   It is in this context of the battle for foreign exchange and for a monopoly on the deployment of national economic resource that we have to place Negrín's confrontations across the war — first with the CLUEA (union fruit-exporting consortium in the Levante)[30] and then much more bitterly with the Consejo de Aragón and, perhaps worst   of   all,   the   morale-grinding,   resource-sapping jurisdictional dispute with the Catalan Generalitat.   From Negrín's perspective, its unwillingness to submerge its licit historic and cultural demands in the face of the *force majeure* of war   had   turned   the   Catalan   Nationalists   into   petty provincialists.

Negrín's constant attempts, from the start, to bring all channels of arms procurement under the direct control of the Treasury and thus under his personal control brought him into

---

28   All these points of Negrín's strategy were reinforced in his speech to the Cortes, 30 September 1938.

29   The closest we come to Negrín's own political-economic testimony is via one of his treasury deputies, the Socialist Jerónimo Bugeda at the important PSOE national committee meeting held in July 1937 in Valencia. See the stenographic record of Bugeda's speech in the Archivo Histórico de Moscú, Fundación Pablo Iglesias, Madrid; see also H. Graham, *Socialism and War*, 108.

30   Aurora Bosch Sánchez, *Ugetistas y libertarios: guerra civil y revolución en el país valenciano 1936-1939* (Valencia: Institució 'Alfons el Magnànim'/Diputació Provincial de València, 1983), 117-23, 336-40; Walther Bernecker, *Colectividades y revolución social: el anarquismo en la guerra civil española 1936-1939* (Barcelona: Editorial Crítica [Grijalbo], 1982), 123-26.

conflict with the Republic's procurement committee [*Comisión de Compras*] in Paris. This had originally been set up in September 1936 by Luis Araquistain, Largo's political lieutenant and Republican Ambassador in Paris (until May 1937). Araquistain's objective had been to end the chaos he had encountered on arriving in Paris where scores of individual Spaniards were milling around attempting to purchase arms in the name of the myriad Republican committees which had dispatched them. Indeed these agents often ended up driving the already high prices higher by bidding against each other — such was the general dislocation and lack of communication as a consequence of state fragmentation after the coup. Araquistain complained that Negrín had simply ignored his requests for funds with the result that potential arms purchases were lost.[31] While it is true that funds were on numerous occasions not released to the Paris *comisión*, it is not possible to substantiate Araquistain's accusation with the currently available documentation.

The lack of trust between Araquistain and Negrín was in part the product of pre-existing political and personal antagonisms. Their estrangement dated back to the May 1936 Cabinet crisis and the Socialist Left's obstruction of Prieto's bid for the premiership — something Negrín and his parliamentary colleagues held Araquistain to have been primarily responsible for engineering.[32]

If, however, Negrín did deliberately hold back funds, (rather than the problem arising from fractured communication channels), such 'parsimony' would be entirely in keeping with his long-term economic strategy, especially as Negrín was well aware of the staggering waste involved in arms procurement via

---

31 See Araquistain's requests to Negrín, 9, 25 February 1937 and his sarcastic comments to fellow left Socialist Julio Álvarez del Vayo, Foreign Affairs Minister (22 February 1937) (legajo 70/81, Araquistain's correspondence [political documentation, Archivo Histórico Nacional, Madrid]).

32 See Araquistain's letter to Negrín, 2 March 1937 accusing him of sabotaging his ambassadorial work and claiming this was because he disapproved of Araquistain's having ever been appointed (legajo 35, 8-20, Araquistain correspondence [political documentation, Archivo Histórico Nacional, Madrid]).

the commissions.   While the Paris commission may have constituted an improvement on the state of affairs Araquistain had encountered, like Largo Caballero's Cabinet, the commission was unwieldy since its membership also had to reflect the full constitution of the Popular Front. This meant there was a great deal of internal politicking and dissention which significantly reduced its efficacy, while the problem of the committee duplicating material purchased through other sources remained. In the spring of 1937, in a bid to improve matters, the central control Negrín sought was increased as the procurement committee saw its functions taken over by the defence ministry's newly-established sub-secretariat of armament. Its Paris office was run by Defence Minister Prieto's and Negrín's Socialist colleague, Alejandro Otero (who, like Negrín, and Marcelino Pascua, the Republican Ambassador in Moscow, was also a medical doctor).[33]

But we should remember that, ultimately, the inefficiency and waste involved in Republican procurement was a structural consequence of the embargo itself. Non-Intervention, in ruling out most of the useful government-to-government avenues (Soviet aid notwithstanding), obliged the Republic to submit to the vagaries of the arms market and to the dealings of some extremely dubious private intermediaries. And we should also remember that, at the outset, the Republic's leading cadres — most of whom were liberal professionals — were ill-equipped to deal with this jungle, having neither adequate contacts nor the requisite technical expertise. The Republican purchasers were made doubly vulnerable to a startling array of middle men and assorted opportunists (many of whom made considerable fortunes in the process) precisely because of their lack of alternative channels.

The fact that Non-Intervention forced the Republic to rely on a series of ever more byzantine routes and procedures to obtain arms and war materiel meant cumulative qualitative, as well as quantitative, disadvantage: weapons arrived with incompatible ammunition, or with the instructions in some obscure foreign language or materiel arrived without technical

---

33 José Fernández Castro, *Alejandro Otero: el médico y el político* (Madrid: Noguer, 1981), 108.

or logistical back-up thus vastly reducing its utility. To add insult to injury, moreover, the ratchet effect produced by Non-Intervention meant these substandard goods also habitually cost the Republic 'over the odds'.[34]

The wave of popular violence — anti-clerical, revolutionary and otherwise — which exploded in the Republican zone under the impact of military coup and state collapse had posed a serious dilemma for Negrín, leading him to question for a time the validity/quality of his commitment to the Loyalist cause. As a minister, Negrín continued to participate — with the attendant personal risk involved — in informal nightly patrols in the capital which sought to prevent or at least diminish the occurrence of *paseos* (executions at the margins of the judicial process).[35] Their eradication was for Negrín the essential pre-condition of reconstructing a legitimate state authority in the Republican zone. From 23 August 1936 the Tribunales Populares began functioning with precisely this objective:[36] to return to the state its defining function and basis of power — the monopoly on 'legitimate violence' in national (i.e. Republican) territory. For Negrín, 'legitimate violence' had always included the state's recourse to the death penalty for exceptional crimes which threatened its stability. (For example, in 1932 Negrín had argued strongly that the Republic was too weak to do other than execute the military ring-leaders of the

---

34 So although Negrín's centralizing drive undoubtedly cut down on waste through duplication, the Republic still had to pay crippling 'market' prices (plus commission) for its arms. For his assistance in fathoming the obscure history of the *comisiones de compras* I am indebted to Gerald Howson. His monumental research on the impact of Non-Intervention/arms embargo on the Republic also informs this section. Pending the publication of his book, see G. Howson, *Aircraft of the Spanish Civil War* (which, in spite of its specialist aeronautical format, has a considerable amount of his research on the effects of Non-Intervention embedded in it). See also my review in 'Spain and Europe: The View from the Periphery', *The Historical Journal*, XXV (1992), No. 4, 969-83.

35 M. Pascua in S. Álvarez, *Negrín (Documentos)*, 280 and *cf.* (re. Valencia) M. Ansó, *Yo fui ministro de Negrín*, 165-66.

36 Alberto Reig Tapia, *Violencia y terror. Estudios sobre la guerra civil española*, (Madrid: Akal, 1990), 121; see also various pieces in 'Justicia Republicana', in *Justicia en guerra* (Madrid: Ministerio de Cultura, 1990) (proceedings of conference on judicial process during the Civil War, Archivo Histórico Nacional, Salamanca, November 1987).

failed August coup attempt led by General José Sanjurjo, then leader of the civil guard.) For Negrín, as a liberal, legitimacy in this context resided in the fact that violence as a facet of state power was not arbitrary: the limits on state authority were established in constitutional law and subject to revision by collective consent, which was not the case with committees.

Negrín's own political and ethical reservations about the Republic in 1936, thus, did not concern the violence emanating from a reconstructed state but rather *popular* violence. And these reservations did not outlast the first months of the conflict. In part this was because the road to Republican normalization — though clearly long and hard — was decidedly being undertaken. But the resolution of Negrín's dilemma was also due to the course of events in the rebel zone which rapidly clarified what the Nationalists' meant by 'order'.

The *Africanista*[37] rampage in July through Triana — the most important working class district of Seville — heralded a sustained repression in the province.[38] The barbarity of Franco's southern war of agrarian counter-reform and the Badajoz massacre in mid August 1936 (the latter intended specifically as a message to those in Madrid contemplating resistance), represented the most extreme version of a dantesque repression enacted wherever the Nationalists took control. Yet there had been no real fracturing of state control or public order in the rebel zone. The military authorities were themselves sanctioning widespread terror and it was directed as much against certain civilian sectors as against combatants. As Negrín himself indicated, the rebels were, in this way, redefining 'the enemy'. There was of course a great deal of violence in both zones after 18 July 1936 — but this should not

---

37 The Army of Africa — North African (colonial) troops commanded by career army officers — constituted the Nationalists' shock force in the war once they had been airlifted to the Peninsula courtesy of German and Italian planes.

38 See Antonio Bahamonde y Sánchez de Castro, *Un año con Queipo: memorias de un nacionalista* (Barcelona: Ediciones Españolas, n.d. [1938]), 23-27; Julio de Ramón-Laca, *Bajo la férula de Queipo: como fue gobernada Andalucía* (Seville: Imprenta del Diario Fe, 1939), 18-20; Ian Gibson, *Queipo de Llano: Sevilla, verano de 1936* (Barcelona: Grijalbo, 1986), 80-92; Nicolás Salas, *Sevilla fue la clave: República, alzamiento, guerra civil (1931-1939)*, 2 vols (Seville: Castillejo, 1992) I, 281-363; II, 409-91.

lead us to suppose that the violence always meant the same thing. In this first phase of rebel warfare we can see it as signifying two things: 'colonial' war (especially in the south) against a social class — the proletariat produced by modernization and perceived (by the rebels and their civilian backers) as 'out of control' — and war against liberalism's plural and inclusive cultural option, not least because this required an acceptance of change rather than offering a guarantee of its containment.[39]

For someone of Negrín's intellect, temperament and experience, the notion that the flux produced by Spain's contemporary social and economic development could be 'solved' by resurrecting a monolithizing myth of imperial glory and projecting this inwards violently to repress sectors of the Spanish population and exclude them from the definition of the nation, was both intellectually sterile and ethically repugnant.[40] Negrín was not alone of course in rejecting this vision of 'medieval' intolerance — indeed such a rejection united liberals with those on the Left. But the fact that this perception remained so sharp in Negrín[41] sets him apart from most other liberals — including Azaña and, ultimately, I would argue, Prieto too — whose mounting personal and political crises would bring them by mid 1938 to believe that the Nationalists still shared with the Republicans enough of a common political and cultural language to make a negotiated settlement viable.[42]

---

39 The meanings of violence in Nationalist Spain are explored more fully in my forthcoming book on the Spanish Republic at war.

40 One can read triumphalist Francoism as signifying the 'internalization of empire': i.e. the Spanish proletariat — and particularly the urban proletariat — was itself constructed, through the war, as the colonized class/people, the internal 'other' excluded from nationhood/the nation. This idiosyncratic 'alternative' to social imperialism was at the root of the brutal social relations which dominated the 1940s in Spain.

41 *Cf*. Negrín's remarks in 1938 to the French military attaché Colonel Morel, concerning the complete mind-set ['otro modo de pensar'] which separated the Republic from the Nationalists, cited by Juan Marichal, *El intelectual y la política*, 100.

42 When the Law of Political Responsibilities was promulgated by the Nationalists in February 1939 and Franco gave assurances of the 'distinction' to be made between political and common crimes, it was Negrín who saw most clearly the meaninglessness of such a comment in the context of a civil war: *cf.* 'en una guerra como la nuestra, con los caracteres de una despiadada y salvaje

Other factors, such as the Nationalists' increasing reliance on Axis support and the territorial violation this signified would, of course, reinforce a whole liberal Nationalist agenda of resistance in Negrín.   But always underlying this was his perception — quite singular for the time — of the cultural horror which underlay Francoism and which, if the Republic let go, would be visited violently on the bodies of the defeated en masse.   This was the thought behind his unanswerable comment, '¿Pactar? Pero ¿y el pobre soldado de Medellín?'.[43] Medellín was the most remote point on the Republic's furthest front in Extremadura and what Negrín was implying was if the war ended without guarantees (i.e. of no reprisals) then the leading cadres would mainly get out, those with private resources would make their arrangements, and take the route to exile if necessary, but what awaited the bulk of the civilian population, not to mention the Republican army, after such an outcome?

Negrín and his Socialist, Communist and republican Cabinet colleagues knew that, of the three fronts on which the Republic was resisting — military, home and international/diplomatic — ultimately the most decisive would be the last of these.   Soviet aid had prevented defeat at the time of the battle for Madrid in November 1936, but by May 1937 it was quite apparent that the material and logistical disadvantages under which the Republican army was forced to operate, largely as a result of Non-Intervention, made outright military victory against the Nationalists an impossibility.   The *sina qua non* of Republican victory was, therefore, a change of heart on the part of the Western democracies — and predominantly Britain — in the first instance to secure the lifting of the arms embargo but Negrín also hoped that this would herald a more general political shift in favour of the Republican cause.   When appeasement failed, as Negrín firmly

---

guerra civil, delito común es todo o delito común no es nada', speech by Negrín in Palacio de Bellas Artes, Mexico, 1 August 1945 (*Documentos políticos para la historia de la República Española* [Mexico: Colección Málaga, 1945], 25-26).

43   F. Vázquez Ocaña, *Pasión y muerte de la segunda República española*, 62.

believed it must,[44] the Republic would be assured of a political victory more valuable than any military triumph the Nationalists could win on the battlefields.

In the meanwhile, then, while the Republic's representatives, and sometimes the Prime Minister himself,[45] fought propaganda and diplomatic battles in international forums, the Republic's most vital task was to concentrate all its efforts on sustaining its long-term defensive capabilities. Negrín, whose ministerial responsibilities also included the treasury (from May 1937 encompassing Trade and Industry) and the Defence Ministry during the last year of the war, sought to sustain a defensive military effort (which nevertheless included some significant offensives) and to fortify civilian resistance on the Republican home front until the European climate changed.

The alliance which was to sustain this wartime strategy across 1937-39 was the Popular Front. In terms of its reformist, state-building content the 1937 Popular Front alliance of Socialists, Communists and republicans recalled the very first progressive republican-Socialist alliance back in 1931. But the developments of the six intervening years had radically altered its form. This time the Front's political axis was formed by the Socialist and Communist movements rather than by republicans and the PSOE. By 1936 Republicanism had entered terminal crisis in most of Spain in that it had failed to create (principally between 1931 and 1933) a political project which could mobilize a viable social base. In fact the republicans had been entirely unable to deal with the levels of mass mobilization occurring under the Republic.[46] This final

---

44 Negrín's European perspective was significantly informed by the reports sent by the Republican Ambassador in Prague (until September 1938), the law professor and (until August 1938) PSOE vice-president, Luis Jiménez de Asúa. These are to be found in the Archivo de Barcelona (Ministry of Foreign Affairs, Madrid), Apartado 1, archivo de la SIDE [Sección de Información Diplomática Especial] boxes 58-69.

45 Most notably Negrín's outstanding performance at the League of Nations, September 1937 (J. Marichal, 'Ciencia y gobierno: la significación histórica de Juan Negrín [1892-1956]', in *Estudios sobre la II República Española*, ed. Manuel Ramírez [Madrid: Tecnos, 1975], 197-98).

46 Cataluña is arguably an exception, but Republicans there were obviously not concerned to strengthen the central state. For

failure of historic Republicanism underlay the process between 1934 and 1936 which we usually term 'polarization'. Its collapse was consummated by the military coup which saw swathes of the republicans' natural constituents — small holders and tenant farmers, traders, shopkeepers, small entrepreneurs — side with the rebels and, in consequence, an ill-fated attempt by the leadership (in the person of Diego Martínez Barrio, leader of Unión Republicana and President of the Cortes) to treat with the rebel chiefs, thereby losing Republicanism its last shreds of political credibility in the eyes of the Republic's proletarian defenders.

As a result of the coup the state lay in ruins. Yet it was rapidly becoming clear in the first months of the conflict that the Republic would have to fight on the rebels' terms, thus taking on the might of their Axis backers. By the time Largo had assumed power in September 1936 it was already clear the Republic would have to gear itself for total war (something unprecedented, of course, in Spanish experience). An essential precondition of successful reconstruction and wartime policy implementation was, thus, the articulation of new government cadres both directly to meet the increasing functions of a state at war and to organize national mobilization to this end. Given Negrín's understanding of the PSOE's modernizing function which, years back, had prompted his own membership of the party, the prime minister naturally looked to the Socialists to support his work and provide the necessary cadres.

But for a series of reasons the PSOE could not, on its own, deliver the major functions that Negrín's project required. The birth of the Republic in 1931, by accelerating a process of mass political mobilization, had also precipitated a major crisis in the Socialist movement. For, like Republicanism, Spanish Socialism too was ill-equipped to meet the challenge of encadring the

---

centrist/progressive Republicanism's fear of and failure in the face of mass mobilization, see H. Graham, 'Community, State and Nation in Republican Spain 1931-38', in *Nationalism and National Identity in the Iberian Peninsula*, ed. A. Smith and C. Mar-Molinero; and Paul Preston, 'The Creation of the Popular Front in Spain', in *The Popular Front in Europe*, ed. H. Graham and P. Preston (London: Macmillan, 1987), esp. pp. 99-100. Nor can we see the Radical Party as 'disproving' this Republican failure, since it was regionally very disparate and essentially clientelist.

previously unorganized.[47] Most of the potential new recruits — in the first instance to the union organization (UGT) — had very low levels of political, and often also general, education which was perceived by the leadership as a threat to the identity ('historic traditions') and thus the coherence of Spanish Socialism.

By spring 1936 the Socialist movement was indeed suffering severe organizational dislocation. This was not, however, the result of the new membership, but rather the resurgence of the deadly ideological and strategic confusion at the heart of Spanish Socialism. Spain's experience of acutely uneven development had, over time, produced highly internally fragmented social class formations and these endured into the 1930s. If the Socialists were to carry reform forward successfully, in a situation where highly disparate socio-economic and cultural levels remained the given, then they had to develop a means of addressing contradictory popular demands (i.e. those of small entrepreneurs, rentiers, shopkeepers, small peasants alongside those of industrial workers and the rural landless) in order to provide a sufficiently broad social support base for the Republic to withstand oligarchic assault. But between 1931 and 1936 the Spanish Socialist movement, like the republicans, proved unable to elaborate a discourse which could reach and mobilize across these disparate constituencies. Yet it was precisely this populist ability simultaneously to sustain 'contradictory' discourses which was the essential precondition of democratic modernization/social reform in such a context of uneven development — and this was even more the case once war had erupted.

After 18 July 1936, moreover, the underlying problem of how to handle mass mobilization became more urgent. For one crucial 'meaning' of the outbreak of Civil War itself was to accelerate the very process of mass political mobilization which had underlain the tensions of the pre-war Republic, as well as to render such mobilization indispensable to its survival. Republicanism had been eclipsed by a military coup which

---

47 For a fuller analysis of the crisis in the Socialist movement, see H. Graham, *Socialism and War*.

consummated the process of polarization its own political failures had originated. But once there was war then the PSOE/UGT too was confronted by an imperative of mass mobilization which it could not adequately handle either conceptually or practically. Yet Negrín's bid to build a strong Republican state demanded precisely this. It was about winning the war but also about creating a framework for a viable liberal capitalist project which could — looking to the post-war period of reconstruction — 'contain' and channel the popular protests and initiatives which had in the spring and summer of 1936 been manifest in the extra-parliamentary dimension of Popular Front — much to the alarm of the republicans and parliamentary Socialists alike[48] — and which would resurface in various ways in the first year of the war in the form of a variety of popular resistances to the extension of central state control of which the Barcelona May Days and the dismantling of Aragonese cantonalism in August 1937 are only the most well-known instances. The poverty of the veteran Socialist leadership response — to batten down the hatches of the organization *until the war is over*[49] — is staggering, not least because it suggests they did not really understand that the mobilization of the Republican population for total war was the essential precondition of victory.

The fact that the Spanish Socialist movement lacked the material political skills necessary to develop a discourse and means of mass mobilization which could sustain (for the duration of the War at least) the contradictory interests/policy agendas of the various social groups constituting the Republic's support base provides the key to the wartime ascendancy of the Spanish Communist Party (PCE). The party was vital to Negrín precisely because it possessed to a high degree the organizational skills required to implement the Republican

---

48 Helen Graham, 'Spain 1936. Resistance and Revolution: The Flaws in the Front', in *Community, Authority and Resistance to Fascism in Europe*, ed. Tim Kirk and Tony McElligott; and Paul Preston, 'The Creation of the Popular Front in Spain', in *The Popular Front in Europe*, ed. H. Graham and P. Preston, esp. pp. 99-100.

49 It was best not to 'pescar en río revuelto' [fish in troubled waters] — the implications of this often-repeated adage contrast sharply with Negrín's own instrumental view of the PSOE's function.

mobilization on which his own project for building the state depended. Without the crucial Soviet aid of autumn 1936 there would of course have been no material basis for such a state-building project (since the Republic would have been defeated militarily), but the PCE's protagonism is not reducible to its function as a conduit for this aid nor to the *kudos* it derived thereby. For Soviet aid alone would have been insufficient to secure the Republic had it not also been for the massive internal effort to articulate a national war effort (i.e. Republican-zone wide). The PCE not only argued for a wide inter-class alliance (as did the parliamentary PSOE), it also went far down the road to realizing it. In the PCE Negrín found a party which could be used as an instrument of change in a way the PSOE could not because of its organizational 'puritanism' and 'identity crisis'.

Not only did the PCE's party membership expand dramatically in the war,[50] but even more importantly, via the umbrella organizations of the Popular Front, the United Socialist Youth Organization (JSU) and the unions, the PCE was instrumental in bringing the previously unorganized — middle and working classes alike, but above all the young[51] — to the state.

In this sense the PCE inherited from the PSOE (which had, ironically, always constructed itself as the 'inheritor party') the still unrealized ideological task of historic Republicanism to mobilize the 'people'. In fulfilling this task, the PCE not only

---

50 PCE membership was recorded (at the plenary session of the party's central committee) in March 1937 at 249,140 of whom over half (an estimated 131,600) were at the front. By the end of June 1937 the PCE claimed 301,000 members, excluding the Basque and Catalan Communist parties (with c.22,000 and 60,000 members respectively). Recruitment was notably from among those of no previous political affiliation and, linked to this, particularly from among the conscripted young (see note 51 below for separate JSU figures). Wartime membership figures for Madrid (capital and province) for the period up to May 1938 also reinforce this picture (PCE archive [Madrid], microfilm XVII [214], frames 108-13).

51 By January 1937 the JSU was estimated to have some 250,000 members incorporated into military units — this amounting to seventy per cent of the total membership. For a discussion of the 'modern' (social and cultural) implications of this youth mobilization, see H. Graham, 'Community, State and Nation in Republican Spain 1931-38', in *Nationalism and National Identity in the Iberian Peninsula*, ed. A. Smith and C. Mar-Molinero.

delivered to Negrín[52] vital human resources for state-building and the war effort but also undertook — via the process of mass mobilization these required — the equally essential task of legitimizing the Republican state/political project itself. This was the challenge facing the Popular Front — to mobilize state cadres and war workers and to project a vision of what the Republican order could offer in return, to fulfil its part of the social contract with those fighting and dying for the Republic. Through this reciprocal process could thus be begun the long-overdue making of the Republican nation.

In the face of the evident physical threat from the Axis-backed Nationalists, the PCE's military discipline appealed across class lines both to workers and sectors of the republican middle classes.   The latter were especially attracted to the PCE's moderate republican discourse. Its call to re-articulate state power offered a defence of liberal property and values, with which Negrín was already identified, against the — albeit politically unfocused — currents of social and economic radicalism released by state collapse in July 1936. Thus the PCE attracted the urban and rural lower middle classes whom it organized in peasant, commercial and professional/white collar unions (the latter two often inside the UGT) and in a variety of Popular Front social/welfare organizations servicing the Republican home front — of which the women's organization, Asociación de Mujeres Antifascistas (AMA), is a good example of significant middle class mobilization.[53] But, at the same time, the PCE retained a proletarian constituency to whom it held out a promise of social and economic reform as the fruits of victory in the war — although these reforms were couched in somewhat imprecise language. In sustaining these lines simultaneously the PCE was accused of being either incoherent or, much more often, consciously duplicitous and

---

52 Apart from Cabinet level exchanges (through the Communist ministers) communication between Negrín and the PCE occurred mainly via the national Popular Front committee and the liaison committees [comités de enlace] which existed (from January 1937) at local, provincial and national levels between the PCE and PSOE in order to facilitate state administration and the mobilization of war resources.

53 So much so that it was dubbed by some Socialists and others on the Left, Mujeres Antes [previously] Fascistas.

opportunistic (the PCE's underlying 'reality' being radical or moderate depending on the provenance of the criticism).

In fact, rather than expressing confusion or duplicitousness, the PCE was responding strategically to the structural consequences of uneven development. The highly fragmented constituencies with conflicting aspirations and perspectives produced by this process over time simply could not be reconciled, nor the disparities resolved, within the period of the war itself. What was needed then, if Negrín's project of a Republican state was to be realized, was a political force which could engage the different and 'contradictory' social sectors of the Republican base in dialogue, sustaining that simultaneous mobilization for the duration of the war at least. It was, moreover, precisely the PCE's democratic centralism which allowed it to bear these contradictions. Such a tactical populism was beyond the capacity of republicans and Socialists. Indeed these structural contradictions had already provoked republican eclipse and Socialist dislocation. In short, what Negrín required was a political force which could be populist and bear/mediate the contradictions that ripped the Socialist organization apart between 1931 and 1937.

This failure of Spanish Socialism which the needs of war threw into sharp relief, was revealed further in Juan Negrín's own inability as premier to differentiate between mobilizing discourses appropriate for domestic consumption (in broadcast/ printed prime ministerial speeches and the like) and those fitted to address international and diplomatic forums. Instead the Prime Minister employed in them all a universalist rhetoric of abstract constitutional rights and liberties which, in this form, had little purchase on popular minds. Negrín's failings in this respect — scarcely surprising given his origins, education and career — locate him clearly within a republican-Socialist continuum and, again, shed more light on the PCE's importance to the Prime Minister's state-building goals.

The PCE's stress on organization was crucial here: all the apparently redundant committees, councils, meetings and conferences were in fact indispensable in sustaining popular mobilization and morale — the Republic's greatest resource. Their maintenance required constant and untiring efforts — hence the PCE's use of repetition and ritual, techniques that brought only condescending criticism from the Socialists. Yet as time went on, the constant rehearsal of organization was even more crucial to sustaining the Republic — as the material and psychological fabric of the Republican zone eroded further during the second half of 1938 under pressure from the accumulated effects of blockade, territorial loss, the consequent increase in refugees, aerial bombardment, disrupted agriculture, urban food and housing shortages, galloping inflation and an emergent black market.

The PSOE's failure to grasp the importance in a situation of 'total war' of popular mobilization, seeing it exclusively as evidence of the Communists' sectarian opportunism, is clear in the following extracts from a letter of complaint, sent to the PSOE's national executive by the provincial leadership in Almería in March 1938 and which perfectly illustrates the attitude permeating the PSOE throughout the Republican zone:

> The [Socialist] Party, somewhat startled by Communist methods — so given to excessive publicity and dramatic gestures, to vulgar and ornate ritual ... — has become even more sparing in its public declarations, which were always austere and dignified. But what we disdain in terms of methods employed, we cannot ignore in terms of the effects produced. The people here are uneducated and impressionable. Until very recently they were in thrall to a religious mysticism — which, for all that it was distorted, met a certain need in them. Communist propaganda, full of puerile, rhetorical flourishes, peppered with clichés and accompanied by impressive gestures, has filled the void left in these simple people — *and principally in the young, male and female alike*. The Socialist Party has resolved to take part in each and every initiative, to be present wherever and whenever any sort of meeting or gathering is held — *however ridiculous these appear to us to be*. The Party ... will keep itself apprised of all the 'popular movements' which are organized. Thus will it attempt to keep a check on all public demonstrations in order not to be taken unawares.[54]

---

54 AH-13-63, p. 80, Archivo Histórico de Moscú (AH), Fundación Pablo Iglesias, Madrid (italics and translation mine). *Cf.* 'We have never plastered the insignia of our Party over walls — but let those who have seen us act bear witness for us', *Avance* (Socialist press, Ciudad Real), 10 June 1938.

The Almerian Socialists were unconsciously describing the way in which the PCE was central to the making of a new political practice of mass engagement. Ultimately, this process was about the transition from an older clientelist political system based on patronage — typical of agrarian-dominated Mediterranean societies — to a 'modern' politics of mass movements whose social mobilization was based on occupational and generational categories. Finally, in the reality as well as the intent, politics was ceasing to be the preserve of an elite. The Spanish Socialist organization — apart from the Communist-controlled unified youth (JSU) — found itself superseded precisely because a series of factors, analysed above, prevented it from adequately adapting organizationally, ideologically or culturally to the needs of the new environment. Rather than seeing the PCE's presence in the JSU or the UGT as 'evidence' of a sectarian conspiracy or ideological conquest we need to understand it as a part of this broader process of change whereby social provision (via women's associations, youth and women's training schemes, public health clinics, nurseries, canteens etc.) was becoming the proper and necessary preserve of national political parties and organizations.

The PCE was not the only force which understood the imperative of mobilization of course. Anarchist organizations such as Mujeres Libres or the libertarian youth federation (FIJL), were engaged, ideological differences notwithstanding, in a similar process of mobilization and education. And for those thus mobilized for the first time the experience offered would have been similarly emancipatory. (And even though the scale of mobilization in these anarchist organizations was smaller than the Popular Front's it was still numerically significant.)[55] The singular importance of the PCE's activity lay rather in its connecting this mobilization 'bottom-up' with the requirements of new state structures 'top-down'. Through the organizational networks of the Popular Front articulated by the PCE, the still very incomplete structures of state bureaucracy were crucially reinforced. In functioning thus the PCE was both symptom and instrument of a wider process of social, political and cultural modernization. Practically and organizationally

---

55   FIJL had c.100,000 members and Mujeres Libres c.20,000.

the PCE was not only underpinning Negrín's policy of resistance, it was also coming to embody his vision of a *modern* Spain. What the PSOE found so distasteful — and not only its Almería section — was the PCE's preparedness to engage at the existing cultural level of its interlocutors among the popular classes, many of whom did indeed have very low levels of basic education. But such engagement was essential if a concerted national Republican war effort was to be achieved.

In view of the PCE's organizational strengths and mobilizing capacity one could also reasonably surmise that the prospect of Socialist-Communist unification would for a time have held a certain pragmatic appeal for Negrín. (After all, Prieto, significantly less instrumental in his view of the PSOE, had also seriously proposed such a course in spring 1937, believing it could reinforce the war effort.[56] Moreover, a Popular Frontist PCE seemed to confirm the long-expressed 'old Socialist' view that the Communists' departure from the fold in 1921 was unwarranted and unnecessary in ideological terms and had thus weakened Spanish Socialism without any real cause.)

Yet by the autumn of 1937 Negrín had definitively ruled out such a unification, declaring that it was more suited to the Nationalist zone than the Republican one.[57] But, in fact, there was a striking similarity between the social bases, mobilizing process and state bureacracy-in-the-making function of the PCE and the Falange in the two respective zones. This did not make the PCE 'Fascist' because there were qualitative differences in the underlying culture of mobilization: the Republican stress on self-education and the liberating potential of social change had no equivalent in the impersonal, monolithizing discourse of Falange. Nevertheless, Negrín's negative overdrew the contrast and it is probably the case that the Prime Minister downplayed his own views on unification for two related reasons. First, because of serious discontent throughout the PSOE and its UGT components — a product of their organizational rivalry with the PCE, exacerbated by the latter's sectarianism[58] — and, second,

---

56   H. Graham, *Socialism and War*, 132.

57   D.T. Cattell, *Communism and the Spanish Civil War* (New York: Russell & Russell, 1965 [first pub. 1955]), 186.

58   Such views were transmitted to Negrín by his friend and colleague, PSOE general secretary, Ramón Lamoneda. In addition to the PSOE's loss of

because of the negative impression which the creation of a single party [*partido único*] would have had both in British and French governing circles and the dominant anti-Communist sectors of Northern European social democracy, whose favour Negrín was courting in the hope of securing an end to Non-Intervention and embargo.

But the intense anti-Communism to which Negrín was reacting here would prove an impenetrable barrier, preventing the real complexity of the PCE's role in the national context of Republican Spain from being even remotely understood in those Western European policy-making circles on which the premier was ultimately pinning his hopes. Nor, since the end of the war, has that barrier ever really been dismantled: the PCE's role in sustaining a progressive liberal agenda of state construction and national mobilization still lies buried beneath a monolithic historical interpretation of the party which casts it — and, by association, Negrín — solely as the instrument of Soviet policy.[59]

This monolithic interpretation would arise from the way in which Stalin utilized the Soviet Union's especial political influence in the Republican zone (derived from its status as major supplier of vital war materiel) to extend to it the violent purge of Trotskyist and other left dissident Communists already underway in the Soviet Union. In Spain this translated as the persecution of those grouped in and around the Marxist-Leninist POUM. But the criminalization of the POUM, after its participation in the anti-government protest/street fighting in Barcelona in May 1937, also belongs to another story: the domestic class struggle being waged between a reconstructing bourgeois state — supported by a significant and varied social

JSU and PSUC (the United Socialist party of Catalonia), relations were deteriorating between Socialists and Communists on the inter-party liaison committees [*comités de enlace*]. The abortive attempt at party unification in Jaen in August 1937 damaged relations further (see H. Graham, *Socialism and War*, 122-23).

59 The most influential example of this view being Burnett Bolloten's work, the final version of which was published as *The Spanish Civil War. Revolution and Counterrevolution* (Hemel Hempstead: Haarvester Wheatsheaf, 1991).

base in the Popular Front[60] — and, on the other side, all those
fragments within the Socialist, Anarchist and Communist
movements who had aspired to more radical social and political
change in the wake of the July Days.   Comintern agents
imprisoned and sometimes assassinated dissident Communists,
most infamously in the case of POUM leader Andreu Nin. The
especially brutal treatment meted out to Nin was bound up
with his dissidence being perceived as a betrayal from the inner
circle. (Nin had lived in the Soviet Union throughout the 1920s
and was an executive member of the Red International of
Labour Unions. In 1926 he had joined the Left Opposition,
acting for a time as Trotsky's secretary.) But the definitive
work of suppressing the radical Left as a political force in Spain
was carried out not by the PCE's *checas* [clandestine party
prisons] but by the Republican courts which endorsed the
criminalization of the party by sentencing and imprisoning
many of its leading members for political rebellion *against the
state.*[61] And nor was this a mere semantic or procedural detail
whereby the Republican Government pragmatically distanced
itself from being seen to obey the 'will of Stalin'. In some ways
the horrific nature of Nin's fate has obscured the fact that the
repression of the POUM responded to an internal political
dynamic: the bourgeois state was being reinforced through the
exercise of coercive authority.[62]

The very occurrence of the Barcelona May Days had
undermined the credibility of the Republican state because,
once again, doubt was cast on its ability to keep 'order'. To
repair the damage, to restore faith in the Republican state at
home and abroad (among Western democratic policy makers),
the authorities had to be seen to be forcibly reimposing liberal

---

60 For an analysis of the counter-hegemonic project and of the Popular
Front as the 'least weak option', see H. Graham, 'Spain 1936. Resistance and
Revolution: The Flaws in the Front', in *Community, Authority and Resistance
to Fascism in Europe*, ed. Tim Kirk and Tony McElligott and 'Community,
State and Nation in Republican Spain 1931-38', in *Nationalism and National
Identity in the Iberian Peninsula*, ed. A. Smith and C. Mar-Molinero.

61 Andrés Suárez (pseud. of Ignacio Iglesias), *El proceso contra el
POUM. Un episodio de la revolución española* (Paris: Ruedo Ibérico, 1974).
(This is primarily a dissident left critique of Stalinist activity.)

62 One index of this was the increasing number of remand prisoners
held in Republican jails (A. Reig Tapia, *Violencia y terror*, 121).

economic and constitutional order and castigating those who had sought to break it. Negrín, whom the May crisis had brought to the premiership, understood this very well. This was the Republican regime's objective in targeting the POUM and, ultimately, bringing them to trial in 1938. Compared to the CNT, whose social constituencies had played a much larger part in the May events, the POUM was a much clearer and more 'manageable' target for state action. Clearer because the POUM leadership had publicly supported the May rebellion once it was in progress while the CNT's national leadership had not. More manageable because the POUM's mobilizing capacity was small and fairly circumscribed compared to that of the anarchists. (Negrín and his Cabinet colleagues knew full well that many CNT militants were unhappy with their leadership's pro-government line, and if pushed too far, the CNT still had the mobilizing capacity to wreck Republican war production.) In targeting the POUM Negrín was also attacking the recalcitrant separatism of the POUM militia on the Aragon front. They were an enduring obstacle not only to the extension of the state's military control but also to its political authority in that militia arms were what ultimately guaranteed the existence of the Consejo de Aragón.

For Negrín, however, due legal process against the POUM was one thing, while the activities of Soviet police agents, imprisoning and assassinating with virtual impunity on Spanish sovereign territory, were quite another. Negrín had no sympathy for the radical politics of the POUM. But the activities occurring under the Comintern 'umbrella' were daily violating the basic principle of his liberal philosophy — that the Republican state was legitimate because it was constitutional. Moreover, public knowledge about this state of affairs, whose 'lawlessness' seemed to recall the early days of the *paseos*, would, Negrín knew, alienate the very Western powers whom he was hoping to win over in order that the Republic might be able to forego Soviet aid. But as this aid could not be jeopardized until the West definitely lifted the arms embargo, Negrín found himself obliged to turn a blind eye to the Comintern's illegal persecution of the POUM, while at the same time knowing that in doing so he was giving hostile opinion in Britain and France more anti-Republican ammunition, and further undermining his own long-term objective — the creation of a strong, centralized liberal state in Spain. Stalin's obsessive concern to liquidate dissidents notwithstanding, however, we must be clear that the *criminalization* of the POUM itself obeyed the logic of a domestic state agenda: for too long a failure to recognize the repressive potential of the Republican state-in-the-making between 1937 and 1939 has led commentators wrongly to label its products as 'Stalinist [or 'Communist'] violence'.[63]

It was, nevertheless, the reconstruction of state structures and national mobilization through the Popular Front which allowed the Republic under Negrín to fight a long war in extremely unfavourable conditions. To understand why this finally ended in defeat, rather than our having recourse to an ultimately unsubstantiable argument about what an (always hypothetical) revolution might have achieved, it makes more sense to open up the largely unexplored period between 1937 and 1939 — which constitutes two thirds of the whole war we should remember — and to examine the dynamic and cumulative effects of defeat on the battlefield combined with mounting home front crisis. We should also remember that both of these outcomes were substantially shaped by the policies of Western capitalist democracy. The Republic under Negrín struggled not only to combat the Axis-equipped Nationalist armies but also a crippling economic embargo. This not only prevented the Republican army from ever engaging on an equal military footing, but in the end also savagely undercut Negrín's attempts to sustain the physical fabric and morale of the home front, crucial to its war of resistance — the only war that the Republic's limited resources allowed it to fight. Indeed, the effect of our perpetually focusing on the intra-Republican conflict of 1936-37 when we seek to explain the defeat of 1939 is

---

63 In Ken Loach's recent film, *Land and Freedom*, a virtually exclusive anti-Stalinist narrative leads precisely to this misassigning. A further necessary differentiation between 'Stalinist' and 'Communist' violence (i.e. the latter term defining the PCE's organizational sectarianism and the former the specific, clandestine political activities of Soviet/Comintern agents (interrogating dissidents, running *checas* etc.) in which members of the PCE were sometimes involved) will be provided in my forthcoming book on the Spanish Republic at war.

to preclude — rather too conveniently — any discussion of the savagely erosive impact of Western policies on Republican Spain from 1937 onwards.

Wars distort all economies, but war under embargo conditions magnified the distortion by forcing Negrín to allocate an even more disproportionately high percentage of convertible resources (gold pesetas) to the direct purchase of war materiel.[64] Between 1937 and 1939, then, the policies (as well as the 'unspoken assumptions') of British, French (and American)[65] liberal democracy played a key role in undermining the Republican war effort and the fabric of its civilian front and thus in delegitimizing the emergent Republican state. The fault line in liberalism between capitalist economic defence and a politically inclusive vision which the 1930s economic crisis opened up, and which the Spanish liberal Republican project — inherited and refined by Negrín — had always tried to bridge, was instead widening to become the chasm that would engulf it.

By April 1938 Franco's armies had reached the coast at Viñaroz (Castellón), splitting the Republican zone in two and cutting off the Centre-South zone from its only friendly land frontier (with France). Thereafter, Negrín's prioritization of military supply in order to maintain resistance in a situation of ever more acute material shortage, with supply problems exacerbated by the division of Republican territory, meant rapidly deteriorating conditions and serious hardship for large sectors of the Republican population — and especially in the increasingly refugee-crowded cities (above all in Cataluña). The Republic had to feed a substantial urban population with ever fewer internal food resources. Nationalist military conquest had steadily deprived it of food-producing land, aerial bombardment disrupted and diminished agrarian production and industrial dislocation and inflation encouraged rural hoarding which, in turn, aggravated a series of social tensions between rural and urban communities and also between the peasantry and the Republican armies and state authorities over

---

64 See earlier in this article for discussion of the economic implications of Non-Intervention.

65 Douglas Little, *Malevolent Neutrality. The United States, Great Britain and the Origins of the Spanish Civil War* (Ithaca/London: Cornell U. P., 1985).

the requisitioning of supplies. Negrín did not have access to adequate credit facilities to meet the growing shortfall in food and essential supplies — Soviet aid notwithstanding — and by December, when the gold was dwindling and silver reserves were being mobilized to meet military expenditure, Negrín was desperately trying to secure a new credit package from the Soviet Union to cover essential requirements on the home front.[66] In such dire conditions, the burgeoning black market was, inevitably, another focus of mounting social and political tensions.

Material emergency exacerbated the political crisis of the Republican state. Negrín had overseen its basic reconstruction, but the very dynamic of a war fought in conditions of such inequality massively escalated the scale of functions that same state was required to fulfil. The shortfall between necessity and delivery did not only mean material hardship, it had a political charge too. That the Republic was visibly failing — daily — to deliver food, shelter, physical security meant that it was also failing — daily — to deliver a vision of its own worth/superiority. And ultimately, rather than military crisis or logistical difficulties, it was the social and political disintegration of the home front — symbolizing the state's material and ideological failure — which permitted Colonel Casado's coup against Negrín that prematurely ended the Republic's war of resistance.

One strand in this desperate story does concern the consequences of Communist sectarianism[67] — what one might call its 'dysfunctionality', as contrasted with the structural functionality of the PCE's democratic centralism in the context of Republican state-building and national mobilization. But dysfunctional sectarianism alone did not 'cause' the Casado coup. Rather it functioned as a catalyst for a multi-faceted popular discontent and profound war weariness. These reached

---

66   Over the last year of the war Negrín sought to diversify the Republic's financial strategy, in particular by securing new Soviet loans (Ángel Viñas, 'Gold, the Soviet Union and the Spanish Civil War', in *European Studies Review*, IX (January 1979), No. 1, esp. pp. 120-21 and 'The Financing of the Spanish Civil War', in *Revolution and War in Spain 1931-1939*, ed. P. Preston (London: Methuen, 1984), 271-73.

67   See note 63 above.

their 'critical mass' after the territorial division of April 1938, thereby finally precipitating the latent conflict between the advocates of resistance (symbolized by the figure of Negrín and organizationally sustained by the PCE) and those who wanted to negotiate the peace with Franco which they wrongly believed was possible.

This essay has sought to show that the failures which have often been personally attributed to Negrín as wartime premier were in fact symptoms of the crisis of the Republican state itself. Negrín sought to consolidate a liberal democratic order and to mobilize the Republican population behind a war effort in its defence. But this project was undercut by the historic weakness of the Spanish state, by the intense fragmentation of the Republic's social constituencies, and by the massively draining conditions of material inferiority and shortage in which the Republic was forced to wage a long, gruelling, 'modern' war.[68] Material crisis finally delegitimized the Republican state. It was the collapse of the home front which ultimately ended the Republic's war of resistance.

---

68 As Negrín pointed out to Prieto in his letter of 23 June 1939, *Epistolario Prieto y Negrín*, 41.

8

Civil War, Violence
and the Construction of Francoism[1]

MICHAEL RICHARDS

... for a social elite the features of subordinate groups
always display something barbaric and pathological.
(Antonio Gramsci)[2]

I

Introduction: Problems and Perspectives

Francoist repression during the Spanish Civil War (1936-1939)
and in its aftermath was far more extensive than anything
which may have been 'justified' by military strategists in the
interests of victory. The use of terror and violence in what was,
above all, a class war, derived from a policy of *purging* society.
Reconciliation was explicitly and consistently rejected as an
option. Social integration under Francoism would be strictly
limited. According to the ideology of the Catholic Church,
which supported the Francoist 'crusade', it was 'impossible to
negotiate with evil'. The words 'forgiveness' and 'amnesty' were
to be erased from the Spanish language.[3] Ideologically
informed repression, which took many forms, accompanied a
rapid reclaiming of power by society's traditional élites. It was
upon these foundations that Spain's future development was

---

1   The research on which this paper is based was partly facilitated by
financial assistance from the British Academy and the Cañada Blanch
Foundation for which I am grateful.
2   *Il Risorgimento* (Turin: Einaudi, 1950), 200.
3   *ABC*, 1 November 1936.

based. During the conflict, and in the first post-war decade, ideology, industrialization and violence interacted within a context of complete social and political domination as the parameters within which social change might take place were established.

The problems of quantification and interpretation of the Francoist repression revolve around three main issues: first, the question of the location and use of sources arises. Following Franco's victory in 1939 Spain was ruled by a dictatorial regime for almost forty years which was able to shape and control both the formation of collective memory and the writing of history itself much more efficiently than in post-war Germany or Italy. Indeed, under Franco, the history of the 1930s, or the little which was permitted publication in Spain, was written by policemen, soldiers, state functionaries and priests.[4]   Their depiction of the Civil War as a religious crusade avoided any necessity to talk of the *class nature* of the conflict. Moreover, rigidly restricted access to records, until very recently, has favoured particular historians who employ a methodology which eschews explanation. An obsession with the accumulation of 'known facts' has led to an almost complete absence of context in studies of this kind. This 'neo-positivist' approach has often, effectively, produced little more than propaganda in the interests of the Francoist state.[5] The question of the social function of the regime and of its violence has not been posed in these accounts.

Second, the magnitude of the brutality, the manner in which it was directed from above, and the ideological discourse which surrounded it suggest that some kind of explanatory framework based upon an analysis of *the social and ideological roots of the repression* is required. Is it persuasive, or sufficient, to attempt

---

4 Paul Preston, 'War of Words: The Spanish Civil War and the Historians', in *Revolution and War in Spain, 1931-1939*, ed. Paul Preston (London: Methuen, 1984), 2.

5 Alberto Reig Tapia, *Ideología e historia: sobre la represión franquista y la guerra civil* (Madrid: Ediciones Akal, 1984). The work of Reig Tapia has constituted the principal systematic critique of the methodology and political bias behind many of the 'scientific' accounts of the repression in Spain and this paper owes a great deal to his work. See also Reig Tapia, *Violencia y terror: estudios sobre la guerra civil española* (Madrid: Ediciones Akal, 1990).

to explain the depth of the violence by reference to a perceived collapse of state authority, or to the 'brutalization of warfare'; or might it be more useful to look at the *ideological* influences which were prevalent?[6]

What significance, for example, did the construction of the Civil War as a religious crusade to *reconquer* Spain have, in terms of the violence? It is quite clear, in relation to this question, for example, that those who carried out the killings were effectively given the blessing of the Catholic Church.[7] Moreover, what was the meaning of notions like *purification* and how did this relate to the whole canon of pathological vocabulary which accompanied the purges? These are questions which ought to be asked in an analysis of the violence of the 1930s and 1940s.

The third issue which makes the study of violence, terror and repression during the Civil War and in the 1940s difficult is the *internalization or evasion of the past,* both at a collective and individual level.   As oral historians have pointed out, memories of pain, or of shame are not easy to recapture, articulate or interpret.[8]   The Spanish Civil War and its devastating aftermath represented an overwhelming sense of *loss,* at a great many levels and in very many ways. This was not only about *losing* the war, about military defeat, but about the loss of ideals, of visions of the future. The regime, through the imposition of its totalitarian institutions, attempted to implant an alternative vision, although the effects of this kind of institutional indoctrination were impossible to predict or

---

6   Part of the 'mission' of the Spanish Fascist Party, the Falange, was to bring about a revaluation of violence. The founders of Spanish Fascism were among the first to call for violence following the proclamation of the Spanish Second Republic in 1931. See, for example, Ramiro Ledesma Ramos, *Discurso a las Juventudes de España* (Madrid: Ediciones Fe, 1954). War was seen as 'an element of progress' and violence as creative and purifying.

7   Antonio Bahamonde y Sánchez de Castro, *Un año con Queipo: memorias de un nacionalista* (Barcelona: Ediciones Españolas, 1938), 71, for example.

8   See, for example, *Our Common History*, ed. Paul Thompson (London: Pluto Press, 1982), 16.

control.[9] The working class was so cowed materially that it was impossible to mobilize behind *any* concrete set of ideas. Ultimately, Francoism enforced an actual loss of the future itself, a loss of hope, as millions of Spaniards were robbed of a sense of identity and of dignity. But loss was also highly personal. It was the loss of family members, not only for those who supported the Republic but also for those who found themselves on the other side, either through conviction or through geographic accident.

Memory, for countless people, implied an encounter with a reality which they would rather have forgotten. The appalling conditions under which most of the lower classes, were forced to live under Franco determined a *necessary obsession* with mere survival in the immediate post-war period. The victory of Franco was re-created in the day-to-day degradation of the defeated. It was chiefly this enforced retreat into the private domestic sphere in order to survive which made resistance all but impossible.[10] The extreme interventionism of the State in economic relations, which was an intrinsic feature of autarky (economic self-sufficiency), facilitated an economic violence which was ideologically determined. Indeed, the repressive social function of autarky needs to be considered in determining the extent of the totalitarian pretensions (or Fascism?) in Francoism.[11] In addition, part of the effect of this retreat was a

---

9   For some women, in particular, Francoist organizations offered greater possibilities for social interaction outside of church and home. See, for example, M. T. Gallego Méndez, *Mujer, Falange y franquismo* (Madrid: Taurus, 1983). On Spanish youth under Franco, see J. Saíz Marín, *El Frente de Juventudes: política de juventud en la España de la postguerra (1937-1960)* (Madrid: Siglo XXI, 1988); G. Germani, 'La socialización política de la juventud en los regímenes fascistas: Italia y España', in *Revista Latinoamericana de Sociología*, V (Nov. 1969), 542-58. The effects of a rigidly imposed education based on Nationalism and Catholicism are, perhaps, clearer (Gregorio Cámara, *Nacional-catolicismo y escuela: la socialización política del franquismo [1936-1951]* [Jaén: Hesperia, 1984]).

10   It was partly this enforced retreat which explains the prominence of women in the sporadic expression of resistance which occurred in the 1940s.

11   See Michael Richards, *Autarky and the Franco Dictatorship in Spain, 1936-1945*, doctoral thesis (Univ. of London, 1995). 'Totalitarian' is used in this paper to refer to a will by the regime to 'total control' within society and

suppression of consciousness. The politically-induced environment of scarcity broke down popular collective solidarities. The hopelessness of the situation dulled the senses. Personal memories of what was a nightmare world for millions were partly shaped by the almost dream-like state which people were forced to enter into in order to get by.

This sense of evasion is suggested by Manuel Vázquez Montalbán in writing of Barcelona in the 1940s: 'The city *survived* and pretended not to hear the firing squads shooting, not to notice the queues outside the Model Prison, or the systematic destruction of its own identity'.[12] The suggested relationship between pain, fear and evasion is reinforced by personal testimonies. One woman from Seville, for example, recalls the days following the occupation of her working-class *barrio* in the summer of 1936: 'We were five days without going out at all ... There were executions against the wall, right opposite where we lived. But I never saw them. There were those who got up in the morning and went to see who had been shot. They left them there for two or three hours so that the people could see them ... The lorries loaded with people destined for the cemetery also passed down my street ... But we didn't want to see them either. When the shots sounded at night we covered up our ears ...'.[13]

Very little of this repressed, hidden or distorted memory has been recovered in the new democratic Spain. The transition of the mid-1970s from a brutal dictatorship to a liberal constitutional democracy rested upon a tacit agreement that, in return for relinquishing its power, the Francoist political class would be compensated by an obligatory exercise in collective amnesia.[14]

Therefore, considerable problems have to be overcome, in terms both of methodology and interpretation, in analysing the

---

not as a way of resurrecting the Cold War construct of 'totalitarianism' which saw no essential distinctions between state Communism and Fascism.

12 Manuel Vázquez Montalbán, *Barcelona* (Barcelona: Empuries, 1987), 168.

13 Cited in A. Braojos Garrido, L. Álvarez Rey, F. Espinosa Maestre, *Sevilla '36: sublevación fascista y represión* (Seville: Muñoz Moya y Montraveta Editores, 1990), 218-19.

14 See the article by Antonio Elorza, *El País* (4 January 1990).

Francoist repression during and after the Civil War. The paucity of sources, both because of the destruction of material and rigid control of access to archives, has been and continues to be an enormous obstacle to research.[15] This situation has allowed for the perpetuation of a distinct political bias in some writing about the war and dictatorship. The neo-positivist tendency in writing about the repression has meant that questions about motivation and the origins of the violence have largely been avoided. This series of problems and obstacles in writing about the brutality of the Civil War presents a difficult terrain upon which to attempt a more historically grounded understanding of the nature of Francoism.

II

Positivism and Propaganda

The debate about the repression has largely been dominated by historians who have attempted to limit discussion to the abstract quantification of the terror. This has produced a situation which, according to one dissenting voice, is characterized by a series of 'macabre accounting exercises'.[16] Some of these 'scientific' attempts to 'quantify' the repression have, in reality, constituted little more than a perpetuation of regime propaganda which sought to create a particular image of the Civil War.[17]

---

15 Ironically, perhaps, the relative opening up of official archives since the transition has encouraged many historians to adopt a rather drily value-free empirical approach, producing a great deal of published material consisting of, or based upon, copies of those documents which have survived the activities of Francoist censors. While this has revealed much which is of interest, there is occasionally a complete absence of analysis. See the critical comments of Paul Preston, 'The Politics of Revenge: Francoism, the Civil War and Collective Memory', in Paul Preston, *The Politics of Revenge* (London: Unwin Hyman, 1990), 33-34.

16 Manuel Tuñón de Lara, prologue to Reig Tapia, *Ideología e historia*, *op. cit.*, 10. See also *Violencia y política en España*, ed. Julio Aróstegui, *Ayer* 13 (1994), 15.

17 On systematized regime propaganda and the Francoist re-writing of history see Herbert Southworth, *El mito de la cruzada de Franco* (Paris:

In this kind of account the terror is always discussed in isolation from any social context. These studies, limited to what is described as 'precise quantification', deliberately do not enter into the specific characteristics of repression in each zone. No distinctions are drawn between terror and violence in the Republican zone and the systematic purging of Nationalist society. To enter into such discussion would involve facing up to some difficult questions about the role of ideology, about social and political motivations, structures of power, decision-making processes, and, indeed, about the very nature of the Civil War itself. Historians sympathetic to Franco have been reluctant to do this.[18]

Before elaborating upon these distinctions it is worth making a few prior observations about the potential problem here in the use of terms. Specifically, an undifferentiated use of the words 'violence', 'terror' and 'repression' is not useful. Obviously, the fighting of a war involved the use of physical *violence*. This kind of violence was primarily in the interests of *military* objectives and was carried out by both sides.[19] At the same time, while the war was still being fought, violence was also used, again by both sides, in the pursuit of *more plainly political and social goals*, although these were often not particularly well-defined. (Anti-Marxist purges and symbolic acts of anti-clericalism, for example.) This use of what I have

---

Ruedo Ibérico, 1963); *Guernica! Guernica! A Study of Journalism, Diplomacy, Propaganda and History* (Berkeley: Univ. of California Press, 1977); Paul Preston, 'War of Words: The Spanish Civil War and the Historians' in *Revolution and War in Spain, op. cit.* and 'The Politics of Revenge: Francoism, the Civil War and Collective Memory' in *The Politics of Revenge, op. cit.*

18 See, particularly, Ramón Salas Larrazábal, *Pérdidas de la guerra* (Barcelona: Editorial Planeta, 1977); Ricardo de la Cierva, *La historia se confiesa* (Barcelona: Editorial Planeta, 1976); *Historia ilustrada de la guerra civil española*, 2 vols (Barcelona: Ediciones Danae, 1990), particularly volume 2, 215-16; *Francisco Franco: Un siglo de España*, 2 vols (Madrid: Editorial Nacional, 1973), II, 172.

19 The distinction between 'military violence' and 'political violence' is clearly also far from free of problems, particularly when talking of *civil war*. This distinction is difficult to encapsulate within a heuristic model of violence, the construction of which is not possible in this paper. For a discussion of the problems and possible approaches see Aróstegui, *Violencia, op. cit.*

tended to refer to as *political terror* is occasionally difficult to distinguish from the violence of warfare. However, there is no doubt that this terror was frequently applied, particularly by the Nationalist forces, *during* the Civil War itself. In other words, we cannot simply argue that all violence in the Civil War period, strictly defined as between 17 July 1936 and 1 April 1939, was just the 'violence of warfare', and that only *subsequent* violence was political. Finally, I have used 'repression' here to refer to that brutality which was applied *at the clearly articulated behest of a well-defined state authority*, or primary institutions thereof, such as the Nationalist army. This was state-directed oppression in the pursuit of a reactionary *political* project 'justified' by a clearly articulated code of values and ideas; by an *ideology*. The Republican government never called for the use of brutality in this sense and its public ethics were contrary to the use of political terror.[20]

Republican terror was unleashed, often in the form of spontaneous outbursts, to some degree, as a result of the years of frustrations created by the devastating way of life which Spain's social and political structure imposed and as a response to the violent attempt by rebel generals to destroy the Republic which offered some remedies for this social malaise.[21] Violence

---

20 This Nationalist *repression* obviously overlapped with what I have described as 'political terror', in the Nationalist zone, but, although continuing to be guided by the 'ideological symbols' constructed by Nationalist Spain — the 'crusade', the 'revitalization of the spirit', etc. — it constituted a more strictly organized *system of repression*. These distinctions will become clearer in the course of this article.

21 The point is not to deny that there were specifically targeted groups which were victims of the revolutionary terror in the first months in the Republican zone (Francisco Cobo Romero, 'La justicia republicana en la provincia de Jaén durante la guerra civil. La actuación de los Tribunales especiales populares [1936-1939]', in *Justicia en guerra* [Madrid: Ministerio de Cultura, 1990], 127-38). However, this kind of 'popular' violence, undirected by the state and carried out by workers, was of a distinct nature to the violence of middle-class Falangists or employers whose killing received the blessing of the Church (Reig, *Violencia*, 16-17). In the Republican rearguard there was an embryonic and unevenly pursued social revolution going on which one historian has preferred to describe as 'a state of generalized subversion' (Glicerio Sánchez Recio, 'Justicia ordinaria y justicia popular

in the Nationalist zone, and, subsequently, in Franco's Spain, in contrast, was carried out at the behest of the highest authorities and according to a pre-conceived plan to purge society.[22] This contextual difference would seem to be the essential point of departure for an historicization of Civil War and post-war violence in Spain.

Resistance to the tendency of isolating the repression in an interpretative vacuum has entailed both a reconstruction of the attitudes towards violence of the political and military leaders of the two sides in the Civil War and of the processes of the brutality itself.[23] In essence, this implies a need to situate the repression within an analysis of the particular political and social conjuncture of Spain in the 1930s and 1940s. Francoist political terror and violence performed a similar function to violence in Nazi Germany and Fascist Italy. It both facilitated the political disarticulation of the enemy structure and the paralysis of the reflexes of the Republic and of its social base within the working class. In other words, it disorientated Republican strategy *and* wiped out much of its social support. Thus, the repression was never 'inevitable' in the way that

---

durante la guerra civil', in *Justicia en guerra*, 87-108, cited by Joan Sagués San José, 'La justicia i la repressió en els estudis sobre la guerra civil espanyola i la postguerra', in *Violència política i ruptura social a Espanya, 1936-1945* [Lleida: Edicions de la Universitat de Lleida, 1994], 9).

22 This important distinction between the cold, methodical and organized violence in Nationalist areas and the poorly controlled 'popular justice' of Government Spain, is made by writers who spent time in both zones during the Civil War. See, for example, Antonio Bahamonde, *Un año con Queipo: memorias de un nacionalista, op. cit.* Bahamonde, a devout Catholic, was the Propaganda Delegate of General Queipo de Llano. He had been in the Falange militia and was involved in guard duties in prisons and cemeteries but did all he could to escape because of the horror he witnessed there. See also *Lo que han hecho en Galicia: episodios del terror blanco en las provincias gallegas contados por quienes los han vivido* (Paris: Editorial España, 1938), 31-32.

23 See Ian Gibson, *Granada en 1936 y el asesinato de Federico García Lorca* (Barcelona: Editorial Crítica, 1979); Manuel Tuñón de Lara, *La España del siglo XX, 1914-1939* (Paris: Librería Española, 1973), 450-55; Francisco Moreno Gómez, *La guerra civil en Córdoba, (1936-1939)* (Madrid: Editorial Alpuerto, 1985); Josep María Solé i Sabaté, *La repressió franquista a Catalunya* (Barcelona: Edicions 62, 1985).

many claim. It was only viewed as 'necessary' by the Nationalist military rebels and ideologues because of the *social* and *political* possibilities it was seen as opening up. In contrast, the terror in the Republican zone was never 'bankable';[24] it was much more spontaneous and less selective and could therefore perform no particular social function. It never effectively contributed to the achievement of any of the objectives of the besieged Republican government.

Although there were doubtless 'irrational' violent episodes, Nationalist (and, subsequently, Francoist) repression, in the main, was a *political* activity. The terror was programmed, thought-out, and intentional.[25] In contrast, in the Republican zone violence was never planned as a political weapon.[26] The considerable, and lamentable, violence unleashed against priests and members of religious orders, in particular, was often perpetrated by marginal groups and individuals outside of the legal and moral code as developed by Republican political leaders.[27]

The contrasting nature of authority in the two zones at the height of the political terror is, therefore, an essential consideration within any framework of explanation. The decision-making process in Nationalist Spain was put in place by what was a coherent state in formation.[28] The Republic, in contrast, constituted an incoherent power in a process of virtual

24 Tuñón de Lara, prologue, *Ideología*, 9. In contrast, the 'social shock' of Nationalist/Francoist brutality in this period could be seen as having a lasting 'value' in terms of social control into the 1950s and 60s.

25 Pierre Vilar, *Spain: A Brief History* (Oxford: Pergamon, 1977 [2nd ed.]), 113.

26 Political violence was used in Republican Spain as part of the state's reconstruction of bourgeois authority after May 1937. However, of course, *this* violence was against anarchists and supporters of the dissident Marxist parties, *not* against Francoist supporters.

27 This is not to suggest that Republican violence is not in need of analysis. However, to an extent, our view of terror in the Republican zone has been distorted by Francoist propaganda. A study which sets this violence too within a context of living conditions, political participation and popular cultural and political ideas would be very useful.

28 Ramón Serrano Suñer, *Entre Hendaya y Gibraltar* (Madrid: Ediciones y Publicaciones Españolas, 1963 [6th ed.]), especially pp. 33-70; Stanley Payne, *Franco's Spain* (London: Routledge & Kegan Paul, 1968), 23.

disintegration. Martial law was declared immediately in July 1936 in the Nationalist zone.[29] Ultimate power passed to the military which guaranteed a rigorous system of authority based on honour, order and discipline. The Army was quite accustomed to assuming this role in moments of social and political crisis. In Republican Spain, however, martial law was not declared until January 1939, only months prior to Franco's victory. Virtually from the beginning of the conflict the Nationalist system of authority was more secure, solid and stable than that of the Government itself.[30] As Pierre Vilar has suggested, in Nationalist Spain '... contrary to what happened in the Republican camp, democratic forms didn't exist — a pluralistic press, parties, open ministerial crises ... there were no open discussions about methods and ends. The violence of class hatred, when it is exercised from above, is much more coherent and durable than in the other direction'.[31]

The Question of Quantification

Criticisms of 'scientific' method, along these lines, are not designed to weaken the need for intellectual rigour. Quite the reverse is the case. First, some sense of the magnitude of the killing is obviously essential in making judgments about the nature of a divided society at war. However, perhaps as important, a *genuinely* 'scientific' methodology would have to take account of the severe limitations of the available sources.

---

29 In Seville the state of war was declared in article 1 of a decree of 18 July 1936. The priorities were quite clear; article 2 decreed that strikers would be shot (Julio de Ramón-Laca, *Bajo la férula de Queipo: como fue gobernada Andalucía* [Seville: Imprenta Comercial, 1939], 16).

30 See Gerald Brenan in *Manchester Guardian*, 31 August 1936: 'Those who point to atrocities [...] on the Government side often forget the provocation and the circumstances. When soldiers and police have to go to the front because other soldiers and police have rebelled, who is left to keep order among an enraged population?'. Following the military rebellion there was a collapse of bourgeois Republican power which was not recaptured from the street, as it were, until May 1937.

31 Pierre Broué, Ronald Fraser and Pierre Vilar, *Metodología histórica de la guerra y revolución españolas* (Barcelona: Editorial Fontamara, 1980), 90.

Some of the authors who have insisted upon the need for 'scientific' quantification of the victims of Francoist repression appear to have been suffering from what Arthur Koestler called 'objectivity neurosis'.[32] Scientific method ought not to be simply reduced to the use of quantitative techniques. The material to be found in those archives which are open to public view in Spain has, in the vast majority of cases, been systematically scrutinized by authorities loyal to the dictatorial state. An enormous number of records have been purposely destroyed.[33] Some accounts have used global demographic figures as the basis for calculating total losses resulting from the Civil War and its aftermath. However, this manner of proceeding is of strictly relative value since the census statistics upon which such calculations are based are notoriously unreliable.[34] Only a partial and sanitized version of the reality can be reconstructed from the use of such records in isolation. Simply isolating the 'known facts' gives a highly distorted image of the repression; an image, in part, constructed by the Franco regime itself. The relationship between the social crisis in Spain and the development of rightist ideology, prior to the conflict, needs to be taken into account in explaining both the magnitude of the violence as well as its origins and objectives. The available anecdotal evidence suggests that the brutality was of a dimension far in excess of that which it is possible to quantify precisely, and that it was related to the generalized crisis of the first third of the twentieth century in Spain. The estimates of critical historians which suggest that as many as two hundred

---

32 Koestler, *Spanish Testament*, 84. In other words, 'objectivity' is used as a way of 'justifying' the refusal to countenance the possibility that the reality was something more than is demonstrable by trawling through the archives and counting entries on lists.

33 See, for example, Josep M. Solé i Sabaté, *La repressió franquista a Catalunya, 1938-1953*, 16-17; Joan María Thomàs, 'Memoria que quema', in *El País*, November 1, 1992.

34 Ramón Tamames, *La república*, 348-53. This fact was even recognized officially (Reig Tapia, *Ideología*, 72). In an attempt to obtain more rations from central authorities in the harsh aftermath of the Civil War, local governments often inflated regional population figures wildly. See also, Jesús Villar Salinas, *Repercusiones demográficas de la última guerra civil española* (Madrid: Sobrinos de la Sucesora de M. Minuesa de los Ríos, 1942), 110-12.

thousand men and women were killed in the Nationalist repression do not then seem unreasonable.[35]

The most obvious form of repression was physical extermination.[36] This did not cease with Franco's declaration of the end of the Civil War, as such, in April 1939. Thousands of executions took place in Spain during the next five or six years, in particular, although the regime continued to put its enemies to death until the very end of the dictatorship in the 1970s. Since we know for sure that many officially sanctioned executions took place outside the dictatorial legal framework during the war and in the 1940s and were often not recorded we will certainly never know the true number of those killed.[37]

---

35 Charles Foltz, the American journalist, gave, in the 1940s, the figure which an unnamed official of the Spanish Ministry of Justice mentioned. That is, between 1 April, 1939 and 30 June, 1944 precisely 192,684 executions were carried out. See Foltz, *The Masquerade in Spain* (Boston: Houghton Mifflin, 1948), 97. Foltz also points out that the Ministry of Justice had nothing to do with the recording of executions of prisoners held by the Falange, the Ministry of the Interior, or of the army. See also Bowker to Eden, 12 December 1944, Public Record Office (PRO) FO371/49575/Z89/41. An early, and sympathetic, biographer of Franco, Brian Crozier, on mentioning the figure quoted by Foltz was contacted by the Spanish Ministry of Information to insist that the number of executions was not more than forty thousand, a view which has been supported by some historians since. Gabriel Jackson calculated that a minimum of 150,000 and a maximum of 200,000 were killed in reprisals and formal executions in the Nationalist zone from 1936 to 1944 (see his *La República Española y la Guerra Civil 1931-1939* [Barcelona: Editorial Crítica, 1976], 14). Ramón Tamames, employing a reasoned and critical viewpoint towards official demographic statistics, estimates the number of executions in the period 1939-1945 alone at 105,000 (*La República. La Era de Franco* [Madrid: Editorial Alianza, 1973], 323).

36 Political repression encompasses more than extermination, physical violence and the deprivation of liberty. It also encompasses coercion through work, material deprivation, and in the dynamics of culture and gender. None of these forms of repression were mutually exclusive. They were all based upon a totalitarian conception of power which assumed value and utility in violence and ideological control imposed against and upon enemies defined according to a particular conception of what (and who) constituted 'the nation'.

37 Gabriel Jackson, *The Spanish Republic and the Civil War, 1931-1939* (Princeton: Princeton U. P., 1965), 526; see also the Spanish edition, at p. 13; Tamames, *La República*, 348-56.

The lowest recently suggested figure has been that given by the ex-Nationalist militia (*requeté*) volunteer and Francoist General, Ramón Salas Larrazábal.[38]   Salas calculated that in the Nationalist zone during the war itself (in the period July, 1936 to April 1, 1939) there were 57,662 executions.[39] Subsequently, he calculates, 23,000 further 'judicial executions' took place during the period 1939 to 1961 in the whole country.[40]   This figure has been accorded a great deal of authority by other historians who have doubted the claims made by observers in the post-war period.[41] Of course, by any calculations, the magnitude of the repression was enormous. Of this there is no doubt.   In the argument over 'exact' quantification this should not be lost sight of. As one historian has pointed out, the scale of repression claimed in the account of Salas, in itself, would mean that ten individuals, on average, were shot each and every day throughout the entire period of seven years from 1939 to 1945.[42]

Executions were carried out in a manner designed specifically to avoid leaving traces.[43] Within the bureaucracy of

---

38 Ramón Salas Larrázabal, *Pérdidas de la guerra*. See the critical comment in Paul Preston, *The Politics of Revenge*, 33, fn. 13. The general approach of Salas is suggested by the title and spirit of such publications as *Los datos exactos de la guerra civil* (Madrid: Ediciones Rioduero, 1980).

39 *Pérdidas*, 372.

40 *Ibid.*, 428-29.

41 See, for example, the account of the respected American hispanist Stanley Payne in his important and influential recent book, *The Franco Regime, 1936-1975* (Madison: Univ. of Wisconsin, 1987), 635. See also Ricardo de la Cierva, *La historia se confiesa* (Barcelona: Editorial Planeta, 1976), in which the author suggests that a figure of around 20,000 is more accurate. He also takes the opportunity to castigate other historians for their 'notorious irresponsibility' in giving figures up to ten times greater. La Cierva was an official of the regime's Ministry of Information in the 1960s, placed in charge of the so-called Centre for Civil War Studies (see Paul Preston, 'War of Words: The Spanish Civil War and the Historians', 3-5).

42 See Juan Pablo Fusi, *Franco: autoritarismo y poder personal* (Madrid: Ediciones El País, 1985), 79.

43 Tamames, *La república*, 349. An illustrative example cited by Reig Tapia is that of the Republican Civil Governor of Valladolid who was arrested and tried before a Nationalist tribunal in 1936 and executed. The events were well publicized and reported in the newspapers but his death was not recorded

the 'New State' loyalty to leaders and to their ideology counted for much more than efficiency in terms of adherence to legal forms and procedures. In very many cases only the immediate and purely clinical cause of deaths were recorded in the civil registers.[44] The ambiguities involved in making calculations are numerous. How many men and women were shot after summary 'judgments' on their political affiliations and recorded as 'killed in action'?

Although some of these studies have provided a record of the deaths of some of the individual victims of the repression — a formal remembering which had often been previously denied — the manner in which the repression was unleashed makes impossible anything approximating to precise quantification. Often relatives of victims were too afraid to identify the bodies of loved-ones for fear of being arrested as equally culpable.[45] Even publicly to express mourning for the executed was to risk punishment in the immediate post-war period.[46] In these cases deaths were often not registered. In the environment of fear created by the state many brutalities were committed which

in the civil register. It seems reasonable to assume that thousands of other executions of less prominent individuals surely took place and were similarly not recorded (*Ideología*, 102). In Galicia an order was given that no death certificates be issued even to those family members brave enough to identify the bodies of the executed (see *Lo que han hecho*, 46). Civil War deaths have continued to be registered by families even in the last ten years. In the mining districts of Asturias, for example, more than fifty per cent of the victims were registered in the civil registers *after* 1975. Ramón García Piñeiro, *Los mineros asturianos bajo el franquismo (1937-1962)* (Madrid: Fundación 1º de Mayo, 1990), 175.

44 According to the register in Granada, for example, Federico García Lorca '... died in the month of August of 1936 as a consequence of wounds produced by a fact of war' (Ian Gibson, *Granada en 1936*, 192-93). Luis Companys, the President of the Catalan regional Government during the Civil War, was detained in Belgium by the Nazis and handed over to the Francoist authorities and summarily executed in Barcelona in 1940. The death certificate noted simply that he had died in Montjuich Castle from a 'traumatic internal haemorrhage'. This was an example of the language of double-think used to obscure the reality (see Vázquez Montalbán, *Barcelonas*, 169).

45 Thomas, *The Spanish Civil War*, 261.

46 See García Piñeiro, *Los mineros*, 175.

were never recorded and are now impossible to prove or quantify. However, a considerable amount of anecdotal evidence suggests that original estimates may be very close to the truth. Salas uses the provincial records of the civil registers to quantify the death toll in each area. However, contemporary claims went far beyond even the extraordinary degree of repression suggested by his calculations. One Spanish exile wrote to the British Foreign Office claiming, for example, that forty or fifty were being shot each day in Madrid alone in 1941. The informant continues:

> It is said that in Asturias alone 60,000 have been killed. According to the Franco press, there were 60 and 70 executions in Gijón and Oviedo every day for four months.[47] In one Gijón factory 12 out of 15 men were killed. In Huelva there have been 15,000 executions; in Ferrol from 9,000 to 10,000; in Santander 6,500. In Navalvillas de Pela, Badajoz, 1700 of the 6,000 inhabitants were executed, including various women. As a result of the Civil War and the subsequent repression, only 9,000 inhabitants remain in Tortosa out of 45,000. In Larrióaga, Bilbao, out of 1,200 prisoners, 600 were killed. In the Canary Islands more than 1,000 from the Communist Party alone were shot. From October 11th to December 31st, 1939, 417 men from 6 small villages were buried in the cemetery of Ciriego, Santander. In Laguna de Teza, a village in the same province, 150 of the 400 inhabitants have been killed. In January 1940 12 condemned men in Celanova, Orense, were forced to carry their own coffins to the place of execution ... A favourite day for these mass murders is a political celebration, such as the anniversary of the death of Primo de Rivera or Calvo Sotelo, the first of May, etc. During the time that the remains of Primo de Rivera were being carried amid great pomp and circumstance to the Escorial, 2,000 men were killed in two days in Madrid alone ...[48]

While it is obviously important to evaluate critically the significance of what are exaggerated claims, the alternative of

---

47 Asturias was a traditionally militant mining area which had often historically led the way for working-class protest, most spectacularly, prior to the Civil War, in October 1934 when a political rising by workers was crushed by General Franco and his troops.

48 PRO/FO371/26890/C3986/3/41, 15 April 1941. This informant was the ex-Republican Ambassador to Britain, during the Civil War, the moderate liberal Pablo de Azcárate.

simply ignoring them and relying solely upon surviving records is clearly insufficient. The intervening period of almost forty years of dictatorial censorship, as well as the context of the unleashing of the repression itself, and the manner in which executions were carried out, have to be taken into account in any such evaluation. This may be anecdotal evidence but in most cases it is virtually all that has been left to us.

III

Contextualizing the Repression

The attitudes of Nationalist political leaders towards violence was quite different to that of Republicans. There was no comparable reaction among the rebel leaders to the moral crisis suffered by the Republic's President Manuel Azaña on hearing of the killings carried out by Government supporters in the aftermath of the military rebellion in Madrid.[49] There were no protests from Nationalist leaders; only encouragement.

From the initial stages of the planning of the rebellion against the democratic Government a determination to carry out an extermination campaign was declared. This process of 'purification' was seen as necessary in order to purge Spain of 'sick bodies', of 'unhealthy organisms', and received the blessing

---

49 Republican leaders repeatedly tried to put an end to the terror. Josep María Solé i Sabaté and Joan Villarroya, in *La repressió a la reraguarda de Catalunya (1936-1939)* (Barcelona: Publicacions de l'Abadia de Montserrat, 1989), do show that not all illegal violence was carried out by the so-called 'incontrolats', and that the political leaders of revolutionary groups have some responsibility. However, they also show how the Republican authorities, by and large, investigated 'excesses' and attempted to put structures in place which would stop such violence. Many of Azaña's speeches, for example, were concerned with questions of brutality. See, for example, that given at the University of Valencia on 18 July 1937, particularly the sections on 'La reconstrucción moral' and on the condemnation of what he recognized as the Nationalist policy of extermination, 'Reprobación de la política de exterminio'; also the speech given in the *ayuntamiento* of Madrid, 13 November 1937, 'Monstruosidad de la guerra civil'; and in Barcelona, 18 July 1938, 'Paz, piedad y perdón'. Other Republican leaders, like Indalecio Prieto, Juan Negrín and the Anarchist Joan Peiró, made constant efforts to limit the revolutionary violence in the Republican zone.

of the Catholic Church.[50]   A pathological vocabulary of purification continued to inform the notion of reconstruction in the post-war period. Extreme violence was seen as a tool to bring about social 'improvement'. The best thing about what was called 'Hitlerism' was its 'task of moral and political cleansing'.[51]   Fervent admiration for Nazi Germany was expressed because 'personal security' was 'completely defended' there, 'order rules all public life' and 'property is guaranteed'. The suppression of political parties, imprisonments and anti-semitic measures were the logical outcome of a need to 'renovate the state'. At least one leading intellectual of the Spanish Right saw Dachau as 'a truly educating establishment' where prisoners lived as in a kind of 'hygienicized village'.[52]

---

50 Liberalism, which bred Communism, was seen as an infection or a virus. See, for example, Eloy Montero, *Los estados modernos y la nueva España* (Vitoria: Montepío Diocesano, 1939); Ernesto Giménez Caballero, *Genio de España* (Madrid: Ediciones Jerarquía, 1932, 1938, 1939); Ramiro de Maeztu, *Defensa de la Hispanidad* (Madrid: Renovación Española, 1934); Joaquín de Azpiazu, *El estado católico* (Madrid: Ediciones Rayfe, 1939); Marqués de Eliseda, *El sentido fascista del Movimiento Nacional* (Santander: Aldus, 1939). The sense of the perception of the War as a campaign against a psychological sickness at the root of extremism is reinforced by some of the state's scientific endeavours. Among the many state documents which have been destroyed, or disappeared, over the long course of the Franco dictatorship (and subsequently?) was a report (still listed in the archive of the Servicio Histórico Militar) written in 1938 dealing with the creation of an office or laboratory of 'psychological investigations' charged with analysing 'the bio-psychic roots of Marxism' ['Creación de un gabinete de investigaciones psicológicas para investigar las raíces bio-psíquicas del marxismo'] (Reig, *Ideología*, 28). See also 'Psiquismo del fanatismo marxista: investigaciones psicológicas en marxistas femeninas delincuentes', in *Revista Española de Medicina y Cirugía*, II (May 1939), No. 9.
51 See, for example, Montero, *Los estados modernos*, 24.
52 Vicente Gay y Forner, *La revolución nacional-socialista: ambiente, leyes, ideología* (Barcelona: Bosch, 1934). Gay was a professor of economics and had been Under-secretary of Economy, Director General of Industry and Tariffs, and Secretary of the National Assembly during the dictatorship of Primo de Rivera in the 1920s. After the rising in July 1936 he was rapidly appointed first Delegate of Press and Propaganda. Concentration camps were to be a prominent feature of Francoist society as territory fell to the Nationalists during the Civil War and in the 1940s.

The primary objective was not simply to defeat but to exterminate the enemy. Nationalist repression was seen as being a social and political prophylactic on a national scale. The Civil War had been an operation to 'surgically eradicate' the 'putrefaction' in society.[53]   The German Nazi press understood and admired the purposes of the Spanish repression, which, in a sense, was seen as providing an example to be followed: 'The Generals looked for guarantees of victory not primarily in military successes, but in a systematic and thorough cleaning up of the hinterland ...'.[54] 'Fortunately the old attitude of sentimentality has been dissipated among the Nationalists, and every soldier realizes that a horrible end is better than endless horrors ...'.[55] 'The Marxist parties are being destroyed and exterminated down to the very last cell far more drastically even than here in Germany. Every house, every flat, every office is kept under constant observation and supervision ... Every single citizen, moreover, is drawn into the whirl of political excitement, made to participate in triumphal celebrations and mass demonstrations. The principle of modern Nationalism, "No opponent but shall be destroyed", is thoroughly carried out ... Just as here in Germany'.[56] Franco boasted in November 1938 that the Nationalist government had built up a file with more than two million names of those who were considered enemies, '... with the proof of their crimes and the names of the witnesses'.[57] The purpose was to 'clean the

---

53 See the comments of Wenceslao González Oliveros, Franco's first Civil Governor in Barcelona in 1939 (*Catalunya sota el règim franquista* [Paris: Edicions Catalanes de Paris, 1973], 292).

54 Kurt Kranzlein in the *Angriff*, 10 November 1936 (see Arthur Koestler, *Spanish Testament* [London: Golllancz, 1937], 83).

55 The *Angriff*, 17 September 1936, *op. cit.*

56 *Essener National-Zeitung*, 13 October 1936, *op. cit.*

57 *Palabras del Caudillo* (Barcelona: Ediciones Fe, 1939), 284-85; PRO/FO371/24126/W1215/8/41, January 1939. The British Foreign Office received a report warning that 'only a peace which was achieved without unconditional surrender or a fight to a finish can avert such a disaster for Spain. That will not be achieved unless Italy is made to withdraw her planes and troops'. In accordance with the policy of appeasement over Spain, the Foreign Office decided on sending a warning to Franco but that the point about Italians 'be ignored'.

site ready for our structure'.[58] This was to be the foundation upon which the 'modern state' in Spain would be constructed.

Even before the 1936 military rising itself the conspirators made clear their belief in the need for exemplary violence directed against the working class, its organizations, and the leaders of Republican groups in general. Emilio Mola, the general directing the military conspiracy, insisted: 'It is necessary to propagate an atmosphere of terror [...] Anybody who openly or secretly defends the Popular Front must be shot'.[59]

Mass executions became a central component of the theory and practice of the operation undertaken by the rebels. Colonel Juan Yagüe, one of Franco's leading officers, ideologically close to the Falange, and the man responsible for the massacre of about two thousand leftists who were rounded up, herded into the bullring of Badajoz and shot,[60] gave a sense of the priorities and purposes of the Civil-War repression: '... the fact that the conquest of Spain by the Army is proceeding at a slow pace has this advantage; that it gives us time to purge the country thoroughly of all Red elements'.[61]

This kind of 'cleansing' (or *limpieza* — the word was also used in the 1930s and 40s to refer to 'purity of the blood') was linked to a desire to 'regenerate' Spain.[62] Many of the generation of Spaniards which politically and militarily led the ideological struggle in the 1930s and 40s had passed their formative years, in the aftermath of the loss of Spain's last colonies in 1898, amidst an environment of Regenerationism which viewed Spain as a decaying entity. Regenerationist

---

58 Speech, 24 January 1942.

59 This was the so-called 'Instruction Number 1', signed by Mola on 25 May 1936 and carried to the front on the person of rebel officers. See *El Colegio de abogados de Madrid*, Report (Madrid, October, 1936); *Franco's Rule: Back to the Middle Ages* (London: United Editorial, n.d. 1938?), 154.

60 See Paul Preston, *The Spanish Civil War* (London: Weidenfield Y Nicolson, 1986), 61.

61 *Franco's Rule*, 154.

62 Thomas, *Spanish Civil War*, 279. On Franco and regenerationism, see Manuel Vázquez Montalbán, *Los demonios familiares de Franco* (Barcelona: Dopesa, 1978), 10-11, 47-51; 'Franco i el regeneracionisme de dretes', in *L'Avenç*, (December, 1992), No. 165, 8-15.

thought as developed in the decades around the turn-of-the-century revolved around four principal factors: (i) A belief that there existed a peculiar Spanish essence which could be defined and perpetuated; (ii) the absorption of the natural sciences, particularly Darwinist biology, which were perceived as determining the future of national fortunes; (iii) disillusionment with constitutional politics; and (iv) Spain's military defeat of 1898. Franco was six years old in 1898. The interaction of these elements produced a synthesis which called for a reversal of decline by combining Castilian traditions with the modernity of science and authoritarian rule. A nation constructed of 'weak organisms', it was believed, was condemned to disappear sooner or later. An 'Iron Surgeon' would be called upon to impose an authoritarianism which would cut away society's diseased tissue. Not surprisingly, regenerationism has been seen by some writers as constituting Spain's own 'pre-Fascism'.[63]

The rebel generals, by the 1930s, saw the working class as virtually sub-human,[64] a factor which had contributed to this decline. The Spanish people, according to Mola, considered itself weak and had therefore 'degenerated'. The situation required the resurrection of what was seen as 'natural law' (*derecho natural*), that is, the 'law of force' which had been undermined by decadent parliamentarianism.[65] The notion of politics had been substituted by that of 'extermination and

---

63 For example, Enrique Tierno Galván, 'Costa y el regeneracionismo', in *Escritos, 1950-1960* (Madrid: Tecnos, 1971).

64 Franco described the Civil War as essentially a 'frontier war'. Accordingly, he and his generals applied a similar strategy, based upon a similar perception of the enemy, to that previously employed in the colonial campaigns of Morocco. Among the Spanish *africanistas* there was a fierce pride in brutal violence against the dehumanized villagers, which was typified by the decapitation of prisoners and the exhibition of severed heads (see Preston, *Franco*, 29-30). This kind of brutal rule was, in a social, political and economic sense, applied as *internal colonization* in Spain after the Civil War.

65 Emilio Mola, *Obras completas* (Valladolid: Librería Santarén, 1940), 945-46, cited in Reig Tapia, *Ideología*, 147. When, in an effort to avoid more bloodshed, Indalecio Prieto, at the end of July 1936, suggested to Mola that the two sides might attempt some negotiation, the general responded that '... this war had to end with the extermination of the enemies of Spain'. This extremism could be seen as a symptom of a process in the bastardization of regenerationist thought.

expulsion'.[66]   Accordingly, the work of 'purification' was systematically continued after the formal cessation of war on 1 April 1939. Francoist Spain would be characterized, above all, by a refusal to countenance any reconciliation. Society would be divided as between 'Spain' and 'anti-Spain'.[67]   This was the basis for the massive post-war repression.

This brutality was overwhelmingly targeted on the lower orders of society.[68]   In order to 'make Spain work' the insurgents and their supporters intended to use violence to establish and safeguard what they considered to be a stable social order. Accordingly, the Nationalist Burgos government rapidly decreed, in September 1936, the illegality of all those organizations which had participated in the legally elected Popular Front government, or which had opposed the insurgent 'National Movement'. Thus, from the beginning, the concept of legality was stood on its head.[69] The state produced legislation to give a veneer of legality to a repression which condemned the working class on the principle of guilt by association with the political parties and trade unions of the Republic. The claim that justice would be applied to those 'without blood on their hands' was meaningless in a situation where violence was utilized to confirm the defeat of a political order and a social class.

The purposes of the repression were summarized succinctly by Franco himself: only those '... capable of loving the Fatherland, of working and struggling for it, of adding their grain of sand to the common effort ...' would be tolerated. The others could not be allowed back into 'social circulation ... Wicked, deviant, politically and morally poisoned elements ... those without possible redemption within the human order ...'.

---

66 Azaña, 'Reprobación', cited speech; José María Pemán, *Arengas y crónicas de guerra* (Cádiz: Ediciones Cerón, 1937), 13; Reig, *Ideología*, 153.

67 Effectively, half of Spain was to be denied any collective identity.

68 Josep Fontana, 'Reflexiones sobre la naturaleza y las consecuencias del franquismo', 24; Solé i Sabaté, *La repressió franquista a Catalunya*, particularly pp. 51-62; Manuel Tuñón de Lara, *La España del siglo XX*, 450-55; Francisco Moreno Gómez, *La Guerra Civil en Córdoba, 1936-1939*; Stanley Payne, *The Spanish Revolution* (London: Weidenfield & Nicolson, 1970), 231.

69 Ramón Serrano Suñer, *Entre el silencio y la propaganda* (Madrid: Editorial Planeta, 1977), 244-45.

Salvation for such people could only come through labour.[70] It was the working class which needed to be 'disciplined' in this process of the national 'expiation of sin'. According to Franco, '...the suffering of a nation at a particular point of its history is no caprice; it is spiritual punishment, the punishment which God imposes upon a distorted life, upon an unclean history'.[71]

The Spanish proletariat, in particular, it was claimed, was 'sick' — contaminated by 'Bolshevism'. Franco's first Minister of the Interior, Ramón Serrano Suñer, who was to be mainly responsible for constructing the formal institutions of the Francoist state, gave his view on the situation in Barcelona after its fall in January 1939 to a German journalist: 'The city is completely bolshevized. The task of decomposition absolute ... In Barcelona the Reds have stifled the Spanish spirit. The people ... are morally and politically sick. Barcelona will be treated by us with the care with which one attends to an invalid'.[72]

The 'reconquest' of Southern Spain was viewed as an opportunity for a definitive settling of accounts between landowners and their representatives and the landless population.[73] In Seville civilian volunteers, many associated with the area's powerful landowning elite, co-operated with the local military and the Falangist organization in establishing local power through brutal repression of the working-class

---

70 *La Vanguardia Española*, 4 April 1939. Franco had already made clear in 1937 to the Italian Ambassador in Nationalist Spain that victory for him meant the annihilation of large numbers of Republicans and the total humiliation and terrorization of the surviving population (Preston, *Franco*, 276). The Caudillo evidently saw the bloodiest battles of the Civil War as part of a necessary 'cleansing operation', 283. On the centrality of 'work' linked with 'redemption', see El Patronato Central de Redención de Penas por el Trabajo, *La obra de la redención de penas — La doctrina, la práctica, la legislación* (Madrid: El Patronato Central, 1941).

71 Speech, Jaén, 18 March 1940.

72 *Catalunya sota el règim franquista*, 229.

73 Antonio-Miguel Bernal, 'Resignación de los campesinos andaluces: la resistencia pasiva durante el franquismo', in the edited volume, *Causa general y actitudes sociales ante la dictadura* (Univ. of Castilla-La Mancha, 1993), 148.

population.[74] Categoric orders were issued to officers insisting that upon the occupation of every town, information be obtained from priests and 'other reliable persons' as to the attitudes of the community.[75]

There were two general phases of terror and repression in Seville.[76] First, the period from July 1936 to January or February 1937 was characterized by a wave of executions among the working class. This phase saw the 'disappearing' of hundreds (perhaps thousands) of men and women. Mass shootings in the streets and in the cemeteries, without any formalized bureaucratic processing, were typical of this era.[77] Only a fraction of these deaths were recorded in the civil register. This was not violence which was 'necessary' in any military sense. Nor was it indiscriminate. It was organized to the extent that both political militias (principally the Falangists) and the army utilized lists drawn up by those locals with influence; principally landowners and their representatives. A second phase began from February 1937. Repression now was partially undertaken beneath an appearance of 'legality'. This was the era of the Councils of War. Files were called for, at a formal level, but in most cases the 'evidence' was never heard since pre-judgment had been made beforehand.[78] Although from this time onward the

---

74 On Falangist involvement in purges see, among an ever-mounting quantity of evidence, Moreno Gómez, *La guerra civil*; Juan de Iturralde, *El catolicismo y la cruzada de Franco*, 2 vols (Bayonne: Egi-Indarra, 1955), II, 107-20; Gibson, *Granada en 1936*; Braojos Garrido *et al.*, *Sevilla '36*; Herbert Southworth, *Antifalange: estudio crítico de Falange en la guerra de España* (Paris: Ruedo Ibérico, 1967); Julián Casanova, Ángela Cenarro, Julita Cifuente, María del Pilar Maluenda and María del Pilar Salomón, *El pasado oculto: fascismo y violencia en Aragón, 1936-1939* (Madrid: Siglo XXI, 1992); Bahamonde, *Un año con Queipo*, 100-01, 113-20.

75 *Franco's Rule*, 155.

76 Braojos Garrido, *Sevilla '36*, 238.

77 According to the testimony, among others, of the Falangist official Antonio Bahamonde (see *Un año con Queipo*, 92). The watchword was 'abreviar trámites' (cutting short procedures). See also *The Times*, 9 December 1936.

78 Bahamonde (*Un año con Queipo*, 92, 108), describes the 'parody' of the Councils of War. He claims that in Seville the Delegado de Orden Público, Captain Manuel Díaz Criado, signed some sixty death sentences a day without

records of the civil registry begin to reflect the reality a little closer, we know that men and women continued to be killed and not recorded here since the rough figures of what was known as the Common Grave (Fosa Común) of the San Fernando Cemetery are markedly higher than those of the civil register.[79]

The initial 'pacification' of Seville and its environs took a week. In some hamlets, according to the personal secretary of the director of the rising, General Mola, the repression was so thorough that virtually the entire worker population was wiped out.[80] The officer in control of repression in the occupied South was the notoriously brutal Gonzalo Queipo de Llano, who became infamous for his threatening, drunken and half-crazed radio broadcasts made from Seville. On 19 August 1936 Queipo declared his determination to carry through the most fundamental objective of the rebels: 'Eighty per cent of the families of Andalusia are already in mourning. And we shall not hesitate, either, to adopt even more rigorous measures to assure our ultimate victory. We shall go on to the bitter end and continue our good work until not a single Marxist is left in Spain'.[81] This provided an answer to the question posed by Francisco González Ruiz, the Republican former Civil Governor of Murcia who found himself in rebel territory during the early part of the Civil War, only to be disillusioned by what he witnessed: 'Why do they go on shooting after twelve, fourteen months of war, and in Seville, where they were the masters of the situation from the very beginning?'[82]

---

studying the files. He described his task as 'thoroughly cleansing (*limpiar*) Spain of Marxists'.

79 These common graves became a feature of the landscape throughout Spain as the Nationalist campaign proceeded. The general belief, even amongst those civil servants who administer the civil records, is that there were possibly three times as many deaths as have been recorded during this period (*Ideología*, 111).

80 José María Iribarren, *Con el General Mola* (Zaragoza: Editorial Heraldo de Aragón, 1937), 187; *Franco's Rule*, 187.

81 Tuñón de Lara, *La España del siglo XX*, 450.

82 Francisco González Ruiz, *Yo he creído en Franco: proceso de una gran desilusión — dos meses en la cárcel de Sevilla* (Paris: Ediciones Imprimerie/Coopérative Étoile, 1938), 128. The same question might be asked in relation to Granada or Córdoba or Zaragoza: see Gibson (*The Death of*

Queipo rapidly took to ordering mass executions in the streets of working-class districts of the city, rather than within the precincts of the prisons and cemeteries, and the bodies were left for several hours where they fell as an example to the population in general. While the General Strike called by workers in defence of the city was maintained bodies littered the street and had to be piled up against the side of houses so that army trucks could pass. The initial declaration of a state of war by the Nationalists on 18 July, the priority of which was to announce the death penalty for strikers, was reiterated by subsequent decrees in the next few days. In mobilizing workers in factories and the railways, 'blind obedience' was demanded and 'the ultimate penalty' threatened to those who did not co-operate.[83] Resistance under such violent conditions was extremely difficult. However, workers in other parts of Spain too attempted to organize in the face of such brutality.[84]

While recent 'scientific' study has suggested a figure of around two thousand, four hundred executions during the Civil War in Seville, local estimates at the time suggested that the magnitude of the repression was at least three or four times greater.[85] José María Varela Rendueles, the Republican Civil

---

Lorca, 68), Moreno Gómez (Córdoba), Bahamonde (op. cit., 123-24), Casanova (El pasado oculto), for example. Queipo claimed that cities like Mérida would cease to exist; that he would leave nobody alive. In Seville the number of executions decreased simply because there was an ever-dwindling number of workers left to shoot (Bahamonde, 90-93).

83 Ramón-Laca, Bajo la férula, 20-27.

84 In the main population centres of Galicia, for example, the main resistance was manifested by a refusal to work. The first worker shot was a striking tram driver. Executions followed as a systematic purge of each section of the economy in turn followed. Workers in the metallurgy sector followed the tram drivers in this process. Then the guns were turned on railway workers. In La Coruña workers organized collections of money to help feed strikers. These donations were made illegal but they continued as did the strike until the authorities took five workers as hostages. In spite of the executions workers' passive resistance continued to prevent a return to normality (see Lo que han hecho, pp. 30, 45-46, 181-82, 199-200).

85 Salas Larrazábal gives the lower estimate (Pérdidas), but see also Franco's Rule, pp. 148, 151. These estimates range from 7,000 victims by August 1936 to 15,000 by November and 30,000 by 1937. See also Nicolás

Governor of Seville in 1936, claimed that it was enough to be found with a membership card of the socialist union, the UGT, to be killed on the spot. He states that between July 1936 and February 1937 more than six thousand were killed in the city of Seville without appearing before any court whatsoever.[86]

The authorities in Seville devised the tactic of organizing motorized squads, or 'Brigadas de Depuración', (Purification Brigades), of one hundred men each which descended upon 'dubious' villages in order to 'clean up' the population by exterminating all suspect elements in so-called 'executions of national salvation'.[87] Despite later propaganda attempts to depict the volunteer forces which helped carry out the fiercest acts of extermination as being composed of a mix of social groups, it now seems clear that these squads were co-ordinated and largely composed of local grandees, noblemen and landowners and their sons.[88] A typical case was that of the son of the administrator of the estates of a marquis of Jaen in Andalusia who, after the military rising, became a Falangist and was assigned to an execution squad and was responsible for hundreds of deaths.[89]

Salas, *Sevilla fue la clave*, 2 vols (Seville: Editorial Castillejo, 1992), II, 644-55, which gives a figure of 8,000 dead between July 1936 and December 1941.

86 Reig Tapia, *La represión franquista y la guerra civil: consideraciones metodológicas, instrumentalización política y justificación ideológica*, doctoral thesis (Univ. Complutense, Madrid, n..p, 1983), 710. The Falangist Antonio Bahamonde, from conversations with the authorities involved in the repression, suggested that in Andalucia 150,000 had been killed by 1938. In the city of Seville alone he reckoned that 20,000 had fallen victim to the repression (*Un año*, 94).

87 *The Times*, 12 August 1936; *Franco's Rule*, 145-46.

88 The propaganda effort was led by Luis Bolín, a personal friend of Franco and of Queipo who was made Director-General of the Spanish National Tourist Department in 1938 and held the post for fifteen years. See his *Spain: The Vital Years* (London: Cassell, 1967), a brazen attempt to falsify the history of the Republic and the Civil War. On Seville, see particularly pp. 183-84.

89 See Francisco González Ruiz, *Yo he creído en Franco; Franco's Rule*, 177. See also Antonio Ruiz Vilaplana, *Doy fe ... un año de actuación en la España nacionalista* (Paris: Ediciones Imprimerie/Coopérative Étoile, 1938), 124-34; Julio de Ramón-Laca, *Bajo la férula de Queipo*. In Cadiz the mayor put in place by the Nationalists was the principal *cacique* of the province. He took a leading role in promoting the repression (Bahamonde, 124-25). In the

The repression did not cease after the initial wave. Three years later, in the summer of 1939, Mussolini's Foreign Minister, Count Ciano, reported that eighty executions a day were still being carried out in Seville. He pointed out that this scale of repression was unleashed despite the fact that the city had never been 'in the power of the Reds'.[90] Foreign witnesses, however conservative and often despite their general support for Franco's 'crusade', reported torture and death within Seville's overflowing prisons. Dozens were dragged off daily for execution. One told of a common nameless grave on the outskirts of the city which stretched for fourteen kilometres.[91]

Equally, the repression in much of the remainder of *latifundista* Spain was motivated by a desire to castigate the rural proletariat for having dared to challenge the social *status quo*.[92] In Córdoba province, for example, it was legendary that when land workers were led at gun point to the common grave where they were to be executed they were told by their *señorito*

province of Pontevedra, in Galicia, executions were organized by the established Monarchist parliamentary deputy who accompanied the Falangist squads into the towns and villages in search of leftist agricultural workers. After execution, workers' houses were often destroyed (*Lo que han hecho*, 51-52). Extermination was one side of Queipo's policy. He was also responsible for articulating legislation concerning the production and commercialization of wheat in Andalucia. His Ley de Ordenación Triguera of August 1937 put in place a rigid structure which welded the nascent Francoist state to the interests of the big growers (Higinio París Eguilaz, *El desarrollo económico español, 1906-1964* [Madrid: 'Edición del Autor', 1965], 163-65). In a sense, this heralded the resolution of the central conflict of Spanish society in this era, in favour of landed élites. The result was huge profits, economic repression and starvation in the 1940s (see, for example, Carlos Barciela's introduction to part 2, vol. III of the *Historia agraria de la España contemporánea* [Barcelona: Editorial Crítica, 1986], 383-413).

90 *Ciano's Diplomatic Papers*, ed. Malcolm Muggeridge (London: Odhams, 1948), 294. See also, 'Matanzas franquistas en Sevilla' in *Interviú*, (5-11 January 1978), No. 86.

91 *Franco's Rule*, 147.

92 On repression in Jaen, for example, see Francisco Cobo Romero, *La guerra civil y la represión franquista en la provincia de Jaén* (Jaén: Diputación Provincial de Jaén, 1992). On Málaga, see Encarnación Barranquero Texeira, *Málaga entre la guerra y la posguerra* (Málaga: Editorial Arguval, 1994), 199-228.

captors that they were being led to a distinct kind of 'agrarian reform'.[93] Landowners themselves provided black lists of so-called 'troublemakers' whose lives they demanded. Workers who had been involved in measures of land collectivization were particularly singled out for the most severe measures and torture was utilized to extract information.[94]

In Granada, much of the brutal repression was carried out by Falangists and by former affiliates of José María Gil Robles' Catholic Party of the 1930s, the CEDA. Although the records in Granada show 2,314 assassinations carried out, the testimonies of local people suggest that a figure of around 8,000 would be more accurate.[95] Indeed, the province was the site of some of the most brutal acts of the war and its aftermath. As was habitual throughout that part of Spain occupied by Francoist forces, the repression was exhaustive and systematic but, at the same time, not fully recorded. For many months all formalities were dispensed with. The generalized environment of a requirement to punish which was emitted from the very highest authority of the nascent 'New State' made possible a very thorough purging of society. Repression was, in fact, 'controlled'

---

93   Francisco Moreno Gómez, 'La represión en la España campesina', in *El primer franquismo: España durante la segunda guerra mundial,* ed. J. L. García Delgado (Madrid: Siglo XXI, 1989), 192.

94   Moreno Gómez, 'La represión', 190-99.   See also his magisterial accounts of the provincial repression, *La Guerra Civil en Córdoba*; and *Córdoba en la posguerra* (Madrid: Francisco Baena Editor, 1990).   See also Bernal, 'Resignación', 149-51.

95   The first figure was calculated by Ramón Salas Larrazábal in *Pérdidas de la guerra,* 208.   Ian Gibson estimates the figure to be between 5,000 and 6,000 (*Granada en 1936* ..., 126).   In July 1936 there were 16,000 affiliates of the Anarchist union, the CNT, in the city of Granada as well as 12,000 of the Socialist UGT. The Republican Government at first refused to arm the workers as the military rising was unleashed.   See also 'Granada: las matanzas no se olvidan', in *Interviú,* (December 1977), No. 81.   Local people were anxious to remind the writer of this last article that it was not only García Lorca who was shot in Granada, but thousands of others.   Their memories of the events of 1936 were alive and they wanted to know why *these* executions were not spoken about.

to the extent that it was directed by local society's most influential social and political élites towards the lower orders.[96]

Class-based repression was not only unleashed in the 'backward' south of Spain.[97] In San Sebastian on the North coast, for example, one of the country's most 'European' and 'modern' cities, Basque and Catalan industrialists who had fled from the Republican zone mingled with semi-organized groups of traditional power holders and helped develop ways of supporting the Nationalist war effort financially.[98] The relative weakness of the Falange in the Basque country did not mean however that there was not brutal repression in San Sebastian. Nearly 1,000 executions took place in the first three months of the Nationalist occupation in the autumn of 1936. By the beginning of 1945 there had been more than 4,500 'mostly illegal' killings of supporters of the Republic.[99] In Vigo, one of the major port cities of Galicia, the first head of the Falange was a rich manufacturer. He was succeeded by the son of a

---

96   Ian Gibson, *The Assassination of Federico García Lorca* (London: W. H. Allen, 1979), 61-111; Reig Tapia, *La represión*, 727-30; Ángel Gollonet Megias and José Morales López, *Rojo y azul en Granada* (Granada: Ediciones Imperio, 1937).

97   See also, for example, Casanova *et al.*, *El pasado oculto: fascismo y violencia en Aragón, passim*; Carlos Fernández, *El alzamiento de 1936 en Galicia. Datos para una historia de la guerra civil* (A Coruña: Ediciós do Castro, 1982).

98   See, for example, D. Pastor Petit, *Los dossiers secretos de la guerra civil* (Barcelona: Argos, 1978); Joan M. Thomàs, *Falange, guerra civil, franquisme: FET y de las JONS de Barcelona en els primers anys de règim franquista* (Barcelona: {Publicacions de l'Abadia de Montserrat, 1992); J. M. Fontana Tarrats, *Los catalanes en la guerra de España* (Madrid: Samarán, 1952).

99   British Consul in Bilbao to Eden, 11 January 1945, FO371/49575/Z1893/89/41. In the industrial centre of the Basque Country, in the city of Bilbao too there was considerable repression. Within a month of the fall of the city in June 1937 nearly a thousand leftists and Basque Nationalists had been executed and a further 16,000 imprisoned. Large numbers of executions were still being carried out six months later (Juan de Iturralde, *La guerra de Franco: los vascos y la Iglesia*, 2 vols [San Sebastián: n.p., 1978], II, 285-99; Guillermo Cabanellas, *La guerra de los mil días*, 2 vols [Buenos Aires: Editorial Heliasta, 1973], II, 861, cited by Preston, *Franco*, 280; Tuñon de Lara, *La España del siglo XX*, 453).

prominent factory owner. Indeed, all the principal Falangist leaders in the region were from the 'moneyed' classes. Mechanical repression was carried out here under their supervision by docile and disciplined underlings.[100]

The situation was similar in other provinces, although systematized repression was harshest both in Barcelona and in Valencia. This had much to do with the fact that these large cities were the places where Republicans of all sorts — from leading politicians to workers — had congregated in fleeing the advance of Franco's Axis-backed forces. In Valencia, when the city fell, the public was urged to denounce all supporters of the Republic. Those denounced had been imprisoned up to the highest possible limits of prison capacity. The main prison in Valencia, the Cárcel Modelo, which had eight hundred cells, housed eight thousand prisoners by June 1939. In the province as a whole so many were incarcerated that bullrings, convents and monasteries were converted into prisons. Two hundred death sentences were officially announced for the month of April 1939 and a further two hundred and seventy for the first fortnight of May. It was generally accepted that the actual number of executions in the city greatly exceeded these figures.[101]

The anecdotal evidence, upon which an appreciation of the scale of the repression relies, suggests a substantial repressive wave in the Spanish capital too. The British Ambassador reported to the Foreign Office in mid-June that while probably thirty thousand were in prison in Madrid alone, awaiting trial, the number of what the regime labelled 'political assassins and gunmen', tried by court-martial and executed, amounted to fifteen thousand. In the light of later declarations, even by the regime itself, this seems a rather conservative estimate. The

---

100 *Lo que han hecho*, 137-40.

101 PRO, *ibid*. For more information on Francoist repression in Valencia, see Vicente Gabarda Ceballan, 'La continuación de la Guerra Civil: la represión franquista', in *Estudis D'Història Contemporánea del País Valencià*, VII (1986), 229-45; and *Els afusellaments al País Valencià (1938-1956)* (Valencia: Edicions Alfons el Magnànim, 1993). Similarly, the British Consul in Tenerife reported that there had been 'some hundreds of murders with the presumptive connivance of the military authorities' in his area (PRO/W9548/3921/41, 19 June 1939; 39742/C16811).

English journalist, A. V. Philips, who spent four months in the prisons of Madrid in 1940, claimed that death sentences were pronounced in the capital at the rate of several thousand per month. He calculated that during just the first eleven post-war months, close to one hundred thousand had been executed. Ciano, during his visit to Spain, had claimed that in Madrid, in the summer of 1939, two hundred to two hundred and fifty executions were taking place each day.[102] In just one of the twenty or so prisons in the capital full with political prisoners, five hundred victims of executions are actually listed for the period 1941 to 1944. This relatively unusual written source suggests something of the real scale of the brutality in Madrid.[103] Moreover, many received no trial.

The Caudillo's determination to achieve total victory was borne out by his refusal to countenance the possibility of negotiating a peace and establishing a neutralized zone in the north-east of Spain as refugees fled from Barcelona, the principal industrial city of Catalonia, towards the French border in January 1939.[104]   According to Franco's Interior Minister, Ramón Serrano Suñer, Catalonia's local nationalism was 'a sickness'. 'Secessionism' had 'lived as a parasite' off of what he viewed as an ostentatious and false local patriotism. The 'secessionist virus' had to be treated: 'Today we have Catalonia on the points of our bayonets. Material domination will take little time. I am sure that the moral incorporation of

---

102 The informant in touch with the British Foreign Office in early 1941 wrote, 'To the inhabitants of Manuel Becerra Square in Madrid the six lorries which carry off men and women every day to the East Cemetery for execution are a familiar sight. On July 18th last (the fourth anniversary of the military rising against the Republic) more than forty lorries were needed for this ghastly work ...' (PRO/FO371/26890/C3986/3/41, March 1941).

103 Sueiro and Díaz Nosty, *Historia del franquismo*, 130.

104 Josep Pernau, *Diario de la caída de Cataluña* (Barcelona: Ediciones B, 1989), 219-20.   Franco's aim remained the total annihilation of the Republic and its supporters (Servicio Histórico Militar, *La ofensiva sobre Valencia* [Madrid: Servicio Histórico Militar, 1977], 16-18, cited in Preston, *Franco*, 304).

Catalonia into Spain will be achieved as quickly as its military incorporation ...'.[105]

Preparations for a post-war purge of the region were put in hand by the organization of the 'exiled' Catalan Falange[106] which could boast in 1938 of having built up an archive of thirty thousand names of 'red elements'.[107] The official entry into the city, at the end of January, 1939, was led by General Solchaga's Navarra corps. According to the British Assistant Military Attaché in Burgos, the city where Franco's headquarters were situated, '... The Navarrese march first not because they have fought better, but because they hate better. That is to say, when the object of this hate is Catalonia or a Catalan'.[108]

The first priority of the occupying forces was the 'disciplining' of the population. The first months of military occupation would be used to deliver what was to be labelled by the regime itself: 'Franco's Justice'. Within days of the fall of the city of Barcelona, the new authorities declared that forty thousand Republicans who 'have blood on their hands' had been unable to escape from the city before the arrival of the 'liberating army'. The British Consul did not doubt that they would be unable to escape 'the extreme penalty'. Mass executions without prior opportunity for defence would continue until 1943 when the numbers of 'enemies' disposed of in this way would begin to decline.[109] The round-up of 'political enemies' began straightaway. According to the US Vice-Consul, the new administration organized seemingly hundreds of trials and thousands of executions were carried out in just a few months. Firing squads could still be heard regularly in the city

---

105 Declarations of Serrano Suñer, early January 1939, cited by Rafael Abella, *Finales de enero de 1939: Barcelona cambia de piel* (Barcelona: Editorial Planeta, 1991), 59-60.

106 FET y de las JONS, Barcelona, *Informe* (17 September 1940), Secretaría General del Movimiento, Archivo General de Administración (AGA), Presidencia, caja 30.

107 See *'Informe acerca de FET de las JONS en Cataluña'* (June 1937); and *'Informe de FET-JONS sobre las delegaciones provinciales de Barcelona, Tarragona, Lérida y Gerona'* (undated, but 1938), AGA, Presidencia, caja 31.

108 FO371/W1610/8/41, 24 January 1939.

109 Solé i Sabaté, *La repressió, passim*; Preston, *Franco*, 319.

as late as 1942.[110] According to a representative of a Catalan exiles' organization, writing in September 1939, the execution of Republicans and Democrats was continuing at the rate of thirty a day.[111] Count Ciano, after visiting Spain during the summer of 1939, and meeting with Franco and Serrano Suñer, had reported that one hundred and fifty executions a day were taking place in the city.[112] The correspondent of the London *Times*, Lawrence Fernsworth, reported to the British Parliamentary Committee for Spain that about two thousand, five hundred people had been executed in Barcelona by June 1939, a period of only four-and-a-half months. The Committee was very concerned by evidence that armed bands of Falangists were carrying out 'reprisals' over the heads of the police and the military authorities.[113] The British Consul General in Barcelona confirmed that executions, of which there was no official information available, were taking place throughout the province.[114]

The social objectives of the regime were clearly laid out in the details of the first pronouncements of the military authorities in the city. The provisions of the military order establishing the Special Regime of Occupation in Barcelona had as a priority the insistence upon a reversion to the pre-1931 situation with regard to the ownership and control of property. All the legislative actions of the Republican state in the city were annulled.

A central preoccupation, following the military rising in July 1936, was the imposition of an authoritarian corporativist labour structure in the 'New Spain'. This is what employers and rightist political leaders had been calling for throughout

---

110 James W. Cortada, *A City in War: American Views on Barcelona and the Spanish Civil War, 1936-39* (Wilmington: Scholarly Resources, 1985), 179.

111 Cortada, *City in War*, 205.

112 'Les archives secrètes du Comte Ciano, 1936-1942' (Paris: Plon, 1948), cited in *L'Avenç* (January 1979), 47.

113 PRO/24160/W9646/3921/41, 16 June 1939; W9033/3921/41, 6 June 1939.

114 PRO/FO371/24160/W9033/3921/41, 6 June 1939. Shootings also took place in Falangist headquarters. In Calle Ballester in Barcelona, for example (Victor Alba, *Sleepless Spain* [London: Cobbett Press, 1948], 109).

the 1930s.[115]   In September, all organizations which had supported the Popular Front Government were expressly made illegal and the first state union structures put in place.[116]   In April 1937 the state's new Centrales Nacionales Sindicalistas were created, integrating workers and employers in a vertical union structure (CNS).[117] There was no democratic provision in the functioning of these bodies in each industry, and they were dominated by employers and Falangists.   This structure, in closing off any opportunity for the articulation of working-class dissent, provided the essential framework for ensuring that the burden of the economic crisis fell squarely upon workers' shoulders.   The panoply of state intervention in the labour process was completed by the declaration of a 'Labour Charter' (*Fuero del Trabajo*), in March 1938, based on the Italian *Carta del Lavoro*.   This heralded the formal outlawing of strikes.   The nationalistic 'mysticism' represented by autarky allowed the regime to claim that, in the pursuit of this patriotic economic crusade, all threats to production were acts of treason and strikers, therefore, were to be executed as traitors.   The unifying notion of the *Patria* was the central axis around which Francoist ideology was to revolve.[118]   Economic national self-sufficiency contributed to this way of determining that which would endure and that which had to perish.   Thus, autarky was, from the very first, vital to the way in which the 'New

---

115 For example, see Eduardo Aunós Pérez, *Calvo Sotelo y la política de su tiempo* (Madrid: Ediciones Españolas, 1941); José María Gil Robles, *No fue posible la paz* (Barcelona: Ariel, 1968), 150-51; Francesc Cambó, *En torno al fascismo italiano* (Barcelona: n.p., 1925), pp. 42-46, 183-85; Gil Robles' prologue to the Fascist Ramón Ruiz Alonso's *Corporatismo* (Salamanca: Ed. Luiz Alonso, 1937).

116 *Boletín del Estado*, 16 and 28 September 1936.   This was only formalizing what was a *de facto* repression of trade unionists from the outset.

117 Employers were permitted to maintain some level of organization through professional guilds (*agremiaciones profesionales*) although, in fact, they came to rely heavily on more informal mechanisms of economic power.

118 The unity represented by the traditions of the *Patria* — Catholicism, *Hispanidad*, and a mythical social harmony — became the ideological reference point for the imposition of repression.   As Franco proclaimed, 'freedoms opposed to the *Patria* could not be' (see Carles Viver Pi-Sunyer, 'Aproximació a la ideología del franquisme en l'etapa fundacional del règim', in *Papers: Revista de Sociología*, XIV (1980), 20.

State' would cement its authority. The regimentation of labour, through corporativism, legislated in the *Fuero*, and the autarkic trade and industrialization strategy, were two sides of the same authoritarian coin.[119]

The families of 'the guilty', those killed or incarcerated for political crimes, were also made to suffer. In Seville, prisoners' families had Nationalist soldiers billeted on them.[120] Under the provisions of the iniquitous Law of Political Responsibilities, proclaimed in January 1939, those 'convicted' had their possessions confiscated. This, in effect, gave *carte blanche* to Falangists to go to family homes and make off with whatever they pleased. Often a woman deprived of the principal breadwinner of the household would lose her only means of making a living in this way. A sewing machine, for example, used as a way of making ends meet through taking in piece-work from a local textile factory might be confiscated as a way of 'redeeming' the 'crimes of the family'. This was an element of the economic violence which was inflicted upon the defeated day-by-day in the 1940s. Women were seen as being guilty of failing to maintain a moral vigilance over their menfolk. Being the wife of a 'Marxist' was enough to be shot.[121] Families were subjected to a constant vigilance by state authorities so as to ensure no 'campaign against the state'.[122] The authorities were indignant when the families of Republicans displayed any sense of confidence. In the first years of the Spanish post-war Falangists were ever-watchful of signs of optimism within the working-class population that the Axis powers would be

---

119 See Richards, *Autarky*. The Rome correspondent of the principal Barcelona daily newspaper, *La Vanguardia Española*, suggested the possible function of autarky as economic *and* ideological or political, through viewing Italian society under Mussolini: '... that vague concept of autarky was translated into a graphic image which was inserted into the senses of the people ... sublimating it, even converting it into a true catechism, a true guide to politico-social perfection; in a word: into a mysticism ...' (17 September 1939).

120 *Franco's Rule*, 147.

121 González Ruiz, *Yo he creído*, 124.

122 'Informe de la Delegación General de Seguridad', 29 April 1942, Toledo, in Fundación Nacional de Francisco Franco, *Documentos inéditos*, (1994), III, 425.

defeated. This optimism, it was claimed, was often manifested in '... an insolent manner', an example of which was that when '... families go to take things to the provincial prison to their detained relatives, they do so with ostentation instead of concealing their status as the relatives of prisoners'.[123]   The 'defeated' were stigmatized and expected to suffer.

Repression against families was often more direct. In areas where the armed anti-regime *guerrilla* movement was active the state took the opportunity to make the populace in general suffer. The tactic of starving out the 'Reds' was used, subjecting entire villages to martial law and curfew regimes.[124]   Any shelter given to the *maquis* was punishable by death.[125] Women were particular targets for this repression against families as the extreme misogyny of regime ideology blended with its outright class brutality.   In the Spanish post-war period it was not unusual for women found out in the streets after eleven at night to be arrested and have their heads shaved and be made to drink castor oil or even petrol as a punishment for infringing the moral or political code of the state.[126]

The course of the world conflict had major repercussions within Spain.   In some ways 1943, as the war began to go against the Axis, marked something of a turning point.   The fall of Mussolini in Italy sent shock waves through the Francoist

---

123 *Boletín* No. 491, DNII, 28 February 1942, AGA, Presidencia, caja, 16. Women also resisted in other ways. Wives and mothers who queued outside the prisons were often informed that their loved ones had been 'given their freedom' (the euphemistic phrase used to refer to the fate of the executed) the night before. In La Coruña the women protested by staying day and night at the prison gates, effectively as a guard against Falangist killing expeditions to the cemeteries (see *Lo que han hecho*, 195-96).

124 See Heine, 'Tipología y características', 316.

125 PRO/FO371/73356/Z659/596/41, 15 January 1948. See also Moreno Gómez, *op. cit.* In Málaga and Granada small tenant farmers caught up in this class conflict between rebellious landless labourers and the state, often fled their properties as a result.

126 PRO/FO371/26890/C3986/3/41, March, 1941. The prevalence of prostitution in the Spanish post-war period was a further element of the economic violence of autarky; an element of the imposition of power and the disarticulation of resistance through economic marginalization.

regime.[127]   However, in terms of repression, change was very slow to come about.   The fate of the Italian dictatorship produced a repressive reaction from the Franco regime.   There was immediately a wave of arrests of potential opposition groups.[128] There was a stepping-up of Falangist activity and a sharp increase in political executions, in an effort to terrorize 'Red' elements of the population.[129]   Meetings were rapidly arranged among the heads of each sector, sub-sector and street.[130]   The traditionally important strategic points of the city of Barcelona were posted with Falangist guards.   The provincial party chief gave a speech to raise Party morale in the city to an assembled gathering of six thousand militants.[131] There was an attempt to strengthen the profile of the symbols of the Party and of the 'victory'; in Málaga the local Party Secretary ordered that militants wear the Blue Shirt of the Falange every day.[132] In Seville Falangists were distributed with additional small arms and were promised the assistance of Falangist army officers in the garrison if tensions with local Monarchists came to a head.[133]

The Falange would again be armed as the World War came to its conclusion in May 1945 with the defeat of the Axis powers.   The sensational news revealing the manner of the execution of Mussolini and the way in which his remains were

---

127 Preston, *The Politics of Revenge*, 118; Javier Tusell and Genoveva García Queipo de Llano, *Franco y Mussolini: la política española durante la segunda guerra mundial* (Barcelona: Editorial Planeta, 1985), 208-09.

128 Samuel Hoare, *Ambassador on Special Mission* (London: Collins, 1946), 211.

129 Yencken to Eden, 4 October 1943, PRO/FO371/34789/C11465/63/41. In Madrid the doors of certain flats and houses were marked with a cross or 'R.I.P.' in order to facilitate the early extermination of the occupants at the outset of any serious trouble.

130 Under Franco, alongside the police, every rural village had designated someone who acted as party boss. In urban areas every block of flats had a Party representative who reported to an area controller or district officer (José María Molina, *El movimiento clandestino en España, 1939-1949* [Mexico: Editores Mexicanos Reunidos, 1976], 34).

131 *Parte*, FET-JONS Barcelona (November 1943). AGA, Pres., caja 376.

132 PRO/FO371/C10340/63/41, 5 August 1943.

133 PRO/FO371/34789/C9796/63/41, dispatch from British Consul General in Seville, 14 August 1943.

treated by the people aroused fears amongst Party militants.[134] Again, those areas with a tradition of worker militancy would witness the most Draconian clamp down.   In Asturias pistols were handed out to Falangist militants as the hunt for men and women in hiding was stepped up.   Frequently their relatives were made homeless by the merciless burning to the ground of the family homes of those in refuge.   Villagers unwilling to assist the Civil Guard and the Party in their search would have their cattle carried off, thereby denying them of their livelihood.[135] The repression had already been stepped up prior to the final outcome of the war.   It was seen as almost inevitable that the regime would be forced to consider some kind of liberalization in the aftermath of the defeat of Nazism and Fascism. It was considered that the 'external form' of the Movement would have to be reformed leaving intact 'the substantial essence of Falangism'.[136]   Therefore, the Francoist authorities were determined to continue the purge before this necessity imposed itself.[137] During the first few months of 1945 the executions continued apace.   On 17 January no less than twenty-three executions were carried out in Madrid. A reliable police source claimed that between 13 and 19 January forty-two

---

134 Still, in view of the treatment of Mussolini there was confidence, at least, that Franco would not easily loosen his grip on society (*Parte*, Barcelona [May 1945], AGA, Pres., caja 165).

135 In the area of Cabrales an entire village was arrested after one such expedition to discipline the population ended in an all-out gun-fight (PRO/FO371/49575/Z7624/89/41, May 28, 1945).   There is no doubt that hostages were taken by the authorities in an attempt to force fugitives to give themselves up (PRO/FO371/49575/Z7167/89/41, Bowker to Eden, 16 June 1945).   After two Falangists were killed in Madrid in May there were 350 arrests in Gijón as reprisal.

136 *Parte*, FET-JONS Barcelona, May 1943, AGA, Pres., caja 376; *Parte*, FET-JONS Barcelona (May 1945), Pres., caja 165.

137 Two people were executed in Zaragoza on 21 March 1945 expressly because it was believed that an amnesty would come into effect on the 30th under the pressure of the Spanish bishops. According to the informant to the British Foreign Office, '... orders were given to execute as many prisoners as possible, and, above all, educated persons ...' (PRO/FO371/ 49575/Z5339/89/41, 19 April 1945).   In fact, Franco rejected the letter of the Bishops.

executions took place. There were many more executions in February in the capital.[138]

Conclusion

Repression in the Spanish Civil War has, during the last ten years, begun to be written about. The opportunities offered by the relative opening up of archives since the transition to democracy have been taken advantage of. However, many of these accounts have amounted to only the partial recounting of series of specific violent episodes. Attempts to explain the *origins* of this violence or to suggest what it signified in terms of *the nature of the regime* which was being put in place or to define its role in terms of *social development* have been, for the most part, lacking.[139] It is in relation to these questions that the problems outlined at the beginning of this article were posed.

It has been suggested here that violent acts were perpetrated by both sides during the Spanish Civil War, and by Francoists in its aftermath, which cannot be explained in terms of strictly military strategy or, indeed, as products of 'the heat

---

138 Two executions were reported in Barcelona on 20 January; one in Valladolid on New Year's Day; two from Granada on 21 December; and ten on the 26 and 27 January. A further seventeen were killed at a Seville cemetery on 17 February. It was reported that seventy-three political prisoners had been taken from the Dirección General de Seguridad to the Carabanchel cemetery on 27 April to be shot (PRO/FO371/49575/Z7167/89/41, 16 June 1945). The Director of Prisons, while unable to confirm these figures, would neither deny that they were accurate (PRO/FO371/ Z2952/89/41, 3 March 1945). According to the Director of Prisons, about three hundred and fifty death sentences were examined at each meeting of the Council of Ministers presided over by Franco himself, in early 1945. Meetings took place, on average, every six weeks. About forty of the sentences were confirmed and the victims executed immediately. According to this official, Franco was the leading spirit in the small group of ministers who insisted on the continuation of the merciless purge which these executions represented.

139 Julio Aróstegui (*Violencia y política*, 13), suggests that these kind of questions ought to be asked in relation to any historical study of political violence.

of battle'. This violence was motivated by political and social objectives. Individuals and groups within Republican Spain employed political violence against those who were seen as enemies of the Republic and of the revolution. This terror was a response to the rebellion of the military. It was a part of the revolutionary upheaval which was sparked off by the rising against the elected Government.[140] In the early part of the war it was largely uncontrolled. The central Republican state authorities gradually intervened as a moderating force within a context of contested power within Government Spain. 'Popular justice', in spite of its unpredictability, was seen by the Government's leading figures as a sop to the working class, the excesses of which were to be discouraged whenever possible. The more organized 'popular justice' became the less brutal it was. *Organized* Republican political repression, as such, involving the central state power, was limited to the liquidating of what was seen as the leftist threat posed in Barcelona in the first eleven months of the war. Only in this case was there a clearly articulated political objective which was achieved through an organized *ad-hoc* plan devised by the political authorities of the state.

In contrast, violence as perpetrated by Nationalists (subsequently, Francoists) against those social groups which supported the legal Government was overwhelmingly carried out according to political or ideological criteria and was encouraged as such by the authorities of the nascent Francoist state. The notion of 'purification' was invested with a multiplicity of meanings. These were unified under the Catholicism of the state (its surrogate Nationalism) in a determination to reverse national 'degeneration'. This crude attempt at social engineering was tinged with a vague technicism which produced a pathology of development under

---

140 It was the military rebellion which was the primary cause of the destructuring of the Republican state institutions, including the legal institutions (see Sánchez Recio, 'Justicia ordinaria', *op. cit.*). The working class was, at first, denied weapons in response to the rising, and was, thus, in many places, left defenceless. These two factors need to be borne in mind when considering the uncontrolled nature of Republican terror in the first months of the Civil War.

Francoism in the pursuit of brutal punishment and industrialization at any cost.

As we have seen, leading figures within local economic elites played a significant part in directing the purges. They drew up the black-lists which were used by the army and the para-military groups in rounding up 'Reds'; they sat on local commissions to decide upon 'responsibilities' for 'Marxist crimes' and helped dish out penalties; they even decided who would eat and who would go hungry according to political criteria; finally, many of them joined the Falange and participated in militia activities. This is not to say that the majority of the bourgeois élite did these things, but they were disproportionately represented within the higher echelons of local power, as well as influencing the conduct of national policy too.[141] Terror was employed against particular social groups, defined ideologically. The objective was to systematize and institutionalize repression, directing it, principally, towards the working class and its political organizations. Free trade unions were made illegal. Strikes became acts of treason; strikers were therefore to be shot.[142] This was the institutionalized punishment of those who had dared to challenge the socio-economic and political *status quo*. It was systematized, mechanical, political repression and was instrumental in securing power for the Francoist 'New State'.[143]

---

141 See, for example, Amando de Miguel, *Sociología del franquismo* (Barcelona: Editorial Euros, 1975); Carles Viver Pi-Sunyer, *El personal político de Franco, (1936-1945): contribución empírica a una teoría del régimen franquista* (Barcelona: Vicens-Vives, 1978); Joan Thomàs, *Falange, guerra civil, franquisme*; Barranquero Texeira, *Málaga*.

142 We have already given examples in Galicia and Seville. Such was the case in other parts of Spain. The main organizers of the first strike in Barcelona under Francoism, for example, in the major industrial plant of La Maquinista in March 1941, were shot without trial (Borja de Riquer, 'Dossier: el franquisme i la burguesía catalana, [1939-1951]', in *L'Avenç*, [January 1979]).

143 In general, the issue of repression has not figured prominently even in attempts to *theorize* Francoism which have utilized an historical perspective. See, for example, Javier Tusell, *La dictadura de Franco* (Madrid: Alianza Editorial, 1988).

In analysing violence and terror during the Spanish Civil War, and in the aftermath of the conflict, it is woefully insufficient to view all acts of brutality, on both sides, as part of an inevitable decline into barbarity. The explanatory power of this kind of 'analysis' is extremely weak. For a number of reasons violence in the Republican zone and Nationalist terror were distinct phenomena. The political leadership of the Republican side was consistently guided by a sense of striving for some kind of social and political *reconciliation*. In contrast, extreme violence was an integral part of the plan of the Nationalists to purge Spain of the threatening 'other' which was the working class and its political leadership. This was in accord with the social objectives of those groups which supported the military conspirators. The intellectual laziness which only too often gives rise to the comment that extreme brutality is 'inevitable' in any war situation can only serve to obscure what is, in many cases, in fact, a programme of terror with definable social and political objectives.

9

'Obligación de opinar': The Limits of Pluralism in Manuel Azaña's *La velada en Benicarló*

JAMES WHISTON

The circumstances of the Spanish Civil War placed great restrictions on Manuel Azaña's public life, over and above the normal ones relating to his Presidential functions, as outlined in the Republic's Constitution. As a former minister and Prime Minister, with an outstanding reputation for parliamentary debate and action, the combination of the Civil War and of his constitutional office left Azaña in a position that contrasted sharply with the early years of the Republic, in which he was the pre-eminent figure. Azaña's only major public opportunities for pronouncing on the course of the war (apart from a short *alocución* delivered at its outbreak) were his four speeches, three of them made during 1937. Detached from the Government during most of the winter and spring of 1937 by virtue of his residence in Barcelona, while the former was based in Valencia, Azaña took the opportunity to compose *La velada en Benicarló* towards the end of that period of separation, during a period of enforced confinement, brought about by the internecine conflict between Trotskyites, Anarchists and Stalinist Communists in the city. These events were in sharp contrast with Franco's much more expeditious unification of Carlists and Falangists under his leadership just two weeks earlier. The actual battle in Barcelona (and — who knows? — Franco's Declaration of Unification of 19 April 1937) prompted Azaña to complete and put *La velada* into a finished state.[1] In

---

1   Azaña's account of this conflict may be found in his *Cuaderno de La Pobleta*, in *Manuel Azaña, Obras completas*, ed. Juan Marichal, 4 vols (Madrid: Giner, 1990), IV, 575-88. He summarized the affair as follows:

his diary entry for 17 June 1937 Azaña suggests that this radical shift in his life from man of decision and action to constitutional President of a country at war, also meant a necessary shift from actions to words, in which Spain now only exercised Azaña's 'juicio, y ... emociones, y ... pronósticos, pues de Presidente, y en guerra, poco tengo que promover y resolver' (IV, 629). One can see in this reflection the source of the lengthy discourses in *La velada*: during the Civil War words, and words alone, were all that Azaña had to contribute to resolving the Spanish tragedy.

Bearing in mind that many of Azaña's decisive contributions to Spanish politics were in the field of parliamentary and government debate, his choice of a dialogue format for *La velada* was a natural extension of that experience, incorporating elements of debating procedure in Cabinet and parliament and also, perhaps, the practice of the direct oratory of the political meeting. In his diary, dated 20 May 1937, Azaña lamented the loss of regular Parliamentary life caused by the Civil War:

> El Parlamento, muy a mi pesar, no funciona. Cuantas veces le he dicho al Gobierno que convenía convocarlo, ha ido difiriéndolo; yo no tengo potestad para convocarlo personalmente. La cuestión actual [Largo Caballero's position as Prime Minister], planteada en las Cortes, se resolvería de un modo normal ... Así, todos los elementos del juego político de que el Presidente de la República se asiste en trance de crisis, están en suspenso o han desaparecido. No me quedan más que mis observaciones personales. (IV, 592-93)

The substantive dialogue of the five main interlocutors in *La velada* is like an ideal Government Cabinet, with Azaña as its unseen moderator. (In the diary entry just quoted, Azaña mentions his recommendation to Largo Caballero to reduce the size of the Republican Government's Cabinet from eighteen to as few as eight members, and also during the same May crisis Azaña describes how he presided over the last hours of the Largo Caballero administration and his address to the incoming

---

'¡Conclusión de diez meses de ineptitud delirante, aliada con la traición! Las radios facciosas lo celebraban con entusiasmo' (IV, 587). All quotations from Azaña's writings are from volume III of this edition unless otherwise indicated.

Negrín Cabinet [IV. 600-06].) The style of formal debate in *La velada*, the fluent and thoughtful exchange of practical and philosophical reflections on the war, constitute in their overall impact an image of the Republic as a civilized meeting place for a plurality of views, including those views that could not find an outlet in the circumstances of the war, but which enjoy the equivalent of parliamentary privilege in Azaña's Republic.

Jesús Gómez, in his book on the sixteenth-century Spanish dialogue, reminds us that many of the dialogues of that period are associated with an age of reform, Erasmian in particular,[2] and it is possible that Azaña was attracted to the dialogue form because of its association with humanist culture, and with what Gómez has noted in the most interesting of the dialogues as 'una preocupación por reproducir la variedad de lo real'.[3] The crucial links between Spanish Erasmian reformism and Alcalá de Henares (where Azaña was born and whose roots went back several generations)[4] have been amply documented by Marcel Bataillon.[5] Indeed, in Azaña's first of a series of lectures given in 1911 in the Casa del Pueblo of Alcalá, he claimed to sense another decisive period of history about to open again: 'Parece que estamos en un momento crítico de la historia. Diríase que la civilización en su marcha, va á cerrar uno de los grandes ciclos en que se desenvuelve y á abrir otro nuevo'.[6] Gómez's examination of sixteenth-century dialogues also leads him to

---

2   *El diálogo en el Renacimiento español* (Madrid: Cátedra, 1988), 163.

3   Gómez, *op. cit.*, 160.

4   See Franco Meregalli, 'Manuel Azaña', in *Azaña*, ed. Vicente Alberto Serrano and José María San Luciano (Madrid: Ediciones Edascal, 1980), 160-223, at pp. 166-67.

5   *Erasmo y España*, 2 vols, (Mexico/Buenos Aires: Fondo de Cultura Económica, 1950), I, 12-26, and 395-403; Bataillon's book *Erasme et l'Espagne* first appeared in 1937, the same year as the composition of *La velada*, and was reviewed by Antonio Machado in the September 1938 issue of *Hora de España*, where Machado was not slow to link its publication with the Civil War, describing Bataillon's intellectual integrity as proof that he was 'un egregio amigo de España, y de la España nuestra, que no es precisamente la que se ha vendido al extranjero al par que gritaba en Salamanca: ¡muera la inteligencia!'; see *Antonio Machado, Poesía y prosa*, ed. Oreste Macrí in collaboration with Gaetano Chiappini, 4 vols (Madrid: Espasa-Calpe/Fundación Antonio Machado, 1988), IV, 2397-98, for the full text of the review.

6   *El problema español*, republished in facsimile, in *Azaña, op. cit.*, 21-59, at p. 28. (Original orthography has been retained.)

conclude that the typical dialogue of that period 'es un espacio abierto a la discusión, al aire libre de la retórica forense',[7] a reminder, for readers of *La velada*, of the importance of legal studies in Azaña's intellectual formation. Writing on Antonio Machado's creation of apocryphal figures, José Luis de la Iglesia connects them with 'autores desconocidos que han pensado a contracorriente',[8] the word *apocrypha* taken as signifying writings that are not part of the accepted canon, unofficial or alternative accounts, and it may also be helpful to view the interlocutors of *La velada* in this sense.

In his *Preliminar* Azaña claimed that *La velada* was not the product of an 'arrebato' nor a 'vaticinio', but was rather intended as a 'demostración' (381). The two words rejected by Azaña, in favour of the third, point towards a search for a measured, exact assessment of those opinions in Republican Spain towards which he was most sympathetic or which he viewed as being compatible with the idea of a Republic,[9] but in fact he allows his interlocutors plenty of scope to develop their views of the Civil War to extremes of enthusiasm and pessimism. The word 'Diálogo' in the sub-title of the work, (*Diálogo de la guerra de España*) and the heading 'Diálogo', which comes after the *Preliminar* and as a headline for the list of the interlocutors in the work, are essentially emblematic words, not only in the context of *La velada*, but of the Republic's primary political characteristic, or at least one that the Republic at war wished itself to be distinguished by, especially with foreign opinion in mind: its spirit of pluralism, independence of thought and freedom of debate. Or as Azaña expressed it in the introduction to his final Civil-War speech: 'estas verdades las hemos descubierto entre todos, cada cual a su manera: unos, por puro raciocinio; otros, las han descubierto por los implacables golpes de la experiencia' (365). (Incidentally, the use of the phrases 'entre todos' and 'cada cual

---

7   Gómez, *op. cit.*, 50.

8   *Antonio Machado y la filosofía* (Madrid: Orígenes, 1989), 11.

9   For a brief discussion of Azaña's exclusions from the dialogue, see Manuel Azaña, *La velada en Benicarló*, ed. Manuel Aragón (Madrid: Castalia, 1974), 41-42, and John. H. Seekamp, '*La velada en Benicarló*: The Political and Personal Testament of Manuel Azaña', *Mid Hudson Language Studies*, VIII (1985), 89-102, at p. 100.

a su manera' in the quotation is a small but telling example of the blend of inclusivism and pluralism in Azaña's make-up, and which commanded his utmost allegiance, even though the times appeared to demand the virtues and vices of *Realpolitik*.)

By using a fictional form in *La velada* (the author states in the *Preliminar* that 'Sería trabajo inútil querer desenmascarar a los interlocutores' [381]) Azaña was able to develop lines of thought about the Civil War that were greatly sharpened in their focus through being linked to the character in question. Thus the professional military man, Blanchart, voices disapproval of the indiscipline of the Republic's militia; the attitude of the medical academic, Lluch, to the war is influenced greatly by his experience of hospital work during it. Garcés, the Republican ex-minister, exhaustively argues for the survival of the Republic as a legally constituted State. The intellectual and creative writer Eliseo Morales shows the keenest sensibility, where the destructive nature of the War is concerned, and attempts to think through the consequences of such destruction for the Spanish nation; while the lawyer Marón's repeated belief in the irresistible march of history leads him to have an unshakable confidence in Spain's future. The other two main interlocutors, Pastrana and Barcala, are the political activists in the group, and help to bring the dialogue closer to the *Realpolitik* of national and international aspects of the Civil War. The juxtaposition of rational and emotive views (the latter represented by Marón and Barcala) is another 'dialogue' within the overall structure of the work. José Antonio Pérez Bowie, in an illuminating article, sees the kind of focus provided by the interlocutors as a general gain in expressiveness for the work. He argues that Azaña chose a fictional form rather than the form of the essay, which would have seemed to be the logical choice for a work 'exclusivamente al servicio de las ideas', because the fiction allowed Azaña to 'intensificar la expresividad de la argumentación y la pasión que los personajes ponen en su interpretación'.[10] The essay form, although of course an implicit dialogue between narrator and reader, lacks the sense of direct, mutual exchange of the dialogue, which is

10 'Géneros y perspectivismo en *La velada en Benicarló*', *Ínsula*, DXXVI, (1990), 19-20, at p. 19.

essential to the ethos and political character of *La velada*. Jesús Gómez also reminds us that the sixteenth-century Spanish dialogue represented a transitional bridge from the formerly dominant culture of speech to the newly emerging dominance of print.[11] Azaña's choice of the dialogue form has an analogous effect on his text, but in reverse, enlivening the printed word and helping to make it more immediate by the spoken context of the dialogue. While it cannot be called an 'antología de urgencia', because the text was not published during the Civil War, the various spoken contributions combine to give *La velada* a testimonial character which is of a piece with the circumstances of its composition and with the nature of Azaña's Republicanism.

In the last of his Civil-War speeches Azaña dedicated some of his opening remarks to what the headline summarized as 'Obligación de opinar' (365), and these remarks are also a valuable introduction to the   wide array of opinions, apportioned to the eleven interlocutors that we encounter in *La velada* (the norm for the Spanish Renaissance dialogue was two, according to Gómez).[12]   'El derecho de enjuiciar públicamente subsiste a pesar de la guerra' (366), Azaña writes; not only is it the private citizen's right, but for those in public life it is an obligation, in order to promote the well-being of the Republic. In this partnership between the individual and civic leaders, Azaña states, 'es indispensable que la verdad se depure y se acendre en lo íntimo de la conciencia y se acicale bajo la lima de un juicio independiente' (366). The variation in the use of the verbs, *depurar*, *acendrar* and *acicalar* is not just an elegant or emphatic technique of oratory: it is itself an image of the process of sifting, refining and assaying that for Azaña was an integral part of civilized political life. The non-conformist strain in Azaña's character, with possible Protestant overtones of the primacy of conscience and of private judgment, are also well revealed in the phrases 'un juicio independiente' and 'lo

---

11 Gómez, *op. cit.*,170-73.
12 *Ibid.*, 61. Azaña used the phrase 'obligación de opinar' in his diary entry of 14 June 1937, when recording his observations to Negrín and José Giral (Minister of Foreign Affairs) about the importance of diplomatic initiatives in the conduct of the war: 'Yo no gobierno, no resuelvo; pero tengo la obligación de opinar ante ustedes y aconsejarles' (IV, 621).

íntimo de la conciencia'. Azaña's interest in George Borrow (his translation of *The Bible in Spain* was published in 1921) could be seen on one level as the sympathetic response of a fellow dissenter having to survive in the midst of the deep-rooted orthodoxies of the Spanish religious temperament.[13]

The sequence of verbs in the quotation is useful to bear in mind when following the highways and byways of the speeches in *La velada*. On occasions the interlocutors themselves are aware that they may have exceeded the limits of verbal exchange, because what Azaña has done is to push the development of their opinions to the limit — what Pérez Bowie calls 'afirmaciones maximalistas' —,[14] and in so doing give the best advertisement possible for the survival of democratic politics, putting the style of democratic exchange and division through its paces, and showing its fitness to continue in the trust and esteem of all. Azaña's faith in the freedoms of democracy allows him to give the doubting voices of Morales and Garcés a more extended hearing than those of the activists, Pastrana and Barcala. In his first Civil-War speech Azaña had expressed this confidence in the democratic process by a provocative irony, in which he humorously holds the audience in suspense, before the reassurance of the irreconcilable paradox (democracy and dictatorship) in the second half of the following sentence: '¡Ah! Si dicen [los franquistas] que quieren la dictadura militar, yo me comprometo a subscribirla, porque estoy seguro de que poquísimos españoles votarían en favor de la dictadura militar!' (337). This is effectively what Azaña does in *La velada*: he allows unorthodox or dissenting views about the War to be freely expressed, be seen, recognized, assessed, challenged if need be, and assigned a value by one of the other interlocutors.

John H. Seekamp, however, has sounded a note of caution

---

13   In his 'Nota preliminar' to the translation, Azaña commends Borrow's artistic energy in the hostile environment of the Spain of that time: 'Es difícil encontrar otro caso en que un escritor haya triunfado con más brillantez de la hostil realidad presente' (*La Biblia en España*, Introducción, notas y traducción de Manuel Azaña [Madrid: Alianza, 1987], 21). Meregalli also notes that Azaña's translation 'tenía sus motivos más en la referencia española que en el deseo de tomar contacto con el mundo inglés' (*art. cit.*, 185).

14   Pérez Bowie, *art. cit.*, 19.

with regard to Azaña's brand of liberal democracy in *La velada*, and claims that 'Instead of a dialogue, the play [*La velada*] might be better described as a disguised monologue by a government leader increasingly isolated from the leftward evolution of Republican politics after the uprising of July, pessimistic about the chances for ultimate Republican victory, repulsed by violence on both sides, and possessing a cold and aloof personality that had led him to remain distant from those he disliked or scorned'.[15] Seekamp argues that it is precisely Azaña's 'limitations of personality and political bias' as shown in *La velada*, that help the reader to a greater understanding of the course and outcome of the Spanish Civil War for the Republic.[16]   The issue of whether *La velada* tends predominantly towards inclusivism or exclusivism is a large one, with arguments for and against.   One is certainly aware, for example, that secessionist or libertarian philosophies are excluded from, or generally criticized in the work.   The purpose of this present paper is firstly to show how Azaña uses *La velada* to present an ideal broad-church political philosophy as an example of Republicanism in action, and secondly to argue that Azaña's philosophy transcends conventional party-political considerations, being more concerned with areas such as self-criticism, intellectual debate, historical reflection, and dialogic truth.[17]

Manuel Aragón has drawn attention to what he sees as the special quality of *La velada*: that in spite of the intensely conflictive context of its composition it does not seek to divide Civil-War Spain into Manichean zones of good and evil: 'Nada más lejos ... de una literatura de guerra, fanatizada, banderiza, propagandística', he writes.[18]   In this context, however, it is not so different from many of the writings that appeared in *Hora de España*, for example.   Pérez Bowie's description of *La velada* is nearer the mark, in my view, when he writes that, not only does

---

15   Seekamp, *art. cit.*, 90.

16   *Ibid.*, 100.

17   Compare José-Carlos Mainer's view: 'No creo que deba ser estrictamente política la posteridad que celebramos en Azaña' ('Manuel Azaña y la crítica de la cultura' in *Azaña*, *op cit.*, 359-93, at p. 392).

18   '*La velada en Benicarló* o la agonía republicana', *Ínsula*, DXXVI (1990), 18.

Azaña 'analizar con lucidez extraordinaria la caótica situación sino, además, exponer sin pudor alguno, a través de esa visión perspectivística que de la suma de voces se obtiene, la incertidumbre en que se debatía su ánimo'.[19] What does make *La velada* such an unusual Civil-War text is the presence of self-criticism or self-examination in the work. In this way, too, *La velada* transcends the politics of conventional democratic parliamentary practice, because such criticism is as a rule directed against the opposition, not against one's own side, no matter how much the latter may deserve it. Franco Meregalli has commented on Azaña's 'habitual necesidad de autoanálisis'[20] in the diaries, and this mood spills over into *La velada*, in relation to both personal and national considerations. Almost from the beginning of the work we encounter Lluch's view, expressed to Rivera, that 'los hombres como nosotros ... Sobramos en todas partes' (386). One of Pastrana's replies to the gloomy prognostications of Morales is full of the self-analytical tone, whether in the name of the individual or of the nation, that characterizes the independent spirit of the work:

> Nosotros, ya en la madurez, recibimos únicamente sinsabores. Tenemos formados o encarrilados los gustos, los hábitos, la ambición. Trastornarse todo, nos deja abandonados en el camino, no sabemos qué hacer. En el fondo de muchas repulsas late el despecho del egoísmo y un poco de miedo. (433)

This note of philosophical detachment, of a willingness to admit that some of the interlocutors at least, including himself, may not actually be well placed to judge the import of the upheavals around them because of their age, culture and other predispositions, is of a piece with Pastrana's cold and sober assessment of things throughout. His last sentence, in particular, places a question mark against any motivation that underlies the negative response to change. It seems typical of Azaña's openness towards another view (and another political party) that Pastrana's critical realism is given such a sharp cutting edge, and that this realism is portrayed as being in consonance with Pastrana's socialist beliefs.

On the occasion that Pastrana replies to Morales' concerns

---

19 Pérez Bowie, *art. cit.*, 19.
20 Meregalli, *art. cit.*, 192.

for the fate of the nation's artistic treasures in the War he bases his reply on a critical examination of the phrase 'lo que hay en España es de los españoles' (455), itself a phrase, or its like, that had in all probability been turned into a slogan in the Republic, to oppose the German and Italian military presence in Spain. Pastrana proceeds to demolish the slogan by asking: what is the *patrimonio nacional*, and who are these *españoles*? Answering his own question from a socialist viewpoint he states that a considerable portion of the national heritage is created by the workers of the nation, whereas those who own that part of the heritage not in State control amount to 'unos cientos de miles de Juanes y Pedros' (a small percentage of the twenty million   population) who hide behind the slogan of national solidarity in order to preserve the fiction that Spain belongs to the Spaniards (455). Although Manuel Aragón's summary of Azaña's politics — 'para Azaña la línea divisoria entre izquierda y derecha no pasa por la propiedad, sino por la libertad' —[21] seems essentially correct, Azaña's openness to the socialist questions of ownership and State control is evident in the example given. Aragón goes on to suggest that Azaña, the architect of the Frente Popular, had no other option than to contemplate coalition with the Socialists: 'Como el liberalismo de Azaña resulta inconciliable con la derecha española de entonces, ciertamente reaccionaria, no hay más remedio que concluir que estaba, literalmente, condenado a entenderse con los socialistas'.[22] The portrayal of Pastrana in *La velada* allows us to view Azaña's attitude to Socialism as emanating from his openness to any political philosophy that sought to extend popular participation in the organization and government of the State.

An instance of Azaña's willingness to contemplate the failure of his own political philosophy is his inclusion in *La velada* of an attack on the Popular Front by Pastrana. Having been the decisive figure in welding this coalition of liberals and the Left in Spanish politics,[23] Azaña puts in Pastrana's mouth

21   'Manuel Azaña y su idea de la República', in Azaña, *op. cit.*, 226-54, at p. 231.

22   *Ibid.*, 237.

23   See Paul Preston, 'Manuel Azaña y la creación del Frente Popular' in *Azaña, op. cit.*, 267-85: 'La victoria del Frente Popular fue, en definitiva, la

the assertion that the Front was choked with 'ambiciones, divergencias, rivalidades, conflictos e indisciplina' (425) before the War, effectively admitting that his work was built on sand. No matter how intimately the Popular Front might have been a part of the promotion and defence of the Republic, it could not put itself out of the range of Azaña's critical armoury, even if Azaña himself is marksman and target at the same time. Azaña's English translators go so far (rather too far in my view) as to say that with Morales, Azaña is making 'bitter fun of himself and his own ideas [because] the very name *Eliseo Morales* stands as a ubiquitous pun on the way this character thinks and talks'.[24]   Such was the importance that Azaña placed on the critical imperative that in his last Civil-War speech he gave it equal status with courage in battle in defence of the Republic, calling for habits of 'higiene moral, el ejercicio cotidiano de actos de valor cívico, menos peligrosos que los actos de valor del combatiente en el campo de batalla, pero no menos necesarios para la conservación y la salud de la República' (366). Garcés practises this moral cleansing, accepting that he has no role to play in the present conflict (407), while Morales, in his condemnation of fanaticism and intolerance, joins all Spaniards together, including himself, within his unfavourable judgment on their inability to be sensitive to the give-and-take of social exchange: 'Los segundos términos, los perfiles indecisos, la gradación de matices, no son de nuestra moral, de nuestra política, de nuestra estética' (450).

One of the most corrosive social remarks in *La velada*, made by Lluch, again shows a character standing aside from his views, however self-evident they might appear, and subjecting them to critical assessment. Lluch is a mixture of detachment from and strongly opinionated attitudes towards what he has experienced as the pettiness, misery, vanity and inefficiency of the defenders of the Republic, essentially the trade-union led militia, and he sees old mistakes being repeated, as when he puts forward his view that 'El orden, o sea la tranquilidad de los

---

victoria de Manuel Azaña, nacida por igual tanto de su diplomacia desde detrás de la escena, como de su masiva popularidad en el campo' (285).

24 Manuel Azaña, *Vigil in Benicarló*, translated with an Introduction by Josephine Stewart and Paul Stewart (London: Associated University Presses, 1982), 22.

venturosos, se funda en la desventura de los miserables' (391). Lluch's statement, incidentally, contradicts Víctor Alba's contention that Azaña could not understand the Civil-War revolution because he was too wrapped up in his own conservative habits of thought. Alba writes that 'Azaña no comprendió nunca — no podía comprender, sin duda, habida cuenta de su formación — que lo que la gente "de orden" llamaba desorden era la busca de un orden distinto, un orden para todos y no sólo para unos cuantos'.[25] Although Lluch's observation is probably directed mainly at one of the Republic's new Civil-War ruling class of militia committees, his remark is applicable to all degrees of order that are designed for the convenience of their proponents. One should add, too, that Garcés, who speaks after Lluch, does not reject Lluch's theory.

La velada eschews any element of sentimentality about Spain, her history or her peoples, her cultural heritage, the romantic nature of the Civil War, the staunch friends of Spain abroad. Lluch also asks Morales at the end not to romanticize what he has heard and seen that evening, by writing of the hopes of young love, as they watch two of the minor interlocutors, the wounded aviator Laredo and the actress Paquita Vargas, together by the water's edge (458). It is typical, one feels, of his search for a pluralist truth that much of the colder, sharper thought in *La velada* is given by Azaña to Pastrana the socialist, rather than to Garcés, whose political background and opinions seem closer to Azaña's Republicanism. (Garcés' consistent defence of the constitutional integrity of the Republic may certainly be taken as reflecting Azaña's view also.) Pastrana's cool appraisal of any rose-coloured view of the Spanish Civil War as a galvanizing agent for grand democratic alliances abroad or as a glorious struggle for the victory of democracy at home (409-10) is very much in line with the note of independent honesty that Azaña sounded in his *Preliminar* to the work, and in his Civil-War speeches, when explaining in the latter the international repercussions of the War.

In the *Preliminar* Azaña draws attention to the extremes of debate in *La velada*, referring to the 'formación polémica' of the work. The writer and intellectual, Morales, represents an

---

25 *Los sepultureros de la República* (Barcelona: Planeta, 1977), 68.

extreme, that of the pacifist or near-pacifist view that the War is not worth the devastation that it is causing in Spain, the main argument arising from the destruction, or potential destruction, of the country's artistic treasures: since the day that the Prado was bombed, Morales says, he has been demoralized (442). He is also given plenty of space to put forward his idea that the Spanish nation should take precedence over accidental forms of government such as monarchy or republicanism. Morales regularly refers to both sides of the conflict in the same breath, in phrases such as 'uno y otro campo' (127), 'la bandera tricolor o la otra', or in the phrase referring to the 'triunfo de su hermano enemigo' (127), doing so in terms, as the last quotation suggests, that are conciliatory to the insurgents. Azaña, in his Madrid Civil-War speech, also claimed that as true Republicans 'no hemos renegado de ningún valor español, de lo que sea noble, grande y lleve el sello propio del genio de nuestro país' (361); indeed throughout the Civil-War speeches this note of inclusivism is present in a quiet and undemonstrative way. Morales takes the inclusivist argument to the extreme of claiming that the nation has rights that are not being recognized by either side and that 'cuanto ocurre en España es ventajoso o satisfactorio para unos (y en igual medida desastroso y penoso para otros), pero nocivo, mortífero para el ser nacional' (445-46).

Morales' 'sentimientos lastimados de un artista' (445), as Pastrana calls them, convey the suffering and the waste of war through the sensibility of the creative writer, keenly attuned to its pathos, and plumbing its depths of division and destruction with arguments that others in the dialogue only either touch upon or ignore. Pastrana, at the end, expresses his disdain for those such as Morales, who, he says, would prefer to live under a military dictatorship with all Spain's monuments intact than in a Republic that emerged from the ruins of artistic Spain. Morales' arguments are also rejected by Marón (442) as examples of appeasement and defeatism, and he is rebuked by Barcala for the apocalyptic scenario — 'Hipótesis monstruosa', Barcala calls it (444) — that he draws of the possible total destruction of the historic cities of Spain in the War. Morales presses his arguments to the limit in order to provoke opposing responses and gain the reassurance afforded by dialectical debate. Almost at the end of the dialogue Morales admits that he was hoping that his hypotheses might have been knocked over by the others and that he could 'cobrar fuerzas en la contradicción de ustedes' (456). And when Pastrana replies to a question from Morales towards the end with the comment 'es peligroso extremar el argumento' (454), the phrase reminds us that this is what Azaña has been doing throughout the dialogue, whether or not it is considered dangerous by a political 'prohombre' of the Republic, as Pastrana is described in the list of interlocutors.

If Morales pushes his arguments beyond the limits of the patience of such as Pastrana, the former's insistence on precision in weighing up 'la proporción exacta entre el objeto y el sacrificio para conseguirlo' (441) is an important element in the unsentimental approach to the Spanish Civil War in *La velada*. Garcés is another who insists on 'exactitud' (414) in the debate in order to think through the consequences of the course and conduct of the War for all Spaniards. One of Morales' fiercest attacks is on the romantic idea that Spaniards are somehow linked with a glorious national past, immediate or historical, by taking part in the Civil War. Such a notion reduces the national spirit to 'cierta virtud cuasi zoológica' (446), as Morales puts it. And he continues: '¿Dónde están los muertos? Se han convertido en polvo ... Puestos a imaginar su humanidad, es lícito creer que la proporción de sinvergüenzas, tontos, miserables, perversos etcétera, no fue entre los que ya vivieron menor que entre los vivientes de hoy'. A possible context for these comments may have been Miguel Hernández's celebrated poems 'Sentado sobre los muertos' and *Nuestra juventud no muere* which had appeared in the previous months in *El Mono Azul* and *Ahora*.[26] It is not difficult to imagine Azaña's response to the poem in *Ahora*, along the lines that 'nuestra juventud ¡sí que muere!'. Morales' references to the emotion of such telluric heroism are echoed, although given a very different slant, in the famous final words of Azaña's last Civil-War speech. Here, the dead are imagined as sending from the graves the message of peace, mercy and pardon. Indeed, the

---

26 For full details of publication, see Miguel Hernández, *Viento del pueblo*, ed. Juan Cano (Madrid: Cátedra, 1989), 62-63 and 77.

rhetoric of that ending (the dead are described as being 'abrigados en la tierra materna' [378]) is altogether softer and quieter than Morales' scathing references, even though the message of a common humanity is the same. *La velada* has been described as a 'political testament':[27] the term is certainly illustrated in Morales' passionate concern with exactitude, unsentimental reflection, equilibration, clearsightedness and the debunking of myths.

This is not to say that, although downplayed, the positive emotional response to the Civil War is missing from *La velada*. Barcala's interventions are characterized by his own enthusiasm and a simply expressed faith in the people and the revolution. As one would expect from someone described as a 'propagandista', Barcala stresses the positive aspects of the Civil War, where the Republic is concerned: opportunities for participation for the proletariat, solidarity and community of interest among the classes in the face of a common threat of military dictatorship, and he believes that enthusiasm and emotion, indeed all energies, should be harnessed towards the victory of the Republic. In common with Pastrana he is not interested in lengthy historical analysis of why Spain has come to such a pass: 'Borrón y cuenta nueva' (413) is a typical slogan that he uses, when shrugging off the mention of losses or inadequacies on the Republican side. Garcés' earlier remark that 'Un cartelón truculento es más poderoso que un raciocinio' (407) shows that Azaña was fully persuaded of the power of the emotive image. If Barcala's brief, blunt speech has at times the air of a persuasive slogan, it is nevertheless difficult to agree with those who contend that Barcala's views are easily blown away in argument.[28] His replies to Garcés are a timely perspective on the latter's interventions (the longest in the work), finding that Garcés' speeches lack a basis in reality (414), accusing him of pontificating from above (415), of being

---

27 See Seekamp, *art. cit.*, and Juan Espadas, '*La velada en Benicarló*: ¿Teatro, ensayo dialogado o testamento político?', in *Estudios en homenaje a Enrique Ruiz-Fornells*, ed. Juan Fernández Jiménez, José J. Labrador Herraiz and L. Teresa Valdivieso (Erie, Pennsylvania: Publicaciones de la Asociación de Licenciados y Doctores Españoles en los Estados Unidos, 1990), 175-81.

28 Stewart and Stewart, *op. cit.*, 23; also Seekamp, *art. cit.*, 93, and Manuel Aragón, *ed. cit.*, 43.

over-fastidious, and of failing to understand the significance of the revolution (416-17). Barcala's contributions also lend a greater air of urgency to the dialogue, a more direct sense of the work at hand. What Hugh Thomas has called Azaña's 'política de la tolerancia'[29] evidently compelled him to go at least as far as including the propagandist's persuasive affirmations of faith, enthusiasm, commitment and solidarity as an important constituency of opinion in the Republic of the Civil War.

The conservative lawyer Marón is another figure who revels in the extremes of debate and in the emotional conviction that democracy will finally triumph in Spain. Azaña uses him to make what is a debating *tour de force*, subtly suggesting that even conservatives have everything to lose, when they lose their freedom in a military dictatorship. Marón compares the military insurgents to the Anarchists, because of their attitude to the law of the land: 'Patean la ley para sustituirla con su capricho despótico. Es el mayor desorden posible, lo más anárquico' (431). In other words, Marón's very conservatism leads him to reject such an anarchic prospect as Francoism offers to Spain. For this reason I cannot agree with Azaña's English translators when they write that 'Marón ... serves as a Republican representative of the kind of men who served with Franco'.[30] Marón certainly represents the optimistic, even opportunistic, figure who is willing to move with the tide of history, as he sees it; but he is also portrayed as one who is not afraid of the revolution, and who is prepared to be available to direct and order it. A self-proclaimed conservative, he nevertheless believes that the time has come for the 'people', pronouncing that 'La masa puede y debe forjar la legitimidad futura' (432). Marón also expresses his faith in an innate sense of justice that glows like a divine, hence inextinguishable, spark in our souls. Carried away by his own rhetoric, perhaps, but still grounded in democratic convictions, he voices his belief in the logic of historical processes as providential, leading forces of salvation that will surely come to the rescue of the people in their time of trouble (427-28). Azaña himself had expressed this idea, but in much more sober and less populist terms, in his

---

29   'El Presidente desposeído', in *Azaña*, *op. cit.*, 288-96, at p. 296.
30   Stewart and Stewart, *op. cit.*, 23.

final Civil-War speech: 'Es seguro que, a la larga, la verdad y la justicia se abren paso' (366). The mode of expression here, although couched in terms of certainty, reveals a significant emotional gap between Azaña and his character Marón with regard to their beliefs in the future of justice and democracy. We can also see other thoughts, negative and positive, about the type of character represented by Marón, in Azaña's diary for 17 June 1937 (IV, 627-28). Although in the final Civil-War speech Azaña appears to distance himself from Marón's attitude when he admits that he does not have 'el optimismo de un Pangloss ni voy a aplicar a este drama español [the War] la simplísima doctrina del adagio, de que "no hay mal que por bien no venga" ' (378), he made space in *La velada* for the optimistic voice of Marón as a voice of the future, a representative of that blind, quasi-religious faith in the final vindication of democratic processes: the victory of the will of the people.

If we were to suggest a direct contrast between Marón and one of the other interlocutors, the choice would fall on Garcés. Marón's motto could be summed up in his optimistic assessment of the future: 'De experiencias terribles saldrán energías nuevas' (433), which is akin to Azaña's own hopes expressed at the end of his final Civil-War speech. Garcés, on the other hand, is described in terms of the past (in the list of interlocutors he is called an 'ex ministro') and he tells us himself that he is not a man of action. Is Garcés meant to be viewed as one of yesterday's men, an old Republican whom the events of the second half of 1936 and beyond have left behind?[31] Garcés claims that 'El fondo de mi pensamiento data del siglo IV antes de Jesucristo' (418), thereby linking himself no doubt to the philosophical ideals of Plato and Aristotle, but underlining the anachronism by the way in which he expresses his view. Other pointers that Garcés' sympathies are not with the present age can be observed in his longing to see someone of the administrative capacity of the Emperor Trajan return again to Spain (435), and his description of the Spanish language as 'este latín estropeado que escribimos los españoles' (435). His

---

31 Meregalli states bluntly that 'Garcés es el Azaña histórico, el personaje político salido repentinamente de la sombra y rápidamente quemado' (*art. cit.*, 213).

attitude to socio-economic progress and to the incapacity of the Gross National Product to bring about advances in civilization also puts Garcés out of the mainstream of industrial and agrarian development and concomitant social changes. 'La civilización', he contends, 'no consiste en fabricar tractores sino en cultivar los sentimientos y domesticar los impulsos feroces' (437).

Garcés' belief in the legitimacy of the Republic and of its rights in law, brings him into direct conflict with the revolution, and hence with Marón's benign view of it. For Garcés, revolution in the Republic has not only materially undermined the war effort, but has also taken away from the legitimacy of the Republic. The Civil War, seen in this light, rather than a war between rebellion and legitimate authority has now become one between revolution and counter revolution: the revolution has given a spurious, retrospective legitimacy to the rebels. Garcés allows for one war aim only: military victory, based on the universal acceptance in the Republic of its legitimacy as a legally constituted State. All other aims distract and detract from victory over the rebels. Garcés also takes the view that the defence of the legitimacy of the Republic has positive, practical effects: as a unifying force within which everybody can be incorporated, as an existing legal framework which can bring the rebels to justice, and as a means of enhancing the authority of the State. The Non-Intervention Committee in London is condemned by Garcés as the greatest enemy because it effectively denies the legal status of the Republic, by agreeing not to sell arms to either side. Azaña's famous pluralist dictum, from his first Civil-War speech, 'Ninguna política se puede fundar en la decisión de exterminar al adversario' (413), as appeared to be the case with Francoist intransigence, is appropriately assigned to Garcés in La velada, because Garcés' argument seeks its legitimacy from the legality of the Spanish Republic, which, he contends, as the embodiment of law, cannot respond to terror with terror, even though its cause is manifestly just. Since the rule of law, national and international, is Garcés' theme throughout, both rebellion and revolution are condemned as a focus for criminal activity. In Garcés, therefore, we find the most striking example of the development of the theoretical extremes which Azaña allows his interlocutors.

It is left to the socialist Pastrana to conclude the discussion of the war with the view that the Civil War will solve none of the questions that gave rise to it, because these will re-emerge from its ruins, and Spain itself will be so enfeebled by the conflict that a dictatorship will be established, no matter who wins (457). As if to emphasize the gravity of Pastrana's views, Azaña reduces the dialogue to two interlocutors, and to one of its more traditional formats: that of the experienced teacher (Pastrana) and the student eager for knowledge (Rivera).[32] Coming from an authoritative political figure such as Pastrana is supposed to be, it is not surprising that 'Guárdeme el secreto' (458) is part of his reply to his scandalized listener. Thus the discussion of the War finishes with a reference to the kind of dialectic that has informed the whole of the dialogue as a piece of Civil-War writing: Azaña's expression of polemical views on the War is an integral part of what he sees as the 'Obligación de opinar', yet these opinions can only be consigned to the privacy and secrecy of the unpublished text. In Pastrana's last confidence to Rivera, Azaña mirrors, if not necessarily his own views, his own situation as dissenter in the War. Thirteen years before, Azaña had written: 'La piedra de toque de la libertad es el respeto que se tenga a la conciencia de los disidentes'.[33] Pastrana's speculation about the War is Azaña's recognition of the kind of freedom of expression that, in his view, a democracy must embrace in some form or other, in order to escape the cruel and unfeeling destiny of dictatorship.

On 17 June 1937, the month following the completion of *La velada*, Azaña committed a thought to his diary that seems like a reflection of, as well as a reflection on, the work that he had just finished: 'El drama profundo, insoluble, está reservado a los que saben emanciparse de la ansiedad del momento, rastrean el origen de los sucesos, aquilatan su valor, y se anticipan al pasado mañana' (IV, 627). In *La velada* Azaña invests his interlocutors with some of the insights mentioned in this quotation, sharing them among the participants in the dialogue. Garcés and Morales, who because of their respective

---

32 See Gómez, *op. cit.*, 53.
33 Quoted in Aragón, 'Manuel Azaña y su idea', 235.

experiences of the sacking of Madrid's Modelo Prison (429) and of the bombing of areas adjacent to the Prado Gallery (442), are especially sensitive to the negative emotions of the War, search in Spain's past for explanations of the present barbarism. Pastrana, Barcala and Marón face the future impassively or with enthusiasm. The key to this apportioning procedure may lie in the word 'insoluble' in our quotation, and it is true that democratic politicians in governments in Europe at this time found it impossible to cope with the rise of militarism on the continent. From the evidence of Azaña's own expressed views, in his 1934 address, 'Grandezas y miserias de la política', on the essentially unpredictable nature of democratic politics, his was an intellectual temperament for which collaboration, dialogue and plurality of opinion were not only an antidote to the dogmas of authoritarianism but were also essential to authentic political experience, which latter he saw as forever evading the grasp of the dictator:

> La política no admite experiencias de laboratorio, no se puede ensayar, preparar en pequeña escala, observar sus consecuencias para luego aplicarla, como se dice, industrialmente, en gran escala a la totalidad del país; no se puede hacer eso. La política es un caudal de realidades incontenibles, irrestañables, y la mayor parte indomables para el que las quiere dominar. (15)

The uncomfortable and unorthodox political views in La velada — 'incontenibles, irrestañables' — represent a unique blend of political memoir, of democratic, pluralist exchange and literary organization, making an important contribution to the history of the Republic at war, both in their freedom of expression and in the dialectical form employed. In La velada en Benicarló Azaña, presiding over the union of an ideal parliamentary-style debate and the literary form of the dialogue, set an important example of independent opinion in a period of populist sloganism, and also breathed unexpected literary life into the venerable cliché la república de las letras.

10

'The Grand Camouflage': Julián Gorkin, Burnett Bolloten and the Spanish Civil War

HERBERT RUTLEDGE SOUTHWORTH

There are books, the text and notes of which should be read and analysed like the fine print of an insurance policy. The three volumes which form the corpus of the work of Burnett Bolloten, *The Grand Camouflage: The Communist Conspiracy in the Spanish Civil War* (1961); *The Spanish Revolution: The Left and the Struggle during the Civil War* (1979) and *The Spanish Civil War: Revolution and Counter-Revolution* (1991), together with their different editions and translations, and an article or two, some letters to publishers, personal letters to and from Bolloten, all can be of interest to the critic. I have assembled for this study the essential material available today.[1]

To the best of my knowledge, none of the critics of Bolloten's posthumous book,[2] myself included, have up to now commented on the fine print in that volume. The careful reader should

---

1   I am deeply grateful to Linda Wheeler, Reference Librarian, and to Ronald M. Bulatoff, Archival Specialist, of the Hoover Institution on War, Revolution and Peace who have made available copies of correspondence with Mr Bolloten, as well as correspondence with Mr Julián Gorkin and others. I am also greatly indebted to Ms Susan Mason, who has spent many hours gathering this material for me.

2   There are two printings of this text. The first in Spanish (Madrid: Alianza Editorial, 1989) contains the only Spanish translation of the prologue written by H. R. Trevor-Roper to the second edition of *The Grand Camouflage* (1967). The second printing was published at Chapel Hill, by the University of North Carolina Press in 1991. It is to this latter that I shall refer throughout this essay. The best succinct evaluation in English is by Adrian Shubert, York University, in *American Historical Review* (April 1992).

above all concentrate on a note numbered 48 on page 810, which reads as follows:

> The Communists and their supporters claim that El Campesino's articles and books were ghost-written by Julián Gorkin, one of the leaders during the Civil War of the anti-Stalinist Partido Obrero de Unificación Marxista (POUM). This is true. El Campesino was to all intents and purposes an illiterate and incapable of giving literate expression to his thoughts and experiences ... See his book, *La vie et la mort en URSS, 1939-1949*, which was written by Gorkin on the basis of El Campesino's oral testimony after the latter's escape from Russia (see Gorkin's letter to me of 18 October 1984, Hoover Institution). It is important to record that during the Civil War El Campesino's brutality in carrying out Communist policy was proverbial ...[3]

Further attention is called to this note by another note in Bolloten's book: note 21 on page 884 which reads: 'See chapter 17 for the claim that El Campesino's articles and books were ghost-written by Julián Gorkin'. The two notes are offered in reference to El Campesino's article in *Solidaridad Obrera* (Paris), 11 March 1951. However, it is note 48, p. 810, that contains the essential, more affirmative, information; it is to this that I shall refer in the rest of this article.

This note was not preceded or followed by any immediate explanation or amplification. I shall therefore attempt to interpret it for the reader through an exposition of its background and consequences. The background of the note can be found in a polemic which I nurtured with Bolloten in the *TLS* in 1978. I was reviewing the French edition (1977) of the second version of his book.[4] In this review, I wrote in the *TLS* on 9 June 1978:

---

3   In his 1979 book, when Bolloten was quoting El Campesino as his witness, he referred to him as 'a much publicised Communist and somewhat charismatic figure during the war' (174). Later, apparently unwilling to express his justified irritation with Gorkin, he attacked El Campesino and Communist policy.

4   Burnett Bolloten, *La Révolution espagnole et la lutte pour le pouvoir* (Paris: Ruedo Ibérico, 1977). This printing contains material not found in *The Grand Camouflage*, but has less of such new material than does the 1979 U.S. edition.

Bolloten's book cannot be dissociated from the Cold War, above all because of his sources. Many of these are the confessions of ex-members of the Spanish Communist Party or Russian *transfuges*. It would be of historiographical interest some day to pin down exactly which of these volumes were in reality inspired by secret funds from certain United States agencies.

Bolloten's pride was piqued and he replied with indignation, (25th August):

Mr Southworth asserts that the book 'cannot be dissociated from the Cold War' and throws out an innuendo that it was 'inspired by secret funds from certain United States agencies', by which of course he means the CIA ... I must ask Mr Southworth which sources inspired his innuendo.

I, in turn, answered Bolloten on 13 October:

Among Bolloten's sources that I consider suspect are 'confessions' of various Spanish Communists published during the Cold War, especially those connected with the propaganda outlets of the associations for 'Freedom of Culture'. Above all, I distrust the book attributed to Valentín González (El Campesino) originally published in 1950 in French, *La vie et la mort en URSS (1939-1949)*. This book was transcribed by Julián Gorkin, whose links with Freedom of Culture groups are undeniable; it has an introduction by Gorkin and was translated from, one supposes, the language of El Campesino, that is, Spanish. It was later translated from French into Spanish by Gorkin. But then in which language had El Campesino written or dictated his book? Moreover, in the English and German editions of this book, the introduction signed originally by Gorkin forms a part of the text supposedly written by El Campesino. This manipulation of the text of a book should have caused Bolloten to use it with caution; instead, he cites it frequently.

Again, this time in the *TLS* of 17 November, Bolloten defended his use of the quotations from El Campesino:

Finally, I should perhaps reply to Southworth's objections to my use of the evidence of various former Spanish Communists. He takes particular exception to Valentín González (El Campesino) the former Communist military leader. I naturally examined the circumstances of the editing and publishing of González's work with the utmost care.   I have therefore concluded that Southworth's objections amount to no more than an attempt to confuse the layman with editorial detail irrelevant to the authenticity of the material.

The Times and the *TLS* then entered into a period of strikes that lasted for weeks and my polemic with Bolloten was not revived in the magazine.

I have now given the reader some background facts which will, I hope, clarify note 48, page 810 of Bolloten's 1991 book; this note itself being based on the letter written by Julián Gorkin, dated 18 October 1984. But this is not all of the truth. Some other parts of the letter, which Bolloten did not quote, are also essential to an understanding of the footnote. I shall now copy the pertinent extracts from Gorkin's letter which Bolloten omitted.[5] 'I shall tell you the truth', thus began that part of Gorkin's letter of 18 October 1984 that deals with his relations with El Campesino. It continued:

> In April 1949, on learning that El Campesino had escaped from the Soviet Union and had arrived in Teheran, I obtained from a French Socialist Minister, a friend of mine, two photographs of El Campesino. I recognized him and, thanks to the financial help of some North American friends, I arranged for him to be brought to a place near Frankfurt. We spent about a month together. I took note of his Odyssey in the USSR and I transcribed the account in *La vida y la muerte en la URSS*, which thanks to the agency Opera Mundi obtained an international success. We then went at once to Germany [*sic*] and in Berlin we recorded ten radio programmes to be broadcast to East Germany, and we also smuggled in a pile of texts of these programmes on Bible paper. We [El Campesino and Gorkin] travelled through several cities and we were even received in the Bundestag. I was a great friend of Willy Brandt,[6] who, among others, helped us enormously ... We toured Italy in the same way and finally, invited by the Cuban Confederation of Labour and by President Carlos Prío Socarrás, we visited all of Cuba. Putting together my knowledge of Soviet reality and the testimony of El Campesino, each day I wrote an article for the daily *Prensa Libre*. Every day the team which accompanied us through the country in two automobiles used to say to El

5   All of the letters to and from Gorkin were written in Spanish. I have done the translation.

6   Brandt was one of the 'men of the anti-Communist' Left aided financially by the CIA (Kai Bird, *The Chairman* [New York: Simon & Schuster, 1992], 358).

Campesino: 'Valentín, read your article for today in case somebody questions you about it'.

This last sentence reveals the contumelious attitude of Gorkin towards his protégé, perhaps his victim.

Gorkin had already written an account of his relations with El Campesino in the introduction to a book titled *Comunista en España y antistalinista en la URSS*, published in Mexico City in 1952, and in Spain in 1979. In each edition, El Campesino was named as the author and Gorkin as the transcriber. The 1979 edition had, in addition, a short prologue by Gorkin, dated 1978. In this prologue, Gorkin revealed that *Comunista en España* was based on the articles first published in the Havana daily *Prensa Libre*, during the El Campesino-Gorkin propaganda cam-paign in the island. They were signed by El Campesino but written by Gorkin. The 1979 prologue, signed by Gorkin, ends with this highly sardonic phrase, 'It goes without saying that these revelations are entirely the responsibility of El Cam-pesino, and that for my part I assume the entire responsibility of transcription'.[7] Apart from the question of authorship, the most significant difference between what Gorkin had written in 1952 and 1978-79, and then what he wrote in 1984, lies in the fact that in his 1984 letter to Bolloten, Gorkin acknowledges that El Campesino's trip from Teheran to Western Europe was carried out with financing from United States sources, quite the contrary of what he had pretended in 1952 and 1978-79. In 1952, Gorkin had written that, on hearing that El Campesino was in Teheran,

I abandoned my literary work and my pro-European political tasks. I placed at El Campesino's service not only my pen, but all of the resources which it had brought me. I likewise put into play all my influence to get him out of Teheran, where he could encounter certain dangers, and bring him discreetly to Western Europe ... Seven or eight times the Moscow radio insisted that he owed his salvation to the North Americans ... that he had been converted into a well-paid agent of Washington. Always the same story! Meanwhile, we were living modestly in the suburbs of Paris ... we were preparing together, on the basis of his story and of his

---

7   Valentín González, 'El Campesino', in *Comunista en España y antistalinista en la URSS* (Gijón: Ediciones Júcar, 1981), 11.

rich documentation, the book *La vida y la muerte en la URSS*, today published in more than sixty periodicals all over the world and edited time and again in various countries.[8]

It is difficult to understand how a man in flight for his life, on foot, unable to read or write, would have ben able to load himself down with 'valuable documentation'.   Gorkin was always the first to pat himself on the back. He wrote, 'the bold escape of El Campesino and his sensational revelations have found a universal response', and he continued, 'from this point of view, my satisfaction is immense, above all because this result has been achieved by the joining of our two unaided forces'.[9] He went on, in the same blustering vein, 'Not only did I spend, for the trip from Teheran to Western Europe and for his sustenance, all of my money, but I also contracted debts for three hundred and fifty thousand francs'.   And as for the expenses involved in Gorkin's activities in Germany with El Campesino, these, he said, were underwritten by 'our editor, by two important broadcasting companies in Berlin and by working class organizations and anti-Stalinist entities'.[10]

To sum up, Gorkin in 1952, and again in 1979, repeatedly and publicly denied that any North American funds were involved in El Campesino's escape from Teheran to Western Europe and for his campaign of propaganda of many years that

---

8   Valentín González, 'El Campesino', *Comunista en España y antistalinista en la URSS* (Mexico, D.F.: Editorial Guarania, 1952), 13.

9   *Ibid.*, 14. Gorkin wrote to Bertram D. Wolfe, 24 May 1952, 'Opera Mundi tells me that "The Voice of America" intends to make a dramatization of *La vida y la muerte en la URSS*, by El Campesino, which, as you know, has had a great success in the United States press (and in Latin America, where the Spanish edition printed in Buenos Aires has sold more than 50,000 copies'. Gorkin added, 'I think Opera Mundi is negotiating through the services of the Embassy'. These last four words would seem to be Gorkinese for the CIA. Twenty-six years later, Gorkin wrote, in his new prologue to El Campesino's second book, that *La vida y la muerte en la URSS* had been published and republished in fourteen countries, and that, by means of a great news agency, large extracts of the book had been reproduced in more than seventy newspapers all over the world. Gorkin's figures for the distribution of his propaganda should not be confused with the sales figures of an editor dependent on the market.

10   *Ibid.*, 26

followed. Gorkin insisted that he had financed all of this from his piggy-bank. In 1984, thirty-two years later, he wrote, confidentially, the exact contrary.

It seems reasonable to imagine that when Bolloten read Gorkin's letter informing him that he, his trusted friend, had not always told him the truth about his relations with El Campesino, Bolloten could have wondered about other books by ex-Communists who had profited from Gorkin's friendship, for example, Jesús Hernández (a member of the PCE executive and a minister in Largo Caballero's government during the Civil War) and Enrique Castro Delgado (first commander of the Communist Quinto Regimiento). Bolloten had already quoted from both sources in the two versions of his own book and would continue to quote from them in the new edition he was then preparing.

Gorkin had also boasted of his role in the preparation of the books by Hernández and Castro Delgado. According to Gorkin, after he had returned from Mexico on one of his frequent trips — that is, after he had begun his work for the Congress, which entailed numerous visits to Spanish America — José Bullejos, Secretary-General of the Spanish Communist Party from 1925 until his expulsion in 1932, informed him that Jesús Hernández wanted to talk with him. It was common knowledge among the Spanish groups in Paris that Gorkin could help to publish anti-Communist books. Gorkin, according to Gorkin, replied to Bullejos: 'I cannot clasp the hand of Jesús Hernández so long as he has not denounced in a book the Stalinist crimes in Spain and, precisely, the details about the imprisonment and assassination of Andrés Nin'.

Gorkin, in effect, had indicated to Hernández, the conditions under which his book could be published. 'Six months later', Gorkin continued, 'after my return to Paris, I received the text of Hernández's book *Yo fui un ministro de Stalin*'. Hernández had followed the instructions given by Gorkin, who noted 'I intervened in the French translation of the book and in its publication under the title *La Grande trahison*. The revelations contained in the book, and especially those dealing with the torture and assassination of Andrés Nin, as well as the setting up of the *Procès de Moscou dans l'Espagne en guerre* caused a sensation'.[11]

Another Spanish ex-Communist, Enrique Castro Delgado, who had distinguished himself politically and militarily during the Civil War, also collaborated with Gorkin. After the war, Castro Delgado had found refuge in the Soviet Union and, then like Hernández, had left. He arrived in Mexico after the end of the Second World War.

Among Gorkin's friends and fellow ideologues was the writer Bertram D. Wolfe, who was living in New York City. On 23 March 1948, when Gorkin was preparing to leave Mexico to go to Paris, he wrote to Wolfe that he would send him in a month or so, 'a sensational manuscript ... signed by Enrique Castro, an ex-leader of the Spanish Communist Party, who has been living for seven years in Russia and from where he has miraculously escaped ... I have requested the author to send you a copy as soon as the book is finished. He will send me another copy in Paris'. He added this highly interesting sentence: 'They are making German translations of both books, mine[12] and Castro's, for distribution in the non-Soviet zones of Germany'. Clearly, Gorkin's North American friends were already giving to Castro Delgado's work the same treatment they would give to the works of El Campesino, when, a year later, Gorkin was in Europe.

My admonition to Bolloten in 1978 to be more prudent in quoting from the works of El Campesino went unheeded. Not only did he repeat in 1991 the four quotations from El Campesino that he had used in the previous edition, but he also introduced four new citations from *Comunista en España y antistalinista en la URSS*, the book signed by El Campesino which Bolloten preferred to quote at that time, inasmuch as its contents concerned more frequently the newer parts of the 1991 book.

Of the four new references to El Campesino's literary production found in Bolloten's 1991 book, two are worthy of further study: in one of them Bolloten elaborates on his

---

11   Julián Gorkin, *El proceso de Moscú en Barcelona* (Barcelona: Ayma, 1973), 14; *Les Communistes contre la révolution espagnole* (Paris: Belfond, 1978), 17.

12   This was probably Gorkin's book on the murder of Trotsky.

methodology in dealing with the confessional works by Spanish ex-Communists and Soviet dissidents; in the other, he reveals how Gorkin used El Campesino to trick Indalecio Prieto.

Bolloten had recourse to El Campesino as an authority on the alleged low morale among the Republicans in April 1938, when Negrín formed his second government; the quotation from El Campesino was preceded by Bolloten's revival of our dispute in the *TLS* in 1978. Bolloten began by insisting that the testimony of El Campesino and other ex-Communists was not essential to prove his thesis, and went on,

> But to ignore their testimony entirely would be tantamount to yielding to those who would exclude all books from the historiography of the Civil War that do not conform to the party line. One such book is *Comunista en España y antistalinista en la URSS* by Valentín González (El Campesino), the well-known Communist militia commander, who escaped from the Soviet Union after World War II. Despite numerous inaccuracies and distortions, like countless books on the Civil War, it nonetheless contains material of undoubted historical value, which deserves recording.[13]

After perusing the above words, wherein Bolloten acknowledged his conviction that El Campesino's book contained numerous inaccuracies and distortions, and after studying the extract from my letter in the *TLS* of 13 October 1978 already quoted, in which I enumerated a number of reasons for mistrusting the writings attributed to El Campesino, the reader may wonder why Bolloten at this place in his new book, years later, defiantly summoned up El Campesino as his leading authority for the argumentation that he was developing.

The explanation probably is that Gorkin's letter left Bolloten in a state of confusion and, during the three years he had still to live, he came to no decision. By his own irresolute behaviour, he left his readers as bewildered concerning the true nature of the collaboration of Gorkin and El Campesino as he showed himself to be. The reader, at this point, may plead that by 14 October 1984, Bolloten had already incorporated the additional

---

13 Burnett Bolloten, *The Spanish Civil War: Revolution and Counter-Revolution* (Chapel Hill: Univ. of North Carolina Press, 1991), 632.

references to El Campesino into his new text and had not had the time to erase them before his death. I shall a bit further along demonstrate the instability of such a position.

Bolloten then, and for the only time in his posthumous book, makes extensive reference to our 1978 polemic in the *TLS*. He does not quote from his own letters to the *TLS*, nor from mine; he does not quote from my review of his book, but he does quote from the letter that Robert Conquest wrote to refute my review of Bolloten's book, a work which Conquest defined as a 'profound and thorough work on the Spanish Civil War'.[14] Bolloten wrote:

> ... replying to Southworth, Robert Conquest, the famous sovietologist stated: 'Mr Southworth is very choosy about evidence. Everything written by ex-Communists, but also by anyone else connected with Western organizations, thought to have been involved in the Cold War, is to be ruled out. Cold War here signifies as usual the voicing of opinions or retailing of facts unpalatable to the Soviet leadership. Anyone who has been connected with a broader view of the period knows that *some* defector material is false ..., when it comes to the disputed issues; any real historian must pick his way very carefully. On the other hand, neither the opinion, nor even the imperfect character, of one or another witness in themselves refute his testimony. Nor are we to exclude those who may tend to put themselves in a better light than we might accept — to do so would be to disqualify virtually the entire human race. Mr Southworth's criteria, even if they were not so patently partisan, would enable him to exclude anyone he wished, under cover of an insistence on immaculate certainties'.[15]

Who can quarrel with Conquest when he states that 'when it comes to the disputed issues any real historian must pick his way very carefully'? Bolloten did not know how to 'pick his way very carefully'. Nor did Robert Conquest, who, in his letter to the *TLS* offered this egregious evaluation of Bolloten's qualities as a researcher:

> Mr Bolloten, naturally with his massive and careful checks, and counter-checks, survives more unscathed still and is hardly to be hurt by such footling ploys as Mr Southworth's new rule that a

---

14 *TLS*, 17 November 1978, 1340.
15 *Ibid*.

writer must quote every book in his bibliography — yet another sign of his inability to understand what a history is for or about.

Conquest suffers from the same disability that afflicted Bolloten, verbal exaggeration. When Bolloten increased the material of his first book, *The Grand Camouflage*, after sixteen years of additional labour, by more or less a hundred pages, he described it as a 'vast expansion'.[16] As the reader of this article will perceive, Bolloten's research concerning the trustworthiness of El Campesino's memoirs and political pronouncements was practically less than nothing. The first recorded effort that he made to verify El Campesino's reliability was in a letter to Gorkin, dated 15 August 1984, which reached Gorkin only on 17 October. In the meantime, Bolloten had written again, on 10 October. In this letter, he asked Gorkin for an answer to his earlier letter, described as containing 'several very important questions'. He also enclosed a copy of his earlier letter, apparently without making another copy for himself. This is indicated in a manuscript note written later on the letter of 10 October. It is evident from Gorkin's answer to Bolloten's letter of 15 August 1984, now unfortunately misplaced, that among the questions posed by Bolloten was one concerning El Campesino and Gorkin.

Despite Bolloten's reassurance to the readers of the *TLS* that he had examined the circumstances of the editing and publishing of González's work with the utmost care, it is evident today that Bolloten had taken no steps at all to verify the writings signed by El Campesino. There were no 'massive and careful checks and counter-checks' save in Conquest's imagination. Here we are concerned with but one aspect of Bolloten's work, but it is representative of a flaw that appears persistently therein.

Bolloten was reminded by reading Gorkin's letter of 18 October 1984 that he had publicly fibbed in writing in the *TLS* that he had examined the circumstances of the editing and publishing of González's work with the utmost care. In his first letter to the *TLS*, Bolloten wrote:

---

16   *TLS*, 25 August 1978, 953.

> In the preface to my new book, I state: 'In preparing this volume, I have allowed myself to be guided solely by a desire to reveal the truth. I have endeavoured by the most diligent research and by the most conscientious selection of materials to maintain the highest possible standard of objectivity'.
>
> I have presented the facts without manipulation or omission and am confident that the unbiased reader will draw his own conclusions. I am likewise confident that the integrity of the book will be upheld and that Mr Southworth will be thoroughly discredited.[17]

This defensive affirmation reads as if Bolloten felt that he had been accused of lying, as if any questioning of his written work, any suggestion that he might have been mistaken constituted an all-out assault on his moral probity. Many historians would have deemed such a declaration superfluous. The same preoccupation appears in his correspondence. 'My objective has been no other than to tell the truth and nothing but the truth', he wrote to Julián Gorkin on 17 February 1977, at the same time reassuring the latter that 'there is no one more qualified than yourself to judge the historical value of a book on the Civil War'. More than eight years later, on 21 November 1985, he wrote to Gorkin, 'My only intention during so many years of labour, has been to attain to the truth'. This was written a year after he had read Gorkin's revealing letter about El Campesino's responsibility as an author, and Gorkin's responsibility as a memorialist.

Above, I have quoted from Bolloten's letter to the *TLS* (25 August 1978), in which he protests that he has presented the facts without manipulation or omission. This was not true. He was guilty of being an accessory to the manipulation of the facts presented by Gorkin, in the guise of El Campesino. As for omission, Bolloten certainly knew that Gorkin was salaried by an organization dependent on the CIA. He omitted this information from his text, while refusing to admit that his work was tainted by this relationship. In the end, he had abandoned the search for the truth.

Among the numerous contradictions found in Bolloten's work, between one page and another, are those based on his

---

17 *TLS*, 25 August 1978, 953.

experiences during the Civil War as a journalist in Spain and his first months or even years in Mexico. As I have shown in an article on his 1991 book (*Journal of the Association for Contemporary Iberian Studies*, IV [1991], No. 2), in early 1940 Bolloten was busily engaged in writing a history of the Spanish Civil War, tailored to the tastes of his friends General Ignacio Hidalgo de Cisneros and his wife, Constancia de la Mora; both militant members of the Spanish Communist Party, in Mexican exile. Thus, Bolloten at that time could be said to have held a travelling fellowship in the Spanish Communist Party just as, later, in his correspondence with Spanish anarcho-syndicalists, such as Federica Montseny, he gave the impression of sympathizing with their movement.[18]

An event took place, later on in 1940, according to friends of Bolloten in whom he confided, that completely changed his interpretation of the Spanish Civil War. This event touched in some way on the murder of Leon Trotsky. One version is that Communist friends sought to coerce him into helping the assassin Mercader to escape — for instance, by offering him a safe house. It seems probable that Bolloten may have left papers concerning this matter, but to my knowledge, nothing has been published.

In his introduction to the second printing of *The Grand Camouflage*, the well-known historian, H. R. Trevor-Roper, asserts that Bolloten's long years of study had forced on him a 're-interpretation' of his material. He wrote, 'When [Bolloten] left Spain, he was, he says, profoundly influenced by official propaganda, from which only time and diligent research could free me. He took his time and was diligent in research; and as he studied, he found himself, as every good historian does ... gradually modifying the views originally based on personal involvement'.[19] In fact, a close study of his life and works, from all the evidence available, reveals Bolloten to have passed from one personal involvement to another personal involvement. His 'diligent research' was tainted by his negligent acceptance of the

---

18 *Espoir*, Toulouse, 7 September 1961; H. R. Southworth, *El mito de la cruzada de Franco* (Paris: Ruedo Ibérico, 1963), 276-77.

19 H. R. Trevor-Roper, 'Introduction', Burnett Bolloten, *The Grand Camouflage* (London: Pall Mall Press, 1968), 4.

unreliable manuscripts of Julián Gorkin.

Bolloten was more forthcoming about his past in his posthumous book than in his previous writings, but he still failed to recognize publicly the importance of the friendship that united him with the Hidalgo de Cisneros couple. He offered this information in driblets, in notes to his book. He wrote in one place, 'I visited Constancia de la Mora and her husband ... at the beginning of 1940' (892). In another note, he said that he interviewed her in Cuernavaca in March 1940.[20] Jay Allen, one of the most significant of the newspapermen who covered the Spanish War,[21] and who was also a Negrinista, received a letter from Constancia de la Mora, dated 14 January 1940, in which she wrote that Bolloten and his wife had been their house guests for the last three days, and that he had shown to her and her husband seven chapters of his book. She described the manuscript as 'simply marvellous' and wrote that 'it will be, really, *the* historical documentary study of the war'.[22] It is evident that the seven chapters that Bolloten gave to Hidalgo de Cisneros and his wife to read were not those which he later published, although traces of this first manuscript remained in Bolloten's mind. These traces are evident in *The Grand Camouflage* and impelled me to write, in *El mito de la cruzada de Franco*, 'Bolloten's book is, in my opinion, the most pro-Republican book yet to be published openly in Franco's Spain'.[23]

There are other confessional items here and there in Bolloten's last book. Referring to an incident that took place on 18 June 1937, he wrote: 'I was at that time the United Press correspondent in Valencia and sympathetic to the Communist Party line' (500). He also wrote: 'I was not a long-term sympathiser, least of all a party member' (501). He explained, more fully as follows:

---

20 Bolloten (1991), 896, n. 18.

21 Jay Allen wrote the first interview with Franco after his arrival in Morocco from the Canaries, the frequently anthologized account of the massacre of Badajoz, and the last interview with José Antonio Primo de Rivera before his execution.

22 See my article in *ACIS Journal*, IV (Autumn 1991), No. 2, 59.

23 Southworth, *El mito de la cruzada de Franco*, 151.

> It is true that when I first began to write about the Civil War and Revolution in 1936 as a British correspondent for United Press, I was very much influenced by the wartime propaganda of the Communist Party, as indeed were many other journalists who supported the Republic, and that it took several years to cast off the slough of distortions and lies that encumbered my thinking.
> (297)

Unfortunately, Bolloten, in casting off the slough of distortions and lies that encumbered his thinking, adopted the distortions and lies of Julián Gorkin, transmitted through the false personality of El Campesino.

Gorkin showed considerable ingenuity in his exploitation of the propaganda possibilities he had unearthed in El Campesino, however illiterate the latter might have been. Not only were two books published under his signature, but also the anarcho-syndicalist press in exile in Paris, *Solidaridad Obrera*, was used successfully. Another impudent exercise in historical revisionism was perpetrated by Gorkin and El Campesino by means of a letter sent to the Spanish Socialist leader in exile, Indalecio Prieto, on 10 October 1950. Prieto had been Defence Minister at the time of the Republican capture of Teruel late in December 1937 and of its subsequent loss in late February 1938. In 1950, Prieto was living in France near the Basque frontier. He was the outstanding personality among the Spanish exiles opposed to Negrín. In this missive, El Campesino informed Prieto that he, the famous militia leader, one of the protagonists of the capture of Teruel, had also been involved in a Communist plot to abandon Teruel to the Franco forces, in order to discredit the Minister Prieto. In his letter, El Campesino described himself as the scapegoat of a plan gone awry.

El Campesino stayed in Teruel while Franco's forces were encircling the city they had lost some weeks earlier. Then, according to El Campesino, Juan Modesto and Enrique Líster, Communist militia leaders like himself, were to counter-attack and save him and his men:

> I served as a scapegoat in order to displace you from the Ministry, and to do so, I had to display heroic efforts together with my *compañeros* of the division. Hundreds of times I was within inches of losing my life — all of this to prove that the Communist

divisions were good and the Minister bad. All this *tinglado* was prepared at the cost of thousands of lives of the poor Spanish people, because the Minister, Comrade Prieto, did not let himself be manipulated by the GPU of the Kremlin.[24]

The trap set by Gorkin (and El Campesino) proved a success. Prieto, who was a professional journalist, wrote, in an article in *El Socialista* (Paris, 2 November 1950), that he had been greatly surprised by the loss of Teruel:

> How could such an unexpected event have taken place? I could find no explanation. Officers of highly balanced judgement gave as their firm opinion that the Communists, implacable enemies of mine, had conceived the loss of Teruel in order to discredit me, to destroy me. But in spite of much evidence supporting the assertion I did not believe it, because I could not believe it. Impossible! Now El Campesino seems to confirm it in his letter ... So many things I thought impossible have become reality.[25]

El Campesino's letter to Prieto was accompanied by a copy of *La vie et la mort en URSS*, which had just been published. Gorkin's introduction to this book contained a short summary of El Campesino's version of what had happened at Teruel (14). Much later, Gorkin 'revealed' that the letter to Prieto was sent 'at my suggestion'.[26] A fuller account of El Campesino's version of what had happened in Teruel was included in his second book, *Comunista en España y antistalinista en la URSS* (65-72). These pages inspired Prieto to further reflections on the Battle of Teruel, under the title 'Why we lost Teruel'. This article was probably first published in *El Socialista*. It was dated 14 February 1953. The article was reprinted in Prieto's *Entresijos*

---

24 Indalecio Prieto, *Convulsiones de España*, 3 vols (México, D.F.: Ediciones Oasis, 1968), II, 111. 'La pérdida de Teruel' (107-13) is a copy of the article by Prieto which appeared in *El Socialista*, 2 November 1950. The PSOE press in exile, like that of the anarcho-syndicalists, was at the service of Gorkin. Prieto had sponsored Gorkin's entry into Mexico in 1940, and later, in France, Gorkin and most of the Poumistas joined the PSOE in exile.

25 Bolloten (1991), 573. Bolloten does not quote the preceding sentence to which I allude further on. It reads, 'one night, without any forewarning, I received news that Teruel had passed to the hands of the enemy' (*Convulsiones de España*, II, 111).

26 Julián Gorkin, 'La verdad de España y las mentiras del Kremlin', *España Libre* (New York) (julio-agosto, 1972).

de la guerra de España,[27] and much later in 1968 in the second volume of his collected articles, *Convulsiones de España*.[28]   In this second article about El Campesino and the Battle of Teruel. Prieto displayed an unquestioning faith in El Campesino's account of the events in Teruel, with a sub-heading 'Teruel is lost in order that I be lost', and a full page of Prieto's collected essays was filled with extracts from *Comunista en España*.[29] Prieto's full acceptance of the Gorkin-El Campesino theses on the Battle of Teruel is found in a section of *Convulsiones de España, II*, labelled 'Los rusos en España'.   In this section there are three articles; the third is '¿Por qué perdimos Teruel?'.

These paragraphs from Prieto's book caught the attention of Colonel José Manuel Martínez Bande, an official Francoist military historian of the Civil War.   His considerable work was sponsored by the Servicio Histórico Militar.   The tenth volume of Martínez Bande's series of *Monografías de la guerra civil* was devoted to the Battle of Teruel.[30]   In that work he reproduced the paragraph that Prieto had reprinted from El Campesino, preceded by a few lines which, if we accept the punctuation used in *Entresijos* and *Convulsiones, II*, were written by Prieto. These read:

> In order to find the way to deal me the final blow, there was a Russian-Spanish consultation. 'We must utilize the loss of Teruel', decreed Gueré [Gerö] one of the delegates of the Kremlin, seconded by Stepanov, who had just come back from a very rapid trip to Moscow, from which he brought strict instructions.[31]

Although not clearly indicated by Prieto, Gerö's phrase comes from Jesús Hernández.[32]

Gerö's remark, quoted above, was allegedly made *after* the

---

27   Indalecio Prieto, *Entresijos de la guerra de España* (México, D.F.: n.p., 1953), 63-70.

28   *Convulsiones de España,* II, 101-06.

29   *Ibid.,* II, 103-04, quoting *Comunista en España*, 68-71.

30   Juan Manuel Martínez Bande, *La batalla de Teruel* (nueva edición, Madrid: Editorial San Martín, 1990).   A first edition of this monograph was published in 1974.

31   *Convulsiones de España,* II, 103.

32   *La Grande trahison* (Paris: Fasquelle, 1953), 136; Jesús Hernández, *Yo fui un ministro de Stalin* (Madrid: G. del Toro, 1974), 232.

fall of Teruel and therefore has nothing to do with any *plot* to lose Teruel in order to discredit Prieto. Anyway, Martínez Bande attributed the phrase to Prieto, and, with these few lines, Martínez Bande placed his seal of approval to the Gorkin-El Campesino account of the Russian-Spanish Republican conspiracy to oust Prieto from the Ministry. Martínez Bande wrote, 'El Campesino's version [on Teruel] is full of stupid mistakes, if not to say lies, but it is worth reading'.[33] And at more length, he stated, 'Probably Valentín was neither a coward, nor still less, a hero. He endured much in Teruel, but his *estado de ánimo* was not that of Colonels Barba and Rey d'Harcourt'.[34] 'Neither Modesto nor Líster could reproach him too much, since neither of them had carried out the missions they had been given'.[35]

I want, at this point, to take note briefly of what El Campesino, Modesto and Líster wrote, later, about the final hours of the battle for Teruel. El Campesino, in *Comunista en España*, recounted that, abandoned by Modesto and Líster, who were supposed to come to save him, he and his men had fought for five hours during the night of 21 February to escape from the siege that the counter-attacking Nationalists were forming around Teruel. He asserted, 'I lost in the fight some thousand men, but the siege was lifted and I saved around 11,000 men'.[36] Both Modesto and Líster told their stories about the final days of the battle of Teruel, after the compositions of El Campesino-Gorkin had been published. Modesto accused El Campesino of having 'evacuated Teruel without orders or necessity'.[37] Líster, more harshly, charged Valentín González of having fled from Teruel, leaving behind hundreds of his men to fall into the hands of the enemy, and of having run away as far as fifty kilometres behind the lines. Líster expressed his indignation that El Campesino had not been punished for his behaviour and had not even been relieved of his divisional

---

33   Martínez Bande, *La batalla de Teruel*, 205, n. 264.

34   Barba and Rey d'Harcourt were in command of the Francoist garrison at Teruel.

35   Martínez Bande, *La batalla de Teruel*, 205, n. 6-1.

36   *Comunista en España*, 70.

37   Juan Modesto, *Soy del Quinto Regimento* (Paris: Éditions du Globe, 1969), 149-51.

command.[38]

These three versions of the final hours of the Battle of Teruel can be compared with Martínez Bande's version of the same period of the time, based on captured Republican army communications and Nationalist army dispatches. Martínez Bande did not accept El Campesino's version of his escape from Teruel. Basing his text on official Republican communiqués between Minister Prieto and General Vicente Rojo, in charge of the withdrawal from Teruel, he shows that both Prieto and Rojo were uneasy about the first facts emerging about El Campesino's leaving his post at Teruel on 21 February. He wrote, 'But Prieto is sceptical, and still more so, when, on 22 February, Rojo speaks to him of the "large numbers of fugitives on the roads south of Teruel, most of them without armament". Many are from El Campesino's division and almost all of them have thrown away their arms ... On the 23rd, the disorder continues ... The 24th, Prieto again talks with Rojo about "El Campesino's case". The Minister wants El Campesino to write a report on the reason for his abandonment of the city and for the manner in which the evacuation was carried out, "because the event has not been sufficiently clarified" and there are contradictions between the statement that the withdrawal was carried out in an orderly fashion, and the reality of the fugitives disarmed and demoralized.[39]   This material obliges us to serious doubts about El Campesino's post-war revelations and also about the sincerity of Prieto's exclamations of surprise about these same revelations (see note 25 and related text).

Martínez Bande, as an army officer, judges El Campesino severely on the charge of having abandoned his troops. He poses the question, 'Were any forces left in Teruel? Independently of whether or not the city should have been evacuated and of the manner in which the evacuation was carried out, there is another question: Did El Campesino leave behind part of his men?'.[40] He then refers to Nationalist army dispatches. One confirms that some 1,200 men from El Campesino's division, on the morning of 22 February, attempted

38   Enrique Líster, *Nuestra guerra* (Paris: Éditions du Globe, 1966), 182.
39   Martínez Bande, *La batalla de Teruel*, 203.
40   *Ibid.*, 204.

to leave Teruel. According to this source, most of them were made prisoners. Martínez Bande comments, 'thus there were at least 1,200 men left behind when El Campesino fled'.[41]   A dispatch from another unit reported that on entering Teruel that morning, 400 prisoners were taken, some from El Campesino's division. Still another Nationalist *parte* says, 'The enemy, broken and shattered, surrendered in large groups, others managed to flee by the river-bed during the night'.[42]

This evidence is at times highly contradictory. In summing up, Martínez Bande states: 'Perhaps at nightfall on 21 February, El Campesino flees with an ill-defined number of men, and from then on contact with him is lost; finally, he will reappear far in the rearguard'.[43]   Martínez   Bande's condemnation was of course in part political.[44]

A more even-handed evaluation of El Campesino's career can be found in *Testimonio de dos guerras*,[45] written by Manuel Tagueña Lacorte and published posthumously in Mexico in 1973. Tagueña came from a middle-class family and by 1933 was *licenciado* in Physical and Mathematical Sciences. In 1932 he had joined the Communist Youth Movement, with his 'best friend' Fernando Claudín and in the Spring of 1936 became a member of the Spanish Communist Party. He had received some basic military training and when the Franco rebellion broke out, he immediately joined the ranks of the anti-Fascist army of the Republic.   He finished the war as a lieutenant-colonel and after some months of adventure, found himself in Moscow, where he spent the World War II years, as a student at the Frunze Military Academy and eventually in the Soviet army.

Tagueña was not present at the Battle of Teruel and wrote but a few lines on the last days of that event. 'Some part of its defenders were able to escape with El Campesino; the rest perished or were taken prisoners'.[46] He does not mention El

---

41 Martínez Bande, *La batalla de Teruel*, 204.

42 *Ibid.*

43 *Ibid.*

44 See Alberto Reig Tapia, *Ideología e historia* (Madrid: Akal, 1984), 69-74, for an informed opinion on the Servicio Histórico Militar.

45 (Mexico, D.F.: Ediciones Oasis, 1974).

46 *Ibid.*, 167.

Campesino in his detailed account of the Battle of the Ebro and the fighting for Catalonia and the final defeat and the withdrawal into France. This lacuna is explained by his remark later on in the book; on entering the Frunze Academy in Moscow in 1939, he 'had not expected to see El Campesino, who had been separated from his command since the Battle of the Ebro, but his fame weighed in his favour as did the insistence of the Russians'.[47]

Taguena also gave information on El Campesino's experience at the Frunze military academy, far more credible concerning the same episode than the pages by El Campesino and Gorkin. For example, at the end of the summer of 1940, there were examinations. 'A number of our companions received very low grades and in three cases, the results were practically nil. One of them was El Campesino, whom I had tried to support because I did not agree with the growing hostility against him. It is certain that he did not have the capacity to follow higher studies, but he was not the only one, and while he was our fellow student, I thought he should be treated as such. Two of the students had to leave the academy, one of them was El Campesino'.[48]

Taguena mentioned El Campesino again, in referring to the events of 1943 when, after the Battle of Stalingrad, changes were made in the organization of the Spanish refugees and elements of the Frunze Academy, who had been transferred to the Uzbek Republic in 1942 when Moscow was threatened by the advancing Nazi armies. At the time, Taguena wrote, 'certain elements such as El Campesino' were excluded from the group. Taguena amplified in this manner, 'El Campesino had been sent to Kokand and it was reported that he was a figure in the local low-life and the black market', but he immediately added, 'it was also said that when other Spaniards came to him, he helped them to solve their problems'.[49]

Taguena did not refer to Gorkin or to El Campesino's writings but he had probably read them, for he wrote, 'in time, El Campesino showed that during the war, he had not

---

47 Taguena Lacorte, *Testimonio de dos guerras*, 385.
48 *Ibid.*, 398.
49 *Ibid.*, 453.

distinguished himself by chance and that he was capable of exploits that not one of his critics would ever have attempted.[50]

This benevolent, almost fatherly, attitude towards El Campesino on the part of by Tagueña was, to a much lesser extent, adopted by another Communist officer, Antonio Cordón. Cordón was qualified as an industrial engineer and was retired from the Army Corps of Engineers when the Civil War broke out.   He immediately entered the Republican ranks at the Ministry of War and at the same time the ranks of the Communist Party.   He was highly regarded by Negrín who promoted him to general during the last weeks of the conflict. Although Cordón was not at the Teruel front during the battle, his post (he was director of *matériel* in the Subsecretariat of Defence) ensured that he was well informed of what had happened there.   He judged El Campesino's conduct at Teruel to have been repugnant and confirmed that 'completely demoralized, he [El Campesino] had abandoned his forces, and these men, lacking a leader, had withdrawn in disorder and at an inopportune moment'.[51]

Cordón analysed at some length the case of Valentín González.   I shall quote a few lines, 'the prestige of El Campesino had its origin in the first days of the fighting when the war still had, in so far as it concerns the Republican side, a *guerrillero* character'.[52]   This coincides with the opinion of Tagueña.   Cordón described Valentín González's problem as concerning a 'case of the false prestige of an individual created substantially by the reflection of the authentic prestige and bravery of the mass led by him, more in appearance than in reality'.[53]   And at greater length, 'El Campesino had a highly developed ability for self-propaganda and he developed it ever more intensely.   Exaggeration and falsehood, which were congenital features of his person, were elements which served him for that purpose.   Hyper-sensitive to praise and extremely

---

50   Tagueña Lacorte, *Testimonio de dos guerras*, 399.

51   Antonio Cordón, *Trayectoria (recuerdos de un artillero)*, Prólogo, Santiago Carrillo (París: Librairie du Globe, 1971), 382.

52   *Ibid.*, 385.

53   *Ibid.*, 384.

vain, he felt himself at each moment "a hero of the people" '.[54] Another excerpt: 'It is necessary also to recognize that in maintaining the false prestige of Valentín González, we, the Communist Party, must bear some of the blame ... The error was, I believe, in maintaining, far above all reasonable limits, aid to a man so lacking in any capacity for development in any aspect: moral, intellectual, political or military as was Valentín González'.[55] Cordón made an effort to be fair-minded about El Campesino, recognizing that he was better prepared for guerrilla than for organized warfare. He told an enlightening anecdote about Valentín González that clarifies somewhat Gorkin's statement about the unlettered state of El Campesino. Shortly after the loss of Teruel, Cordón was on a visit to the divisional headquarters of El Campesino who 'firmly resisted indicating to me the disposition of his brigades on the map'. The reason: 'El Campesino did not know how to read a map'. His chief of staff told Cordón what he wanted to know.[56]

On 4 April 1938, after the loss of Teruel, El Campesino was in charge of the defence of Lérida. When its fall seemed imminent, Cordón came to visit El Campesino, who had been ordered not to abandon his command post on the Segre without authorization. Cordón wrote: 'I was aware of the terror that, since Teruel, could seize Valentín González, with his back to the river, when the enemy was attacking'. He found that El Campesino had crossed the river two or three days earlier, 'practically out of touch with his forces, just as he had done at Teruel'. Cordón finally found him in an isolated farm-house: 'He was thrown, dressed, on a bed complaining of great pains, exactly where, he could not say, again pretending to be ill. Ill he undoubtedly was, ill of an irrepressible fear ... I ordered that he be placed in an ambulance and taken to Barcelona'.[57] This was undoubtedly the incident to which Tagueña had referred in expressing his surprise at seeing El Campesino among those admitted to the Frunze Academy, and it explains in detail what Tagueña meant when he wrote that 'El Campesino ... had been

---

54   Antonio Cordón, *Trayectoria (recuerdos de un artillero)*, 384.
55   *Ibid.*
56   *Ibid.*, 382.
57   *Ibid.*, 384-85.

separated from his command since the Battle of the Ebro'.

Castro Delgado, who was Political Commissar during the Battle of Teruel, in his 1960 book, *Hombres made in Moscow*, does not mention El Campesino by name in the thirteen pages he allots to the Battle of Teruel, but he does refer to him in a coded manner. He described, 'The heroism of the Republican forces, chiefly of the 46th Division, which held on in Teruel until the encirclement by the enemy was completed and which then was itself obliged to break the circle by dint of sheer tenacity ...'.[58] The 46th Division was El Campesino's. This sentence reads as if Castro Delgado had read *Comunista en España*. But fifty pages further on in this not highly readable prose — Tagueña and Cordón are much better — there is a direct reference to El Campesino, 'who since he lost Lérida, said he was suffering from tuberculosis, in spite of his marvellous appearance'.[59] And forty pages later, this time during the battle for Catalonia, when Líster's wife had prepared a dinner: 'El Campesino began to talk of when he was chief of staff for Ed-el-Krim [*sic*], an old rebel who was at the heart of the disaster at Annual. It was a lie but marvellously told ... El Campesino was a terrific imposter (*embustero*).[60]

Another commentator on El Campesino, Gorkin, Prieto and the Battle of Teruel is Santiago Carrillo in his *Memorias* (1994). Carrillo referred to *Comunista en España* as 'a book signed by Valentín González *El Campesino* and written [*redactado*], as was well-known at the time, by Gorkin — since *El Campesino* could barely read or write ...'. He added that 'all those who knew about the progress of the Battle of Teruel know that El Campesino abandoned the city before his troops and that he was severely criticised for that'.[61] There is agreement here between Carrillo and Martínez Bande on the following, where Carrillo wrote, 'It is difficult to believe that Prieto might take up so easily this stupid version, since he followed the operations of those days so closely, and in view of the precision of El

---

58 Enrique Castro Delgado, *Hombres made in Moscú* (Mexico D.F.: Publicaciones Mañana, 1960), 609.

59 *Ibid.*, 660.

60 *Ibid.*, 701.

61 Santiago Carrillo, *Memorias* (Barcelona: Planeta, 1994), 271.

Campesino's version'.[62] There is also a large consensus among the viewpoints that I have cited to support a condemnation of El Campesino's behaviour at Teruel. And Cordón's account of what happened at Teruel and at Lérida, as well as his analysis of El Campesino's comportment are helpful in understanding the later career of Valentín González in the Soviet Union and in Western Europe. There is nothing here to encourage belief in the stories concocted by Gorkin and El Campesino.

But Gorkin was himself the most eager promoter of El Campesino's reconstruction of the Battle of Teruel. This was perhaps natural, for he, as we have seen, claimed to have written it. 'El Campesino, ha esclarecido la diabólica maniobra soviética dirigida, en efecto, contra Prieto', asserted Gorkin in his short book *España, primer ensayo de democracia popular*, referring to the Battle of Teruel, which he also described as 'la maniobra más desleal y monstruosa'.[63] This booklet was published in Buenos Aires by the Asociación Argentina por la Libertad de la Cultura, a satellite of the Congress for Cultural Freedom.

Bolloten commented on El Campesino's letter and Prieto's reaction in this ambiguous way: 'Although it is debatable whether the Communists went to the extremes of ordering the abandonment of Teruel in order to destroy Prieto, there is no question that the loss of the city was the starting point of their drive against him'.[64] But if Bolloten was uncertain about whether he should adopt as gospel truth the testimony of El Campesino concerning the Battle for Teruel, he was confident that there was a Communist plan to oust Prieto from the Ministry of Defence. But could not this effort to replace Prieto as Defence Minister by Negrín have been motivated by a desire to win the War? Unfortunately, Bolloten's interpretation of El Campesino's testimony about Teruel corresponds to a theme running throughout most of his book: the positions of the Negrín Government were always designed to create a Spanish Soviet, with the control of the victorious Republican army in

---

62 Santiago Carrillo, *Memorias*, 271.

63 Julián Gorkin, *España, primer ensayo de democracia popular* (Buenos Aires: Asociación Argentina por la Libertad de la Cultura, 1961), 73.

64 Bolloten (1991), 573.

Communist hands.

There was undoubtedly a possibility that, had the Spanish Republic defeated Franco in 1938(?) or 1939(?), the Communists might have controlled Spain. Had the Republican armies defeated Franco, what would have been the situation in the rest of Europe? Nobody knows, neither Bolloten nor myself. Certainly, Spain would have been in demolition and shock as severe as that which the country knew when Franco won the war in 1939. After his victory, Franco was powerless to help his own creditors in more than menial tasks. What would have been the state of Nazi Germany or the Soviet Union? We can be certain of one thing: the Soviet Union would always have been plagued with logistical problems of aid to Spain. It always shied away from actual involvement on the ground far from its borders, and its efforts in Afghanistan, though close to home, proved disastrous. Counterfactual history is always a game.

Nevertheless, Bolloten stakes a large share of his arguments on the credibility of his contention that had the Spanish Republic won its resistance struggle against Franco and the Spanish Right, Spain would have become overnight a Soviet satellite. This standpoint is untenable not only because it is developed out of context,[65] but also because all the text of Bolloten's book shows that Stalin was not interested in Spain as such, but in averting a Nazi attack on the Soviet Union. Stalin wanted to persuade Great Britain and France, still powerful colonial powers, to join an anti-Nazi coalition. A Communist Spain was not part of his agenda. Even Bolloten's chief interpreter, Trevor-Roper, wrote 'Stalin's immediate fear was of Germany, and the defeat of Fascism in Spain was more important to him than the victory of Communism'.[66]

Julio Aróstegui of the Universidad Complutense de Madrid, in the most considered analysis of Bolloten's work that I know of,[67] rightly underlines the fact that Juan Negrín is the 'gran

---

65 It is unacceptable to compare Stalin's position in Spain in 1938-39 with his position on the Eastern front in 1945. Furthermore, Bolloten's books are all written out of context, for he ignores ninety-nine per cent of what was happening on the Franco side.

66 Trevor-Roper, in Bolloten, *The Grand Camouflage*, (1968), 7.

67 Julio Aróstegui, 'Burnett Bolloten y la Guerra Civil Española: la persistencia del gran engaño', *Historia Contemporánea* (Bilbao) (1990), No. 3.

villano de la obra bollotiana'.[68]   Bolloten, in his chapter 55, where he attempts to dissect Negrín's work, wrote:

> My own judgement of Negrín, based on oral and written testimony, garnered and digested over fifty years, is that he did more than any politician, whether willingly or unwillingly, to extend and consolidate the influence of the Communist Party in the vital centers of power — the army and the security services — during the final year of the war.[69]

In his treatment of Bolloten's analysis of Negrín's relations with the PCE and the Soviet Union, Aróstegui notes that 'Bolloten ends by recognizing, nevertheless, that the central objective of Negrín's policy was to obtain arms from the Soviets'.[70] Further on, he observes: 'The truth is that Negrín as a stand-in for the Communists was an idea put into circulation by Indalecio Prieto after his departure from the Ministry, and the famous polemic that followed'.[71] (As I have already demonstrated, concerning the siege of Teruel, Prieto was easily seduced by any evidence, even the most doubtful as in the case of Gorkin, if advanced by Negrín's enemies.)

Aróstegui points out that Bolloten challenges 'all the opinions of the essayists who have differed with him concerning Negrín (Marichal, Viñas, Malefakis, [Herbert L.] Matthews)'.[72] The Spanish historian then affirms, 'But the salient point is that Bolloten's antinegrinista diatribe ends with a paragraph which is, in the last resort, the equivalent of a thesis that leaves practically all of his arguments devoid of meaning'. The paragraph in question reads 'Despite Negrín's value to Moscow and the PCE during the Civil War and his friendly relations with the Soviet Ambassador, it would be a mistake to argue that during the Spanish conflict he blithely offered his services

---

68 Aróstegui, *op. cit.*, 155.
69 Bolloten (1991), 587.
70 Aróstegui, *op. cit.*, 175.
71 *Ibid.*
72 Aróstegui, *op. cit.*, 176. After quoting Juan Marichal and Ángel Viñas in praise of Negrín, Bolloten wrote, mockingly, 'These encomia were later transcended by U.S. historian Edward Malefakis, who affirmed that Negrín was "without equal in Spain since Olivares in the XVII century" and of the same calibre as such wartime leaders as Winston Churchill' (Bolloten [1991], 905, n. 17).

to Moscow and that he did nothing to preserve a measure of political independence for himself.[73]

I now propose to study the reactions of Bolloten to Gorkin's letter of 18 October 1984. I know of nothing in Bolloten's correspondence in general, or in his correspondence with Gorkin, which reveals irritation, or even slight annoyance with the situation in which he then found himself. There are historians who would have thought themselves obliged to make some form of public repentance for having so firmly misrepresented the testimony of El Campesino, especially in his polemic with myself in the *TLS* in 1978. During the three years that passed between his reception of the letter of Gorkin and his death, Bolloten did little to correct the record.

Bolloten's reaction *vis-à-vis* Gorkin himself, following the latter's letter of 18 October 1984, is difficult to understand. Bolloten could easily have been displeased with Gorkin for having duped him concerning the works of El Campesino. He could have become distantly polite with him. On the contrary, in his next letter (11 December 1984), Bolloten apologized for not having replied sooner to Gorkin's 'very kind' letter, and thanked him 'very much' for the 'highly favourable terms in which you speak of my book', and went on 'so much more inasmuch as they are written by someone for whom I have the greatest respect and admiration'.

In the following paragraph, Bolloten continued, referring directly to the contents of the letter he had received:

> And now I wish to express to you my most sincere gratitude for your answers to the different questions that I posed. Not only have you confirmed matters for which I needed confirmation, but you have clarified many important things which are going to enrich my book.

There is in this letter no sign that Bolloten was in any way troubled by Gorkin's revelations about El Campesino, and he ended the letter with 'your friend greets you very affectionately'. It was true that Gorkin had mentioned his failing health, but Bolloten's reply indicates a strange indifference to the implications of Gorkin's confession about the doctored testimony of one of Bolloten's chief witnesses.

---

73 Bolloten (1991), 591.

Bolloten's attitude described above a few weeks after receiving Gorkin's letter, remained the same a year later, as is shown by his letter of 21 November 1985:

> ... I am indebted to you for all that I have learned from your magnificent books and from your explanatory letters during several years. I am happy to have had the good fortune of your friendship and of your inestimable help, and I want you to know this, in case it gives you some satisfaction to have helped me to write the truth about events so twisted by historians and politicians.

This quotation demonstrates the incomprehensible incoherence that permeated Bolloten's thinking. How could a rational man (Bolloten) have written on the subject of the truth to the very person (Gorkin) who had knowingly been feeding him (Bolloten) material which both, by Gorkin's confessional letter, knew to be forged, in every legal sense of the word?

It cannot be argued that the four new citations attributed, without explanation or disclaimer, to El Campesino in the 1991 book of Bolloten are merely the results of composition achieved before Bolloten had received and comprehended the crucial letter from Gorkin in 1984 or that Bolloten had not had time or strength sufficient to embody this upsetting information in his work in progress before his death in 1987. The proof that Bolloten quoted anew from El Campesino's writings as late as January 1986 — more than a year after Gorkin's letter — is found in another note in his 1991 book:

> The most recent attempt to resituate Negrín was on the occasion of a colloquium held in the Canary Islands in honour of the former Prime Minister and attended by Tuñón de Lara, Juan Marichal, José Prats and Juan Rodríguez Doreste (the last two, one-time aides of Negrín) at which the well-known historian Javier Tusell found himself outnumbered by Negrín apologists. According to Tusell, the most tendentious speaker was not Tuñón de Lara but Juan Marichal (letter to me). It was because of the long-standing effort to revamp Negrín, whose principal apologists studiously avoid any testimony that conflicts with their immutable position, that I delivered a paper in Madrid at the 16th Annual Conference of the Society for Spanish and Portuguese Historical Studies on the Strange Case of Dr Juan Negrín. The paper was published in

Historia 16 in January 1986 together with eighty-nine source references.[74]

One of these eighty-nine references, No. 52, reads as follows: 'Valentín González (El Campesino) *Comunista en España y antistalinista en la URSS* (Mexico D.F., Editorial Guarania, 1952), pag.72'. The text relating to the note was the following:

> In view of the evidence of the hostility [to the Communist Party, which existed among certain socialists and anarcho-syndicalists], it is by no means essential to have recourse to the testimony of prominent ex-Communists. But to ignore their testimony entirely would be tantamount to yielding to those who would exclude from the historiography of the Civil War all the books that do not conform to the Party line. I shall cite, therefore, Valentín González ... who wrote:
>> The hatred of the Communists by the mass of the people reached such a point that during a meeting of the Politburo one of the leaders had to declare: We cannot retreat! We must carry on and stay in power at all costs. Otherwise, we shall be hunted like predatory animals in the street.[75]

This latter quotation is also found in Bolloten's 1991 book (633) with the same source indicated, p. 72 of *Comunista en España y antistalinista en la URSS*. It had already been reproduced in part in the chapter which Bolloten contributed to the book *The Republic and the Civil War in Spain* (1971) edited by Raymond Carr. The previous paragraph is also quoted in Bolloten's book (632). The significance is that the material in *Historia 16* was published in January 1986 during Bolloten's lifetime and reaffirmed in his book. Bolloten, despite his frequent breast-beating about his devotion to the *truth*, incorporated, in his address before the SSPHS, and in the text which appeared in *Historia 16* in 1986, testimony of El Campesino which he had known since 1984 to be from the forgery department of Julián Gorkin.

I have mentioned above the short book published and partly written by Gorkin for the Congress for Cultural Freedom, entitled *España, primer ensayo de democracia popular*, published in Buenos Aires in 1961. This book contained not

---

74 Bolloten (1991), 882, n. 13.
75 *Historia 16* (Madrid), (January 1988), 18.

only Gorkin's article of the same title, but also thirty pages from Jesús Hernández's *Yo fui un ministro de Stalin*, the manuscript of which, as I have indicated above, was corrected following Gorkin's instructions to overstate the significance of the murder of Andrés Nin, turning it into the pivotal incident of the Spanish Civil War.   Unsurprisingly, these pages from Hernández's opus gave exaggerated importance to the POUM and to the political role of Julián Gorkin.

The title of this book became, with Bolloten's helping hand, a frequently repeated political slogan, of dubious logic, with which to attack the Spanish Republic by comparing it with Eastern European states in the late 1940s.   Any serious comparison of the position, real or potential, of Soviet power and influence in Spain in 1938-1939 with that of the Soviet armies on the Eastern Front in 1944-1945 — at that moment probably the strongest armed force in existence — is absurd.

Gorkin's South American propaganda effort (on behalf of Washington and the Monroe Doctrine) was also useful for certain elements in the United States.   For example, it was reproduced in a 1963 book of essays, *The Strategy of Deception. A Study of Worldwide Communist Tactics*, edited by Jeane J. Kirkpatrick, later President Reagan's Ambassador to the United Nations.[76]   Bolloten parroted the slogan invented by Gorkin.   Invited, in late April 1978, by one of the stars of French television, Jean-Marie Cavada, to participate in a programme called *Grand Témoin*, Bolloten gave as his principal contribution the following: 'The Spanish Republic during the Civil War was the first experiment of a popular democracy'.[77] Bolloten also endorsed Gorkin's argument in his 1979 and 1991 versions of his book, in which he quoted the Poumista as follows:

---

76   Jeane J. Kirkpatrick, *The Strategy of Deception. A Study of Worldwide Communist Tactics* (New York: Farrar Straus, 1963).   Gorkin is described by the editor as 'representative of a generation of Spanish working class and democratic leaders who have neither forgotten nor forgiven the Spanish betrayal of the Spanish Republic by its *soi-disant* ally [sic]'. Ms Kirkpatrick made no reference to Gorkin's affiliation to the Congress for Cultural Freedom (CIA).

77   I quote from memory. I have been unable to obtain the exact wording

It has been repeatedly said that the Spanish Civil War was a general rehearsal for the Second World War; what is not clearly understood is that it was also the first testing ground for popular democracy, perfected forms of which we have been obliged to witness in a dozen countries during the post-war period. The men and methods used to convert these countries into Kremlin satellites were tested in Spain. For this reason, among many, the Spanish experience had and continues to have historical and universal significance.[78]

Gorkin's thesis is invalid because the counterfactual basics are contradictory and out of context. Bolloten, writing after the defeat of Fascism, reconstructs the Spanish struggle as one that could have ended with a triumphant, menacing Soviet army on the Spanish slopes of the Pyrenees. I cannot imagine a scenario in which a victorious Spanish Republic would have menaced the capitalist democracies. But I make no pretence at expertise on counterfactual history, a pseudo-science on which Bolloten's book, in its three appearances, depends for its progress and *dénouement*. The Spanish Civil War had historical and universal significance because it was the first armed struggle against Fascism on European soil. In stressing the sinister concept of 'popular democracy, Bolloten forgets that the forces of the United Nations accepted the sacrifice of twenty-five million Soviet citizens as part of the anti-Fascist fight — but, for Bolloten, the enemy of the Spanish people had become not Franco, but the anti-Fascists.[79]

---

from Mr Cavada

78 Bolloten (1979), 295; (1991), 214. Bolloten's narrow view of the Spanish Civil War kept him from writing that Hitler also used against the Soviet armies tactics and men that had served the Fascist cause in Spain. The División Azul, composed of Spanish Falangists, equally utilized their experience in the War in Spain on the Eastern Front.

79 Trevor-Roper wrote, 'By the end of the war, General Franco was really fighting not against the Popular Front, but against a Communist dictatorship' (Bolloten [1968], 7). Trevor-Roper's prelude to Bolloten's arguments first appeared in the second printing of Bolloten's first book, under the imprint of a relatively unknown London firm, Pall Mall Press. Trevor-Roper's comments were copyrighted by Frederick A. Praeger, who had already in 1961 published Bolloten's first book in the United States, and was to publish that book in a new printing in New York in 1968, with Trevor-Roper's new contribution. Bolloten and his friends have written about

Bolloten's conversion from anti-Fascism (anti-Francoism) to militant anti-Communism (pro-Francoism) was in the classic mold, but his was a special case. During his lifetime, he had never wanted to admit that he had become a partisan of Franco's cause. By limiting his writing to a hostile discourse on the actions of the Republican side of the Civil War, he rarely mentioned what was happening on the Fascist side. It was this posture of not discussing atrocities committed by the Franco side that permitted Bolloten to elevate the murder of Andrés Nin, a Poumist councillor of the Generalitat, into the outstanding political crime of the Civil War. In reality, the assassination of Nin, though appalling, was of minor significance, if placed in the context of the Civil War and the wholesale slaughter of Popular Front deputies and functionaries by Franco's armies. Bolloten's emphasis on the killing of Nin, and his failure to discuss the tortures and mayhem inflicted upon the Spanish people by the partisans of Franco underlines the influence of Gorkin on Bolloten's work.

Bolloten's posthumous book reveals how extremely reactionary he had become during his years in California. I know of no other American historian who has written of Eleanor Roosevelt with so much petty hate and acrimony. He wrote, in a note, about a letter which his friend Constancia de la Mora had addressed to Mrs Roosevelt, dated 14 July 1939, to thank her for having received Juan Negrín and herself at the White House, a few days previously. Constancia de la Mora had

---

his various publishers — for example, the Catholic firm Hollis and Carter, his first English publisher, and his Falangist publisher, Luis de Caralt. Yet, nobody, not even Bolloten himself, has commented on Praeger, who is perhaps the most interesting publisher of them all. Bolloten, in his letters to the *TLS*, seemed quite sensitive to the mention of the CIA. Peter Coleman, author of the official history of the CCF, *The Liberal Conspiracy*, in a list of fourteen books published in the United States 'by The Congress for Cultural Freedom or its affiliated groups', included seven books published by Frederick A. Praeger (272-273). According to William Blum, in *The CIA: A Forgotten History* (London/New Jersey: Zed Books, 1991), 351, n. 13, Frederick A. Praeger Inc., 'it was later disclosed, published a number of books in the 1960s under CIA sponsorship'. In spite of the shocked disclaimers by Bolloten and Conquest in the *TLS* in 1978, the trail linking Bolloten to the CIA, Praeger and the Congress for Cultural Freedom gleams more and more brightly.

used the letter to draw Eleanor Roosevelt's attention to the plight of Spanish exiled writers and intellectuals in Mexico and South America and stressed how their cultural prestige could be utilized in Latin America in the fight against Fascism. Bolloten himself in 1939, an exile in Mexico and a temporary anti-Fascist, perceived, later in the century, these facts concerning Mrs Roosevelt to be highly suspicious. He wrote: 'In view of Constancia de la Mora's Communist affiliation and her devotion to the cause ... the quoted passage has unusual significance'. He then wrote of the visit he and his wife had made to the Hidalgo de Cisneros couple in Cuernavaca in early 1940 and revealed this damning detail: '... I can attest to the fact that she [C. de la Mora] was still corresponding with Eleanor Roosevelt, for she asked me to mail a letter to her.[80]   He should have called J. Edgar Hoover immediately, for the FBI chief had the same derogatory opinion of the wife of the President of the United States that Bolloten, later, adopted. This was, of course, years after Bolloten had been granted an immigrant's visa to the United States, at a time when it was extremely difficult, nay impossible, for a foreigner with his reputation of sympathy for the Spanish Republic to obtain a one-day visitor's pass.[81]

I published a fairly long critique on Bolloten's first book in 1963, in *El mito de la cruzada de Franco*.[82] I was less harsh with Bolloten than I would be later, for I was influenced by what I recalled from a conversation years before with Constancia de la Mora, in which she had praised Bolloten outrageously.   In part, I wrote, 'Can we not suppose that Bolloten's research was carried out before 1952 and that the conclusions of the book were written by another Bolloten, nine

---

80   Bolloten (1991), 852, n. 18.

81   The FBI most certainly has a file on Bolloten dating back to the time when he was a refugee in Mexico, known for his interest in the Spanish Civil War, and on his entry in the United States and his naturalization. The Bureau refuses even to admit that it has ever heard of him, let alone that it has a file on him. On the other hand, it has within the past year, released information on Gorkin, formerly witheld. We now know that he was finally allowed to visit the United States when he was working for the CCF. He arrived in New York, coming from Havana. (FBI file 64-29717-23, 10 October 1956).

82   Southworth, *El mito de la cruzada de Franco* (1963), 148-56.

years older, a Bolloten who had perhaps, in the meantime, changed his convictions?'.[83] Trevor-Roper considered such an explanation 'simple, even naive',[84] but Bolloten's continuing evolution, as shown in his revisions and additions, tends to bear out my hypothesis.

Bolloten ignored for many years what I had written about him in Spanish in 1963, but when I confronted him in English in the *TLS* in 1978, he doubtlessly considered that he could not disregard an indignity of that nature and he vowed to discredit me. Alas, Bolloten's methods of revenge were maladroit. He commissioned a young friend, George Esenwein, to dig into my past. He discovered that I had worked during the last year of the Spanish Civil War as an 'important propagandist' for the Spanish Republican Government. I had indicated as much in my short biography in *Who's Who in France* and *Who's Who in the World*. I had gone into detail about my work in 1938 and 1939 for the Spanish Republican Government in the Spanish translation of *Le Mythe de la croisade de Franco* (1963) which appeared in 1986 in Barcelona.[85] This book is in the bibliography of Bolloten's 1991 book. There is thus absolutely no justification for the suggestion that I was hiding my firm commitment to the cause of the Spanish Republic.   Unlike Julián Gorkin, who wrote that he had refused to shake the hand of Juan Negrín,[86] I was proud to have done so. I was and am proud to have striven, to the best of my modest talents, to defend the record of the Spanish Republic, during the Civil War and later.

The readers of Bolloten's book would, without question, have been more curious about Bolloten's past, which he tried to conceal, than about my own (which could have been found in any good university library). I have tried to reveal some parts of Bolloten's past because it is necessary in order to explain the contradictions and incoherences in his successive works. What

---

83 Southworth, *El mito de la cruzada de Franco* (1963), 277.

84 Trevor-Roper, in 'Introduction' to Bolloten (1968), at p. 10.

85 H. R. Southworth, *El mito de la cruzada de Franco* (Barcelona: Plaza y Janés, 1986).

86 Julián Gorkin, *El proceso de Moscú en Barcelona* (Barcelona: Ayma, 1973), 12.

is inadmissible is Bolloten's effort to hang me for holding the same political convictions that he himself held during the Civil War and for a year or so afterwards. It would seem that all that he has published since he changed his mind about the Civil War has been a desperate search for an amnesty, a general pardon for the sins of his youth.

Bolloten's 1991 comments concerning myself are swollen to 107 lines in three notes: on pp. 789-90, there are ten lines; on pp. 881-82, there are 49 lines, and on pp. 916-17, there are 47 lines. I do not resent Bolloten's writing about me, as he seems to have resented my writing about him; unfortunately, in what is a remarkable example of poor editing for a university press, more than half of the 107 lines dedicated to my person are repeated. The following quotation can be found, word for word, three times in the book: ' "In order to understand Southworth's steadfastly loyal and therefore uncritical support of Negrín", writes George Esenwein, "one must bear in mind that he served as an important propagandist for the Negrín government. Between February 1938 and February 1939, he edited in New York *The News of Spain* (see *Contemporary Authors*, vols. 85-88, 557) a bulletin which, if not financed by or otherwise officially associated with the Spanish Republican government, was unmistakably a mouthpiece for its policies" '.[87]

Bolloten really put his heart and soul — if not his intelligence — into his indictment of myself, without ever discussing any of the three books on the Spanish Civil War that

---

[87] I was not the editor of *News of Spain*. The editor for most of the weekly's life was William P. Mangold, who had been with the *New Republic* before the Civil War and was later with *The New Yorker*. I was his assistant. I edited the last two or three issues. To the best of my knowledge, the publication was financed by the Spanish Republican Embassy. It was my understanding that I was working for the Spanish Republic. On p. 881, note 13, Bolloten wrote of 'clearing' Negrín of 'any stigma of pro-Communism'. I thought and I think today that the Communists wanted to win the Civil War, as did Negrín. Where was the 'stigma'? Was there a stigma attached to Roosevelt, or to Churchill, because they encouraged and armed Stalin? Concerning Bolloten's propensity for accusing persons for no valid reason of being members of the Communist Party, Aróstegui wrote, 'Además el texto de Bolloten, texto historiográfico, se supone, no suele presentar las pertenencias como realidades simples sino como delitos' (*op. cit.*, 174).

I had published and limiting himself to a small portion of what I had written about him in the *TLS*. He seemed infuriated by any disagreement with his pronouncements, however controversial they may have been. Bolloten had a hit list, as seen in his letter to Gorkin on 13 October 1982, 'If men like Juan Marichal (great admirer of Negrín) and Viñas (great admirer of Juan Marichal) and Southworth and Georges Soria monopolize historical truth, as they are trying to do, and with a certain success, there is no hope for freedom ...'. And on 27 January 1986, he wrote again to Gorkin, 'It is necessary to counteract a little bit the enormous influence of Juan Marichal, Ángel Viñas, Tuñón de Lara, Southworth, [Pierre] Vilar and so many others who are trying to resituate the figure of Negrín.'

In order to evaluate Bolloten's execution of his expressed desire to write the truth, it is crucial to be able to estimate the credibility of Julián Gorkin, the man who, directly or indirectly, provided many of the key elements in all his arguments. This is particularly relevant in the light of Bolloten's outrage at the suggestion that sources on which he relied might have been financed ultimately by the CIA. Gorkin seems to have been the person who most influenced the thinking and writings of Burnett Bolloten with the possible exception of Ronald Hilton and a few other people close to him in California. The Spaniard named Julián García Gómez, better known by his *nom de plume* Julián Gorkin, this latter name being, according to biographers, a homage (?) to the Russian writer Maxim Gorki, was born to poverty in the province of Valencia, in 1901 and became one of the founders of the Spanish Communist Party. According to one biographer, he left Spain to express his opposition to the colonial war in the Rif. He militated in the Third International until 1929, at which time he broke with Moscow. With the fall of Primo de Rivera, he returned to Spain, and in 1935 joined the Partido Obrero de Unificación Marxista, of which he became Secretary-General. During the Civil War, he was an active participant in the May 1937 troubles in Barcelona. He was then arrested, with most of the leadership of the POUM and condemned to prison, from which he was able to escape a few days before the Fall of Barcelona in 1939.[88]

---

88 Gorkin has written abundantly about himself in his own books, and

Gorkin shared a decisive experience with two Americans, Bertram D. Wolfe and Jay Lovestone: all three had been active in the early years of the Communist Movement, and all three had left the Movement. (I have already mentioned Wolfe in connection with Castro Delgado and covert anti-Communist activities in post-war Germany.) At the time of the Spanish Civil War, Wolfe was a writer living in New York City, and Lovestone was an important figure in the American Federation of Labor (AFL). There is every reason to believe that Wolfe and Lovestone were among those who militated for the Poumists when they were arrested in 1937 and while they were imprisoned.

David Wingeate Pike, who has written a great deal about the Civil War, and knew Gorkin in Paris during his last years, wrote that Gorkin 'readily admitted that he had friends in the American AFL-CIO who arranged his passage to New York [from France] in 1939 before he left for Mexico'.[89] On 11 August 1940, Gorkin wrote from Mexico City to Wolfe that he was corresponding with Jay concerning his activities in Mexico. Gorkin, like Bolloten, spent the World War II years in Mexico; they did not meet there, and, from all that I have read and learned, they never did meet. The Hoover Institution has a letter, in which Gorkin, who was in Mexico City, wrote a formal letter to M. Burnett Bolloten on 12 June 1946, authorizing Bolloten, whose address is not specified, to quote without restrictions from Gorkin's book *Caníbales políticos (Hitler y*

---

there are many short but laudatory resumés of his life by his admirers. I have not read a single reference (favourable or unfavourable) to his connection with the CIA. In the obituary of Gorkin in *Le Monde* (Paris, 28 August 1987), there is a reference to the CCF, described as an 'anti-Communist movement created at the initiative of conservative American personalities'. In a doctoral dissertation by Geneviève Dreyfus-Armand, *L'Émigration politique espagnole en France au travers de sa presse, 1939-1975*, Gorkin is incorrectly identified, for the years, 1953-1966 as 'secrétaire espagnol du Congrès pour la liberté de la culture'. There is not a word about the CIA, which is significant in the study of Gorkin's life and works.

89   David W. Pike, *In the Service of Stalin* (Oxford: Clarendon Press, 1993), 305.   Gorkin admitted too much too quickly.   CIO stands for the Congress of Industrial Organizations.   It did not merge with the AFL until 1955.   Gorkin was on good terms with both groups.

Stalin en España).[90]   This authorization was granted at the request of the Poumist Jordi Arquer.

Insofar as I know, neither Gorkin nor Bolloten — the latter was a British citizen, and both were labelled anti-Fascists — participated in the struggle against Fascism during World War II. After the end of the Second World War, Gorkin sought to pass through New York, en route to Paris. Despite his friendship with well-placed North American labour leaders, he was repeatedly refused a transit visa through the United States, probably because of his self-proclaimed revolutionary status, and did not find sea passage to France until 1948. He had in the meantime become a Mexican citizen. This decision to become a Mexican citizen was perhaps motivated by his realization that the United States administration had adopted a hostile position against Spaniards 'who had taken an active part in the defence of the Republic', as he had been informed on 10 March 1948, at the US Consulate General in Mexico City. Of course, it is debatable whether Gorkin and his friends had been defending or undermining the Republic. In a letter that he wrote to the US Consul General, after his visit that morning, he described himself as 'a democratic and libertarian Socialist'. This was hardly the magic formula to open the doors of the USA.

Gorkin was in Tampico waiting for a Liberty Ship under French flag en route to Paris, on 3 April 1948. In a letter of that date, he wrote that a German translation of his Trotsky book was being made; it was to be published in the non-Soviet part of Germany. He did not say by whom, but, as in the case of the Castro Delgado book already referred to, this work was almost surely being undertaken by agents of the AFL or of the CIA. Gorkin was already involved in the propaganda war of his North American friends. On 14 April, he was in the port of Galveston, Texas, but not allowed to set foot on the soil of the United States. He finally reached Paris. He wrote to Wolfe on 2 June, that he had been in Paris for twenty days. We can assume that, on reaching Paris, in May 1948, Gorkin immediately got in touch with representatives of the AFL or of

---

90 J. Gorkin, *Caníbales políticos (Hitler y Stalin en España)* (Mexico City: Quetzal, 1941).

the CIA, or with someone of each, or someone who stood in for both at the same time. This contact could have been Lovestone, or more probably Irving Brown, who seems to have been the man in the field for the AFL at that time.

What is not clear is the exact situation in Paris at that moment. The CIA was operative from January 1946. Radio Free Europe was broadcasting from West Germany in 1950, Radio Liberty a year later.[91] Both were financed by the CIA.[92] The first public manifestation of the Congress for Freedom of Culture was held in Berlin in June 1950. The CIA had secretly funded the Congress in Berlin, according to Peter Coleman, an Australian barrister and member of parliament, who wrote the official history of the Congress for Cultural Freedom.[93]

At any rate, we may surmise that Gorkin's North American friends, who sponsored his manipulation of El Campesino, even if they were of the AFL, were supported by the CIA. John Ranelagh, in his study of the CIA, quotes Tom Braden, who had set up the International Organizations Division of the CIA, as follows, 'Allen [Dulles] was giving Lovestone money long before I came into the agency, and I think he was doing only what had been done before ... The secret funding of the AFL and the CIO by the CIA I have always thought preceded the agency'. This is a bit muddled, but it clearly means that the CIA was financing the AFL's covert activities in France when Gorkin arrived there in 1948, and when he began collaborating with El Campesino in 1949. If Gorkin's AFL contact was Irving Brown, it is as if it were Lovestone. Braden stated, 'There was a guy named Mike Ross that ran the CIO and Jay Lovestone ran the AFL side. Irving Brown ran around organizing things and Jay Lovestone sent the money'.[94]

Gorkin, by his own confession, was supported by his North American friends, beginning in 1948-49, and probably until 1953, when he became officially Latin American Secretary of the Congress for Cultural Freedom. This title had nothing to do

---

91 John Ranelagh, *The Agency. The Rise and Decline of the CIA* (New York: Simon & Schuster, 1987), 216.
92 *Ibid.*
93 Coleman, *op. cit.*, 46.
94 Ranelagh, *op. cit.*, 248.

with Spain, which was always off-limits for Gorkin and the Congress. Since his American paymasters were supporting a Fascist-style regime in Madrid, Gorkin and his colleagues were not always at their ease in promoting democracy in Spanish America, where relations between Spain and the United States were always high on the agenda. This fact of life is never invoked by Coleman in his discussions of the Congress's difficulties in Spanish America.

Overtly, Gorkin was in charge of Latin American affairs for the Congress, and director of *Cuadernos del Congreso por la Libertad de la Cultura*; this magazine began publication in 1953 and the last number appeared in 1963. Covertly, Gorkin was charged, or had charged himself, with attacks against the wartime Spanish Republic, above all against the Spanish Communists, who were, whatever the reason, the most zealous prosecutors of the War in Spain against the Fascist side. This was an underhanded way to attack the Soviet Union indirectly by a rewriting and revision of the historiography of the Spanish Civil War. The most blatant example of this type of undertaking by Gorkin was his manipulation of El Campesino; his encouragement of Castro Delgado and Jesús Hernández was in the same line of work.

The Latin American activities of the Congress and Julián Gorkin, have received little attention from historians of the CIA. The English, German and French publications of the CCF, especially the English *Encounter*, were, for obvious reasons, better known and had a wider audience. The only book that can pretend to be a history of the Congress is *The Liberal Conspiracy* (1989) written by Peter Coleman. He had worked closely with the Congress, and he had access to the archives of the CCF, held by the University of Chicago, but he had no help from the CIA.[95] From his point of view, Gorkin's chief task was

---

95 'But when I applied to the CIA under the Freedom of Information Act for records covering the years 1950 to 1969 all I received was a clipping from *The New York Times* published after the dissolution of the Congress and the statement: "No other records responsive to your request were located". Given this absence of cooperation, I have no significant news from official sources about the extent of CIA involvement' (Coleman, *op. cit.*, xii). This apparently means that the CIA material concerning the CCF is 'official' and that the CCF records held by the University of Chicago are completely independent.

to give the readers in Latin America a favourable interpretation of United States policy. He considered Gorkin to have been faced with the problem of 'reducing ... the great distrust' of *Cuadernos* in South America, 'a distrust inevitable in a continent of visceral and increasing anti-Americanism especially among its marxisant intellectuals'.[96]

In his book, Coleman did not give a great deal of attention to Gorkin, which probably reflects the attitude of the directors of the Congress. It reads as if Gorkin were run on a long leash by the persons in charge of the Congress, among whom was Irving Kristol, a co-founder of *Encounter*. Coleman quoted from the neo-conservative magazine *Commentary*, 'an extraordinarily controversial statement on McCarthyism by Kristol, in which he blamed the rise of Senator McCarthy on American liberal fellow-travellers', and accused 'the major segment of American liberalism ... of joining hands with the Communists in a popular front' and of applauding 'the massacre of the non-Communist Left, by the GPU during the Spanish Civil War'.[97] Gorkin could not have stated his own position on the Spanish Civil War more clearly. Nor could Bolloten.

Although Gorkin was more than satisfied with the results of his editorial responsibilities with the Congress, even proud of his work, this opinion was not always held by his colleagues. In 1952, Gorkin was sent on a tour of Latin America, one of many he was to enjoy during his years with the CCF; this time to organize national and regional outposts of the Congress. He was accompanied by El Campesino.[98] Gorkin manifested less enthusiasm when he revisited Latin America in 1954. His work of creating good will towards the United States had been greatly hindered by what Coleman described as 'the US backed overthrow of the Arbenz regime in Guatemala in June 1954 and a consequent explosion of anti-Yankee passions'. In his report to the Paris headquarters of the CCF, Gorkin affirmed, 'I was

96 *Op. cit.*, 85.

97 *Ibid.*, 62-63.

98 El Campesino did not accompany Gorkin on the latter's trip to Mexico because of the pro-Republican sentiment in that country. Gorkin wrote, 'The Stalinists, chiefly represented by the painters Álvaro Siqueiros and Diego Rivera, have lent themselves to the most thuggish blackmail' (*ibid.*, 153).

surprised at the almost unanimously violent reaction of the democratic elements ... in favour of Arbenz ... Whoever waves the anti-imperialist banner is sure of a following'.[99]

On 30 January 1970, Santiago Carrillo, Secretary-General of the Spanish Communist Party, declared in Spain's most important daily, the Spanish journal of record, *El País*, that Gorkin was involved in numerous affairs in which the CIA also participated.[100] Some months later, Gorkin published at some length in the same newspaper, an unconditional denial of what he considered to be a 'libellous statement'. 'I would simply have shrugged my shoulders', Gorkin continued, 'had it been only a question of my person; but I feel within myself and in support of me, the memory of prestigious organizations — Spanish and international — of numerous intellectual personalities who placed their confidence in me, and it is evident that I cannot permit myself this scornful gesture.'

He then went on, from Abd-el-Krim to the murder of Trotsky, from Wenceslao Carrillo to Palmiro Togliatti, and after many paragraphs he came nearer to the point: 'Permit me now to tear to pieces the fairy tale of Santiago Carrillo about "my affairs with the CIA" '. He then divagated as before, from the Berlin meeting of the CCF in 1954 to *Cuadernos*, from the Munich conference of June 1962 to Salvador de Madariaga. He managed to return to the subject in this manner, 'Who financed the Congress? Its activities? Its publications? This is not a secret for anybody: at the beginning, the North American trade-union organizations; later, the Ford Foundation, the Rockefeller Foundation, the Fairfield Foundation, a Swiss committee in Zurich, the Deutscher Künstlerbund in Berlin'.

In the course of this vapid and pointless discourse, he did not forget to recall that he, Julián Gorkin, was a 'professional revolutionary, as conceived by Lenin ...', and at one place admitted that one of the functionaries of the Congress, it was true, had belonged to the CIA, and that this fact had been bruited around, 'principally in Communist circles'. The end of the article was politically correct and ... lachrymose:

---

99 Coleman, *op. cit.*, 154.
100 *El País* (Madrid 30 January 1978), 11.

There is one thing that distresses me and at the same time fills me
with pride: the last letter written by that great liberal universal
Spaniard, don Salvador de Madariaga, affectionate as were all of
his letters, was addressed to me. Together we travelled through
the pathways of the world; together we defended, from the 1950s
onward, European federalism and freedom for the peoples of our
Spain.   May this letter — and many others from the most
illustrious men of our time — serve me as a breastplate against
wretched calumny.[101]

Carrillo was right and Gorkin was out of touch with reality
to think that he could deny a fact so well documented in
newspapers and books. Gorkin was correct in saying that the
Congress for Cultural Freedom was financed by American trade
unions and various foundations in America and Western
Europe. What he had forgotten to add, and which he certainly
knew better than most people, was that these institutions had
previously received from the CIA most of the money they were
generously and publicly donating to the Congress. This fact of
American life became widely reported in the United States and
Great Britain, as in France and Germany, from 1964 to 1966,
and it is amazing that *El País* published the 'Tribuna Libre' of
Gorkin without comment. It is less surprising that Gorkin tried
to brazen it out.

Some months later, Gorkin wrote to Bolloten, enclosing a
copy of the article in *El País*, 'the foremost newspaper today in
Spain, the most independent, the most widely read'.   He
explained, 'You will understand that after 62 years of struggle,
of which 52 in exile in three stages of my life, I could not admit
these accusations or calumnies by this cynical individual'. It is
difficult to believe that Bolloten was as unaware of the funding
of the CCF by the CIA and the subsequent scandal in the last
years of the 1960s as were the editors of *El País*, but when
Bolloten received a copy of the 'Tribuna Libre' which Gorkin
sent to him, he answered Gorkin (5 August 1980), by thanking
him profusely for his 'magnificent reply to the libellous
affirmation by the great calumniator Santiago Carrillo, who
began his apprenticeship half a century ago in the Stalinist

---

101 *El País*, 17 June 1979, 15.

school and has not changed since then'.[102]

Of all the intellectuals and 'professional revolutionaries' who worked for the Congress, Gorkin was the only one, to my knowledge, who denied the overwhelming proofs of the unpleasant, generally considered scandalous, situation. The Congress for Cultural Freedom had, in reality, been financially nurtured by the Central Intelligence Agency. When this fact became admittedly common knowledge, the Congress disintegrated, and with it, Gorkin's propaganda base.

There is further evidence of Gorkin's outrage at the Carrillo article in the book by David Wingeate Pike, *In the Service of Stalin*: '... he [Gorkin] was furious with Carrillo for his insinuation that he had been financed by the U.S. intelligence services'.[103] It is made abundantly clear in Coleman's book that Gorkin knew who was paying him and what he was supposed to do. Gorkin himself was so ashamed of his connection with the CIA that he denied it publicly. Bolloten played down Gorkin's work after the Civil War, describing it merely in terms of the past; as 'a member of the executive committee of the POUM' and a 'left-wing opponent of Soviet policy in Spain'. He did not mention *Cuadernos* among the periodicals that he had consulted in a long list of more than three hundred titles in six printed pages; nowhere did he mention the CCF or Gorkin's connection with the CIA. What was of value for the CIA, far more than the innocuous *Cuadernos*, were Gorkin's relentless efforts to revise Spanish Civil War historiography. From this perspective, Bolloten's book, in its three variations, was the masterpiece of Gorkin's covert work for the CIA.

What was it that Gorkin was doing in Paris, that can be considered blameworthy? He was falsifying elements of

---

102 Bolloten could hardly have been unaware of the CCF scandal, which had been brewing in the American press since 1964, when Congressman Wright Patman began examining American private foundations who were receiving money from the CIA. In 1966, *The New York Times* began a series of articles on the CIA and the CCF. In March 1967, the West Coast publication, *Ramparts*, began a publicity-promoted campaign against the CIA and the 'freedom of culture'. On 20 May 1967, in the popular weekly, *The Saturday Evening Post*, the ex-functionary of the CIA, Thomas Braden, wrote an article called 'I'm glad the CIA is immoral'.

103 Pike, *op. cit.*, 305.

Spanish Civil War history. There was no valid reason for the Government of the United States, even in the frigid conditions of the Cold War, to finance a Poumist conception of the Spanish struggle. The American Government had already during the Civil War itself betrayed its democratic principles, and its international obligations towards the Spanish Republic, and then, as if on a slide without controls, after World War II, despite President Truman's original signs of hostility to the Franco regime at the Potsdam Conference in 1945, adapted its Spanish policies to the exigencies of the Cold War, with no regard for the rights of the Spanish people.

We should not forget that Gorkin was not the 'Spanish delegate' of the CCF. Spain was off-limits for Gorkin, if not for the CIA. Gorkin was not the ideal man for United States propaganda in Spanish America; but it was probably impossible to find a real Latin-American who would have taken the risk to promote Yankee propaganda South of the Rio Grande. The nomination of Gorkin was undoubtedly the result of his being the right man at the right moment. His curriculum vitae was extremely anti-Communist and he had some journalistic experience. Above all, he was friendly with Jay Lovestone and Irving Brown of the AFL, and also with representatives of the CIO. He had been in negotiations with such persons, even before leaving Mexico in 1948. His discovery of El Campesino in Teheran and his intelligent exploitation of the possibilities thereof made him the Spanish-speaking man of the moment for the AFL, the CIO and then for the CIA.

Was it not because of the heroism and nobility which, associated in public opinion all over the world with the Spanish Republican resistance to Fascism, became one of the most impressive intellectual and moral assets remaining to the European Left after the declaration of the Cold War, that the CIA-inspired CCF permitted its 'Latin-American delegate' to focus his efforts, not on the pressing problems of South and Central America, but on the Spanish Civil War, to devote his time to vilifying one of humanity's most inspiring chapters of the battle against Fascism?

But, as Coleman shows, and he was working in the Congress archives, Congress attitudes were generally near to the anti-Soviet positions of Gorkin and the POUM. This afforded them a semblance of Leftism, and justified such phrases as this, 'the mission of the Congress for Cultural Freedom ... was obviously anti-Fascist as well as anti-Communist.' And, 'Many of its supporters had been refugees from Hitler's Germany ... from Mussolini's Italy ... or from Franco's Spain (Julián Gorkin, Salvador de Madariaga). The Congress throughout its life fought against the right-wing dictators General Francisco Franco and Antonio Salazar'.[104] At the same time, Coleman wrote of 'the betrayal of the Popular Front in Spain',[105] meaning betrayal by the Spanish Communists and the Soviet Union, not betrayal by Franco, Mussolini and Hitler.

Gorkin reasoned in the same manner. He had sent Bolloten a copy of his book *Les Communistes contre la révolution espagnole*, a simple rehash of his other books, and Bolloten wrote to him on (8 October 1978) that it was proving to be difficult to find a publisher for it in the United States. In reply, Gorkin philosophized (16 October) 'perhaps the frightful experience of the cold-blooded assassination of the martyrized Spanish people no longer interests anybody?' It is evident from the context of the letter that the martyrizing was done by the Spanish Republicans and not by Franco and his allies.

It is not my intention to discuss the propaganda war between the Soviet Union and the United States during the Cold War. My specific interest lies in the work undertaken by Gorkin to deform and mystify the historiography of the Spanish Civil War, while being paid by the CIA, through the conduits of the Congress for Cultural Freedom. Gorkin was not a cloak-and-dagger spy, and we do not know all the details of how his collaboration with El Campesino and his encouragement of the writings of Castro Delgado and Jesús Hernández fitted into his agenda with the Congress. A possible clarification is that, since the CIA, and its affiliate the Congress, grouped together, constituted a major world-wide influence for right-wing causes, its centralizing force ineluctably, however haphazardly, pulled into its orbit all those persons interested in besmirching the Spanish Republicans. Among the leading candidates for this kind of work were Julián Gorkin and Burnett Bolloten.

---

104 Coleman, *op. cit.*, 10-11.
105 *Ibid.*, 3.

In the *résistance* movement in Spain (fighting against Franco and the mercenaries from Morocco, the German Nazi Condor Legion and Italian Fascist ground troops and airmen) there were men and women as worthy of our admiration and respect as in any of the other *résistance* movements in Europe, and their cause, that of resistance to Fascism, Nazism and Falangism, was as noble and heroic as any other anti-Fascist cause. Of course, Bolloten's position is that the fight of the Spanish Republicans, being at times controlled by Communists, is really not respectable. Such a rule disqualifies the greater part of the European anti-Fascist movements.

On 8 May 1945, the Second World War, in its European phase, ended. There was great rejoicing in all of that part of Europe that had been occupied by Fascist armies, by German National Socialists, by Italian Fascists, and lesser breeds, such as the Slovaks of Father Tiso and the Croatians of Ante Pavelic, the Belgian Rexists of Léon Degrelle, and the French of the LVF, and so on. There was rejoicing everywhere except in the European country of Spain, where Franco the Conqueror was in power, after a sanguinary war of more than thirty-three months. Ironically enough, it was in Spain that resistance to Fascism on a large scale first took form.

Of all the Europeans who opposed Fascism, none, and I weigh my words, fought so courageously against such odds, for so long, as did the Spanish Republicans. Their neighbours were either openly against them, or were neutrally against them. The only European country that did help the Spanish Republic was the Soviet Union (and its help was invoked by others as a reason for them not to aid the Republic). France gave a try at helping. The only other country that tried to help was Mexico but it had little to offer. The country that could have aided the Spanish Republic was my own country, the United States of America. Franklin D Roosevelt, the greatest American President of this century, gave in to pressure from the Catholic Church (for domestic electoral reasons, imagined, rather than real) and let Fascism win its most important long-lived victory.

When the Civil War ended, American public opinion was strongly in favour of the Spanish Republic. This position began to erode after the end of the Second World War when the Cold War engendered an unwholesome atmosphere in the United

States (and elsewhere). The Central Intelligence Agency, founded in 1946, marked a definite swing to the right, reflected in all aspects of American life. The FBI considered sympathy with the Spanish Republic ample reason for opening a file on anybody. The modification in American attitudes towards Spanish Civil War historiography can be traced in a popular medium reaching a vast audience, the cinema.

A wide sector of American — eventually international — opinion was affected by an almost subliminal appearance of a biographical reference to a leading male protagonist in a number of films. Motion picture buffs may recall that during World War II, and for a few years later, the leading men of films with a contemporary background were endowed with a romantic past in, or actual involvement with, the Republican forces in the Spanish Civil War. Humphrey Bogart in *Casablanca* played the role of a man who had fought with Republicans in the Spanish Civil War, and he was given the same background in *Key Largo* and other films. One of Gary Cooper's most acclaimed performances was as Robert Jordan in *For Whom the Bell Tolls*. In the 1946 film, *The Lady from Shanghai*, starring Orson Welles and Rita Hayworth, there is a scene in which the rich friend of Hayworth declares that he was on a pro-Franco committee during the Civil War, and Welles (an adventurer named Michael O'Hara) ripostes by saying that during the Civil War he shot a man in Murcia because he was a Franco spy. The bad guy was for Franco and the good guy for the Republicans. This pro-Republican tendency did not last long. In 1950 Senator Joseph McCarthy began his campaign against subversives in the Government. HUAC (House Un-American Activities Committee) began a parallel work, and the search for 'Reds' began. In Hollywood, the man who wrote the scenario for *Casablanca* was put on the black list and Orson Welles did most of his screen work outside Hollywood. Well-known directors, such as Joseph Losey and Jules Dassin, looked for jobs in Europe. The motion picture scene was but a reflection of American life.

Bolloten's book, in its three versions, represents a massive attack against all the resistance movements in Europe. The history of the Spanish Civil War, if viewed in the context of the annals of the century, becomes the narrative of the first significant armed aggression of Fascist power against a democratically elected government, the chronicle of the first defensive action against the Fascist plague. Bolloten attempts to deflect the argument by stressing Communist growth and influence during the fighting. His line of reasoning, if applied to all of Occupied Europe, constitutes a denial of any justification for the world-wide War against the Fascist Powers. The victory over Nazism and Fascism, would never have been achieved without the collaboration of Communists all over Europe. It was a victory of the forces opposed to Fascism, in Germany, Italy and elsewhere in Europe. (Unfortunately, Spain was excluded.) *Résistance* meant resistance to Fascism. The later resistance movements in Europe, after the fall of France, movements against the Nazi occupiers, were ineluctably patterned upon the Spanish model. The Spanish Civil War was a war against Fascism and cannot be separated from the other anti-Fascist struggles that followed it.

When it is said that the Spanish Civil War was the first battle of the Second World War, what is signified as the joining thread between them? It is the anti-Fascist struggle. This matter can be illustrated by the story of a friend of mine, Col. Henri Rol-Tanguy, a French Communist, who distinguished himself in the International Brigades and later in the resistance battles for the liberation of Paris. He has received two of the highest decorations that France bestows on its heroes. For Rol-Tanguy, resistance in Spain and resistance in France were the same combat. Another example is seen in the story of Professor Bernard Knox, who is now a well-known classical scholar in the United States. He fought with the French in the International Brigades in the Spanish Civil War, and later with the partisans in Italy in World War II. The Spanish Civil War was the first engagement in the anti-Fascist epic. Bolloten's wasted exertions to deny this basic fact of twentieth-century history take from his books any permanent meaning.

INDEX

ABC, 25-26, 35, 197
Abd-el-Krim, 284, 303
Abendroth, Hans-Henning, 59-60, 83
Acción, 150
Acción Popular, 8
Adelanto de Salamanca, El, 123
African Army [Spanish], 3, 21, 25, 88, 177, 217
'Agrupación Cultural Faros', 153
Aguilar, Aurelio Fernando (pseudonym) see Franco, Nicolás
Ahora, 254
Alba, Duke of, 13
Alba, Víctor, 252
Alemania nazi y el 18 de julio, La (A. Viñas), 57
Alfonso XIII, King of Spain, 26
Allen, Jay, 274
Álvarez del Vayo, Julio, 104, 174
Álvarez Junco, José, 140-41
American Federation of Labour (AFL), 298-300, 306
Amery, Leo, 43
Anarchism, 135-62, *passim*
Anarcho-syndicalism, 142-44, 146-47, 149, 157, 161-62, 273, 275-76
Andes, Francisco Moreno y Zulueta, Conde de los, 26
An Enemy of the People (H. Ibsen), 137
Anfuso, Filippo, 28, 31-32
Angriff, 215
AO [Nazi Auslandsorganisation], 56 69, 73, 76, 83-84
Aragón, Manuel, 248, 250
Aranda Sánchez, Vicente, 154
Araquistain, Luis, 165, 274
Arbenz, Jacobo, 302-03
Aristotle, 257

Army of Africa see African Army
Aróstegui, Julio, 286-87
Arquer, Jordi, 299
Arranz Monasterio, Francisco, 56
Ascaso, Francisco, 146, 149-51
Asensio Cabanillas, Carlos, 54
Asociación Argentina por la Libertad de la Cultura, 285
Asociación de Mujeres Antifascistas (AMA), 185
Auden, W. H., 88
Aunós Pérez, Eduardo, 231
Avance, 187
Axis, German-Italian/Rome-Berlin, v, x, xiii, 12, 179, 181, 185, 193, 227, 232-34
Azaña, Manuel, 94, 99-101, 168, 178, 213, 218, 241-60
Azcárate, Pablo de, 212
Azpiazu, Joaquín de, 214

Badoglio, Marshal, 50
Bahamonde y Sánchez de Castro, Antonio, 177, 199, 205, 220, 222-23
Bajatierra, Mauro, 148-49
Bakunin, Mikhail, 139, 146, 149
Balbo, Marshal, 50
Baldwin, Stanley, 111
Balius, Jaume, 135
Ballano, Adolfo, 152
XV Bandera (Irlandesa) del Tercio, 127-30
Barba Hernández, Colonel Bartolomé, 278
Barcelona, Fall of, 297
Baroja, Pío, 138
Barroso, Major Antonio, 36
Batalla, La, 156, 158-59
Bau y Nolla, Joaquín, 81
Behan, Brendan, 131

Beigbeder y Atienza, Juan, 54
Belforte, Francesco (pseudonym)
    see Biondi Morra, Francesco
Belton, Patrick, 121-22
Benzler, Felix, 78
Berardis, Vicenzo, 40-41, 47, 90, 92,
    94
Berenguer, General Dámaso, 1
Berger, 71
Bernhardt, Johannes E. F., 53-56,
    58-60, 62-63, 68, 74, 83
Besnard, Pierre, 142
Bethke, Friedrich, 70-74
Bible in Spain, The (G. Borrow), 247
Biondi Morra, General Francesco,
    36
Blomberg, General Werner von, 56-
    57, 67-68
Blueshirts, 114-15, 118, 121, 131,
    234, 292
Blum, Léon, 10, 31, 37, 46, 96, 98
Blum, William, 293
Bogart, Humphrey, 309
Bohle, Ernst, 56
Boletín del Estado, 231
Bolín, Luis Antonio, 25-26, 29, 31-
    32, 34, 42-43, 223
Bolloten, Burnett, 190, 261-65, 267-
    76, 285-99, 304-05, 307-10
Bolshevik/Bolshevist/Bolshevism, xi,
    xiii, 2, 4, 6, 31, 37, 39, 43-44, 98,
    116, 145, 219
Bonnot, Jules, 145, 150-51
'Bonnot Gang', The, 145
Bonomi, Ruggero, 42
Borkenau, Franz, xii
Borrow, George, 247
Bowker, James, 209, 235
Braden, Thomas, 300, 305
Brandt, Willy, 264
Brenan, Gerald, 207
'Brigadas de Depuración' (Purifica-
    tion Brigades), 223
Brigade, Abraham Lincoln, vi
Brigades, International, v, x, xiii,
    89, 125-27, 130, 132, 310
Britain, *passim*
Brossa, Jaume, 138

Brown, Irving, 300, 306
Bugeda, Jerónimo, 173
Bulatoff, Ronald M., 261
Bullejos, José, 267
Bülow, von, 59-60
Bystrova, E., 87

Cadogan, Sir Alexander, 45
Calvo Sotelo, José, 212
Cambó, Francesc, 231
Cambon, Roger, 45
Campesino, El see Valentín
    González
Canaris, Admiral Wilhelm, 47-48,
    75
Cañada Blanch Foundation, i, iv-v
Canela, José, 151
*Caníbales políticos: Hitler y Stalin
    en España* (J. Gorkin), 298-99
Cantalupo, Roberto, 28, 31, 44, 50-
    51
Caralt, Luis de, 293
Carlist/Carlism, 33, 122
Carr, Raymond, v, 290
Carranza y Fernández-Reguera,
    Fernando de, 62
Carrillo, Santiago, 284-85, 303-05
Carrillo, Wenceslao, 303
Carte d'Amiens, 142, 144
Casablanca (film), 309
Casado López, Colonel Segismundo,
    195
Casticista/Casticismo, 164
Castles in Spain (film), 118
Castro Delgado, Enrique, 267-68,
    284, 298-99, 301, 307
Catalonia Infelix (E. Allison Peers),
    iii
Catholic/Catholicism, iii, ix, 5, 8, 25,
    50, 109, 112, 114-19, 122-23,
    125-26, 131, 197, 199, 204-05,
    214, 225, 237, 293, 308
Cavada, Jean-Marie, 291
CEDA, 8, 225
Centrales Nacionales Sindicalistas
    (CNS), 231
Central Intelligence Agency see CIA

Centre for Civil War Studies, 210
Cerruti, Vittorio, 31, 36-37
Ceva, Lucio, 21
Chamberlain, Neville, xiii, 7, 12, 16, 44, 105, 111
Chambrun, Charles de Pineton, Comte de, 46-47
Chatfield, Admiral Sir A. Ernle, 38
Chetwode, Sir Philip, 17
Chilston, Viscount Aretas Akers-Douglas, 90-91, 97-98
Chilton, Sir Henry Getty, 1, 3
Church see Catholic/Catholicism
Churchill, Winston, 10, 287, 296
CIA, xiii, 263-64, 266, 272, 291, 293, 297-301, 303-07, 309
Ciano, Admiral Costanzo, 27
Ciano, Count Galeazzo, 24, 26-29, 31-35, 37-50, 82, 94, 224, 228, 230
Cierva, Juan de la, 44
Cierva, Ricardo de la, 210
Claudín, Fernando, 103, 280
Clerk, Sir George, 36, 45
CLUEA [union fruit-exporting consortium], 173
Colegio de abogados de Madrid, 216
Coleman, Peter, 293, 300-03, 306-07
Collier, Lawrence, 95
Comintern, 191-93
Commentary, 302
Communist/Communism, ix, xi-xii, xiv, 4-7, 11, 17, 23, 39, 44, 60, 89, 92, 94, 96, 98-103, 105, 116, 120, 125-26, 131, 156, 159-61, 179-80, 183-84, 187, 189-91, 193, 201, 214, 241, 262-63, 267-70, 273-76, 280, 282-83, 285-86, 290, 293-94, 296-98, 302-03, 306-08, 310
Communist Party (Spanish), 161, 183, 263, 267-68, 273-76, 280, 282-83, 287, 290, 292, 296-97, 301, 303 see also Partido Comunista de España
Communistes contre la révolution espagnole, Les (J. Gorkin), 307
Companys, Luis, 211

Comunista en España y anti-stalinista en la URSS (El Campesino [J. Gorkin]), 265, 268-69, 276-78, 284, 290
Condor Legion, 22, 82, 84, 308
Confederación Nacional del Trabajo (CNT), xii, 135-36, 142-59, 162, 192
Congress for Cultural Freedom (CCF), 290-91, 293-94, 298, 300-07
Congress of Industrial Organizations (CIO), 298, 300, 306
Connolly, James, 120
'Connolly Column', 110, 119-20, 122, 130
Conquest, Robert, 270-71
Conquest of Bread, The (P. A. Kropotkin), 146
Conservative Party (British), 43
Convulsiones de España I, II (I. Prieto), 276-77
Cooper, Gary, 309
Cordón, Antonio, 282-83, 285
Cork Examiner, 117, 121
Corpo Truppe Volontarie, 89, 121
Cosgrave, W. T., 114
Cot, Pierre, 31
Coulondre, Robert, 100, 104
Coupette, Captain, 57
Coverdale, John F., 33
Cranborne, Lord, 13-14
Crozier, Brian, 209
Crusade in Spain (E. O'Duffy), 119, 121-22, 128-29, 131
Crusades, The (film), 118
Cuadernos del Congreso por la Libertad de la Cultura, 301-03, 305
Cumann na nGhaedheal, 113

Dachau, 214
Daily Express, 26
Daily Mail, The, 5-6
Darwin, Charles, 140, 217
Dassin, Jules, 309
Davies, Graeme J., iv
Declaration of Unification, 241

Degrelle, Léon, 308
Delbos, Yvon, 41, 45, 105
'Democratización de la Universidad',
    La (J. Negrín), 165
Dépêche, La, 38
De Valera, Eamon de, 111, 113-15,
    122-23, 132
Diálogo de la guerra de España
    (subtitle) see *La velada en
    Benicarló*
Diari de Barcelona, 156, 160
Díaz, José, 102-03
Díaz Criado, Manuel, 220
Dieckhoff, Hans Heinrich, 55-56, 76
Dimitroff, 117
Doll's House, A (H. Ibsen), 137
Dörnberg, Alexander von, 77
Downing, E., 126
Drummond, Sir Eric, 27-28, 44
Dulles, Allen, 300
Du Moulin, 64
*Durchsetzung nationalsozialistischer
    Grundsätze in der Wirtschaft*
    (E. von Jagwitz), 79-80
Durruti, Buenaventura, 136, 146,
    149-51

Ealham, Chris, xii
Ebro, Battle of the, 281, 284
Eden, Anthony, 7, 10, 12-13, 16, 28,
    38, 44-47, 95, 105, 209, 226,
    234-35
Einhorn, Marion, 58
Einzige und sein Eigenthum, Der
    (M. Stirner), 138
Eliseda, Marqués de, 214
Elizabeth I, Queen of England, 118
Encounter, 301-02
Enge, 83
Engels, Friedrich, 119
Entresijos de la guerra de España
    (I. Prieto), 276-77
Época, La, 34
Erasmus/Erasmian, 243
Escobar, José Ignacio, 34
Esenwein, George, 295-96
Esgleas, Germinal, 155

*España, primer ensayo de
    democracia popular* (J. Gorkin),
    285, 290
Essener National-Zeitung, 215
Even the Olives Are Bleeding
    (documentary by Cathal
    O'Shannon), 120

Falange Española, 8, 14, 17, 35, 189,
    199, 204-05, 209, 219-20, 223-
    27, 229-35, 238, 241, 292-93,
    308
Faldella, Colonel Emilio, 29-30, 36
Fanjul Goñi, General Joaquín, 3
Farinacci, Roberto, 50
Fascist/Fascism, viii-ix, xi, 6, 8-12,
    18, 21, 25, 27-29, 36, 42-43, 46,
    50-51, 59, 61, 89, 91-93, 95, 98,
    107-10, 114-15, 125, 130, 132,
    147, 159-60, 189, 199, 201, 205,
    217, 231, 235, 280, 286, 292-94,
    299, 301, 306-08, 310
Faupel, General Wilhelm, 76, 80-83
Faure, Sébastian, 150
FBI, 294, 309
FCA [reserve army force (Ireland)],
    114
Federación Anarquista Ibérica
    (FAI), xii, 135-36, 148-59, 162
Federación Ibérica de Juventudes
    Libertarias (FIJL), xii, 135-36,
    152-59, 162, 188
Federación Local de Grupos
    Anarquistas de Barcelona, 155
Felice, Renzo de, 33
Fenians, 119
Fernsworth, Lawrence, 230
Fianna Fáil, 111, 113, 117, 123-24
Fine Gael, 113, 131
Foix, Pere, 144
Foltz, Charles, 209
For Whom the Bell Tolls (film), 309
France, *passim*
Franco, Francisco, vi-vii, ix-xi, xiii-
    xiv, 1-19, 21-22, 24-26, 28-36,
    38, 40-49, 51, 53-57, 59, 61-65,
    67-68, 71-72, 74-83, 85, 91, 93,
    95, 99, 102-05, 111, 121-23, 127,

129-31, 158-60, 163-64, 177-79, 194, 196-98, 200-03, 205-12, 214-19, 223-25, 227-31, 233-38, 241, 247, 256, 274-75, 277-78, 280, 286, 292-93, 306-09
Franco, Nicolás, 63-64, 66, 77
Franco, Ramón, 1-2
Franco: A Biography (P. Preston), i
Francoism see Franco, Francisco
Fuera de la ley (M. Bajatierra), 148-49
Fuero del Trabajo ('Labour Charter'), 231

García, Elías, 148-49
García Birlan, Antonio ('Dionisios'), 151
García Gómez, Julián   see Julián Gorkin
García Lorca, Federico, 211, 225
García Oliver, Juan, 146, 149, 151-53, 158
Gardenyes, Josep, 153, 158
Gay y Forner, Vicente, 214
Generalitat, 173, 293
Generation of 1898, 164, 217
George V, 1
George, Lloyd, 113
Germany, 53-85, *passim*
Gerö, Erno/Ernst (also known as Pedro Gueré), 277
Gibson, Ian, 225
Gil Robles, José María, 2-3, 8, 225, 231
Giménez Caballero, Ernesto, 214
Giner de los Ríos, Francisco, 164
Giral, José, 171, 246
Glasgow, University of, i, iv
Goded Llopis, General Manuel, 1, 3
Goicoechea, Antonio, 23-24, 32-35, 43
Gollonet Megias, Ángel, 226
Gómez, General Francisco see Conde de Jordana y Souza
Gómez, Jesús, 243, 246
González, Valentín (El Campesino), 262-72, 275-85, 288-90, 300-02, 306-07

González Oliveros, Wenceslao, 215
González Ruiz, Francisco, 221, 223, 232
Göring, Hermann, 44, 56-57, 65-73, 76, 78, 83-84
Gorki, Maxim, 297
Gorkin, Julián (pseudonym of Julián García Gómez), 261-69, 271-72, 274-78, 281, 284-85, 287-95, 297-307
GPU [of the Kremlin], 276, 302
Graham, Helen, xii
Gramsci, Antonio, 197
Grand Camouflage: The Communist Conspiracy in the Spanish Civil War, The (B. Bolloten), 261-62, 271, 273-74
Grande trahison, La (trans.) see *Yo fui un ministro de Stalin*
'Grandezas y miserias de la política' (M. Azaña), 260
Grandi, Dino, 27-28, 45-46
Guariglia, Raffaele, 25, 31, 36
Gutiérrez Ravé, José, 33

Halifax, Lord, 16-17
Hankey, Sir Maurice, 12
Hassell, Ulrich von, 39
Haughey, Jim, 126
Hayworth, Rita, 309
Henke, Alfred, 62
Hernández, Jesús, 267-68, 277, 291, 301, 307
Hernández, Miguel, 254
Hess, Alfred, 69
Hess, Rudolf, 28, 56, 69
Hidalgo de Cisneros, General Ignacio, 273-74, 294
Hilton, Ronald, 297
HISMA (Hispano-Marroquí de Transportes, Sociedad Limitada), 53, 62-80, 82-85
Historia 16, 290
Hitler, Adolf, ix, xi, xiii, 5-6, 21-22, 27, 47, 55-61, 64-66, 69, 82-84, 96-98, 214, 292, 307
Hoare, Sir Samuel, 38, 234
Hodgson, Sir Robert, 15

Homage to Catalonia (G. Orwell), 108

Hombres Made in Moscow (E. Castro Delgado), 284

Hoover, J. Edgar, 294

Hora de España, 243, 248

House Un-American Activities Committee (HUAC), 309

Howson, Gerald, 176

Humanitat, La, 156, 160

Ibárruri, Dolores ('La Pasionaria'), 89-90, 132

Ibsen, Henrik, 137

Iglesia, José Luis de la, 244

Ilgner, Max, 79

In Franco's Spain (F. McCullagh), 129-30

Ingram, Edward, 38, 44, 46-47

In the Service of Stalin (D. W. Pike), 305

Iniciales, 151-52

Institución Libre de Enseñanza, 163, 165

International Brigade Association, 132

IRA, 108, 113-15, 120, 125

Ireland, 107-32, *passim*

Iribarren, José María, 221

Irish Christian Front (ICF), 121-22

Irish Independent, 117-18, 124, 130

Irish Internationals/International Brigade, 110, 118-22, 124-25, 130-32

Irish Press, 119, 123

Iscar, Costa, 145

Italy, 21-51 *passim*

Izvestia, 93, 97

Jackson, Gabriel, 209

Jacobin, 119

Jagwitz, Eberhard von, 69-73, 78-80

Jebb, Gladwyn, 7

Jiménez de Asúa, Luis, 180

Johás el errante (E. García), 148-49

Jordana y Souza, General Francisco Gómez, Conde de, 77, 81

Jover, Gregorio, 151

JSU [United Socialist Youth Organization], 184, 188, 190

Juan Carlos I, King of Spain, 132

Kerenski, Alexander, 2

Key Largo (film), 309

Kirkpatrick, Jeane J., 291

Knox, Bernard, 310

Knox, MacGregor, 21

Koestler, Arthur, 208, 215

'Koltsov', Mijail, 87

Kraneck, Wolfgang, 56

Kremlin, 39-41, 90, 93, 96-97, 99, 102, 276-77, 292

Kristol, Irving, 302

Kropotkin, Peter A., 146

Krupp AG, Friedrich, 60, 75-76

Kühlental, General Erich, 55

Labour Party (British), 5

Lady from Shanghai, The (film), 309

Lamoneda, Ramón, 189

Land and Freedom (film), 107-08, 111, 193

Langenheim, Adolf, 54, 56, 60

Largo Caballero, Francisco, 100, 168-72, 174-75, 181, 242, 267

League of Nations, 29, 98, 180

Léger, Alexis, 103

Leitz, Christian, x

Lenin, Nicolai, 103, 117, 190, 303

Levesey, Charles, 154

Liberal Conspiracy, The (P. Coleman), 293, 301

Lindau, Admiral, 57

Líster, Enrique, 275, 278-79, 284

Litvinov, Maxim, 98, 100, 104

Liverpool, University of, ii

Lloyd, Lord, 18

Loach, Ken, 107, 111, 193

Lorenzo, Anselmo, 136

Losey, Joseph, 309

Lovestone, Jay, 298, 300, 306

Luca de Tena, Marqués de, 26, 34-35

Luccardi, Giuseppe, 29-32, 36, 38, 41, 43, 45, 48-49

Luchador, El, 152
LVF [in France], 308

MacEntee, Seán, 123
Machado, Antonio, 243-44
Mackenzie, Ann L., i
MacNamee, Bishop, 118
MacSwiney of Mashanaglass, Marquis, 119
Madariaga, Salvador de, 303-04, 307
Madrid, Francesc, 145
Maeztu, Ramiro de, 214
Mahony, Major, 17-18
Mainer, José-Carlos, 248
Maisky, Ivan, 95-96
Malefakis, Edward, 287
Manchester Guardian, 207
Mangold, William P., 296
March Ordinas, Juan, 33-35, 65
Margesson, David, 7, 43
'Marianet' see Rodríguez Vázquez, Mariano
Marichal, Juan, 287, 289, 297
Martin, Benjamin, 160
Martínez, Segundo, 151
Martínez Amutio, Justo, 172
Martínez Bande, José Manuel, 277-80, 284
Martínez Barrio, Diego, 181
Marx, Karl, 119, 126, 132
Marxist/Marxism, 26, 32, 58, 94, 101, 109, 139, 190, 203, 206, 215, 221, 232
Mason, Susan, 261
Matthews, Herbert L., 287
McCabe, Fr Alexander, 129
McCarthy, Senator Joseph, 302, 309
McCloskey, Leo, 131
McCullagh, F., 129-30
Mella, Ricardo, 136, 138, 140
Memorias (S. Carrillo), 284-85
Méndez Aspe, Francisco, 172
Menéndez, Teodomiro, 164
Meregalli, Franco, 247, 249, 257
Meyer, 70
Milch, General Erhard, 57
Miranda, Augusto, 75

Mito de la cruzada de Franco, El (H. R. Southworth), 274, 294
Modesto, Juan, 275, 278
Mola, General Emilio, 21, 32, 34, 36, 44, 54, 59, 119, 216-17, 221
Monatte, Pierre, 142
Monck-Mason, Mr, 3-5
Monks, J., 120
Mono Azul, El, 254
Monografías de la guerra civil (M. Martínez Bande), 277
Monroe Doctrine, 291
Montagu-Pollack, Mr, 9
Montero, Eloy, 214
Montseny, Federica, 148, 273
Moore, Christy, 108
Mora, Constancia de la, 273-74, 293-94
Moradiellos, Enrique, ix-x
Morales López, José, 226
Morel, Colonel, 178
Moreno y Zulueta, Francisco see Conde de los Andes
Morning Post, The, 5
Morón, Gabriel, 167
Mounsey, Sir George, 7, 12
Mujeres Libres, 188
Müller, Dr, 71
Mundo Obrero, 102, 160
Munich Pact, 16
Municipios libres, Los (F. Urales), 144
Mussolini, Benito, ix, xi, xiii, 5-7, 21-33, 35-47, 49-51, 82, 91, 98, 115, 147, 224, 232-35, 307
Mussolini, Bruno, 27
Mussolini, Edda, 27
Mussolini, Vittorio, 27
Muti, Ettore, 42
Mythe de la croisade de Franco, Le (H. R. Southworth), 295

Naissance de Notre Pouvoir, La (V. Serge), 145
Nasse, 70
Nationalist/Nationalism (Spanish), 7, 14, 17, 63-66, 68-70, 72, 74-77, 80-84, 108, 111, 122, 126-27,

129, 173, 177-80, 185, 189, 193-
94, 203-07, 209-10, 213-15, 218-
19, 222-23, 226, 232, 237, 239,
278-80
Navarro, Patricio, 151
Nazi/Nazism, ix, xiii, 9, 11-12, 18,
21, 47, 53-85, 92, 97, 104, 106,
132, 173, 205, 211, 214-15, 235,
281, 286, 308, 310
Nazi Party, ix, 21, 54, 83
Negrín, Juan, xii-xiii, 104-05, 163-
96, 213, 243, 246, 269, 274-75,
285-88, 293, 295-97
Neurath, Baron Constantin von, 78,
83
New Republic, 296
News of Spain, 296
New Yorker, The, 296
New York Times, 301, 305
Nietzsche, Friedrich, 137-39, 144,
146-48
Nin, Andrés, 191, 267, 291, 293
NKVD [Russian Secret Police], xiii
Noel-Baker, Philip, 5
Non-Intervention, Policy of, 10, 12,
92-93, 98, 130, 171, 173, 175-76,
179, 190, 194
Non-Intervention Committee, 44,
93, 258
Noticias, Las, 154
Novela Ideal, La, 148
Nuestra juventud no muere
(M. Hernández), 254
Núñez Florencio, Rafael, 140-41

O'Cuinneagáin, Captain, 131
O'Daire, Paddy, 120
O'Donnell Abu, 118-20
O'Duffy, General Eoin, 110, 114-15,
118-19, 121-24, 127-31
O'Duffy Brigade, 110
OKW [High Command of the
German Army], 74
Olivares, Gaspar de Guzmán,
Conde-Duque de, 287
O'Neill, Owen Roe, 118
O'Riordan, M., 120, 124
Orwell, George, xi, 108

O'Shannon, Cathal, 120
O'Sullivan Mór, 118
Otero, Alejandro, 175

Pack, Mr, 9
'pacto del olvido', vi-vii
País, El, 303-04
Palabras del Caudillo (F. Franco),
215
Partido Comunista de España (PCE)
[Spanish Communist Party], 89,
159-60, 183-86, 188-91, 193,
195-96, 287
Partido Obrero de Unificación
Marxista (POUM), xiii, 101,
107-08, 156, 158-60, 190-93,
262, 276, 291, 293, 297-99,
305-06
Partit Socialista Unificat de
Catalunya (PSUC), 159-60, 190
Pascua, Marcelino, 88, 93-94, 99,
101, 163, 166, 169-70, 172,
175-76
Pasionaria, La see Dolores Ibárruri
Patman, Wright, 305
Pavelic, Ante, 308
Payart, Jean, 92
Payne, Stanley, 58-59
Pedrazzi, Orazio, 25, 37
Peer Gynt (H. Ibsen), 137
Peers, E. Allison, ii-iii
Peiró, Joan, 142, 157-58, 213
Pelloutier, Fernand, 142
Pemán, José María, 218
Peppo, Ottavio De, 28
Pérez Bowie, José Antonio, 245,
247-48
Perill a la reraguarda (J. Peiró),
157-58
Pestaña, Ángel, 162
Peterson, Sir Maurice, 17-18
Philip V, King of Spain, 119
Philips, A. V., 228
Phillimore, Lord, 16
Pike, David Wingeate, 298, 305
Pineton, Charles de see Comte de
Chambrun
Pini, Achille Vittorio, 141, 145

Plato, 257
Popular Front (French), ix, 49, 61, 96, 98
Popular Front (Spanish), ix, xii, 2, 60-61, 89, 92, 109, 121, 180, 183-85, 188-89, 191, 193, 216, 218, 231, 250-51, 292-93, 307
Porquet, Ramón, 151
Porvenir Anarquista, El, 141
Potsdam Conference, 306
Praeger, Frederick A., 292-93
Prats, José, 289
Pravda, 87, 98
Prensa Libre, 264-65
Preston, Paul, i, 63
Prieto, Indalecio, xii, 166, 169-70, 175, 178, 196, 213, 217, 269, 275-79, 284-85, 287
Primo de Rivera, General Miguel, 1, 17, 57, 146, 150, 212, 214, 274, 297
Prío Socarrás, Carlos, 264
'Problema español, El' (M. Azaña), 243
Procès de Moscou dans l'Espagne en guerre (J. Gorkin), 267
Productor Literario, El, 145
Pronunciamiento, 21, 101, 146
PSOE [Spanish Socialist Party], 163, 165-67, 169, 173, 180-81, 183-85, 187, 189, 276
Puzzo, Dante, 58

Queipo de Llano, General Gonzalo, 205, 221-24
Quinn, Captain, 131

Radek, Karl, 97
Rambla, La, 156
Ramón-Laca, Julio de, 177, 207, 222
Ramparts, 305
Ranelagh, John, 300
Reagan, Ronald, President, 291
Red International of Labour Unions, 191
Regenerationism, 216-17

Reig Tapia, Alberto, 198, 210, 280
Renovación Española [Monarchist Party], 32
Republic/Republican/Republicanism (Spanish), *passim*
Republic and the Civil War in Spain, The (ed. R. Carr), 290
Republic Besieged: Civil War in Spain 1936-1939, The, iv
Residencia de Estudiantes, 163
Revista Blanca, La, 137-38, 147-49, 155
Revolution, Bolshevik/Russian (1917), 2
Revolution and War in Spain 1931-1939 (P. Preston), i
Rexists, 308
Rey d'Harcourt, Colonel Domingo, 278
RFM [Reich Finance Ministry], 73, 78
Ribbans, Geoffrey, ii-iii
Ribbentrop, Joachim von, 60
Richards, Major, 17
Richards, Michael, xiv
Ritter, Karl, 69, 76, 78-80
Rivera, Diego, 302
Roatta, General Mario, 29-30, 47-48
Roberts, Walter, 14
Rodríguez Doreste, Juan, 289
Rodríguez Vázquez, Mariano ('Marianet'), 152, 154-55
Rojo, Vicente, 279
Rol-Tanguy, Henri, 310
Roman Catholic/Catholicism see Catholic/Catholicism
Roosevelt, Eleanor, 293-94
Roosevelt, Franklyn D., 294, 296, 308
Rosenstone, R., 121
Ross, Mike, 300
Rossa, O'Donovan, 119
Rossi del Lion Nero, Pier Filippo de, 29, 31-32, 36, 40-43, 48-49
ROWAK (Rohstoff-Waren-Kompensation Handelsgesellschaft AG), 53-54, 69-80, 82-85
Ruiz Alonso, Ramón, 231

Ruiz Vilaplana, Antonio, 223
'Rusos en España', Los (I. Prieto),
    277
Russia see USSR
RWM [Reich Economics Ministry],
    71-73
Ryan, Frank, 119-20, 125-26

Sabath, Hermann Friedrich, 73, 76
Sainz Rodríguez, Pedro, 33-35
Salas Larrazábal, General Ramón,
    210, 212, 222, 225
Salazar, Antonio, 64, 307
Salut, Emili, 142, 144
Sanjurjo Sacanell, General José, 1,
    3, 26, 58, 177
Sanz, Ricardo, 151
Saturday Evening Post, 305
Saz, Ismael, 21, 23
Schacht, Hjalmar, 72, 78-79
Schieder, Wolfgang, 58
Schopenhauer, Arthur, 146
Schulenburg, Friedrich Werner von,
    103
Schweickhard, General, 63, 68, 71
Schwendemann, 83
Scott, Oswald, 8-9
Seekamp, John H., 247-48
Seguí, Salvador ('El Noi del Sucre'),
    144
'Sentado sobre los muertos'
    (M. Hernández), 254
Serge, Victor, 145
Serrano Suñer, Ramón, 17, 218-19,
    228-30
Shuckburgh, Mr, 3, 7, 44
SIM [Italian Military Intelligence],
    29, 41, 48
Simón, Lieutenant-Colonel, 91
Sinn Féin, 113
Siqueiros, Álvaro, 302
Smith, Denis Mack, 22
Smyth, Denis, x
Socialist/Socialism, vi, xii, xiv,
    passim
Socialista, El, 165, 276
Solchaga Zala, General José, 229

Solidaridad Obrera, 152, 154-58,
    275
'Solidarios', Los, 146, 149, 152
Sonderstab W [Special Staff W], 57,
    74
Sorel, George, 142
Soria, Georges, 297
Southworth, Herbert Rutledge, xiii,
    263, 270, 272-73, 294-97
Soviet-French Treaty of Mutual
    Assistance (1935), 96
Spain, passim
Spain in Eclipse (E. Allison Peers),
    iii
Spanish Civil War: Revolution and
    Counter-Revolution, The
    (B. Bolloten), 261
Spanish Dilemma, The (E. Allison
    Peers), iii
Spanish Foreign Legion, 42, 54
'Spanish Insurgents' [Franco's
    forces], 5, 49
Spanish National Movement, 7; see
    also Nationalist/Nationalism
Spanish Revolution: The Left and
    the Struggle during the Civil
    War, The (B. Bolloten), 261
Spanish Tragedy, iii, 14
Spanish Tragedy 1930-1936:
    Dictatorship, Republic, Chaos,
    The (E. Allison Peers), iii
SPD [German youth movement],
    163
Sperrle, General Hugo, 82
Spriano, Paolo, 90
Stalin, Joseph, xiii, 89, 91-92, 96-97,
    99-100, 103-05, 116, 190-91,
    241, 286, 296
Stalingrad, Battle of, 281
Stalinist/Stalinism, xiii, 108, 156,
    160, 191, 193, 262, 266-67, 302,
    304
Starace, Achille, 50
Stepanov (pseudonym of S. Mineff),
    277
Stirner, Max, 138-43, 145, 147-55,
    157-58, 161-62
Stohrer, Eberhard von, 83

Stradling, Robert, xi
Strategy of Deception. A Study of Worldwide Communist Tactics, The (ed. J. J. Kirkpatrick), 291
Sullivan, Brian R., 21
Suritz, Yakob Z., 99
Suvich, Fulvio, 26

Tagueña Lacorte, Manuel, 280-84
Tamames, Ramón, 209-10
Teruel, Battle of, 275-80, 282-85, 287
Testimonio de dos guerras (M. Tagueña Lacorte), 280-82
Tetuán, Duchess of, 119
Tierra y Libertad, 152-53
Thomas, 45
Thomas, General Georg, 68, 70
Thomas, Hugh, v, 256
'Three Musketeers' [B. Durruti, F. Ascaso, J. García Oliver], 146, 150, 153
Times, The, 220, 223, 230, 264
TLS, 263-64, 269-72, 288, 293, 295
Tiso, Father, 308
Togliatti, Palmiro, 303
Tone, Wolfe, 119
Trajan, Emperor, 257
Treball, 156, 160
Trevor-Roper, H. R., 273, 286, 292, 295
'Tribuna Libre' (J. Gorkin), 304
Trotsky, Leon, 103, 136, 268, 273, 299, 303
Trotskyist/Trotskyism, xii, xiv, 101, 160, 190
Truman, President Harry S., 306
Tuam Herald, 117-18
Tuñón de Lara, Manuel, 289, 297
Tusell, Javier, 289

UGT [Socialist union organization], 182-83, 188-89, 223, 225
Ullmann, Wilhelm, 79
Único y su propiedad, El (trans. of M. Stirner's *Der Einzige und sein Eigenthum*), 138

United States, xi
Universe, The, 118
Unternehmen Feuerzauber [Operation Magic Fire], 57, 63, 68, 71
Urales, Federico, 136, 138, 140, 143-44, 147-48, 151
USSR, 86-106, *passim*

Vaillant, 75
Valldeperes, Manuel, 160
Valle, General Giuseppe, 42-43
Vanguardia, La, 154
Vanguardia Española, La, 232
Vansittart, Sir Robert, 10, 12, 44, 103
Varela Rendueles, José María, 222
Vázquez Montalbán, Manuel, 201
Velada en Benicarló, La (M. Azaña), xii, 241-60
Veltjens, Josef, 59, 75-76
Veu de Catalunya, La, 154
Viana, Marqués de, 26, 31, 42-43
Vida y la muerte en la URSS, La (trans.) see *La Vie et la mort*
Vie et la mort en URSS, 1939-1949, La (El Campesino), 262-64, 266, 276
Viets, Dr, 70
Vilar, Pierre, 206-07, 297
Viñas, Ángel, 57-59, 68, 171-72, 287, 297
Vitetti, Leonardo, 43-44
'Vive el Quinte Brigada' (C. Moore), 108
Voelckers, Hans Hermann, 59
Volunteer for Liberty, 120

Wahle, Anton, 71
War, Cold, xiii, 201, 263, 270, 306-08
War, First World, 59, 145, 153, 163-64
War, Second World, v, viii, xi, 18, 22, 53, 72, 85, 234, 269, 280, 292, 298-99, 306, 308-10
War, Spanish Civil, *passim*

Warlimont, Walter, 67-68, 82-83
Weizsäcker, Ernst von, 60
Welles, Orson, 309
Wellington, Arthur Wellesley,
    Duke of, 15
Whealey, Robert, 65
Wheeler, Linda, 261
Whiston, James, xii
'Why we lost Teruel' (I. Prieto), 276
Wilberg, General Helmuth, 57, 61,
    68, 74
Wolfe, Bertram D., 266, 268, 298-99

*World Situation and British
    Rearmament, The*, 10
Wucher, Theodor, 81

Yagüe Blanco, Juan, 54, 129-30, 216
Yeats, W. B., 118
Yencken, Arthur, 234
Yo fui un ministro de Stalin
    (J. Hernández), 267, 277
Young, Commandant P., 120

Zunzunegui, Luis María, 33-34